W9-BPQ-177

Profiting from Clean Energy

Founded in 1807, John Wiley & Sons is the oldest independent publishing company in the United States. With offices in North America, Europe, Australia, and Asia, Wiley is globally committed to developing and marketing print and electronic products and services for our customers' professional and personal knowledge and understanding.

The Wiley Trading series features books by traders who have survived the market's ever-changing temperament and have prospered—some by reinventing systems, others by getting back to basics. Whether a novice trader, professional, or somewhere in-between, these books will provide the advice and strategies needed to prosper today and well into the future.

For a list of available titles, visit our Web site at www.WileyFinance. com.

Profiting from Clean Energy

A Complete Guide to Trading
Green in Solar, Wind, Ethanol,
Fuel Cell, Power Efficiency,
Carbon Credit Industries,
and More

RICHARD W. ASPLUND

WILEY

John Wiley & Sons, Inc.

To my father, Lauren Asplund

Contents

Acknowledgments

I would like to thank Mike Artz for his help in the preparation of this book. I would like to thank my wife, Deanna Asplund, who helped with her perspectives and her long-suffering task of editing and proofreading. I would particularly like to thank my father, Lauren Asplund, who was extremely helpful in the preparation of this book.

Introduction

This book uses the term *clean energy* in order to adopt a broad definition for the topic. Other choices such as *renewable energy* or *alternative energy* are more limited and typically do not include some of the subsectors such as power efficiency and cleaner fossil fuels, among others, that are covered by this book.

The focus of this book is a bit more limited than the field of *cleantech.* Cleantech typically includes all the categories that fall under clean energy, but also includes the categories of clean water, environmental cleanup (air, water, and soil), recycling, and even broader areas such as removing toxic materials from everyday products. There are interesting investment opportunities in these areas, but they are beyond the scope of this book.

There is some controversy about whether nuclear power should be regarded as "clean energy." Nuclear power does not emit any greenhouse gases and in that regard it is clean. However, this book does not consider nuclear power to be clean because the nuclear waste produced by nuclear power is one of the most dangerous substances on earth. There is also the possibility of a nuclear leak and the release of large quantities of nuclear radiation into the air. Nuclear power has the potential to be a bigger environmental threat than coal and will not be covered in this book as clean energy.

Clean Energy as a Collection of Industries

Clean energy is not a single industry but instead involves a wide variety of very different industries. Some of the broad subsectors under clean energy include solar power, wind power, fuel cells, geothermal power, wave/tide power, biomass, biofuels, cleaner coal, and power efficiency. Each subsector needs to be addressed separately as to its drivers, technologies, competition, and profit model. This book is therefore organized along the lines of those subsectors.

One of the interesting things about the clean energy sector is that even though there is a broad array of technologies and applications that are under development, no one technology stands out as the silver bullet that will solve all of our energy problems. Instead, a wide variety of technologies are likely to become successful within specific areas of application, thus presenting us with a broad set of potentially successful investment opportunities in the clean energy space.

This book attempts to cover a large amount of ground in a relatively short space. There are some interesting clean energy subsectors or technologies that have been left out of the book simply because there are no easy ways to invest in those areas. This book tries to mention all U.S.-listed publicly traded companies with market caps above $100 million now operating in the clean energy space. However, new clean energy companies emerge everyday and smaller companies become bigger companies. If a reader would like to make a suggestion or comment about a U.S. or non-U.S. company to cover in future editions of *Profiting from Clean Energy*, please use this book's companion Web site at www.ProfitingFromClean Energy.com to submit your suggestion or comment online.

TICKER SYMBOLS AND FINDING COMPANY INFORMATION

This book provides the ticker symbol when a publicly traded company is mentioned. This allows the reader to quickly look up the company on a stock Web site if desired. In the case of non-U.S. stocks, the exchange is identified where the stock is listed. For example, London-traded Clipper Windpower Plc would be identified as: (London: CWP LN). The "LN" portion of the ticker symbol is the way that Bloomberg identifies the stock's listing country. There are quite a few non-U.S. companies that are mentioned in this book. Web sites that carry information on non-U.S. stocks include Google Finance (finance.google.com), MarketWatch (marketwatch.com), Bloomberg (Bloomberg.com), and many others.

www.ProfitingFromCleanEnergy.com

We encourage readers to visit this book's free companion Web site at www.ProfitingFromCleanEnergy.com. On the Web site, you will find an on-line response form to provide us with feedback or ask questions. Feedback from readers is very welcome. On the Web site, there are additional resource links for further research, an industry conference list, and more.

The Web site also has a video section with links to video clips of topics related to clean energy, including tours of solar power plants, wind farms, geothermal plants, and ethanol refineries, as well as demonstrations of all-electric vehicles, solar-powered vehicles and aircraft, algae biorefineries, and more.

At www.ProfitingFromCleanEnergy.com, readers can also sign up for our free email newsletter to receive updates for this book and to receive news on the clean energy industry. By signing up for our email list, you can join our community of investors who have a passion for the clean energy industry.

CHAPTER 1

Clean Energy Investments and Performance

The Show Has Just Begun

There are many different ways to profit from the clean energy sector. These profit opportunities, broadly defined, range from starting a business to investing in private or public companies to trading in the clean energy markets. The decision on how to participate depends in part on one's investment goals and experience. For example, an individual investor with little experience and little time to spare may opt to invest in a green mutual fund or an exchange-traded fund, thus taking a broad and diversified investment approach to the sector. A more experienced investor may decide to pick some particular stocks in the sector to add to his or her portfolio. An experienced trader may approach the sector from the standpoint of going long or short clean energy stocks or trading the biofuel or carbon credit markets. This chapter covers the various ways in which it is possible to profit from the clean energy sector.

CLEAN ENERGY BUSINESS STARTUP

There are many entrepreneurial opportunities in the clean energy industry. An entrepreneur can start a business from scratch, launch a startup business with licensed technology acquired in the U.S. or overseas, or buy an established business.

There are a variety of ways to investigate specific ideas for a clean energy business startup. For example, Shell Springboard offers an interesting program that sponsors research and grants prize money for contests involving the best business ideas for tackling climate change. On their Web site at www.shellspringboard.com, Shell Springboard has a report, "Opportunities for Innovation: The Business Opportunities for SMEs [small- and medium-sized enterprises] in Tackling the Causes of Climate Change."[1] This report makes interesting reading for anyone thinking about starting up a business related to the environment and climate change. The report is written for the market in the United Kingdom, but is equally applicable to the U.S. market. The report concludes that the biggest markets for small- and medium-sized enterprises in the climate change sector in the United Kingdom in 2010 will be very substantial and fall in the following primary categories:

* Building regulations for commercial and industrial use (£950 million British pounds or about U.S. $1.9 million)
* Renewable electricity (£800 million or about U.S. $1.6 billion)
* Renewable road transport fuels (£500 million or about U.S. $1.0 billion)
* Domestic energy efficiency (£400 million or about U.S. $800 million)
* Building regulations for domestic use (£275 million or about U.S. $550 million)

The clean energy industry is a new high-growth industry in which the business opportunities are restricted only by one's imagination. The best advice is for an entrepreneur thinking about getting into the clean energy industry is to leverage one's personal strengths and existing knowledge base. For example, an electrical contractor that specializes in servicing residential and commercial customers could add a wind or solar distributorship to his or her product offering, thus offering customers wind and solar power solutions as well as existing services. A swimming pool company could add solar thermal heating systems for its customers, perhaps partnering with a local contractor. A building contractor might add a range of "green building" services to his or her product offerings.

A finance company or bank could add a financing program for residential solar, wind, geothermal, or efficiency projects. Farmers or land speculators could watch for opportunities to buy farmland at attractive prices, particularly marginal land that is not good for growing high-value crops such as corn or wheat, but that will still be able to grow biofuel crops of the future such as switchgrass. Entrepreneurs who live in rural areas could look for new products and services to sell to the booming U.S. agriculture industry. People who specialize in sales and marketing can partner with existing product or service providers to roll out large marketing programs for clean energy products and services.

The U.S. National Renewable Energy Laboratory (NREL) has a program designed to "move NREL-developed technologies and expertise

into commercially viable products and businesses" (see www.nrel.gov/
technologytransfer/). The NREL is looking for companies that want to li-
cense and commercialize NREL-developed technologies. There are similar
technology licensing opportunities in government and academia that an
entrepreneur can tap for business startup ideas.

There is also an expanding range of new employment or consulting
opportunities in the fast-growing clean energy space. There is a list of employment opportunities available in the clean energy industry, for example, at http://www.sustainablebusiness.com/jobs/, or simply do your own
Web search on the phrase "clean energy jobs," "clean energy consulting,"
or a similar set of keywords. The solar power industry is currently hir-
ing aggressively in the United States and one solar job listing site is at the
American Solar Energy Society (see www.ases.org/jobs.htm). This book's
companion Web site at www.ProfitingFromCleanEnergy.com has a more
complete listing of clean energy employment Web sites.

ANGEL INVESTING

In "angel investing," an individual investor invests his or her cash directly
in an early-stage company run by other people. Angel investing is certainly
not for the faint of heart and it is difficult to find reliable companies in
which to invest. However, there are angel networks and clubs that can
help an interested person learn how to do angel investing and how to find
good investments. Industry associations can also be a good place for finding early-stage companies that need seed money. For example, someone
interested in investing directly in an ethanol plant can check on the Renewable Fuels Association Web site, which has a page listing companies
involved in the design and construction of ethanol plants that may have
projects open to investment.[2]

VENTURE CAPITAL

A venture capital (VC) fund pools money from institutional and high-net-
worth investors, invests that money in startup or early stage companies,
takes an active role in helping to build the company, and then finds an exit
strategy such as a sale to a larger company or going public through an initial
public offering (IPO). Venture capital funds try to target annual returns of
20 percent or more.

Venture capital investment is pouring into the clean energy and cleantech industries. According to Cleantech Network, North American and

European venture capital investment in the cleantech industry in 2006 rose +45% yr/yr to \$3.6 billion, after more than doubling in 2005 to \$1.7 billion.[3] The Cleantech Network is a venture capital investment network with over 8,000 investors, 6,000 companies, and 3,500 professional services organizations that specialize in cleantech, according to the company's Web site. The Web site provides a wealth of information on venture capital investment in the cleantech industry. The group also holds conferences to discuss cleantech investing and to bring together investors and companies.

There are several advantages to investing in a VC fund as opposed to trying to invest one's money directly in a company as an angel investor. First, VC funds are highly knowledgeable in the industries in which they specialize and they are constantly scouring the industry at the ground level for attractive investment opportunities with their extensive networking capabilities. Second, VC funds know how to structure investments so that there are attractive risk-reward parameters and incentives for the project. Third, VC funds provide key expertise in building a business and providing it with ongoing support. Fourth, a VC fund knows how to exit a portfolio company by selling the firm or doing an IPO, thus capturing the returns for their investors.

Unfortunately, it is difficult for the average individual investor to get into the venture capital game. Venture capital funds typically only take investment funds from institutions and high-net-worth investors that can qualify for the SEC's definition of an "accredited" investor. For an individual investor, the securities law currently requires an "accredited investor" to have a net worth of at least \$1 million or have an annual income of at least \$200,000 for the last two years. In addition, an investor in a VC fund is typically required to put up a large minimum investment that can go as high as six figures and the investment is then typically locked up for a period of years.

PUBLICLY TRADED STOCKS

The easiest way to invest in the clean energy sector is simply to buy publicly traded stocks. The advantage is that an investor can scale the size of the investment, spread the money around in various companies, and easily enter and exit positions (assuming there is trading liquidity in the stock). Disadvantages include (1) the stock market is fairly efficient and it is not easy to pick stocks that will have long-term appreciation; and (2) an investor's portfolio is not diversified unless a variety of stocks are chosen to spread out the risk.

There is a perception that publicly traded clean energy companies are all small companies that are burning large amounts of cash and depend on government grant support for their survival. This was true back in the late 1990s, but there are now numerous publicly traded clean energy companies operating on a global scale that are highly profitable, that are producing earnings growth rates exceeding 20 percent, and that have market capitalizations of over $2.5 billion. There have recently been a large number of IPOs in the sector, which has added depth to the clean energy stock sector and even encouraged institutional investors to dip their toes into the water.

The global solar industry, for example, is particularly well developed and has a wide range of publicly traded stocks from which to choose. The combined market capitalization of the 12 largest U.S.-listed pure-play solar companies was a hefty $20 billion as of mid-2007. The combined market cap of the top 11 *non-U.S.* pure-play solar cell and polysilicon manufacturers was even larger at $58 billion, producing a global solar company market cap of nearly $80 billion.[4] Moreover, the majority of these solar companies are profitable and the average industry earnings growth rate is about 30 percent. These figures illustrate that the solar industry has clearly established itself as a solid investment arena, even for institutional investors.

In total, there are more than 60 companies listed on U.S. exchanges with market caps over $75 million that can be considered pure-play clean energy companies. The median market cap for these companies is $500 million. About one-half of these companies are profitable.

In addition, there are many micro-cap companies that are popping up with market caps of under about $100 million. Most of these companies are traded over-the-counter on the OTC Bulletin Board (www.otcbb.com) or the Pink Sheets (www.pinksheets.com). Investors need to be careful about investing in these stocks because these companies typically have limited financial reporting, less SEC scrutiny, low liquidity, and high volatility. In addition, there are outright pump-and-dump scams that are occasionally run with OTC stocks.

Yet, the flipside is that it is easier to find an "undiscovered gem" among OTCBB stocks precisely because information is scarce and because Wall Street does not follow the stocks. The best advice for an investor is to think of an OTCBB or Pink Sheet stock as more of a "lottery ticket" than a stock investment. There is a very real chance you may lose a substantial portion of your investment, but there is also the chance that you will sometimes hit the jackpot with a micro-cap stock that ends up hitting it big by being bought out by a larger company or by moving up to trade on the Nasdaq (National Association of Securities Dealers Automated Quotations) or New York Stock Exchange (NYSE).

CLEAN ENERGY STOCKS LISTED OUTSIDE THE UNITED STATES

The United States is accustomed to being the leader in a variety of fields. However, when it comes to clean energy, the United States is far behind the curve. Europe and Japan have a big head start against the United States in most areas of clean energy. This is particularly the case, for example, in the solar power sector, where virtually all the major global solar companies are based in Europe or Asia.

This book mainly focuses on U.S.-listed investments, but will still point out some of the investment opportunities in clean energy available outside the United States. Investing in companies that are based outside the United States is easy if the company has an American Depository Receipt (ADR) that is listed on a U.S. exchange. An ADR is a certificate representing ownership in the company's common stock. For example, several Chinese-based solar companies have their ADRs listed on U.S. exchanges, thus making it easy for U.S. investors to buy the stock. These companies include, for example, Suntech Power Holdings (NYSE: STP), LDK Solar (NYSE: LDK), Yingli Green Energy (NYSE: YGE), and others (Chapter 5 covers the solar industry in detail).

The situation becomes a bit more complicated when an investor wants to buy a stock that trades on an exchange outside the United States. The investor has to make sure his or her trading account will allow the purchase of non-U.S. stocks and many brokerage firms will charge higher brokerage commissions for trading in foreign stocks. Moreover, an investor takes on currency exchange rate risk when buying an overseas stock since the investor is essentially long the currency needed to buy the overseas stock. For example, Renewable Energy Corp. (Oslo: REC NO) is the world's largest pure-play solar company based on current market cap rankings. In order to buy that stock, a U.S.-based investor needs to first convert dollars into Norwegian kroner in order to buy the stock. The investor will then be long, not only the stock, but also the Norwegian krone. The Norwegian krone has a fairly high degree of correlation with the euro but still trades on its own Norwegian-based fundamentals.

Investing in foreign stocks and being long foreign currencies can actually be a good idea for many U.S. investors since globalization is expanding and is reducing the importance of the dollar's role as a reserve currency in the global financial system. The U.S. dollar also remains vulnerable to the massive U.S. trade deficit, which shows little sign of abating in coming years and is causing the daily outflow of more than $2 billion a day in dollars to foreign recipients. Moreover, Asian central banks are looking to reduce the rate at which their dollar reserves are growing.

In the clean energy sector in particular, investors need to consider investing in non-U.S. stocks since the majority of the world's clean energy stocks are traded outside the United States. While investing in non-U.S. stocks involves some information difficulties and exchange rate risk, the rewards can be large for venturing outside the United States in the field of clean energy. Web sites that have good information on globally traded stocks include www.bloomberg.com and finance.google.com, among others.

LARGE-CAP STOCKS

The clean energy revolution is touching companies of all sizes. Many large-cap companies are actively trying to take advantage of clean energy trends. Investors should consider how clean energy trends affect any large-cap stocks that they may own.

A large-cap company cannot be considered a pure play on clean energy trends since the revenue and earnings that a large-cap company may derive from clean energy is probably miniscule compared with its overall revenue. An investor is therefore not gaining any significant exposure to clean energy by investing in a large-cap company, unless the clean energy component at that company promises to have a very significant impact on earnings down the road. Investors interested in investing in clean energy trends should therefore focus on the small and mid-cap companies that derive a significant portion of their revenue from clean energy.

While large-cap companies cannot be considered a pure-play on clean energy, there are some large-cap companies that will benefit more than others from clean energy trends. General Electric (NYSE: GE), for example, is the U.S. large-cap company that is the most heavily involved in the clean energy industry. GE has collected its clean energy products under the brand name of "Ecomagination" and has devoted an entire Web site to the product line (see ge.ecomagination.com).

GE's Ecomagination brand includes a wide variety of products including wind power systems, lighting, cleaner locomotives, clean coal plants, CO_2 sequestration technologies, clean water technologies, water desalination plants, and others. GE is expanding its R&D in cleaner technologies from $700 million in 2005 to $1.5 billion by 2010. GE originally targeted its Ecomagination product sales at $20 billion by 2010, but GE Chairman and CEO Jeffrey Immelt said in May 2007 that GE will "blow away" that $20 billion target.[5] GE is aggressively pursuing clean technology as one of the main drivers of its overall growth. Yet GE's stock price is driven by much more than its Ecomagination product line, which means there is no guarantee that success in the Ecomagination product line will necessarily drive the stock price higher. For example, GE's financial results for Q2–2007 were good but were undercut by disappointing performance in healthcare and its subprime mortgage lending unit (which it now wants to sell), areas that have nothing to do with clean energy.

In addition to the Ecomagination product line, GE also has an investment division called "GE Energy Financial Services" that is actively investing in clean energy projects and companies around the world (see www.geenergyfinancialservices.com). GE Energy Financial Services has $14 billion in assets and invests "more than $5 billion annually in two of the world's most capital-intensive industries, energy and water."[6] Much of this investment is in traditional energy projects, but GE Energy Financial Services is making a big push into clean energy. GE Energy Financial Services plans to expand its investment in renewable energy to $3 billion by the end of 2008 from $1.8 billion at the end of 2006.[7] Kevin Walsh, managing director of GE Energy Financial Services, said that the growth opportunity in clean energy "is so apparent" that "we're going after it."[8] Regarding solar power financing, Mr. Walsh said his company is doing its due diligence on financing large-utility-scale solar projects and said, "We truly believe utility-scale solar will be an incredible opportunity."[9]

GLOBAL PETROLEUM COMPANIES

The positive mention of petroleum companies in a book on clean energy investing may be heresy. However, from an investment standpoint, the forward-looking integrated petroleum companies are not likely to lose out from the clean energy revolution, and may even thrive as they continue to milk profits out of the petroleum industry (which will last for decades) and use that huge petroleum cash flow to leverage themselves into new clean energy opportunities.

The large integrated petroleum companies can afford to wait and invest in whatever areas of the clean energy industry that turn out to be lucrative, thus ensuring their survival and profits for coming decades, even if the petroleum business slowly dies out. There is an old business lesson about letting the pioneers in a new industry get shot in the back with arrows, and then moving in safely to buy the ones that ultimately become successful.

Some of the global-petroleum companies have already become significant players in the clean energy industry. Marathon Oil (NYSE: MRO), for example, has partnered with Andersons (Nasdaq: ANDE), a modest-sized agri-business company, to build and run ethanol plants. If that partnership works out, Marathon Oil could easily afford some of its pocket change to buy Andersons at some point in the future, thus taking complete control of those ethanol plants and distribution channels. Through such partnerships, which are growing, a major company can get a good look at a small company and decide later whether that small company might be a good acquisition target down the road.

BP PLC (NYSE: BP), formerly British Petroleum, is taking a very aggressive approach in developing its own clean energy business. BP is actually carrying out its "Beyond Petroleum" advertising slogan. This book will not discuss the alternative energy initiatives for all the global petroleum companies, but BP illustrates what legacy petroleum companies can do to make sure they are not rendered obsolete by clean energy trends. Here is a quick overview of BP's alternative energy initiatives.

BP's Alternative Energy Efforts

- *Solar.* BP Solar was a Top 10 global producer of solar cells in 2006 and is targeting 600 megawatts of solar cell production by 2008 (see www.bp.com/solar).
- *Wind.* BP Wind is expanding aggressively and has begun wind projects in the U.S. that will produce a combined operating capacity of 550 megawatts. BP Wind has partnered with Clipper Windpower (London: CWP LN) to supply up to 2.3 gigawatts of wind power projects, which is enough electricity to power about 630,000 homes.[10]
- *Hydrogen power.* BP is working with GE on carbon gasification and carbon capture programs that allow coal and petroleum to be used to produce hydrogen for power generation, while allowing CO_2 to be captured. BP is also working with Edison International (NYSE: EIX) to build a $1 billion 500-megawatt hydrogen-fueled power plant that will use petroleum coke as the feedstock and capture and store up to 90 percent of the CO_2 generated by the process.
- *Natural gas power.* BP helps build and supply efficient natural gas-fired power plants that have lower greenhouse gas emissions than legacy natural gas plants. For example, BP, in a joint venture with SK Corporation, built a large 1.1-gigawatt combined-cycle gas turbine power plant in South Korea, which is the most efficient power plant of its kind in the country. BP is constructing a 250-megawatt steam turbine power generating plant at its Texas City refinery and has approval for a 520-megawatt cogeneration facility in Cherry Point, Washington.
- *Biofuels.* BP plans to spend $500 million over the next 10 years to find better biofuel solutions. BP and DuPont (NYSE: DD) have partnered to develop biobutanol from renewable sources. The companies expect initial commercial-scale production to begin in 2007 with feedstock

from British Sugar (which is a division of Associated British Foods that trades in London under the symbol of ABF LN) in the form of sugar beets. BP is working with auto manufacturers to prove the attractiveness of biobutanol as a gasoline additive. Biobutanol is an alcohol, like ethanol, but BP believes that biobutanol has superior performance attributes for use as a gasoline blending agent as compared with ethanol (see www.bp.com/biofuels).

CLEAN ENERGY EXCHANGE-TRADED FUNDS (ETFS)

There are only a handful of clean energy exchange-traded funds (ETFs) and mutual funds, most of which have been launched in the past two years. However, more clean energy ETFs and mutual funds will be launched in coming months and years due to strong investor interest in the sector and due to the expanding pool of stocks available to buy in the sector. The reader can find the latest list of clean energy ETFs and mutual funds on this book's companion Web site at www.ProfitingFromCleanEnergy.com.

A clean energy exchange-traded fund (ETF) seeks to track an underlying index that is comprised of a list of clean energy stocks. An ETF is not trying to pick good and bad stocks—it is just trying to track the index, for better or for worse. The main advantage of a clean energy ETF is that the investor can invest in the whole clean energy sector at a relatively low cost, as compared with trying to choose a diversified portfolio of individual clean energy stocks. However, investing in an ETF means that both good and bad stocks are averaged together, meaning that performance may only be average. In addition, investors should recognize that the clean energy ETFs hold mainly small, growth stocks, and that the performance of these ETFs can be volatile and even erratic. An investor would be well advised not to use one's core portfolio assets to buy a clean energy ETF and instead use a smaller portion of one's portfolio that is earmarked for taking a swing at one of the more aggressive and speculative areas of the stock market.

Before investing in an ETF, an investor should always examine the list of stocks held by the ETF since an investor is really just buying a basket of these stocks. If the investor does not like most or all of the stocks that the ETF holds, then the investor should not buy the ETF. For example, the PowerShares WilderHill Clean Energy Portfolio as of June 2007 held 40 stocks broadly spread across the subsectors of ethanol, fuel cells, solar, power storage and management, power efficiency, and clean utilities. Top holdings included Echelon Corp. (Nasdaq: ELON), Cree Inc. (Nasdaq: CREE), Color Kinetics (Nasdaq: CLRK), First Solar Inc. (Nasdaq: FSLR),

SunPower Corp. (Nasdaq: SPWR), OM Group Inc. (NYSE: OMG), Cypress Semiconductor Corp. (NYSE: CY), Zoltek Cos (Nasdaq: ZOLT), American Superconductor Corp. (Nasdaq: AMSC), and Itron Inc. (Nasdaq: ITRI).

A list of clean energy ETFs is shown in Table 1.1. Of the six clean energy ETFs shown, the PowerShares WilderHill Clean Energy Portfolio had the largest amount of assets under management at about $950 million, in part because it is the oldest clean energy ETF (started in March 2005). The other ETFs had assets of about $20 million or less.

Advantages of the PowerShares WilderHill Clean Energy Portfolio include its liquidity and the sensible choice of the clean energy stocks in its portfolio, but it also had the highest expense ratio of 0.71 percent versus 0.50 percent or less for the other ETFs that hold U.S.-listed stocks. The PowerShares Cleantech Portfolio has a broader mix of stocks due to its "cleantech" mandate rather than just "clean energy," which is a plus for diversification purposes. The PowerShares WilderHill Progressive Energy Portfolio is not really a clean energy ETF but is more of a progressive fossil fuel fund since it owns companies involved in nuclear power and uranium, coal-to-fuel, and other companies involved with fossil fuels. The First Trust Nasdaq Clean Edge U.S. Liquid Series Index Fund is slanted more towards electronics and power solution companies than the more traditional clean energy mix.

Regarding global clean energy ETFs, the PowerShares Global Clean Energy Portfolio holds a broad range of 76 global clean energy stocks. That ETF is anchored by some large-cap stocks (Sharp and Sanyo) and a 27 percent contingent of clean utilities, which should keep the volatility down but may also limit the upside potential. The Market Vectors Global Alternative Energy ETF, by contrast, holds only 30 stocks, although those stocks are well-chosen as the big global players in the clean energy industry.

GREEN MUTUAL FUNDS

Clean energy ETFs, because of their low expenses, can make attractive investment vehicles for short-term traders and for investors with a relatively short investment horizon. However, the clean energy business is a new and volatile industry and there are a number of companies that are not going to thrive over the long haul and that will drag down the performance of the ETF funds. Therefore, it can make sense for an investor with a longer-term horizon to consider one of the actively-managed clean energy mutual funds, even though the expenses on a mutual are typically higher at 1.50 percent to 2.00 percent of assets and front-end load expenses can be as high as 4.75 percent. Only an investor with an investment horizon of at

TABLE 1.1 Clean Energy Exchange-Traded Fund (ETF)

ETF Name	ETF Ticker	Exch	Index Ticker	Assets (in millions)	Expense Ratio	Fund Inception	Geographic	Comments	Web site
PowerShares WilderHill Clean Energy Portfolio	PBW	AMEX	ECO	$950	0.70%	3-Mar-05	U.S.-listed	Good mix of U.S.-listed Clean Energy stocks	www.powershares. com
PowerShares Cleantech Portfolio	PZD	AMEX	CTIUS	$22	0.60%	24-Oct-06	U.S.-listed	Broader stock mix due to Cleantech mandate	www.powershares. com
PowerShares WilderHill Progressive Energy Portfolio	PUW	AMEX	WHPRO	$23	0.70%	24-Oct-06	Global	Slanted toward nuclear and cleaner fossil fuels; 15% large-cap	www.powershares. com

Name	Ticker	Exchange	Symbol	Price	Expense Ratio	Inception	Focus	Description	Website
PowerShares Global Clean Energy Portfolio	PBD	AMEX	NEX	na	0.75%	13-Jun-07	Global	Broad, diversified list of 76 global stocks.	www.powershares.com
First Trust Nasdaq Clean Edge U.S. Liquid Series Index Fund	QCLN	XNMS	CELS	$18	0.60%	8-Feb-06	U.S.-listed	Slanted toward power stocks	www.ftportfolios.com
Market Vectors-Global Alternative Energy ETF	GEX	NYSE	AGIXL	$16	0.65%	3-Mar-07	Global	Good global list but only 30 stocks; strong on wind (19%) and solar (39%); 40% in U.S.	www.vaneck.com/etf

Source: Company Web sites and Bloomberg.
Note: Please check fund Web site for the latest information.

least several years should even think about getting in a fund with a 4.75 percent front-end load expense.

The clean energy sector lends itself to stock-picking by professional investment managers who closely watch the industries and who are equipped (in theory at least) to separate the wheat from the chaff. Paying a front-end load expense and an annual expense to hire a professional manager can make sense in an industry such as clean energy that has such strong potential and such a wide range of stocks with disparate potential.

There are four clean energy or "green" mutual funds listed in Table 1.2. There are other green or environmental funds that are not listed here that are managed by global banks and brokerage firms

The two largest funds in the green mutual fund group are the Winslow Green Growth Fund and the New Alternatives Fund. However, the new Calvert Global Clean Energy Fund, which was started in March 2007, promises to be a formidable challenger. A brief profile of each fund follows.

- *Winslow Green Growth Fund* (WGGFX). The Winslow Green Growth Fund pursues environmentally responsible investing. The fund was launched in 1994 and now has about $237 million in assets under management. The fund interprets its "green" mandate liberally and invests in a number of food companies such as Whole Foods Markets and Green Mountain Coffee, with lower overall exposure to clean energy and cleantech companies than the clean energy ETFs, for example. The fund at the end of 2006 held 50 companies with top holdings including Isis Pharmaceuticals (Nasdaq: ISIS), SurModics (Nasdaq: SRDX), Green Mountain Coffee Roasters (Nasdaq: GMCR), Fuel Tech (Nasdaq: FTEK), ThermoGenesis (Nasdaq: KOOL), aQuantive (Nasdaq: AQNT), NutriSystem (Nasdaq: NTRI), SourceForge (Nasdaq: LNUX), WFI Industries Ltd (Toronto: WFI CN), Whole Foods Market (Nasdaq: WFMI). The fund has an impressive 10-year annual return record of 18.25 percent. See www.wggf.com.
- *New Alternatives Fund* (NALFX). The New Alternatives Fund was the first environmental mutual fund, launched in 1982. The fund focuses on alternative energy investments on a global basis. The fund has about $200 million in assets under management. The fund's top holdings include Acciona SA (Madrid: ANA SM), Abengoa (Madrid: ABG SM), Gamesa Corporation Technologica (Madrid: GAM SM), Ormat Technologies (NYSE: ORA), Schneider Electric (Paris: SU FP), Brookfield Asset management (Toronto: BAM/A CN), and Conergy (German Xetra: CGY GR). The fund posted a large gain of 33.8 percent in 2006 and its five-year average annual return is 15.86 percent. See www. newalternativesfund.com.

TABLE 1.2 Clean Energy Mutual Fund List

Fund Name	Ticker	Assets	Front Load	Back Load	Expense Ratio	Inception	Web site
Winslow Green Growth Fund	WGGFX	$237 mln	none	none	1.45%	3-May-94	www.winslowgreen.com
New Alternatives Fund	NALFX	$201 mln	4.75%	none	1.25%	3-Sep-82	www.newalternativesfund.com
Guinness Atkinson Alternative Energy Fund	GAAEX	$80 mln	none	none	1.98%	31-Mar-06	www.gafunds.com
Calvert Global Alternative Energy Fund	CGAEX	na	4.75%	none	1.85%	31-Mar-07	www.calvert.com/ alternativeenergy/

Source: Company information and Bloomberg.

- *Guinness Atkinson Alternative Energy Fund* (GAAEX). This fund invests in global alternative energy stocks. The fund was launched in March 2006 and has $80 million under management. As of December 31, 2006, the fund held 55 stocks and the top holdings were Q-Cells (German Xetra: QCE GR), Nordex AG (German Xetra: NDX1 GR), Biopetrol Industries AG (German Xetra: B2I GR), Iberdrola SA (Madrid SMCE: IBE SM), Environmental Power Corp. (AMEX: EPG), Vestas Wind Systems (Copenhagen: VWS DC), Clipper Windpower PLC (London: CWP LN), REpower Systems (German Xetra: RPW GR), Climate Exchange PLC (London: CLE LN), and Fuel Systems Solutions (Nasdaq: FSYS). For more information, see www.gafunds.com.
- *Calvert Global Clean Energy Fund* (CAEIX). Calvert recently launched its Global Clean Energy Fund in March 2007. Calvert has been a pioneer for 30 years in the area of socially responsible investing. The fund intends to invest in about 150 companies, mostly from the United States, Europe, China, and Japan. The fund intends to invest 80 percent in pure plays and about 20 percent in "market leaders" such as GE and BP, according to the fund manager. See www.calvert.com/alternativeenergy/.

In addition to mutual funds that focus on buying green stocks, there are "socially responsible" funds that invest in traditional areas of the stock market but exclude stocks that do not meet certain social or environmental criteria. Environmentally screened mutual funds are operated by the Sierra Club (www.sierraclubfunds.com), Spectra,[11] Portfolio 21 (www.portfolio21.com), and others. Socially responsible investing has grown rapidly in the past few years and assets under management are now as high as $2 trillion. An excellent source of information on socially responsible investing can be found at the Social Investment Forum's Web site at www.SocialInvest.org.

GLOBAL ETFs AND GREEN MUTUAL FUNDS

Investors should seriously consider the clean energy ETF and green mutual funds that are global in scope. As mentioned before, there are only about 60 pure-play U.S.-based clean energy companies, whereas there are many more stocks globally. Mutual funds that invest in global clean energy stocks include the New Alternatives Fund, Guinness Atkinson Alternative Energy Fund, and Calvert Global Alternative Energy. Clean energy ETFs that invest in global stocks include the PowerShares WilderHill Progressive Energy Portfolio, the PowerShares Global Clean Energy Portfolio and the Market Vectors-Global Alternative.

FUTURES AND OPTIONS

There are a variety of futures and options contracts that are tied to the clean energy industry. In the biofuels market, for example, the Chicago Board of Trade has an ethanol trading complex with futures and swaps. There are various futures and options contracts on ethanol feedstock products such as corn and sugar (for ethanol) and palm oil (for biodiesel) at various exchanges around the world. There are carbon allowance futures contracts at the International Commodity Exchange (ICE). Trading opportunities in these areas will be discussed in more depth later in the book.

INVESTMENT CRITERIA FOR PUBLICLY TRADED STOCKS

This book focuses on identifying the clean energy companies that have publicly traded stock and that have market caps at least $75 million. However, not all of the companies listed in this book as participants in the clean energy industry will represent a good investment. In setting out the criteria for choosing attractive clean energy stocks, we start with some standard investment criteria:

- Industry with an attractive and scaleable profit model.
- Company has a protected niche or a unique strategic advantage.
- Company has a current or strong promise of accelerated earnings growth.
- Company has a strong and proven management that can deliver results.

With the clean energy industry, we are mainly operating in the investment style known as *small- and mid-cap growth*. In other words, we are mainly looking at small- and mid-cap companies that are in a high growth mode. This raises some additional investment challenges, as compared with investing in more stable, large-cap stocks. Small- and mid-cap growth companies operate in fast-growing industries where there are a myriad of problems including disruptive technology change, difficulty in commercializing even promising technologies, difficulty in gaining sales traction, unclear paths to profitability, a shortage of capital, volatile financial results, among many others. Quite simply, we need to be very careful about choosing clean energy stocks. We cannot simply invest in a company that tells a good story or that has a technology that looks promising. We need to assess whether there is actually large-scale demand for that company's product and whether that company is capable of commercializing and selling that product or service in a profitable manner.

Here are some additional criteria that a small- to mid-cap clean energy company should satisfy:

- Proprietary technology or a sustainable niche that will allow the company to compete against larger companies that have much greater resources.
- Ability to commercialize a product or service and quickly scale up that product or service to serve a mass market.
- World-class sales and marketing capabilities to ensure sales traction.
- Sufficient financial and human resources to take a product all the way to the commercialized stage.
- Management focus on creating profits and value for public shareholders and not on simply burning cash indefinitely or granting themselves big pay packages.

The stock market graveyard is littered with small companies that thought they had a business but failed due to the following causes:

1. Insufficient financing.
2. An inability to translate a promising technology into a commercially attractive product or service.
3. An inability to execute on sales and marketing.
4. An inability to compete against competitors or a large company, among many other reasons.

Less-experienced investors would be well advised to take a lower-risk strategy of choosing companies that are already profitable and that have proven that they have a product or service that is already succeeding in the marketplace. The potential upside for the stock may be lower than an earlier stage company, but the risks are also significantly lower, meaning the risk-return profile may still be very attractive. Investors that have more experience in analyzing and selecting small-cap companies, on the other hand, will find that the clean energy industry can offer them a host of opportunities.

VALUATION AND BUBBLES

A cautionary word is in order about excess valuation and speculative bubbles. As with any new, hot industry, the clean energy industry is subject to speculative excess, bubbles and overvaluation. Certain subsectors of the clean energy industry have already gone through speculative bubbles and busts. The fuel cell industry, for example, has seen periodic stock run-ups and sell-offs since 2000, and fuel cell stocks on average were very weak from mid-2006 through mid-2007 and traded down to five-year lows. Ethanol stocks soared in early 2006 but then fell sharply later in 2006 and in early 2007. This volatility creates trading opportunities (long and short) for traders with short time horizons, but makes it difficult for the long-term investor to enter a long-term, profitable position.

A long-term investor in the clean energy sector would be well advised to patiently wait for buying opportunities in strategically attractive stocks, put in a good-til-canceled stop for safety well below the entry price, and then just forget about the stock and plan to hold it for three to five years or more. Having a long-term investment horizon means not worrying about the week-to-week fluctuations in the stock, but instead investing in an industry that is likely to do very well in coming decades, knowing there will be various bumps and corrections along the way.

CLEAN ENERGY STOCK PERFORMANCE

In order to look at the stock performance of the clean energy sector, we will use clean energy indexes produced by Melvin & Company, an institutional research and trading brokerage firm based in Chicago. The Melvin Clean Energy Index™ tracks about 50 U.S.-listed clean energy companies. The graph in Figure 1.1 summarizes the annual performance seen from 2003 to 2006. The index performed very poorly in 2002 (−35.6 percent) due to the U.S. economic recession and broad stock market correction but then performed very well in 2003 (+116.2 percent), 2004 (+37.4 percent), and 2005 (+29.8 percent). In 2006, the index rose +8.0 percent, which was below the Russell 2000 gain of +17.0 percent, as clean energy stocks saw some profit-taking pressures. In the first half of 2007, the index was up +9 percent year-to-date.

Figure 1.2 illustrates the performance of the Melvin Securities Clean Energy Index™ relative to the S&P 500 and Russell 2000 over the past five years. The chart illustrates the strength of the clean energy sector from 2003 through the first half of 2006. The clean energy sector then fell back in the second half of 2006 because of weakness in ethanol stocks (due to the rise in corn prices that started in September 2006) and due to profit taking in the other sectors.

The clean energy sector is actually a collection of about 10 completely different industries. It would be a big mistake to assume that these subsectors move together in lockstep. Indeed, Figure 1.3 tracks the Melvin Clean

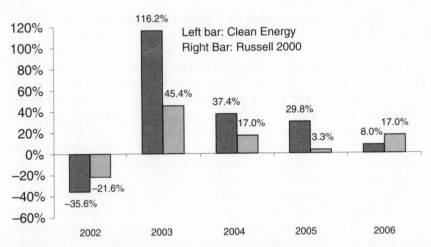

FIGURE 1.1 Melvin Clean Energy Index™ Annual Performance versus Russell 2000 Small-Cap Index

Energy *subsector* stock indexes. The chart illustrates the disparate performance of the various clean energy subsectors. The Fuel Cell and Power Efficiency subsectors have been relatively weak over the past five years. The Ethanol sector soared in the first half of 2006 when ethanol prices surged

FIGURE 1.2 Melvin Clean Energy Index™ vs. S&P 500 and Russell 2000

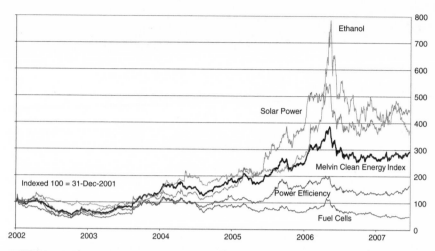

FIGURE 1.3 Melvin Clean Energy Index™ and Subsector Indexes

on the switch to ethanol from MTBE, but ethanol stocks then fell back in late 2006 and early 2007 as corn prices surged and threatened profit margins for corn-based ethanol producers. The solar sector broke out starting late 2004 and has since remained generally strong.

CHAPTER 2

Catalysts for the Clean Energy Industry

I n this chapter, we examine the drivers and catalysts behind the clean energy industry. Every industry has drivers that determine demand and growth rates and, by extension, industry revenues, profits, and stock prices. It is important to examine these drivers to analyze whether the underpinnings of the industry are solid and sustainable, or whether the entire industry is built on a house of cards.

Products and services succeed in the marketplace if they can solve buyers' problems. One of the first rules of sales is to identify the prospective customer's problems so that the sales person can then explain how the product will solve the customer's problems. In the case of clean energy, we need to examine the underlying problems to see if there is a need for a solution and whether clean energy companies can provide that solution. If clean energy technologies can in fact solve serious world problems in a cost-effective manner, then we have indeed found an industry that will have legs for decades to come.

FOSSIL FUEL NEGATIVES: POLLUTION, CO_2 EMISSIONS, CARTELS, PRICE SPIKES, AND RISING PRICES

In the past two centuries, fossil fuel in the form of coal, petroleum, and natural gas has served the world very well in providing a cheap supply of fuel to drive the age of industrialization. The energy derived from burning

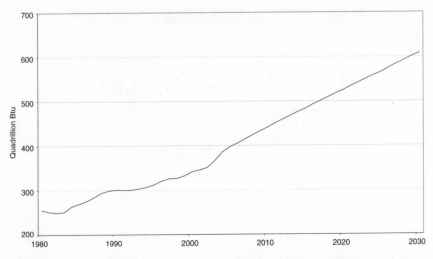

FIGURE 2.1 World Fossil Fuel Consumption: EIA Forecast to 2030

fossil fuels has powered the world's factories, homes and vehicles for many decades. Fossil fuels have helped make citizens in the industrialized world rich beyond the dreams of any person living prior to the modern age.

The U.S. Energy Information Administration fully expects the age of fossil fuels to continue through its forecast period of 2030, with overall fossil fuel consumption by 2030 doubling from the level seen as recently as 1995, as seen in Figure 2.1. Yet the problems caused by fossil fuel are already coming home to roost. The simple fact is that burning fossil fuels, whether in power plants or in internal combustion engines, releases CO_2, other greenhouse gases, and various contaminants into the atmosphere, causing pollution and global warming problems. Energy needs to be derived from cleaner sources that avoid these problems.

Fossil fuels not only pollute the earth's atmosphere but also make the world's economy vulnerable to supply shocks and the price of fossil fuels. Coal prices have remained remarkably inexpensive over the years. However, crude oil prices have been highly volatile in the past several decades, as seen in Figure 2.2. Crude oil prices can single-handedly threaten world economic growth. For example, an upward spike in crude oil prices was the direct cause of three of the last five recessions in the United States (1973–1975, 1980, 1990–1991). The deep 1973–1975 recession was largely caused by the Arab Oil Embargo, the 1980 recession was caused by an oil price spike related to the Iranian revolution against the Shah of Iran, and the 1990–1991 recession was caused by an oil spike tied to Saddam Hussein's invasion of Kuwait and the first U.S.-Iraq War (Operation Desert

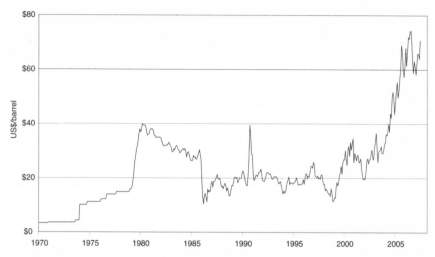

FIGURE 2.2   Crude Oil Prices: West Texas Intermediate

Storm). Those recessions directly caused unemployment, business failures, personal bankruptcies, mortgage defaults, and various other types of misery for citizens.

Crude oil prices are in fact controlled to a significant degree by the OPEC cartel, which restricts the supply of crude oil in order to ensure that oil prices stay high and thus maximize revenue for the OPEC states. The extra revenue that OPEC member states acquire through their anticompetitive behavior comes straight out of the pocket of the average citizen in the U.S., Europe, Asia, Australia, South America, and Africa. Yet the U.S. and European governments have never made a serious effort to break the control of the OPEC cartel, mainly because the Western nations do not want to risk another oil embargo and because they want to ensure that pro-Western governments such as Saudi Arabia stay in power. Yet the price for that subservience to OPEC is that Western consumers and businesses are forced to pay exorbitant prices for petroleum products, which in turn leads to lower consumer income and corporate profits and subpar economic growth.

There is little doubt that the long-term direction of oil prices will be upward, thus providing more pain for global consumers down the road. Crude oil prices over the short-term can go up or down, depending on short-term demand and supply factors. However, crude oil prices from 2004 through 2006 more than doubled from $30 per barrel to a record high of $78 per barrel and have since fluctuated between about $50 to $70 per barrel. The main reason for this rally was strong new demand from China, India, and other emerging countries.

In a well-functioning market, new supply would emerge to meet a surge in demand and that new supply would allow prices to fall back to more reasonable levels. However, the crude oil market is far from being a well-functioning market. OPEC has been pleased with the surge in oil prices and particularly with the fact that oil prices of $70 per barrel have not caused a world recession, contrary to the earlier predictions of virtually all economists. Since the world proved it could absorb high oil prices, OPEC simply raised its effective target price for crude oil from $40 per barrel to about the $60 per barrel area. In fact in autumn 2006, when it became clear that crude oil inventories were excessive and that oil prices were headed to $50 per barrel, OPEC members mobilized to cut production by an overall 5 percent, causing oil prices to rally back up to and above the $60 per barrel level.

The crude oil supply problem has been exacerbated by the fact that the non-OPEC oil producers and global oil companies have not stepped up production significantly despite high prices. Part of that problem is tied to the new nationalism among oil producing countries such as Russia, Venezuela and others. These countries are engaging in a thinly-veiled confiscation of assets from the big global oil companies. The end result of this nationalism is usually lower overall oil production because politically controlled national oil companies are more interested in providing immediate revenue to government coffers to be used for political purposes, rather than using cash flow to invest in new exploration to expand reserves and maximize revenue over the long-term.

The world's oil companies are not only losing control of assets and reserves through nationalism, but are also reluctant to expand investment because they are not sure whether oil prices will remain high enough to give them a sufficient return on investment on the massive quantity of capital that is now required to develop major oil fields. The reality is that virtually all of the world's cheap and easy-to-extract oil has already been found. There is plenty of crude oil left in the world's crust, but it is deep in the earth, far below the ocean or in inhospitable and hard to reach locations. Major oil companies, for example, found huge oil reserves on the order of 3 to 15 billion barrels in the Wilcox formation in the Gulf of Mexico, but the oil is in very deep water some 175 miles off the coast of Louisiana. The oil is under 7,000 feet of water and is then down another 20,000 feet below the sea floor. Major oil companies are developing the technology to drill in such deepwater locales, but the costs are far higher than old onshore oil fields where the oil is close to the surface and cheap to extract.

The reality is that huge amounts of capital are necessary to extract the oil reserves that are being discovered today. The only way that oil producers will spend such large sums of capital on new investment in expensive-to-extract oil is if oil prices are high enough on a sustained basis to allow them to turn a profit on those oil extraction expenses. If they cannot turn a profit, then they will not extract that oil until prices are high enough. In other words, oil prices must stay high or else producers will not bring the new supply to market. This is the main reason why oil prices are likely to stay high and rise further over the long run.

Regarding the cost of coal, coal-fired plants are currently the cheapest way to generate electricity. However, that does not consider the external costs of coal-fired plants. If coal-fired plants were required to capture the CO_2 they emit into the atmosphere, it would cost 40 percent more to build and operate and the plants would produce 20 percent less electricity, according to an MIT study, *The Future of Coal: Options for a Carbon-Constrained World*.[1] If these costs were loaded into the effective cost of coal, then coal-generated electricity no longer looks so cheap and renewable electricity generated by solar and wind power becomes more economical by comparison.

ENERGY SECURITY

The concept of "energy security" has made its way into public discussion in a big way in recent years. Washington politicians even try to get the phrase "energy security" into their proposed bills to make their bills sound more attractive. For example, a recent bill introduced into Congress was called the Biofuels Security Act of 2005.

The dependence of the United States on foreign oil imports is dramatically illustrated in Figure 2.3. U.S. oil production peaked in 1970 at 3.52 billion barrels and has fallen steadily ever since.[2] Meanwhile, U.S. petroleum consumption has steadily risen for the past two decades. The gap between falling production and rising consumption has been filled by a sharp increase in net imports of foreign oil. In 2006, the United States imported a net 4.48 billion barrels of oil, which represented 60 percent of U.S. oil consumption.[3] As things stand now, the U.S. economy simply could not function in any reasonable way without foreign oil imports.

The term "energy security" refers to both economic security and physical security. In an economic sense, western economies would see a huge benefit if they could eliminate their economic dependence on petroleum prices, which are highly volatile and likely to rise over the long run. However, the energy security also refers to geopolitical and physical security. The United States has gone to war over oil in the past and may decide do so again in the future. When Saddam Hussein invaded Kuwait in 1990 and appeared destined to march on to Saudi Arabia, the United States hastily arranged a coalition to go to war with Saddam. The United States and its

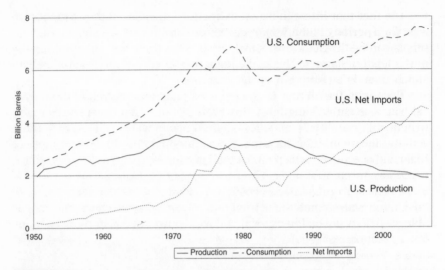

FIGURE 2.3 U.S. Petroleum Import Dependence
Source: U.S. Energy Information Administration, *Annual Energy Review 2006,* May 2007, Table 5.1, http://www.eia.doe.gov/emeu/aer/txt/stb0501.xls.

allies in Desert Storm quickly pushed Saddam's troops out of Kuwait and back to Baghdad.

The reason why the United States went to war to reverse Iraq's invasion of Kuwait was because America's "vital national interests" were at stake. Everyone knows that "vital national interests" often refers to the need for the United States to protect the global supply of oil, without which the U.S. economy would be brought to its knees. The first President Bush used high-minded language such as "aggression will not stand" to justify the first U.S.-Iraq war. But it is doubtful that the U.S. government would have sent its troops into full-scale battle if Saddam Hussein had seized a very small neighboring desert nation with no oil and no strategic importance. There are frequently wars in Africa involving aggression and even genocide, and yet the United States does not go to war there because America's "vital national interests" are not involved.

Regarding the possibility of future wars over oil, there is not much doubt that the United States would be at war within a matter of weeks (regardless of whether the Republicans or the Democrats were in power) if Iran were to blockade the Straights of Hormuz, through which one-fifth of the world's daily oil consumption flows.[4] Oil prices would likely soar above $150 per barrel and gasoline prices could reach at least $5 per gallon on even a temporary shutdown of the Straights of Hormuz. "Vital American interests" would once again be at stake.

The fact that Iran could cut off one-fifth of the world's oil supply, at least for a period of time, highlights the fact that much of the world's oil reserves can be threatened or controlled by countries that are either hostile to the United States or that have serious internal stability problems. The Middle East is a tinder box with low-grade wars going on in Afghanistan and Iraq, with Iran trying feverishly to build a nuclear bomb, with radical Islamists threatening moderate Arab governments in the region, and with hostility toward Israel in the region as high as ever. In Nigeria, rebel activity and political instability have caused a 20 percent reduction in Nigeria's oil output, which is particularly important since Nigeria is the world's eighth largest oil exporter and exports the light, sweet crude that is the easiest to refine into gasoline.[5] Nigeria is particularly important to the United States since Nigeria exports 42 percent of its oil to the United States.[6] In Venezuela, President Hugo Chavez has full control over national oil production and regularly threatens to cut off oil exports to the United States. Venezuela accounted for 11 percent of total U.S. imports in 2005. In Russia, the Russian government over the past several years has used various bare-knuckle tactics to take over private oil and gas operations and consolidate those operations under Russian government ownership and control. In China, government officials have been busy traveling the world to dole out foreign aid and favors in order to lock up sources of oil for direct export to China.

When it comes to "energy security," Brazil is one of the few countries in the world that has it right. Twenty years ago Brazil's government began an aggressive campaign to build its domestic ethanol business. Brazil has now reached its goal of energy independence and no longer needs to import any foreign oil. Brazil's economy and foreign policy are now insulated from oil price shocks and the vagaries of oil politics and threats.

GROWING GLOBAL ENERGY DEMAND

The world could perhaps live with the current energy situation if there were no economic growth in the world and no population growth. However, world demand for energy is growing very rapidly. The supply of energy has to keep pace, not only with current demand, but also with the substantial new demand that will emerge in coming decades.

World energy consumption will increase by a total of 57 percent from 2004 to 2030, according to forecasts by the U.S. Energy Information Administration (EIA), a unit of the U.S. Department of Energy.[7] The EIA breaks down its forecast between the world's industrialized OECD nations (i.e., the 30 industrialized countries that belong to the Organization for

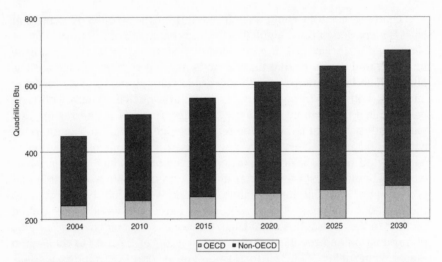

FIGURE 2.4 EIA Forecasted Primary Energy Consumption: OECD vs. non-OECD
Source: U.S. Energy Information Administration, *International Energy Outlook 2007*,
May 2007, p. 1, Table A1, p. 83, www.eia.doe.gov/oiaf/ieo/index.html.

Economic Cooperation and Development) and non-OECD nations. The
EIA's forecast is that energy demand will increase by an extraordinary
95 percent through 2030 in the emerging non-OECD countries, as compared with a 24 percent increase in the OECD countries. Regarding annual
growth rates, the U.S. Energy Information Administration is projecting that
total energy consumption in the OECD countries will grow at an average
annual rate of +0.8 percent, but that annual growth will be more than three
times as large at +2.6 percent for the non-OECD emerging countries. These
forecasts are illustrated in graphical format in Figure 2.4.

The takeaway from this analysis is to recognize how the world's energy outlook is driven far more by new energy demand from emerging
non-OECD countries than from the OECD industrialized countries. Much
of this demand can be tied directly to the fall of the socialist economic system in the 1980s and 1990s. When the socialist economic system fell, some
2.6 billion people (just in China, Russian, and India) were suddenly asking for rapid economic development.[8] India was never officially a socialist
country, but nevertheless suffered from heavy statist government interven-
tion in the economy until free market reforms started to be implemented
in the 1990s. These countries, and many other developing countries, now
have a voracious energy appetite in conjunction with their full-throttle economic development policies.

The alarming extent of non-OECD energy demand is also seen when
narrowing the focus to electricity consumption instead of overall energy

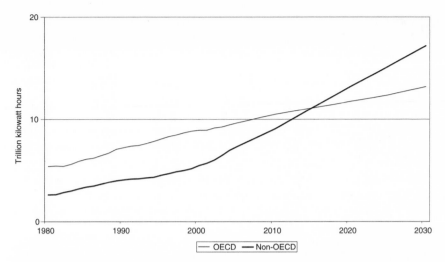

FIGURE 2.5 EIA Forecasted Electric Power Generation: OECD vs. Non-OECD
Source: U.S. Energy Information Administration, *International Energy Outlook 2007,*
May 2007, p. 8, http://www.eia.doe.gov/oiaf/ieo/excel/figure_61data.xls.

consumption. The EIA forecasts that world electricity generation in 2030 will nearly double to 30.364 trillion kilowatt-hours from the 2004 level of 16.424 trillion kilowatt-hours, as seen in Figure 2.5. The EIA is projecting annual growth for electricity consumption in the non-OECD countries of 3.5 percent versus 1.3 percent in the OECD countries.[9] This will cause electric power generation supply in the non-OECD countries to cross above that of OECD countries in about 2015, as seen in Figure 2.5. The EIA says, "Robust economic growth in many of the non-OECD countries is expected to boost demand for electricity to run newly purchased home appliances for air conditioning, cooking, space and water heating, and refrigeration and to support expansion of commercial services, including hospitals, office buildings, and shopping malls."[10]

It is extremely important to recognize the scale of energy demand in developing countries. The population of just China, India, and Russia is 2.6 billion (not to mention the rest of the developing world), which is more than eight times larger than America's population of 301 million people.[11] Many of the people in the developing world aspire to eventually having the same type of homes, electric appliances, and vehicles as Americans, Europeans, and Japanese.

Right now, people in the developing world use a fraction of the electricity used in the developed world. Even though China has more than four times as many people as the United States, for example, it uses one-third less electricity.[12] If China's per capita electricity usage reached the current U.S. level of 12,343 kilowatt-hours, China's national electricity consumption would increase by more than six times from the current level of 2.494 trillion kilowatt-hours to about 16.3 trillion kilowatt-hours. China is already struggling to meet its current electricity demand, let alone meet potential demand running as high as six times the current level.

The enormous size of potential electricity demand in China—and, indeed, from the developing world as a whole—thus becomes clearer. China is already choking on its coal-fired power plants, which are also sending pollution all the way across the Pacific Ocean to the United States.[13] Every 7 to 10 days, China brings another coal-fired power plant on line that is big enough to serve all the households in Dallas or San Diego according to the *New York Times*.[14] Yet the situation can get worse as per capita electricity usage in the developing world rises even further.

The increase in energy demand from the developing world stems from the transportation sector as well as the electricity sector. In the transportation sector, the energy demand takes the form of gasoline rather than coal and natural gas for the electricity sector. For the OECD countries, the EIA forecasts that energy demand for transportation will grow by an overall 27 percent from 57.9 quadrillion Btu (British thermal units) in 2004 to 73.4 quadrillion Btu by 2030.[15] By contrast, the EIA forecasts that in the non-OECD countries, energy demand for transportation will more than double from 39.8 quadrillion Btu in 2004 to 63.1 quadrillion Btu in 2030, swamping growth in the OECD developed world.[16]

The bottom line is that there is extremely strong demand for both electricity and transportation energy coming mainly from the developing countries where there are several billion people who aspire to substantially raising their living standards. The fossil fuel industry might be able to deliver on this demand, but it would take a lot of coal and crude oil extraction, and even then the impact on the environment in terms of greenhouse gas emissions and other environmental damage would be substantial.

GREENHOUSE GAS EMISSIONS AND CLIMATE CHANGE

The American public in 2006 seemed to wake up to the issue of global climate change. Al Gore's book, *An Inconvenient Truth*, was on the *New York Times* bestseller list and his film of the same title won an Academy Award for Best Documentary. Al Gore and the Intergovernmental Panel on Climate Change then won the Nobel Peace Prize in October 2007. Al Gore's book and film certainly had something to do with public awareness of global warming, but so did observable facts such as melting icecaps, shrinking glaciers, and observations by people in their own hometowns.

The American public increasingly recognizes that climate change is real and favors taking action. This support is critical since public demands for action will put pressure on politicians to take action on climate change, thus supporting the clean energy industry. A *New York Times*/CBS News poll found that 84 percent of Americans now believe that human activity is at least contributing to global warming.[17] The poll also found that 92 percent of Americans would be willing to make sacrifices to reduce global warming and that 87 percent favor using renewable energy sources such as solar and wind power and fueling vehicles with ethanol.

Scientists studying climate change now generally agree that global warming is real and that human-generated greenhouse gases are the reason behind global warming. Figure 2.6 illustrates the rise in global temperatures that has occurred in the past several decades. There are a dwindling number of people who deny that global warming is occurring. Most global warming skeptics have given up refuting the data on global warming and have instead started to argue that human-generated greenhouse gases are not the cause of global warming or that the problem is not serious enough to justify government regulation or funding to address the problem.

There is a wealth of information that supports the view that greenhouse gas emissions are the cause of global warming. Some of the most comprehensive information comes from the Intergovernmental Panel on Climate Change, which is a 20-year-old group organized by the United

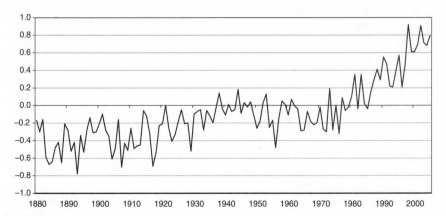

FIGURE 2.6 Global Temperature Variation from Average (Degrees Centigrade) – 1880–2005
Source: NASA Goddard Insttitute for Space Studies, September 10, 2007, http://data. giss.nasa.gov/gistemp/graphs/.

Nations Environment Programme (UNEP) and the World Meteorological Organization (WMO). The group's latest report, which was prepared by hundreds of climate scientists and economists, presents the closest thing to a global consensus on the issue.[18] The Climate Panel concluded in its February 2007 report that human activity is the cause of global warming with near certainty and the group called for action to limit greenhouse gas emissions to avoid substantial risks associated with global warming. The IPCC Web site (www.ipcc.ch) contains a wealth of useful information related to global warming including scientific and technical papers.

Another key report on global warming, the "Stern Report," a comprehensive 700-page analysis of the economics of climate change as opposed to the science of climate change, was produced by a U.K. government group headed by Sir Nicholas Stern, the Head of the Government Economic Service and a former World Bank Chief Economist and released in October 2006.[19] The essential economic message of the Stern Report can be boiled down to a single quote: "The costs of stabilizing the climate are significant but manageable; delay would be dangerous and much more costly."[20]

The Summary of Conclusions of the Stern Report contains the following notable statements:

- The scientific evidence is now overwhelming: climate change is a serious global threat, and it demands an urgent global response. (p. vi)
- Climate change will affect the basic elements of life for people around the world—access to water, food production, health, and the environment. Hundreds of millions of people could suffer hunger, water shortages and coastal flooding as the world warms. (p. vi)
- If we don't act, the overall costs and risks of climate change will be equivalent to losing at least 5% of global GDP each year, now and forever. If a wider range of risks and impacts is taken into account, the estimates of damage could rise to 20% of GDP or more. (p. vi)
- In contrast, the costs of action—reducing greenhouse gas emissions to avoid the worst impacts of climate change—can be limited to about 1 percent of global GDP each year. (p. vi)
- Our actions now and over the coming decades could create risks of major disruption to economic and social activity, on a scale similar to those associated with the great wars and the economic depression of the first half of the 20th century. And it will be difficult or impossible to reverse these changes. (p. vi)
- Action on climate change will also create significant business opportunities, as new markets are created in low-carbon energy technologies and other low-carbon goods and services. These markets could grow to be worth hundreds of billions of dollars each year, and employment in these sectors will expand accordingly. (p. viii)

- The world does not need to choose between averting climate change and promoting growth and development. Changes in energy technologies and in the structure of economies have created opportunities to decouple growth from greenhouse gas emissions. (p. viii)
- Climate change is the greatest market failure the world has ever seen, and it interacts with other market imperfections. Three elements of policy are required for an effective global response. The first is the pricing of carbon, implemented by tax, trading or regulation. The second is policy to support innovation and the deployment of low-carbon technologies. And the third is action to remove barriers to energy efficiency, and to inform, educate and persuade individuals about what they can do to respond to climate change.[21] (p. viii)

One can debate details about climate change, but the observable fact is that most governments in the world have now adopted the view that global warming is real and that government measures are necessary to address the problem. The investment conclusion for our purposes is that the government push to curb global warming is likely to grow in coming years, which will provide a very strong tailwind for the clean energy industry.

CLEAN ENERGY TECHNOLOGY IMPROVEMENTS

In the early 1970s, after the Arab Oil Embargo caused oil prices to soar and caused a painful U.S. recession, there was a rush to encourage energy efficiency and to develop solar power and other forms of alternative energy. The effort largely fizzled, however, because oil prices fell back, and also because technology at the time was not sophisticated enough to truly replace oil and coal.

Since the 1970s, scientists have made enormous strides in semiconductor technology, biotechnology, materials science, nanotechnology, information technology, communications, and other fields. These scientific advances can now be brought to bear on commercializing existing clean energy technologies and inventing new ones. *Nanosolar* was not even a concept back in the 1970s, and now there is a company called Nanosolar, Inc., which has $148 million in venture capital funding and is in the process of building its first factory to produce thin film solar panels using manufacturing techniques based on nanotechnology (see www.nanosolar.com). DuPont has over 100 scientists and engineers working on producing advanced biofuels using biotechnology and other scientific disciplines.[22]

Technology and technological innovation are in fact the backbone of the clean energy industry today. Generating energy is no longer about searching for fuel in the earth's crust, as it was in the days of fossil fuels. Rather, generating energy today is about using advanced scientific disciplines to produce the technological tools and equipment that converts energy from renewable sources such as solar, wind, geothermal, and agricultural crops.

Where do clean energy companies fit into the old Standard Industrial Classification (SIC) scheme of classifying companies into certain industries? Do they fit into industrial, agriculture, electrical equipment, or energy classifications? The answer is that they really fit into *energy technology*, a new classification that involves using technology solutions to produce low-carbon electricity or transportation fuel from renewable sources. Technological innovation is the key driver that will make clean energy technologies less expensive and increasingly competitive with fossil fuels in coming years. The ability to develop and harness new technologies is also what will distinguish the most successful clean energy companies.

DEMAND FOR DISTRIBUTED POWER SOLUTIONS DUE TO GRID UNRELIABILITY

The blackouts in North America in recent years—not to mention the sporadic availability of electric power in developing countries—has driven the demand for distributed, onsite power generation resources that homeowners and businesses can install at their own locations. These distributed power solutions include solar and wind power systems, fuel cells, natural gas or diesel-powered generators, and various types of battery backup systems. Businesses and homeowners can install these systems at their building locations and ensure some degree of protection from the vagaries of the utility power grid. In some areas, any excess power that a homeowner or business generates can be fed back into the grid and the homeowner or business can receive a credit for that power.

Contributors to Wikipedia, the online free encyclopedia, have compiled a long list of serious global power failures that have occurred in the past decade that highlights the poor record of grid electricity.[23] In the United States, the largest blackout in history was the "Northeast Blackout of 2003," which involved 40 million people in eight U.S. states and 10 million people in the Canadian province of Ontario.[24] The blackout caused an estimated $6 billion in losses.[25] A study group eventually concluded that the cause of the blackout was high-voltage power lines that came in contact with overgrown trees in Ohio. Then, because of inadequate transmission system protection measures, the disruption cascaded through much of the regional transmission area and caused the shutdown of more than

100 power plants.[26] The fact that some overgrown trees in Ohio ultimately caused $6 billion in losses is a little difficult to explain to power customers who could only become more doubtful about the reliability of their local power utilities and the entire North American transmission system. Power consumers in developing countries, who may receive power only during certain hours of the day, have even more cause to take matters into their own hands and buy distributed power generation and backup systems.

The cost of power blackouts and brownouts can be enormous for many businesses, with costs including damaged equipment, lost employee time, plant shutdowns, lost inventory, lost sales, and damage to a company's reputation when that company cannot respond to its customers. These high costs make it imperative for many businesses to have some type of self-generated power or at least backup power systems that can hold them over until the grid comes back to life. The unreliability of the grid is a key driver for the industries that sell distributed power generating solutions and power backup solutions.

RISING ELECTRICITY PRICES

Electricity prices in the United States are rising. The higher cost of running a power plant is the main reason for rising electricity prices, both in terms of higher labor costs, higher fuel input prices, and higher administrative expenses in general. In addition, utilities are playing catch-up after years in which regulators blocked electricity price hikes. In fact, the average retail price of electricity on an inflation-adjusted basis (in 2000 dollars) in the United States peaked at 9.24 cents/kilowatt-hour in 1985 and then fell sharply by an overall 27 percent to a trough of 6.78 cents/kilowatt-hour in 1999.[27] The inflation-adjusted retail price of electricity since the trough of 6.78 cents in 1999 moved just mildly higher to 7.63 cents by 2006. That means that electricity in the United States today is about 17 percent cheaper on an inflation-adjusted basis than it was at its peak in 1985. That is a good deal for consumers but a bad deal for utilities that want to raise prices to make up for lost profitability.

United States electricity prices on a nominal basis have in fact risen sharply since 2000 and are presently at record highs, as seen in Figure 2.7. The U.S. Energy Information Administration reports that average U.S. electricity prices were at record highs in 2006 of 10.4 cents/kilowatt-hour for residential customers, 9.4 cents per kilowatt-hour for commercial customers, and 6.09 cents per kilowatt-hour for industrial customers. The average retail electricity price for all U.S. customers in 2006 rose to 8.85 cents from 6.81 cents in 2000, which translates into +4.5 percent annual

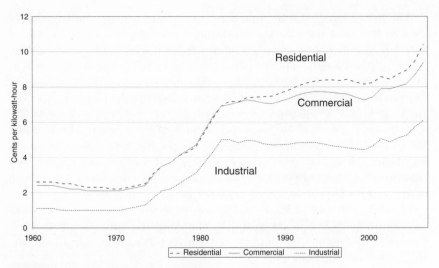

FIGURE 2.7 U.S. Retail Electricity Prices
Source: U.S. Energy Information Administration, *Annual Energy* Review 2006, June 2007, Table 8.10, Average Retail Prices of Electricity, 1960–2006, http://www.eia. doe.gov/emeu/aer/txt/stb0810.xls.

compounded price rise and an overall increase of 30 percent over the 2000–2006 period. That rise in electricity prices significantly exceeds the average U.S. GDP growth rate and U.S. inflation rate.

Rising electricity prices are a driver for clean energy technologies since U.S. electricity consumers are looking for efficiency solutions to reduce their electricity usage and curb the rise in their monthly electricity bill. Rising electricity prices also provide a boost for the solar industry. As solar power becomes more competitively priced, U.S. business and residential electricity users will increasingly consider installing solar power systems at their locations, thus locking in an electricity price for the 25-year life of the equipment and protecting themselves from steadily rising retail electricity prices from the local utility.

COULD THE CLEAN ENERGY MOVEMENT FIZZLE IF OIL PRICES PLUNGE?

While oil prices over the long-term are likely to trend upward due to the increasing costs of extraction, oil prices on a shorter time frame could easily see weakness and perhaps even a sharp decline. For example, in late 2006 and early 2007, oil prices fell sharply to $50 per barrel due to the excessive global inventories that developed after there were no major hurricanes in the United States during the 2006 hurricane season. OPEC responded by pushing oil prices back up to the $60 per barrel area by cutting its production by 5 percent from late 2006 through early 2007. Nevertheless, the drop in oil prices to $50 per barrel in early 2007 showed that oil prices can still fall sharply, particularly if OPEC loses its discipline.

Investors in the clean energy sector must consider whether a sharp drop in oil prices could kill the clean energy movement, which in fact happened in the 1970s and 1980s after the 1973 Arab Oil embargo. There was an initial push for alternative energy and efficiency when oil prices spiked higher on the Arab Oil Embargo, but the push for alternative energy fizzled when oil prices fell back.

In analyzing this issue, it is critical to recognize that the clean energy sector must be divided into two very different segments: transportation fuel companies (ethanol producers), and companies tied to electrical power (solar, wind, power efficiency). A plunge in crude oil prices and gasoline prices would clearly be very bearish for ethanol stocks since ethanol prices closely track gasoline prices. As gasoline prices fall, ethanol prices typically fall as well, thereby undercutting ethanol company revenues and profits.

However, falling crude oil prices should have only a minor negative effect on stocks tied to electrical power such as the solar, wind and power efficiency stocks. Falling crude oil prices do have some minor negative consequences for solar, wind and power efficiency stocks because falling oil prices may reduce the urgency for new government regulations and incentives in favor of solar and wind power. However, clean energy stocks are driven by two other major factors that are not tied to petroleum prices, namely, climate change and energy security. Lower oil prices would do nothing to reduce the amount of pollution and greenhouse gases given off by fossil fuels and would do nothing to insulate western nations from future oil supply shocks or going to war over threats to critical oil supplies. In other words, solar and wind power and power efficiency stocks can still perform very well even if oil prices were to drop sharply.

In the United States, as in most other parts of the world, crude oil prices have very little effect on the generation cost of electricity or by extension the retail price of electricity. In the United States, electrical power in 2006 was consumed from the following sources: 52 percent from coal, 21 percent from nuclear, 16 percent from natural gas, 8 percent from hydroelectric, 1.6 percent from petroleum, and the rest from hydro and other renewable sources.[28] In other words, the generation costs and retail prices for electricity have virtually nothing to do with fluctuations in crude oil prices since petroleum is used for only 1.6 percent of U.S. electricity consumption.

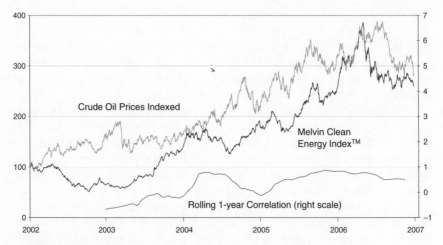

FIGURE 2.8   Melvin Clean Energy Index™ vs. Crude Oil Prices

Falling crude oil prices will not reduce electric power generation costs or retail electricity costs and will therefore not make solar and wind power any less competitive against traditional forms of electricity generation. Fluctuations in crude oil prices should have little direct impact on stock prices for solar, wind and power efficiency stocks. In fact, this thesis is supported by the statistical data.

Figure 2.8 illustrates how clean energy stocks since 2003 have generally risen along with crude oil prices as high crude oil prices have helped spark more global regulation in favor of clean energy and have supported ethanol stocks. The rolling one-year correlation (shown in the bottom line) has fluctuated widely over the past five years, rising to 0.90 through 2005 but recently falling to the current level of 0.51.

The correlation of the Melvin Clean Energy Index™ with crude oil prices is mainly caused by the inclusion of ethanol stocks in the clean energy index. The correlation between the Melvin Ethanol Index™ and crude oil prices is relatively high at 0.86 in the five years through January 2007 and 0.64 in the year through January 2007 as seen in Figure 2.9.

The correlation between crude oil and stocks tied to electricity is much lower, thus supporting our thesis. In fact, in the year through January 2007, the correlation between crude oil prices and the Melvin Solar Power Index™ was only 0.24, as seen in Figure 2.10. The correlation between crude oil prices and the Melvin Power Efficiency Index™ was similarly low at 0.25, as seen in Figure 2.11

The conclusion is that sharply lower crude oil prices would indeed be bearish for ethanol stocks and would perhaps slow the R&D push for

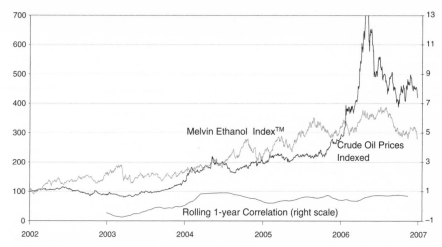

FIGURE 2.9 Melvin Ethanol Index™ vs. Crude Oil Prices

advanced biofuels, but should have little sustained negative impact on stocks tied to electricity such as solar, wind, and power efficiency. A sharp drop in crude oil prices would not have a sustained negative impact on the solar, wind, and power efficiency subsectors because lower oil prices would not make electricity any cheaper and would not halt the other strong catalysts for renewable and efficient power stemming from the need to curb greenhouse gas emissions and improve energy security.

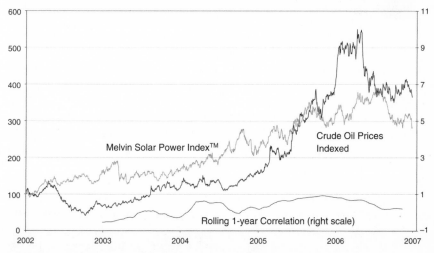

FIGURE 2.10 Melvin Solar Power Energy Index™ vs. Crude Oil Prices

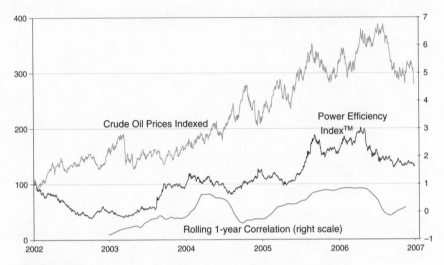

FIGURE 2.11 Melvin Power Efficiency Index™ vs. Crude Oil Prices

CLEAN ENERGY CATALYSTS: INVESTMENT CONCLUSION

The clean energy sector enjoys strong drivers and catalysts that will provide a strong tailwind for the industry for decades to come. These drivers include fossil fuel negatives, energy security, growing global energy demand, climate change, clean energy technology improvements, grid unreliability, and rising electricity prices. The clean energy industry, by providing solutions to these problems, has the drivers that are necessary to create double-digit growth for decades to come.

CHAPTER 3

The Government Push

Strong Enough to Get Clean Energy to Fossil Fuel Parity?

S keptics about investing in clean energy are concerned that the industry is generally not cost-competitive with fossil fuels and that the industry is being propped up only by government incentives, subsidies, regulations, and mandates. The fear is that governments, fickle as they are, may eventually lose interest in supporting clean energy, or the price may become too high for taxpayers to pay, and government support could fizzle, leaving the clean energy industry stranded as an overpriced white elephant.

Government mandates and incentives have undeniably provided a boon for the clean energy industry. Further government mandates and incentives would, of course, be helpful. However, the success of the clean energy industry is no longer fully dependent on government support. Rapid technological progress is being made in the clean energy industry, and huge amounts of private capital are flowing into it. Those efforts should be able to get the clean energy industry to fossil fuel parity even if government support for clean energy peters out in coming years.

There is talk that the U.S. government should support a "Manhattan Project" to promote clean energy or a "Green New Deal" in the words of *New York Times* columnist Thomas Friedman.[1] However, the reality is that the private sector has already started its own Manhattan Project to find cost-effective clean energy solutions since enormous wealth will accrue to those companies and individuals that are successful. That wealth has already started to flow to successful entrepreneurs in the clean energy space. For example, Dr. Zhengrong Shi, founder, chairman and CEO of China-based solar company Suntech Power Holdings (NYSE: STP) has become the wealthiest man living in China, by some estimates, with a fortune near $1.7 billion based on his holdings of Suntech stock.[2]

The entire Manhattan Project, which focused on building a nuclear bomb during World War II, cost $2 billion dollars, which translates into $23 billion in 2007 dollars.[3] By comparison, private sector investment in clean energy technology has already dwarfed the Manhattan Project. The UN Environment Programme says that $71 billion in new investment capital flowed into the renewable energy and energy efficiency industry in the single year of 2006, adding to $50 billion of capital in 2005 and $28 billion of capital in 2004.[4] The group is forecasting $85 billion of new capital in 2007. That totals to $234 billion in just the four years of 2004 to 2007. Private investors and industry are providing a huge complementary effort to the government's push for clean energy.

Nevertheless, there is every indication that the clean energy industry can count on increasing government support in coming years rather than declining support. The United States, for example, is only getting started on serious efforts to support clean energy. Congress may approve a renewable energy bill by late 2007 and the chances are good for a U.S. cap-and-trade CO_2 emissions system by 2009 or 2010 (after the 2008 presidential election). In the meantime, clean energy support efforts are moving full speed ahead at the state level, as states tire of waiting for the U.S. federal government to act. Meanwhile, many governments in Europe and Asia are moving faster than the United States to support clean energy and a new Kyoto global treaty is likely to replace the current treaty, which expires in 2012.

This book cannot describe every government support program on earth for clean energy. There are simply too many of them to catalog in a single chapter or perhaps even in a single book. In addition, government support measures worldwide for clean energy are expanding and changing rapidly and any list will quickly fall out of date. This chapter sticks instead to the big picture with a view toward illustrating the strength of worldwide government support for clean energy. Government support for clean energy is something that has become ingrained in both government and public consciousness, and it is not likely to simply fizzle in a few years.

TYPES OF GOVERNMENT CLEAN ENERGY INCENTIVES AND MANDATES

There are a variety of tools that governments around the world are using to support the clean energy industry, aside from direct funding of scientific research. A more thorough discussion of these policy instruments can be found in a paper on "National Policy Instruments" written by Worldwatch Institute officials.[5] Here is a quick summary of the main government policy instruments to promote efficiency and renewable energy:

- *Greenhouse gas emission curbs through a carbon tax or a cap-and-trade system.* These measures make CO_2 emissions more expensive and raise the cost of using fossil fuels, thus making it easier for renewable energy solutions to become cost-competitive with fossil fuels. The cap-and-trade system also provides economic incentives to companies that reduce their emissions, thus making emission reduction programs more attractive.
- *Environmental regulation.* Greenhouse gas emissions can also be regulated and curbed by direct government order as well. For example, the U.S. Supreme Court in 2007 ruled that the U.S. Environmental Protection Agency must take the regulation of greenhouse gases under its jurisdiction.
- *Renewable Portfolio Standards (RPS) for power utilities.* These measures force a utility to derive a certain percentage of its power from renewable electricity sources.
- *Feed-in tariffs for renewable energy producers.* Feed-in tariffs provide power producers that construct wind or solar farms, for example, with a government-set price at which they can sell their power to the grid, thus effectively providing essentially a guaranteed investment return on the renewable energy investment and making it easier for renewable energy projects to obtain bank financing for the capital costs of the project.
- *Net metering.* Net metering laws and regulations require a utility to provide consumer electricity users with a credit for any excess electricity that the consumer generates with an onsite power generation system (e.g., solar equipment) and feeds into the grid. This makes onsite renewable electricity generation systems more economical and prevents a utility from trying to block consumers from generating their own electricity. Net metering is sometimes referred to as allowing the electric meter to "spin backwards."
- *Subsidies and tax breaks for renewable energy.* A wide variety of incentives and tax breaks exist for businesses and consumers that invest in clean energy solutions (wind, solar, geothermal, hybrid vehicles, biofuels, etc.) or that invest in power efficiency projects. These measures include capital grants, investment tax credits, property tax exemptions, production tax credits, sales tax rebates, excise tax exemptions, and others.[6]
- *Low-interest loans and loan guarantees.* Governments can provide low-interest loans and loan guarantees in order to ease financing of

clean energy projects, thus eliminating the upfront capital cost barrier to projects and making the projects more economical and affordable.

- *Renewable energy credits.* A framework of renewable energy credits allows private investors to invest in projects to reduce greenhouse gas emissions and then sell those credits to buyers who wish to pay to offset their greenhouse gas emissions.
- *Biofuel mandates for fuel blenders and retailers ("Renewable Fuel Standards").* The U.S. government and other governments around the world have set mandates that require transportation fuel blenders to use a certain percentage of biofuels in the fuel they provide to consumers.
- *Building codes and permits.* Federal, state, and local governments use building code regulations and building permits in order to require builders and building owners to implement building techniques that result in improved building energy efficiency.
- *Lighting and appliance efficiency.* Governments implement various laws requiring higher efficiency in lights and appliances, and even go so far as to ban inefficient electrical devices such as incandescent bulbs.
- *Education and information dissemination.* Governments implement various education and information programs to ensure that businesses and consumers are aware of energy issues and are aware of various government support programs.

RENEWABLE ENERGY TARGETS WORLDWIDE

Table 3.1 provides a summary of the long list of countries that have adopted renewable energy targets, which require that a certain amount of the country's electricity comes from renewable rather than fossil fuel sources. Typically a country or state will adopt a renewable energy target and then implement more specific policies designed to meet the goals.

Figure 3.1 illustrates the renewable energy targets for 2010 that each of the 25 European Union countries (EU 25) have adopted. The EU 25 average target is 21 percent of electricity obtained from renewable electricity sources by 2010, which would be up by 7 percentage points from the baseline (actual) of 13 percent in 1997. Most of the renewable energy seen at the baseline in 1997 was from large-scale hydroelectricity and biomass and virtually none of that renewable power was from newer sources such as wind and solar. For the larger EU countries, the targets are as follows: Germany, 12.5 percent; France, 21 percent; Italy, 25 percent; Spain, 29.4 percent; and the United Kingdom, 10 percent.

Aside from renewable energy targets, governments around the world have also been aggressively implementing feed-in tariffs, which provide

TABLE 3.1	Countries (non-EU) with Renewable Energy Targets

North America

United States	5% to 30% of electricity in 18 states (including DC).
Canada	3.5% to 15% of electricity in four provinces; other types of targets in six provinces.

Non-EU Europe

Switzerland	3.5 terawatt-hours from electricity and heat by 2010.
Norway	7 terawatt-hours from heat and wind by 2010.

Asia & Pacific

Japan	1.35% of electricity by 2010, excluding geothermal and large hydro.
China	10% of electric power capacity by 2010 (expected 60 gigawatts); 5% of primary energy by 2010 and 10% of primary energy by 2020.
Korea	7% of electricity by 2010, including large hydro, and 1.3 gigawatts of grid-connected solar PV by 2011, including 100,000 homes (300 megawatts).
Malaysia	5% of electricity by 2005.
Philippines	4.7 gigawatts total existing capacity by 2013.
Thailand	8% of total primary energy by 2011 (excluding traditional rural biomass).
Singapore	35 megawatt-thermal of solar thermal systems by 2012.
India	10% of added electric power capacity during 2003–2012 (expected/planned).
Australia	9.5 terawatt-hours of electricity annually by 2010.
New Zealand	30,000 terajoules of added capacity (including heat and transport fuels) by 2012.

Middle East & Africa

Israel	2% of electricity by 2007; 5% of electricity by 2016.
Egypt	3% of electricity by 2010.
South Africa	10 terawatt-hours added final energy by 2013.

South/Central America, Caribbean

Brazil	3.3 gigawatts added by 2006 from wind, biomass, small hydro.
Dominican Republic	500 megawatts wind power capacity by 2015.

Source: Philippe Lempp, *Renewable Energies: Status and Investment* [slide presentation], REN21: Renewable Energy Policy Network for the 21st Century, 7 March 2007, http://www.ren21.net/presentations/070622_REN21_presentation_ MENAREC4.pps.

a government-set price at which operators of renewable energy projects can sell electricity to the grid. Feed-in tariffs in practice have provided a huge boost for renewable energy projects. A total of 41 countries, states or provinces in the world had a feed-in tariff law as of 2006, which represents a strong incentive for private investors to construct renewable electricity generation units such as solar or wind farms.[7]

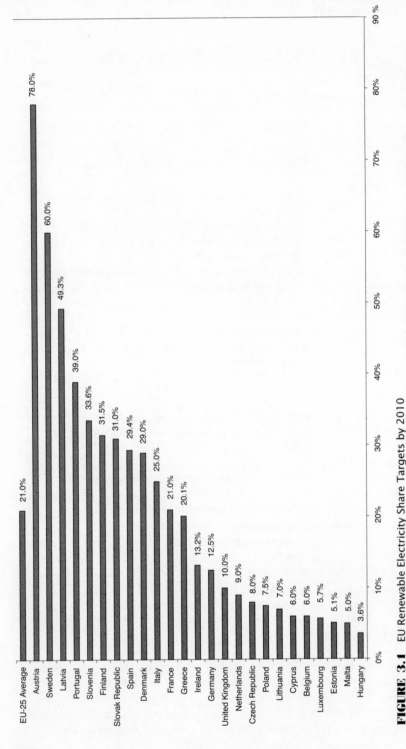

FIGURE 3.1 EU Renewable Electricity Share Targets by 2010

Source: REN21: Renewable Energy Policy Network for the 21st Century, *Renewables Global Status Report, 2006 Update* (Paris: REN21 Secretariat and Washington, D.C.: Worldwatch Institute), http://www.ren21.net/pdf/RE.GSR_2006.Update.pdf.

There are many examples of success stories where governments around the world have implemented support programs that helped produce dramatic growth of renewable energy. Here is a brief description of a few of those success stories.

Government Support Success Stories from Around the World

- *Brazil's energy independence.* Brazil is now completely independent from foreign sources of oil because of an ethanol program that the government started in 1975. The government required ethanol to be blended with gasoline, promoted the manufacture and sale of ethanol-capable flex-fuel vehicles, and provided subsidies and loans for the development of the country's sugar cane farms and ethanol plants. Brazil is now the world's second largest producer of ethanol and the world's largest exporter of ethanol.
- *Germany's feed-in tariff.* Germany approved its first renewable energy requirement in 1990 that contained a feed-in tariff guaranteeing fixed prices to private developers of renewable electricity generation plants. Germany also provided a host of tax breaks and financing measures to promote renewable energy. As a result of these measures, Germany now has leading positions in the world as the producer of wind and solar electricity.
- *European wind power.* Countries in Europe such as Germany, Spain, and Denmark, through renewable power mandates and sustained incentives, helped create the world's wind power business, which is now a multibillion-dollar industry. General Electric, for example, is now on its third generation of wind turbine. General Electric Chairman Jeffrey Immelt credited Europe with the success of GE's wind business by saying, "We grew our wind business in Europe."[8]
- *Japan's solar program.* Japan, in 1992, began promoting solar photovoltaic (PV) power through net metering rules, tax rebates, low-interest loans, and an aggressive public education program. Japan is currently the second biggest market in the world for solar PV demand, behind Germany, and buys more than twice the amount of solar PV equipment as the United States. Solar power is now competitive with the price of retail electricity in parts of Japan without subsidies.

GOVERNMENT CLEAN ENERGY SUPPORT INITIATIVES IN THE UNITED STATES

In the United States, the tide has clearly turned in favor of implementing more clean energy incentives. The pressure for more government action on clean energy is coming in part from the public itself, which has become much more aware of climate change issues and the negative consequences

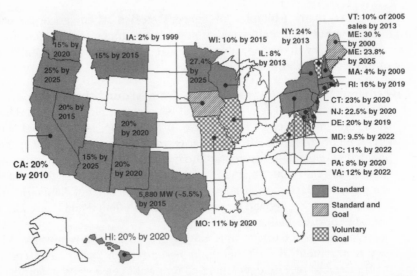

FIGURE 3.2 U.S. State-Level Renewable Electricity Standards (as of July 1, 2007) *Source:* Union of Concerned Scientists, "State Renewable Electricity Standards," http://www.ucsusa.org/clean_energy/clean_energy_policies/res-at-work-in-the-states .html. Reprinted by permission and courtesy of Union of Concerned Scientists.

of U.S. dependence on foreign oil. In fact, a Zogby poll recently found that 77 percent of U.S. voters believe that the United States is not doing enough to promote and utilize green technologies in order to reduce U.S. dependence on foreign fuel sources.[9] Only 17 percent of the respondents in the poll said the United States is doing enough.

The United States federal government has not yet adopted a national renewable energy standard, but 18 states have implemented their own statewide standards and more states are planning to implement such standards. Figure 3.2 shows a map, provided by the Union of Concerned Scientists, showing the states that have adopted renewable energy standards. The Union of Concerned Scientists believes that these renewable electricity standards will lead to a fourfold increase in renewable electricity in the United States by 2020, as shown in Figure 3.3.[10]

The U.S. Congress and President George W. Bush passed the Energy Policy Act of 2005, which contained a wide range of measures to support clean energy. The Energy Policy Act of 2005 included measures to support biofuels, wind power, solar power, wind/tidal power, geothermal power, and power efficiency. Another key measure approved by the federal government was an extension of the 30 percent investment tax credit for solar and wind equipment through January 1, 2009, which was signed by President Bush on December 20, 2006.

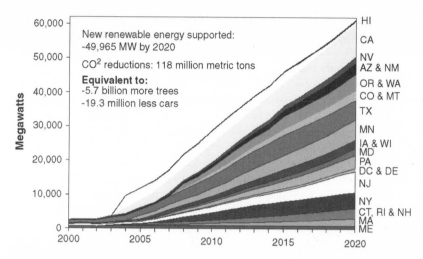

FIGURE 3.3 Renewable Energy Expected from State Standards (as of July 1, 2007) *Source:* Union of Concerned Scientists www.ucsusa.org. Union of Concerned Scientists, "State Renewable Electricity Standards," http://www.ucsusa.org/clean_energy/clean_energy_policies/res-at-work-in-the-states.html. Reprinted by permission and courtesy of Union of Concerned Scientists.

Note: Projected development assuming states achieve annual renewable energy targets.

Congress has recently been working on a new clean energy legislative package. In June 2007, the Senate approved an energy bill that among other items contained (1) the first increase in fuel economy standards (CAFE) in 20 years (to 35 miles per gallon); (2) an increase in the renewable fuels standard (RFS) from 7.5 billion gallons by 2012 to 36 billion gallons by 2022; and (3) $1.5 billion in funding for carbon sequestration solutions. That Senate bill, however, left out a proposed national Renewable Portfolio Standard of 15 percent for the nation's utilities and a proposal to take $32 billion in subsidies away from the petroleum industry and use that money to support renewable energy. The House planned to work on its version of the energy bill through summer 2007 and observers were expecting a unified Senate-House energy package by late 2007.

Pressure on Washington to implement a stronger push for clean energy is coming not only from the public, but also from the state and city levels, and even from big business. Big business would rather see uniform laws approved at the federal level than be bogged down by a hodge-podge of state and local regulations. The states are far ahead of the federal government in promoting a clean energy agenda. The following is a list of some of the higher profile initiatives that are taking place at the state level.

Selected U.S. State Clean Energy Initiatives

- *California's $3 billion Solar Initiative.* The California Solar Initiative, which took effect January 1, 2007, will provide about $3 billion in solar energy rebates over the next 11 years for residential and commercial solar installations in California. The program is the largest solar program ever enacted in the United States and globally is second only to Germany. The program is designed to promote the installation of 3 gigawatts of solar power by 2017 (which is enough electricity to power about 825,000 homes).[11] See www.gosolarcalifornia.ca.gov.

- *Texas wind power.* The Texas legislature and then-Governor George W. Bush in 1999 established a renewable energy portfolio mandate for Texas utilities that required the use of 2 gigawatts of power from renewable sources by 2009. As a result of that mandate, wind power in Texas grew so quickly that the 2-gigawatt mandate was reached by 2005 and the Texas legislature raised the mandate to 5 gigawatts by 2015.[12]

- *Three states with CO_2 emission caps (CA, HI, NJ).* California in September 2006 adopted the nation's first mandatory statewide greenhouse gas emissions cap, which requires a 25 percent cut in CO_2 emissions by 2020 (AB32 Global Warming Solutions Act). The law included provisions for a cap-and-trade system. In mid-2007, Hawaii and New Jersey were the second and third U.S. states to approve CO_2 emissions caps.[13] In the United States, 26 states have now at least set targets for reducing CO_2 emissions.

- *California's Low Carbon Transportation Fuel Standard.* California Governor Arnold Schwarzenegger in January 2007 signed an executive order establishing a Low Carbon Fuel Standard (LCFS) for all transportation fuels sold in California. The standard will require fuel providers to progressively reduce the greenhouse gas emissions from transportation fuels by at least 10 percent by 2020. There are a variety of ways to meet the standard including trading credits, but the main outcome of the LCFS standard will be a big increase in the usage of ethanol and biodiesel. The LCFS standard is due to take effect no later than the end of 2008 after details are worked out. Supporters expect the program to put 7 million more alternative vehicles on the road, including biofuel, plug-in hybrid, battery electric, and fuel cell vehicles.

- *Northeast "Regional Greenhouse Gas Initiative."* Ten Northeastern states are part of a regional plan for a mandatory limit on CO_2 emissions from power plants with a goal of cutting emissions by 10 percent by 2020. The states set up the Regional Greenhouse Gas Initiative (www.rggi.org) as a means to cooperate on a cap-and-trade program.

- *Western Regional Climate Action Initiative.* The Western Regional Climate Action Initiative is a group of six western U.S. states (AZ, CA,

NM, OR, UT, WA) and two Canadian provinces (British Columbia and Manitoba), which are working together on ways to reduce greenhouse gas emissions. The initiative involves setting goals for reducing greenhouse gas emissions and setting up a mechanism to achieve the goals (e.g., cap-and-trade).

- *California's steady per-capita electricity usage.* In an extraordinary accomplishment, California, as a result of 30 years of state-mandated electricity efficiency programs, has been able to hold its per capita electricity usage roughly flat for the last 30 years while the rest of the states in the United States have seen their per-capita electricity usage rise by 50 percent.[14]

A POST-KYOTO CARBON EMISSIONS FRAMEWORK

World officials, working under the auspices of the United Nations, have begun discussions on a new global CO_2 emissions agreement to replace the current Kyoto Protocol, which is due to expire in 2012. The Kyoto Protocol has shown mixed results because key countries such as the United States, China and India are not subject to the Kyoto emissions reduction plan. However, the global clean energy industry would receive a big boost if negotiators can put together a new and more comprehensive global CO_2 emissions agreement that brings the United States, China, and India into the fold with mandatory CO_2 reduction requirements.

The Kyoto Protocol was approved in 1997 and subsequently ratified by more than 160 countries, including Europe, Japan, and Canada. The Kyoto Protocol requires signatories to reduce their CO_2 emissions by an average of 5.2 percent from 1990 levels by 2012. China signed the Kyoto Protocol but was exempt from the accord's binding emission curbs because of its status as a developing country. President George W. Bush, in one of his first acts as president in 2001, announced that the United States would not ratify or abide by the Kyoto Protocol because he did not believe in mandatory caps, because he believed the emissions curbs would hurt U.S. business, and because he objected to the fact that big developing countries such as China and India were not subject to the agreement.

While signatories to the Kyoto Protocol had the best of intentions, the reality is that a global agreement cannot put much of a dent in the world's CO_2 emissions without the help of the United States, China, and India. Table 3.2 shows how China and India's CO_2 emissions over the 1990–2004 period rose by +67 percent and +88 percent, respectively, versus smaller increases of 19 percent in the United States and 6 percent in Europe. A

TABLE 3.2 Carbon Emissions Increases in China, India, Europe, Japan, and the United States, 1990–2004

Country or Region	Carbon Emissions (millions of tons)	Carbon Emissions per capita (tons)	Carbon Emissions Increase (1990–2004)
China	1,021	0.8	67 percent
India	301	0.3	88 percent
Europe	955	2.5	6 percent
Japan	338	2.7	23 percent
United States	1616	5.5	19 percent

Source: International Energy Agency, Worldwatch State of the World 2006 (see www.worldwatch.org).

significant reason for the sharp increase in CO_2 emissions by China and India is the rapid expansion of the use of coal-fired power plants in those two countries. Since the IEA compiled the 2004 data shown in Figure 3.5, China's CO_2 emissions have actually surpassed the United States, making China the world's largest CO_2 emitter. The United States on a per capital basis, however, is still a much larger emitter than China by a factor of four.

China in the past has refused to consider mandatory CO_2 emissions curbs because Chinese officials say the country should be allowed to meet its economic development needs as the United States and Europe did in previous decades without greenhouse gas emission caps. Nevertheless, the rapid rise of China's CO_2 emissions, and growing evidence of climate change, has convinced even Chinese officials that they need to start thinking seriously about how to curb CO_2 emissions. In fact, China's Prime Minister Wen Jiabao on a trip to Tokyo in April 2007 announced that China was willing to participate in negotiations for a new global warming treaty to replace the Kyoto Protocol.[15]

As for the United States, President Bush in June 2007 surprised observers by announcing a plan for the largest nations to start working together to reach a common emissions reduction target within a framework agreeable to China and India. However, the Bush administration continued to oppose mandatory emission reduction targets, leaving the impression that the Bush plan would simply pursue voluntary reductions with no teeth. One European official expressed the opinion that voluntary reductions in CO_2 emissions would be about as effective as a voluntary speed limit. Nevertheless, the odds for binding CO_2 curbs when a new president enters the White House in early 2009 are much better.

In any case, Washington is presently seeing heavy pressure for action on climate change. The pressure is coming from the public, the states, and now major U.S. corporations as well. In fact, a group called the United States Climate Action Partnership (see www.us-cap.org) is calling for federal regulation to help reduce greenhouse gas emissions by 60–80 percent by 2050 with interim targets.[16] The Partnership is a coalition of environmental groups and 10 major companies that include Alcoa, BP America, Caterpillar, Duke Energy, DuPont, Florida Power & Light, GE, Lehman Brothers, PG&E, and PNM Resources.

The stature of the companies involved in the Climate Action Partnership illustrates that U.S. business leaders recognize that the federal government is likely to eventually address the issue of climate change with significant carbon caps or a carbon tax. These business leaders want the opportunity to influence the eventual outcome of the legislation. In addition, large U.S. companies, as mentioned earlier, are worried about being bogged down by a hodgepodge of state regulations on CO_2 emissions. In the words of former Environmental Protection Agency chief Christine Todd Whitman, the varied regulations at the state level are "a nightmare for any business. We need one standard nationally."[17]

The clean energy industry would receive a huge boost if and when the United States approves CO_2 emissions curbs and if the industrialized world including China and India agree to a new post-Kyoto pact. The price of fossil fuels will go up and clean energy alternatives such as solar and wind power, along with efficiency, will become the primary means by which countries will meet their targets for reducing CO_2 emissions.

Note: Please see www.ProfitingFromCleanEnergy.com for updates on the latest developments in U.S. and global clean energy regulation.

CHAPTER 4

Clean Energy Potential

Double-Digit Growth for Decades

The clean energy industry has already seen double-digit growth rates in the past five years. Those double-digit growth rates are likely to continue over at least the next several years, spurred on by strong and expanding government support programs worldwide and by falling clean energy costs tied to improved technology. Even if government support policies start to fade in the next 5 to 10 years, most of the major clean energy subsectors by then should be competitive with fossil fuels without government support, at which point the clean energy industry has clear sailing for at least the next several decades to grow at double-digit rates and start to make major inroads in replacing fossil fuels.

Clean energy technologies are not as far away from parity with fossil fuels as some people believe. Geothermal power is already at fossil fuel parity. Wind power is already fairly close to grid parity and improvements continue to be made in turbine blade technology and overall design. Plug-in gasoline-electric hybrid vehicles, which will easily beat the cost of driving a gasoline-powered vehicle, are expected to emerge in mass production by 2010. Solar photovoltaic power is already competitive with retail electricity rates in some parts of the world such as Japan and should become competitive with retail electricity prices in much of the world within about five years and with fossil-fuel-driven power plants in less than 10 years. Ethanol produced from nonfood cellulosic sources such as switch grass should be in mass production in about five years, which will reduce production costs for ethanol and make it more competitive with gasoline. Fuel cells will be increasingly competitive in certain applications such as power backup and small electronics over the next few years, although there is still little visibility as to when fuel cells may become practical for larger applications such as vehicles and grid power.

OVERVIEW OF GLOBAL AND U.S. ENERGY FLOWS

A brief look at the overall energy situation in the United States and the world will illustrate (1) how dependent the world is on fossil fuels, and (2) the potential market size for the clean energy technologies that aim to supplement and perhaps eventually replace fossil fuels.

Figure 4.1 illustrates the sources and uses of energy in the United States, showing total energy flow for all sectors in a single diagram. The source of energy is shown on the left and the consumers of energy are shown on the right. The chart shows energy units in terms of quadrillion Btu.

Several themes are highlighted by this diagram:

- Fossil fuels (petroleum, coal, natural gas) are the source of 85 percent of total U.S. energy consumption (based on the data in this diagram).
- The U.S. imports 2.7 times more petroleum oil than it produces domestically. U.S. petroleum imports account for a substantial 27 percent of total U.S. energy supply.
- Nuclear power accounts for only 8.2 percent of total U.S. energy consumption (nuclear power accounts for a larger 21 percent of the smaller category of electricity production).
- Renewable energy accounts for only 6.8 percent of total U.S. energy consumption, with most of that renewable energy coming from large hydroelectric dams.
- The transportation sector is a substantial consumer of energy and accounts for 28 percent of total U.S. energy consumption. U.S. businesses (commercial and industrial) account for 50 percent of total U.S. energy consumption, and residential users account for 21 percent of total U.S. energy consumption.

The fact that the United States obtains the overwhelming majority of its energy from fossil fuels is also illustrated in Figure 4.2, which shows that petroleum accounts for 40.2 percent of total U.S. energy consumption, and that coal and natural gas each account for 22.5 percent of U.S. energy consumption. The figures are similar on a global scale as seen in Figure 4.3. The world obtains 86.2 percent of its energy from fossil fuels, with a breakdown of 34.9 percent from crude oil, 25.6 percent from coal and

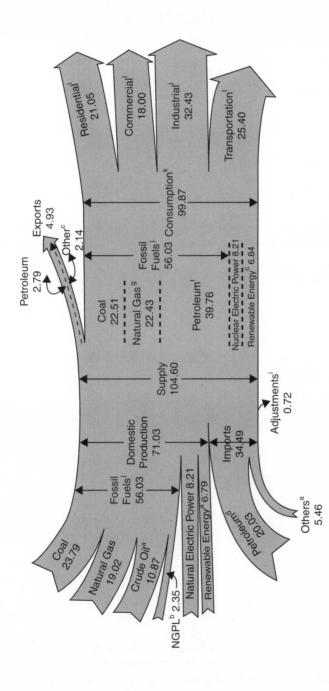

FIGURE 4.1 U.S. Energy Flow, 2006 (quadrillion Btu)

Source: U.S. Energy Information Administration, *Annual Energy Review 2006*, June 2007, http://www.eia.doe.gov/emeu/aer/diagram1.html.

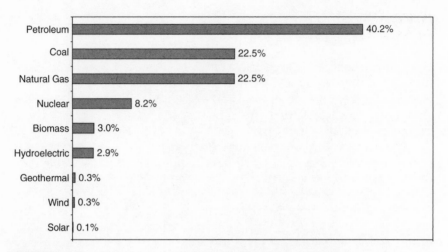

FIGURE 4.2 U.S. Energy Consumption Share by Source (2006)
Source: U.S. Energy Information Administration, *Annual Energy Review 2006,* June 2007, http://www.eia.doe.gov/emeu/aer/txt/stb0102.xls.

23.1 percent from natural gas, and 2.6 percent from natural gas liquids. On a global basis, hydroelectric and nuclear power each account for 6.2 percent of world energy production and geothermal and other renewables (wood, waste, solar, wind) together account for only 1.4 percent of global energy production.

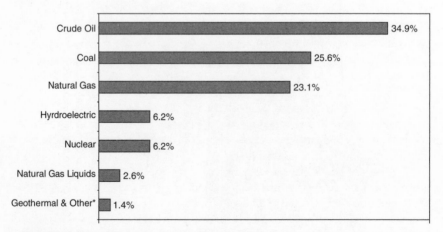

FIGURE 4.3 World Primary Energy Production Share by Type (2004)
Source: U.S. Energy Information Administration, *Annual Energy Review 2006,* June 2007, http://www.eia.doe.gov/emeu/aer/txt/stb1101.xls.

*Other includes wood, waste, solar, and wind.

OVERVIEW OF U.S. ELECTRICITY GENERATION SOURCES

Having looked at total energy use, which includes power generation, heating and transportation fuels, we now focus just on the sources of fuel for electric power generation in the United States. Figure 4.4 provides a diagram of the flow of electricity from the fuel source on the left to the consumers of electricity on the right.

The first thing that jumps out from this diagram is the enormous energy conversion losses that are incurred from the potential energy content of the fuel (left side) to the actual electricity output (right side). This diagram indicates that 70 percent of the potential energy content from the fuel is lost by present electricity production methods and that only 30 percent of the energy content of the fuel actually makes it to consumers in the form of electricity.

Figures 4.5 and 4.6 illustrate the source of the electricity consumed in the United States. Coal is by far the largest source of electricity in the United States at 51.65 percent of consumption. Natural gas accounts for 16.14 percent of U.S. consumption, and petroleum accounts for a negligible 1.63 percent of consumption. Fossil fuels, as a whole, account for a hefty 69.42 percent of U.S. electricity consumption.

Other sources of U.S. electricity include nuclear at 20.70 percent, and hydroelectric power at 7.21 percent. In the renewable electricity sector other than hydroelectric, biomass accounts for 1.07 percent of U.S. electricity consumption, geothermal 0.79 percent, wind 0.65 percent, and solar photovoltaic barely registers at 0.01 percent.

Figure 4.7 shows how the fuels used by the U.S. electric power industry have changed over time. The chart shows that coal has been ascendant with coal usage having more than quadrupled since 1960. Nuclear power has been roughly flat since 2000 due to the halt in construction of new nuclear plants in the United States. The use of petroleum as a fuel source for the U.S. electric power industry has generally fallen since 1980. Renewables (mainly hydroelectric power) have been flat for the past decade. Aside from coal, natural gas is the only other source of fuel that has shown significant gains in the past decade.

Figure 4.8 shows the source of fuels for electricity generation on a global basis for 2004 (the latest available data). Fossil fuels accounted for 66.1 percent of world electricity generation in 2004, which is just slightly below 69 percent in the U.S. Energy Information Administration. The world relies heavily on coal, which produces 39.8 percent of the world's electricity generation. Renewables accounted for only 2.1 percent of world electricity generation in 2004, with most of that coming from geothermal and burning biomass products and very little coming from solar and wind.

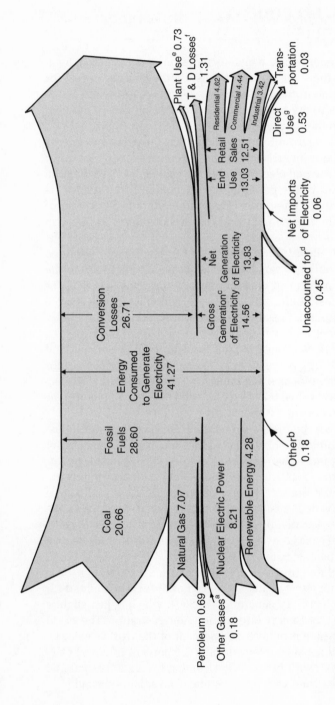

FIGURE 4.4 U.S. Electricity Flow 2006 (quadrillion Btu; data preliminary)

Source: U.S. Energy Information Administration, *Annual Energy Review 2006*, June 2007, p. 221, http://www.eia.doe.gov/emeu/aer/pdf/aer.pdf

aBlast furnace gas, propane gas, and other manufactured and waste gases derived from fossil fuels; bBatteries, chemicals, hydrogen, pitch, purchased steam, sulfur, miscellaneous technologies, and nonrenewable waste (municipal solid waste from nonbiogenic sources, and tire-derived fuels); cEstimated as net generation divided by 0.95; dData collection frame differences and nonsampling error; eElectric Energy used in the operation of power plants, estimated as 5 percent of gross generation; fTransmission and distribution losses (electricity losses that occur between the point of generation and delivery to the customer) are estimated as 9 percent of gross generation; gUse of electricity that is (1) self-generated (2) produced by either the same entity that consumes the power or an affiliate, and (3) used in direct support of a service or industrial process located within the same facility or group of facilities that house the generating equipment. Direct use is exclusive of station use.

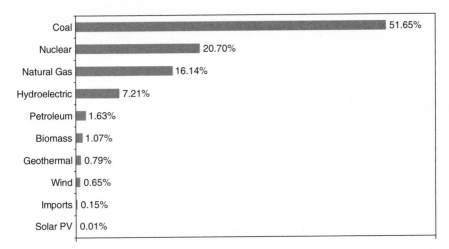

FIGURE 4.5 U.S. Electric Power Consumption Share by Source (2006)
Source: U.S. Energy Information Administration, *Annual Energy Review 2006,* June 2007, Table 2.1f, http://www.eia.doe.gov/emeu/aer/txt/stb0802a.xls.

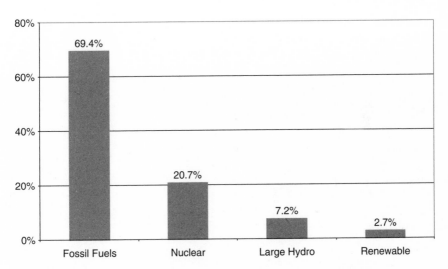

FIGURE 4.6 U.S. Electric Power Consumption Share by Type (2006)
Source: U.S. Energy Information Administration, Annual Energy Review 2006, Energy Information Administration, June 2007, Table 2.1f, http://www.eia.doe.gov/emeu/aer/txt/stb0802a.xls.

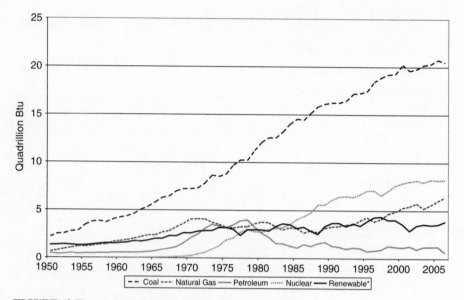

FIGURE 4.7 U.S. Electric Power by Source 1950–2006
Source: U.S. Energy Information Administration, *Annual Energy Review 2006,* June 2007, Table 2.1f. http://www.eia.doe.gov/emeu/aer/txt/stb0802a.xls.

*Renewable category includes Hydroelectric, Biomass, Geothermal, Wind, and Solar PV.

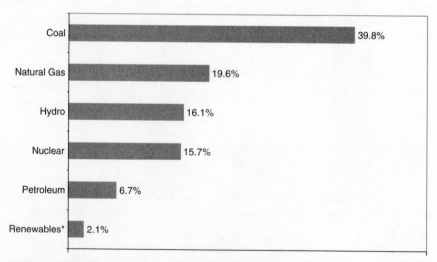

FIGURE 4.8 World Electricity Generation Share by Fuel (2004)
Source: International Energy Agency, *Key World Energy Statistics 2006* (IEA, 2006), p. 24.

*Renewables include geothermal, biomass/waste, solar, and wind.

FOSSIL FUEL MARKET SIZE: EVEN A NOSE UNDER THE TENT IS WORTH BILLIONS

The previous sections of this chapter have illustrated the world's heavy dependence on fossil fuel for its energy. The flip side of this reliance on fossil fuels is that there is enormous upside potential for replacing even part of current fossil fuel energy usage with clean, low-carbon energy solutions. It has become obvious that the cost of fossil fuels is not just the price paid for the fuel itself, but also the external costs paid in terms of greenhouse gas emissions, global warming, geopolitical energy dependence, vulnerability to oil supply and price shocks, and health risks. The overall costs of relying solely on fossil fuels to satisfy the huge increase in energy demand in coming decades would be enormous. This provides a huge upside for the clean energy industry.

The size of the market targeted by the clean energy industry can be estimated based on the size of the current fossil fuel market, which the clean energy industry aims to at least partially replace. The fossil fuel market, which was roughly $2.7 trillion in 2004, will grow to $4.0 trillion by 2030, according to energy unit forecasts by the U.S. Energy Information Administration. Their unit figures were converted to dollar values using recent average trading prices for crude oil, natural gas, and coal. The projected $4 trillion size of the fossil fuel market in 2030 does not assume any rise in fossil fuel prices.

The total fossil fuel market size is calculated by estimating the crude oil, natural gas and coal markets individually. The value of the world's oil consumption was about $1.740 trillion in 2004 and will grow to $2.470 trillion by 2030 according to projections by the U.S. Energy Information Agency in its *International Energy Outlook 2007* and using a crude oil reference price of $60 per barrel.[1] The value of the world's natural gas consumption was about $722 billion in 2004 and will grow to $1.2 trillion in 2030 using a recent average trading price of $7 per million Btu.[2] The value of the world's coal consumption was about $215 billion in 2004 and will grow to $373 billion in 2030 using a coal recent average trading price of $45 per ton.[3]

The size of the fossil fuel markets in terms of final market value is actually much higher. The calculations above were made using the wholesale price of basic fossil fuels, not the value of value-added products such as gasoline and electricity. For example, the annual revenues of just the largest 20 U.S.-listed integrated oil and gas companies in 2006 were $2.3 trillion. In order to calculate the final market value of all fossil fuel energy, we would need to add the revenues of all other oil companies, coal companies, natural gas companies, and the revenue of electricity power utility producers tied to fossil fuel inputs.

In any case, these fossil fuel figures are offered, not as an exact potential target size for clean energy, but simply to illustrate that there is potentially trillions of dollars worth of demand for clean energy solutions in the coming decades if fossil fuels are legislated away and clean energy technologies become cheaper than fossil fuels. In any business plan, an entrepreneur wants a potentially massive market to go after, and that is certainly the case with clean energy.

RENEWABLE ENERGY FORECASTS

The clean energy industry has been growing at double-digit rates for the past 5 years. In those years, the wind industry has grown at an average annual rate of 24 percent and the solar photovoltaic industry has grown at an average annual rate of over 40 percent. Skeptics do not believe that the industry can sustain these strong growth rates and fear a pullback. However, the skeptics are thinking about traditional industry growth rates and are not thinking about the huge amount of room on the upside for the clean energy industry.

Solar power usage in the United States, for example, could grow at the very strong rate of 30 percent every year and it would still account for only 1 percent of total U.S. power generation by 2017, 2.4 percent by 2020 and 9 percent by 2025. (More details on solar power are presented in Chapter 5.) The world is so dependent on fossil fuels that even moderate penetration levels mean literally hundreds of billions of dollars of revenues for clean energy producers.

In fact, the International Energy Agency, a group of economists and statisticians that is not inclined to wild-eyed forecasts, is predicting double-digit growth for key areas of the clean energy industry for the next two decades in their Alternative Policy Scenario. The Alternative Scenario, as opposed to the Reference Scenario, is the IEA's more aggressive forecast based on the assumption that countries around the world "were to adopt a set of policies and measures that they are now considering and might be expected to implement over the projection period."[4] Figure 4.9 illustrates the IEA's Alternative Policy forecasts for wind, solar, geothermal, and tide/wave power. The chart shows how the IEA expects wind energy to capture a big market share relative to the other technologies by 2030.

The IEA's projected annual compounded growth rates over the 2004–2030 period, as shown in Figure 4.10, are as follows: 17.0 percent for solar, 13.2 percent for tide and wave, 11.7 percent for wind, and 4.7 percent for geothermal. It is important to realize that these are *average* growth

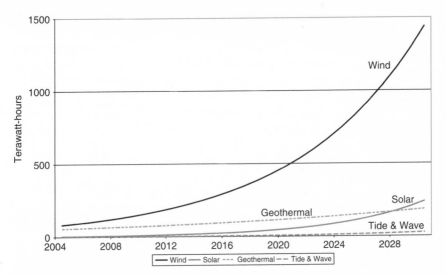

FIGURE 4.9 U.S. Renewable Power IEA Forecasts, 2004–2030
Source: International Energy Agency, *Renewables in Global Energy Supply: An IEA Fact Sheet,* January 2007, p. 12, http://www.iea.org/textbase/papers/2006/renewable_factsheet.pdf.

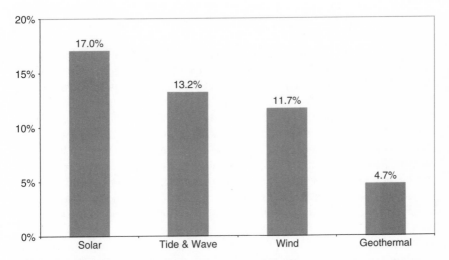

FIGURE 4.10 IEA Forecast for Global Renewable Power Annual Growth Rates, 2004–2030
Source: International Energy Agency, *Renewables in Global Energy Supply: An IEA Fact Sheet,* January 2007, p. 12, http://www.iea.org/textbase/papers/2006/renewable_factsheet.pdf.

rates over the period. What is likely to happen is that growth rates will be much faster earlier in the forecast period when growth is easier to achieve from low base levels and that growth rates will be slower later in the forecast period when growth is more difficult to achieve from higher base levels. Wind power is starting out from a significantly higher base than the other technologies and can therefore reach a higher installed base by 2030. Wind power's base in 2004 was 82,000 gigawatt-hours versus 56,000 gigawatt-hours for geothermal and only 4,000 gigawatt-hours for solar and less than 1,000 gigawatt-hours for tide/wave.

Over the 26-year period of 2004 to 2030, the IEA in its Alternative Policy case is forecasting that wind power will grow by 18 times over, solar power will grow by 60 times over, geothermal will grow by more than 3 times over, and that tide/wave power will grow by 46 times over. There are not many industries in the global economy that even have a remote chance of achieving these growth rates. Moreover, the IEA is not going out on a limb with these predictions and the actual outcome could actually be stronger if government support measures are stronger than expected, if crude oil and electricity prices rise significantly, or if clean energy costs fall more rapidly than currently expected.

Even with these relatively strong forecasts for clean energy growth, fossil fuels would still account for a dominant 77 percent of primary energy demand by 2030 in the IEA Alternative Policy forecast.[5] This indicates there would be plenty of room for additional growth in renewable energy in the decades after 2030.

Estimating the current size of the global clean energy industry is a difficult task because of the wide variety of technologies and industries involved in the sector, the large number of companies involved, the difficulty of identifying companies in other countries where clean energy is a bigger business than in the United States, and because it is difficult to separate out clean energy revenues at large companies such as GE. One group that has tried is Clean Edge, Inc. (see www.cleanedge.com). In its *Clean Energy Trends 2007* study, which is available to the public on the Clean Edge Web site, global clean energy industry sales in 2006 were pegged at $55.4 billion, up 39 percent from $40 billion in 2005.[6] Clean Edge is projecting a compounded annual growth rate over the 10-year period of +15.1 percent, leading the clean energy industry to projected sales of $226.5 billion by 2016. That forecast is just for the biofuel, wind, solar, and fuel cell business, and does not include other clean energy subsectors such as power efficiency, hybrid vehicles, or cleaner fossil fuel technologies.

While it is difficult to produce forecasts for an industry that is growing so fast and is in such a state of flux, it is safe to say that the entire clean energy industry will see double-digit growth rates over at least the next two decades. The biofuels industry is likely to show an average annual growth rate of 10 percent to 15 percent over the next 10 years (assuming cellulosic-based ethanol comes on line within five years), wind power is likely to show an annual growth rate of at least 15 percent to 20 percent over the next 10 years, and the solar industry, which is starting out from a lower base, will likely show an annual growth rate of at least 25 percent to 30 percent over the next 10 years. The growth rates are likely to be higher than the 10-year average annual rate in the first half of the 2007–2017 period and then taper off a bit in the second half of the period as the base levels climb and make high year-on-year growth rates harder to achieve.

Solar Power

The Sky Is the Limit

The energy from the sun that hits the earth *every day* is sufficient to meet the energy needs of the earth's 6.6 billion inhabitants for 27 years according to the U.S. National Renewable Energy Laboratory.[1] Clearly, there is no shortage of energy available from the sun. The mission is to capture this energy and convert it into electricity at a reasonable cost. The fuel for solar power, sunlight, is free. The cost comes in manufacturing and operating the equipment that converts the sunlight to electricity.

There are two main ways to convert energy from the sun into electricity: (1) *thermal solar power,* and (2) *solar photovoltaic power* (or *solar PV*). Thermal solar power uses the sun's energy to heat fluids, whereas solar photovoltaic power uses semiconductor materials to convert the sun's energy directly into an electrical current. Solar thermal power has the advantage of being less expensive than solar PV but otherwise the advantages and disadvantages of the two types of solar power are similar.

SOLAR THERMAL POWER

Within the category of thermal solar power there are two subcategories: (1) *solar hot water/heat,* which involves using hot water or air generated by the sun's rays to provide hot water to a building, to heat to a building, or to heat a swimming pool, and (2) *concentrating solar power* (CSP), which is a utility-scale system that concentrates the sun's rays to create high-temperature water or other liquid, which in turn run turbines to generate electricity.

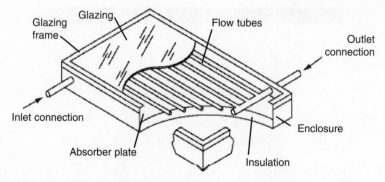

FIGURE 5.1 Solar Thermal Hot Water Panel
Source: National Renewable Energy Laboratory, "A Consumer's Guide: Heat Your Water with the Sun," US Department of Energy, Energy Efficiency and Renewable Energy, Dec 2003, p. 5. http://www.nrel.gov/docs/fy04osti/34279.pdf.

Solar Hot Water/Heat

A simple solar hot water collector unit is made up of a series of thick panels containing water tubes or air baffles under a sheet of blackened, heat absorbent material. These panels are oriented toward the sun so that they receive the maximum amount of the sun's rays. The water or air absorbs the heat and the heated water or air is then piped to where it is to be used. The panels used for hot water and space heating are usually set in a frame and covered by glass. When used for hot water, the solar hot water system can have an electric backup for use at night when the sun is not shining and is not producing hot water.

The utility bill for consumers with solar water heaters is 50 percent to 80 percent lower than for consumers who have traditional electric water heaters, according to the U.S. Department of Energy.[2] Regarding capital costs, a solar heating system for a pool, for example, usually costs $3,000 to $4,000 and has a payback of 1.5 to 7 years, depending on the intensity of the sun and cost of electricity in the area.[3] Researchers at the U.S. Solar Technology Program have set a goal of cutting the cost of solar water heaters in half by using more advanced materials and collectors.[4]

Solar hot water heating is a significant source of renewable energy worldwide. In 2005, solar hot water capacity increased by 14 percent to reach 88 gigawatts-thermal.[5] Most of the solar hot water capacity is in China, which accounts for 63.1 percent of installed world capacity. Europe accounts for 12.7 percent of world capacity, whereas the United States accounts for only 1.8 percent of world capacity where it is mainly used for heating swimming pools.[6] Solar hot water heating in Europe grew

26 percent in 2005 versus the previous year to 1.4 gigawatts-thermal of solar thermal capacity.[7]

Concentrating Solar Systems

Concentrating solar power (CSP) systems are utility-scale systems that use mirrors to concentrate solar energy by 50 to 10,000 times on the solar thermal panels, thus creating fluid temperatures high enough to generate steam for turbines that in turn run electricity generators. There are three different types of mirror configurations: trough systems, dish/engine systems, and power towers.[8]

Trough System. The most common CSP solar thermal system is the trough system, which uses long parabolic shaped mirrors to concentrate the sun's rays on a tube that runs down the center (focal point) of the mirror as seen in Figure 5.2. The tube is filled with a liquid that is heated to

FIGURE 5.2 Concentrating Solar Power System: Trough Style, Mojave Desert, California
Source: U.S. Department of Energy, Office of Energy Efficiency and Renewable Energy, Concentrating Solar Power, Mojave Desert,. http://www1.eere.energy.gov/solar/csp.html.

temperatures high enough to create steam. The liquid is often a type of oil so that a heat exchanger is needed to transfer the heat to the water, but development work is being done to use water in the tube so as to create steam directly. The whole trough can rotate so that it remains oriented toward the sun for maximum heat absorption during the day.[9]

Dish System. The dish system uses mirrors mounted on a large parabolic dish, similar to a satellite television dish, to concentrate the sun's rays on a single focal point above the dish as seen in Figure 5.3. The system

FIGURE 5.3 Concentrating Solar Power: Dish System
DOE photo caption: Dish Stirling solar power system at Arizona Public Service Solar Test and Research Center. This solar technology, capable of producing 25 kilowatts of electricity, uses mirrors to focus sunlight onto a thermal receiver. The heat is used to run a Stirling heat engine, which drives an electricity generator.
Source: U.S. Department of Energy, Image ID 2010501, www.doedigitalarchive.doe. gov.

produces a higher concentration of the sun's rays than the trough system, which means that much higher temperatures can be reached. The sun's rays heat a liquid, which in turn is used to generate steam and drive a turbine. The dish has a motor to keep it oriented toward the sun throughout the day. The dish can be linked to a Stirling engine—made by Stirling Energy Systems, Inc. (see www.stirlingenergy.com)—that is mounted at the focal point of the dish. The sun's rays heat a gas inside the Stirling engine's heater head, which then converts the heat directly into mechanical motion to run an electric generator.[10]

There are several companies that work individually or in teams on dish systems: Science Applications International Corp., STM Corp., Boeing, Stirling Energy Systems, WG Associates, and Sunfire Corporation, according to the National Renewable Energy Laboratory.[11]

CSP Power Tower. The CSP "power tower" is a solar thermal system that uses a large field of mirrors built on the ground around a tower (see Figure 5.4). The mirrors track the sun during the day so as to keep the sun's rays focused on a focal point on the tower. At that focal point on the tower, a liquid is heated and then passed through a steam turbine to generate electricity.

Existing and Planned CSP Plants. Concentrating solar power (CSP) power plants have been operating in the southwestern United States for over two decades. There are nine parabolic trough plants with capacity of 354 megawatts that have operated in California since the 1980s

FIGURE 5.4 Concentrating Solar Power: Power Tower
Source: U.S. Department of Energy, "Solar Two" 10-megawatt pilot system built in 1990s.

according to the National Renewable Energy Laboratory of the U.S. Department of Energy.[12] Prototype dish/Stirling systems are operating in Nevada, Arizona, Colorado, and Spain.[13] Two pilot power tower systems were developed in the 1980s and 1990s ("Solar One" and "Solar Two") near Barstow, California, under a U.S. Department of Energy program. The technology lessons from those pilots are being used to build a full-scale system power tower in Spain.[14] The Department of Energy is currently working on a plan with the Western Governors' Association to build up to 1 to 4 gigawatts of CSP power by 2015.[15]

A major CSP project that was just completed in June 2007 is Nevada One, a 64-megawatt solar thermal electricity generating plant near Boulder City, Nevada. The plant is a trough-style system. The plant is the world's third largest CSP plant and will provide enough power for 18,000 homes.[16] The plant cost about $220 to $250 million to build and will produce electricity at a cost of about 15 to 17 cents per kilowatt-hour according to RenewableEnergyAccess.com.[17] The electricity generated by the plant is being sold to Nevada Power Company and Sierra Pacific Power Company on long-term power purchase contracts. The power purchase will help those Nevada power utilities meet Nevada's Renewable Standards Portfolio requirement that 20 percent of electricity must come from renewable sources by 2015 and that one-fourth of that electricity must come from solar power.

The Nevada One plant was built by Solargenix Energy and Acciona SA (Spain: ANA SM), which purchased a 55 percent ownership interest in Solargenix in February 2006. This book's companion Web site at www.ProfitingFromCleanEnergy.com has a link to a video tour of the Nevada Solar One power plant. Solargenix, a private company based in Raleigh, North Carolina, specializes in manufacturing and installing solar thermal systems (see www.solargenix.com). Acciona SA is a large construction and renewable company based in Spain (see www.acciona.com) with about 35,000 employees and 2006 revenues of 6.3 billion euros.

Another major player in building the *Nevada One* CSP trough plant was the German glass-specialist Schott AG, which supplied about two-thirds of the 18,240 parabolic receivers used in the project. Schott's Chairman, Professor Dr. Udo Ungeheuer, said of CSP: "We are convinced that parabolic trough power plants are on their way to achieving a global breakthrough, thanks to Nevada One. The technology has already proven itself and the costs of generating electricity will soon be competitive."[18] Schott is a major player, not just in solar thermal, but also in solar PV. Schott (www.schott.com) is a large private company with about 17,000 employees worldwide and 2006 revenues of about 2 billion euros.

CSP Costs. The cost of the electricity produced by trough-based CSP power systems, such as the one seen in Figure 5.5, that are currently

FIGURE 5.5 Nevada One CSP solar plant built by Solargenix Energy Inc. and Acciona SA
Source: Acciona Solar.

operating in the southwestern United States is 12 to 14 cents per kilowatt-hour, which is about double the cost of electricity generated by coal-fired or nuclear plants.[19] However, a DOE-sponsored study concluded that CSP technologies could reach production costs of 6 cents per kilowatt with only modest production volumes.[20] A report by the National Renewable Energy Laboratory predicts that the cost of concentrating solar power without subsidies can be reduced to 5.4 cents per kilowatt-hour by 2012 for trough systems, to 4.0 cents per kilowatt-hours by 2012 for tower power systems, and to 6 cents per kilowatt-hours by 2025 for dish systems. These costs are competitive with those of nuclear and fossil-fuel-fired power plants.[21]

Future of CSP. Concentrating solar power is gaining momentum due to the comparatively low power-generation costs and the large scale of electricity that can be generated in remote, desert-type locations. Proponents of CSP are confident that CSP electricity generation costs can be sufficiently reduced to compete head-to-head with fossil fuel without government mandates or incentives, particularly if emissions and other external environmental costs are added to the cost of fossil fuel power plants. Aside from the CSP projects mentioned above, the World Bank's Solar Initiative is pushing CSP for developing nations with financing by the Global Environment Facility.[22]

SOLAR PHOTOVOLTAIC POWER

There is a perception among some that solar photovoltaic power (solar PV) is "not ready for prime time" because it is not powerful enough or because it will always be too expensive. The U.S. Department of Energy notes, however, that a single 100 square-mile solar park in the Nevada desert could satisfy the entire United States with its power needs using even low-efficiency (10 percent) solar modules.[23]

Regarding the cost of solar PV power, there is no denying that solar power is still relatively expensive. However, a huge amount of research and development capital is being spent on finding ways to slash the cost of solar PV. The cost of solar PV has historically fallen by about 5 percent per year and one leading solar research firm has found that solar PV is already competitive with retail electricity pricing in 10 percent of the developed world and will be competitive in 50 percent of the developed world by 2020 (more on this later). The world's largest vertically integrated solar PV company, Renewable Energy Corp of Norway (Oslo: REC NO), has a clearly defined technology roadmap for cutting the cost of solar power by 50 percent by 2010 and has identified further solar cost savings beyond the 2010 roadmap. The global solar PV industry is already in the mass production stage with global sales of $15.6 billion in 2006, according to CleanEdge LLC.[24]

Advantages and Disadvantages of Solar PV Power

Advantages
- No greenhouse gas emissions, which means solar PV is carbon neutral. Solar PV electricity satisfies government-imposed renewable energy mandates placed on power utilities around the world. Solar PV benefits from numerous government subsidies around the world.
- Produces no waste byproducts.
- Equipment typically lasts 25 to 30 years with virtually no maintenance.
- Uses free fuel (sun) and provides energy independence from foreign sources of fuel.
- User-installed solar systems provide distributed electricity to the owner and protect the owner from grid problems such as blackouts, brownouts, and electricity price hikes.
- Generates electricity even on cloudy days and works even in northern climates.
- Generates electricity during the day when electricity is the most expensive, thus avoiding highest electricity generation costs and shaving the peak for utilities.
- Falling solar power costs (5 percent per year on average) have already made solar power competitive with retail electricity prices in some areas of the world (e.g., Japan).

- Uses the same silicon wafers that are used by the semiconductor industry, which means the two industries share R&D knowledge base and investment.
- Already in the mass production stage and the industry is spending large amounts of capital on R&D efforts.

Disadvantages
- Provides electricity only during the day. For power at night, the system must have an ancillary power storage system, or the system owner can draw power from the grid.
- Remains expensive at present and is competitive with existing grid electricity in most areas only after the inclusion of government incentives and rebates.
- Presents a large up-front cash cost, although financing of solar equipment is becoming more available.

How Does Solar PV Work?

Solar cells create electricity by using sunlight to create the flow of electrons between negatively and positively charged layers of semiconductor materials. Electrical contacts are applied to the solar cell, usually through screen printing, in order to collect and transport the electricity from the cell to an output contact (see Figure 5.6 for a photo of a silicon solar cell).

FIGURE 5.6 Silicon solar cell
Source: U.S. Department of Energy.

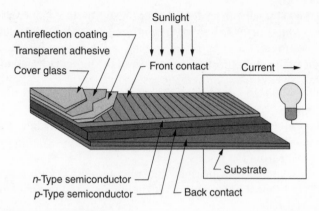

FIGURE 5.7 Solar Module Schematic
Source: U.S. Department of Energy, Office of Energy Efficiency and Renewable Energy,
"Solar Cell Materials," http://www.eere.energy.gov/solar/solar_cell_materials.html.

The solar cells are then assembled into a solar panel or module. As seen in Figure 5.7, the elements of a solar module typically involve a backing plate (substrate), the semiconductor layers, an antireflection coating to improve sunlight absorption, and an aluminum frame box and a glass cover to protect the entire module. Solar modules can be manufactured without solar cells by directly coating a substrate with a thin film of semiconductor material, which is then referred to as "thin film solar" (more on thin film solar later).

The solar modules are then typically combined in an overall system that is placed on a roof or supporting structure, as seen in Figure 5.8. The

FIGURE 5.8 Solar Module System: Supplying Power to Pentagon
Source: U.S. Department of Energy.

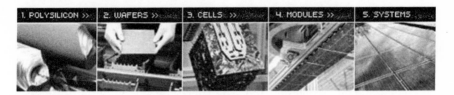

FIGURE 5.9 PV Value Chain Schematic
Source: Renewable Energy Corp. "Analyst Field Trip – presentation material," 28 March 2007. http://hugin.info/136555/R/1115224/203491.pdf]

support structure can have a tracking system that slowly turns the solar modules to directly face the sun in order to obtain the strongest possible sunlight. Also, the system can be constructed so that the sun's energy is concentrated by various methods onto the PV cell/module, which is then referred to as "concentrating photovoltaic" power. A power inverter is typically used to convert the direct current from the solar system into the alternating current that is typically used by the grid and by most electronic devices. A power storage system (e.g. batteries) can be added to the overall system that can be charged during the day and then provide a continuous flow of electricity from the system at night when there is no sunlight.

Solar PV Production Process and Value Chain

The crystalline solar cell industry involves a value chain that begins at a quartz mine and ends with the final product—a solar power system installed at a customer site. It is important to recognize the different stages of the value chain and the stage in which a particular solar company operates. The main stages of the value chain at which solar companies operate are (1) polysilicon (2) wafers, (3) solar cells, (4) solar modules and (5) system integration and installation. There are also companies that sell the production line equipment that solar PV manufacturers use to produce wafers, cells, and modules.

- *Metallurgical silicon.* The silicon PV value chain starts at a quartz mine where a mining company digs quartz out of the ground. Quartz is silicon dioxide (SiO_2), which means there are two molecules of oxygen attached to each molecule of silicon. Silicon is the second most plentiful element contained in the earth's crust (after oxygen) and makes up more than 25 percent of the earth's crust by mass, according to the U.S. Geological Service.[25]

  The mining company then places the mined quartz through a refining process that removes impurities and produces metallurgical-grade silicon (MGS) flakes with 98 percent silicon purity. Metallurgical silicon (MGS) in 2006 cost about 77 cents per pound ($1.70/kg), according to the U.S. Geological Service.[26] The main users of metallurgical silicon are the producers of aluminum/aluminum alloys and the chemical industry. The polysilicon producers that supply the solar and semiconductor industries account for only a few percent of overall metallurgical silicon demand. The supply of mining output of metallurgical silicon is plentiful and is not in short supply despite the sharp increase in demand from the solar polysilicon industry.

- *Polysilicon.* A polysilicon company takes the metallurgical silicon (MGS) and then processes it into pure silicon, typically through the Siemens process. That process involves transforming the metallurgical silicon into either trichlorosilane (TCS or $HSiCl_3$) or monosilane gas (SiH_4) and then using the gas to grow pure silicon crystalline rods in a pressure reactor. Polysilicon is virtually 100 percent pure with any impurities measured in parts per billion. The polysilicon output is usually in the form of long rods, but newer production techniques (e.g., fluidized bed reactors) can produce polysilicon in granular form.

- *Silicon wafers.* The polysilicon is then melted down in a crucible and is allowed to solidify into an ingot block. The two main techniques for creating the ingot are Czochralski (CZ) and float-zone (FZ). In the process of melting down the polysilicon, solar-grade silicon is typically mixed (or "doped" in industry parlance) with small amounts of boron to improve the material's electrical properties. The solid ingots are then cut into very thin wafers with a thickness of only 200 to 280 microns (about one-fifth of a millimeter) using high-precision wire saws. Depending on the solidification technique, the resulting silicon ingot can be either monocrystalline or multicrystalline silicon. There is a different method for creating wafers called the "string ribbon" technique which involves drawing strings through the molten polysilicon to create a solar wafer immediately, thus skipping the process of creating an ingot and sawing it into wafer slices.

- *Solar cells.* In the solar cell manufacturing process, the solar cells are typically created by etching the wafer surface, applying a dopant onto the front side of the wafer to set up the electrical transmission process, applying a thin layer of antireflective material on the front of the wafer to increase sunlight absorption, and then applying electrical contacts through screen-printing.

- *Solar modules.* The solar cells are then placed in a frame under tempered glass and are electrically connected to each other through junction boxes. The typical solar module has a life cycle of more than 25 years and requires virtually no maintenance since rain is usually sufficient to keep the module surface clean.

- *Solar systems.* At a site location, the modules are connected together into an array and are installed on top of a building or on a support structure. As mentioned earlier, the power generated from a solar PV system is direct current (DC), so an inverter may be necessary to convert the DC power into alternating current (AC), depending on the power requirements. The solar system may also use a battery system to store the power for continuous output during night time.

Solar PV Target Markets

The primary target market for solar PV power is for installation at homes and commercial buildings. Typically, the system power range is 2 to 10 kilowatt-hour systems for homes, and 10 to 100 kilowatt-hour systems for office buildings and schools. Solar power equipment has a large up-front capital cost but the equipment typically lasts 25 to 30 years with little or no maintenance. The benefit for homeowners and businesses is that after the up-front capital cost for the equipment, there is no additional cost for the electricity produced by the solar power equipment over the life of the equipment. In addition, the solar PV system owner gains protection from electricity price hikes from the local utility company. Solar power is a distributed means of power generation that allows a homeowner or business to become independent, to some extent at least, from the local grid-based utility.

Solar power is particularly attractive in developing countries for village-scale electricity generation plants in remote areas. China, for example, has an active electrical rural electrification program. Solar power provides an ideal power generation source for remote areas since it requires no fuel and little maintenance. Fossil fuel power plants in remote areas, by contrast, can be expensive because of the need to transport large amounts of coal, diesel fuel, or natural gas to the plant.

Solar power is also attractive for instrumentation devices in remote off-grid locations where it is too expensive or even impossible to run power lines. Such remote locations include (1) microwave repeater stations; (2) TV/radio towers; (3) remote sensors such as pipelines, well heads, and bridges; (4) remote water pumps; and (5) transportation signaling devices such as marine buoys, lighthouses, aircraft warning lights, and road transportation warning lights. The ultimate "remote location" is space, where solar power has been used for many years.

Another important target market is the solar PV park, which involves installing many solar modules on multiple acres of land to provide an overall system that is large enough to provide electricity to the grid. Solar parks are popping up all around the world, largely because of renewable energy mandates and feed-in tariffs. Government feed-in tariffs set the long-term price for the electricity that the solar park can sell to the local utility, thus guaranteeing the investor group or company an adequate return on the project.

Solar parks typically produce electricity on the scale of 10-50 megawatts, which is the size of a very small traditional power plant and is enough to power 3,000–14,000 homes. The Bavaria Solarpark in Germany, for example, is a 10-megawatt complex that covers 63 acres and uses 56,600 PV panels. In another example, First Solar (Nasdaq: FSLR) is providing its solar modules for the Waldpolenze Solar Park in Germany, which is a 40-megawatt solar park that will use 550,000 thin-film solar modules. The Waldpolenze Solar Park solar park will cost 130 million euros to build and is scheduled for completion by the end of 2009. Contributors to Wikipedia are keeping a current list of the world's largest solar parks, which is a good way to keep tabs on the most recent solar park projects (see en.wikipedia.org/wiki/photovoltaic_power_stations).

Research is currently being done on the feasibility of constructing huge 100-megawatt to 4-gigawatt solar parks in desert areas with high sun energy, which are called *very large scale photovoltaic power generation* (VLS-PV) *systems*. These facilities would use the same solar PV technologies that are in use by today's solar parks, but the difference is that these VLS-PV systems would be much larger and would be located in remote desert-type locations where there is intense sunlight and no land constraints or NIMBY ("not in my backyard") objections. One problem with placing these large solar parks in desert locations would be that long power transmission lines would have to be built to transport the electricity from the plant to the cities and towns where the electricity is needed. The main treatise on VLS-PV systems is *Energy from the Desert: Practical Proposals for Very Large Scale Photovoltaic Systems*.[27] The study looks at the possibility of placing huge solar parks in remote desert areas of the world such as the Gobi Desert in Mongolia, Dunhuang in China, the Mediterranean, the Middle East, and Australia.

Solar PV Demand: $4 Trillion in New Electricity Generation Assets Needed by 2030

The world will need a huge amount of investment in new electricity generation in the coming decades. The International Energy Agency (IEA) estimates that from 2001 through 2030 new power generation capacity of 4,700 gigawatts will be built worldwide, which is equivalent to 9,400 medium-sized 500-megawatt power plants.[28] This investment will total about $4 trillion in the period through 2030. The IEA says that about one-third of the new capacity will be built in developing Asia.

In addition to new capacity, the IEA forecasts that over one-third of current total electricity generating capacity in the OECD nations will need to be replaced because of aging facilities. The IEA forecasts that OECD countries will also require more than 2,000 gigawatts of new generating capacity, which is equivalent to 4,000 medium-sized 500-megawatt power plants.

The IEA in its power generation forecast (which was made back in 2003, with no recent update) said that the bulk of the new investment in power plants would be in coal and natural gas fired plants. However, with the increasing global restrictions on greenhouse gas emissions and with the cost of solar and wind power dropping, solar and wind power are likely to take a larger role in meeting more electricity demand than the IEA originally forecasted.

The implication of this huge demand for new electricity generating capacity is that there is a big opportunity for solar power to supply a significant portion of this new capacity. Solar power currently accounts for less than 0.1 percent of world electricity production according to the International Energy Agency.[29] In the United States, solar PV power capacity in 2005 was a negligible 0.44 gigawatts, which was only 0.04 percent of U.S. peak electrical power generation of about 1,000 gigawatts according to the Solar America Initiative.[30]

Total installed U.S. solar power generation capacity could increase by 30 percent per year but solar power would still account for only 1 percent of total U.S. power generation by 2017, 2.4 percent by 2020, and 9 percent by 2025, as mentioned earlier in Chapter 4. Similar figures apply on a global scale. This illustrates the large amount of room on the upside for growth in the global solar industry, particularly given the attractive attributes of solar power relative to the traditional power generation methods of coal, natural gas and nuclear.

SOLAR POWER INDUSTRY GROWTH RATES

The world solar PV cell market grew at an annual rate of 45.5 percent from 2001 through 2006 according to a key solar industry publication, *PV News*.[31] The same publication reports that the solar PV cell production showed year-on-year growth of 41 percent in 2006.[32] Demand for solar modules currently far outstrips supply, meaning that solar module producers (and producers along the entire PV value chain) can easily sell as much product as they can produce.

Figure 5.10 illustrates the growth in global annual solar PV cell production since 2000. In the five years from 2001 through 2006, Europe showed annual solar PV cell production growth of +40 percent, Japan +15 percent, United States +46 percent, and rest of world, which is mainly China, +56 percent. The "rest of world" production soared by +121 percent year-on-year in the single year of 2006, leading the regional year-on-year growth

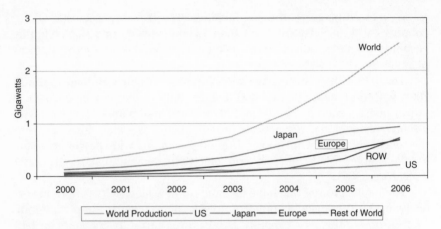

FIGURE 5.10 World Annual Solar PV Cell Production
Source: "23rd Annual Data Collection—Final," *PV News*, April 2007, p. 8, Prometheus Institute, Cambridge MA, http://www.prometheus.org/.

rates in 2006 of +42 percent in Europe, +31 percent in the United States, and +11 percent in Japan.

Looking ahead, global solar module production appears set to show extremely strong growth near 50 percent per year from 2006 through 2010. That suggests the solar PV industry will more than quintuple in size from 2006 to 2010. *PV News* is forecasting compounded annual module growth of +53 percent in the 2006–2010 period, from 2.1 gigawatts of module production in 2006 to 11.3 gigawatts in 2010, as seen in Figure 5.11.

Photon Consulting, in its Solar Annual 2006 report released in September 2006, forecasted 2010 solar PV module production at 10.4 gigawatts,

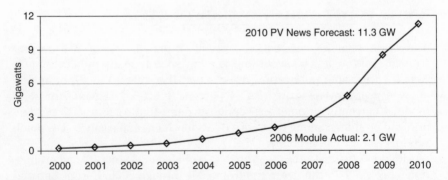

FIGURE 5.11 Global Solar PV Module Production Forecast
Source: "Supply and Demand Reconciliation," *PV News*, Prometheus Institute, August 2007, p. 7-8, Prometheus Institute, Cambridge MA, http://www.prometheus.org/.

which is just moderately below PV News' forecast of 11.3 gigawatts[33] Photon Consulting forecasts that revenues from the solar sector will more than triple from $19 billion in 2006 to $72 billion by 2010.[34] Photon Consulting expects pre-tax margins for the industry to remain strong in the 33 to 38 percent area in 2007 to 2010, with the pre-tax profit pool more than quadrupling from $5.7 billion in 2006 to $27.2 billion by 2010.[35]

DEMAND GENERATED BY GOVERNMENT INCENTIVES AND REGULATION

Growth in the solar industry in the past 10 years has been driven mainly by demand in Germany and Japan. Germany and Japan currently have the largest global demand share for new solar installations at 55 percent for Germany and 17 percent for Japan.[36] The United States had a global PV demand share of only 8 percent in 2006. Figure 5.12 shows that *PV News* is projecting a pickup in United States/Canada demand share to 26 percent in 2010, with Europe still the biggest market by far at 51 percent, Asia at 20 percent, and Rest of World at 3 percent.[37]

Solar PV growth in both Germany and Japan has been driven by aggressive government support programs. Germany began a 1,000 Rooftop program in 1990, which gave a start to solar PV demand. German solar power growth then skyrocketed when the German government implemented the 100,000 Rooftop program in 1999 and the Feed-In Tariff law in 2000. Germany's feed-in tariff offered a guaranteed €0.50 per kilowatt-hour for

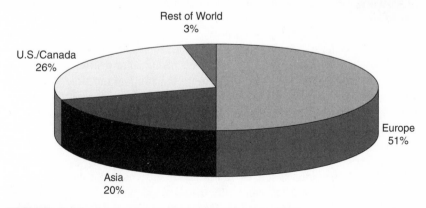

FIGURE 5.12 Regional Solar PV Demand Share in 2010
Source: "PV Market Demand through 2010," *PV News*, July 2007, pp. 5-7, Prometheus Institute, Cambridge, MA, www.prometheus.org.

20 years for electricity fed into the utility grid. The feed-in tariff's guaranteed price falls by 5 percent per year for new projects brought on line to ensure that the solar power providers are receiving benefits only if solar equipment costs fall 5 percent per year, as targeted by the industry.

Japan's 70,000 Roofs program provided a 50 percent cash subsidy for 3- to 4-kilowatt grid-connected residential systems. The program succeeded in growing the Japanese market from 500 to 100,000 solar PV systems over 10 years. Japan's program gradually phased out subsidies and solar PV in Japan is currently competitive with utility electric prices in many areas because of the high retail electricity prices in Japan.

Solar PV growth is now picking up quickly in countries other than Germany and Japan. Solar PV growth is now strong in Spain (+200 percent in 2006), other European countries (Italy, Greece, Portugal, France, and Belgium), and the United States (+33 percent in 2006). California and New Jersey have been the main areas of growth in the United States. California on January 1, 2007, started its $3 billion California Solar Initiative program (www.gosolarcalifornia.ca.gov). The California program aims to have at least 3 gigawatts of solar power installed by 2017. Other states in the United States are also ramping up incentive packages for solar power such as Arizona, New Mexico, Florida and Hawaii. A full list of U.S. state renewable energy incentives is available at the Database of State Incentives for Renewable Energy (www.dsireusa.org).

At the federal level, there is a commercial and residential *investment tax credit* (ITC) of 30 percent (no cap for commercial but residential capped at $2,000) for fuel cells and solar power systems that are installed before December 31, 2008. The solar power industry is currently lobbying for passage of the Securing America's Energy Independence Act (H.R. 550/S. 590), which would extend the solar investment tax credit for eight years.

China's State Electricity Regulatory Commission is expected to release a detailed feed-in tariff and incentive program for solar and wind energy by the end of 2007, which should lead to even faster solar growth in China in coming years. The feed-in tariff represents the implementation of China's larger goal of obtaining 10 percent of its power from renewable power sources by 2010 and 20 percent by 2020. China's Sustainable Energy Programme has mentioned a goal of 450 megawatts of solar power by 2010 and up to 8 gigawatts by 2020, which would create a huge source of demand for the global solar industry.

Table 5.1 provides a list of financial incentives for solar PV in the United States, the length of which illustrates the strong and increasing support that is being given to solar PV in the United States. Table 5.2 provides a list of solar PV incentive programs in Europe, which illustrates the extent of government support in Europe for solar PV. The list of worldwide

TABLE 5.1 U.S. Federal and State Solar PV Incentives

Territory	Sector	System Size	Financial Incentives	Details
U.S. Federal	Residential	All	30% Tax Credit	$2,000 max
	Commercial	All	30% Tax Credit	
Arizona	Residential/Commercial	All	$2.00–2.50/watt	Limited to certain utilities
California	Residential/Commercial	<100kW	$2.50/watt	
	Residential/Commercial	>100kW	$0.39/kWh for 5 years	
Colorado	Residential/Commercial	All	$4.50/watt	Xcel Energy: $2/watt + REC payment of $2.50/watt <10MW
Connecticut	Residential/Commercial	All	$5.00/watt	
Florida	Residential	All	$4.00/watt	Up to $20,000
	Commercial	All	$4.00/watt	Up to $100,000
Hawaii	Residential/Commercial	All	35% personal tax credit	
Massachusetts	Residential	<2.5kW	$2.00/watt	
	Commercial	<10kW	$2.00/watt	
Nevada	Residential/Commercial	All	$3.00/watt	

(Continues)

93

TABLE 5.1 (Continued)

Territory	Sector	System Size	Financial Incentives	Details
New Jersey	Residential/Commercial	0–10kW	$3.80/watt	
	Residential/Commercial	10–40kW	$2.75/watt	
	Residential/Commercial	40–100kW	$2.50/watt	
	Residential/Commercial	100–500kW	$2.25/watt	
	Residential/Commercial	500–700kW	$2.00/watt	
New York	Residential/Commercial	<50kW	$4.00–4.50/watt	
Oregon	Residential	All	$2.00–2.25/watt	Only for PG&E or Pacific Power customers
	Commercial	All	$1.00–1.25/watt	Only for PG&E or Pacific Power customers
Pennsylvania	Residential	All	$4.00/watt	Up to $20,000: $1 kWh up to $5,000 after first $20,000
Texas	Residential/Commercial	All	$4.50/watt	Austin Energy only
Washington	Residential/Commercial	All	$0.15/kWh	
Wyoming	Residential	All	Lesser of $3,000 or 50%	

Source: "Smart Regulation Speeds Growth," *PV News*, November 2006, p. 3–5, Prometheus Institute, Cambridge, MA, www. prometheus.org.

TABLE 5.2	Support Mechanisms for Solar PV in Europe and China (Part 1 of 2)
Austria	The amendment of the Austrian Eco Electricity Law (*Ökostromgesetz*) was passed by Parliament on May 23, 2006, and went into force on July 1, 2006. But the tariff negotiations are still ongoing. It is expected that they will be decided in October 2006.
	Key elements of the Law are: Electricity from all renewable energy sources will be supported with €17million per year. 10 percent are earmarked for PV, with the same amount added by the Federal States because of their cofinancing duty. The support will be constant for 10 years, with a degressive support for three more years and thereafter an obligation for the utilities to accept the electricity from a PV system for another 13 years.
	Some of the federal states have investment support schemes.
Belgium	Green Certificates (with guaranteed minimum price): 0.15 €/kWh; Flanders from January 1, 2006: 0.45 €/kWh for 20 years.
	Additional support in Flanders depends on whether the PV installation is done privately, by an enterprise, or by a farmer.
	The support schemes used are investment subsidies, eco-premiums, tax reductions, and interest reduced mortgages.
Cyprus	Feed-in tariff: 0.22CYP£/kWh (0.391 €/kWh) for households and 0.196CYP£/kWh (0.342 €/kWh for enterprises).
	If an investment grant is taken, the tariff is reduced to 0.012CYP£ /kWh (0.21 €/kWh).
	Investment grants for households, other entities and organizations, not engaged in economic activities are limited to a maximum 55 percent of the eligible costs and the maximum grant is 16.5 k€ (CY£9.500). For enterprises, the grant is 40 percent of eligible costs and the maximum amount of the grant is 12 k€ (CY£7.000).
Czech Republic	New Law on the Promotion of Production of Electricity from Renewable Energy Sources went into effect on August 1, 2005. Producers of electricity can choose from two support schemes:
	Fixed feed-in tariff for 2006: Systems commissioned after January 1, 2006: 13.2CZK/kWh (0.466 €/kWh); Systems commissioned before January 1, 2006: 6.28CZK/kWh (0.222 €/kWh).
	Market price + Green Bonus; Green Bonus for 2006; Systems commissioned after January 1, 2006: 12.59CZK/kWh (0.445 €/kWh); Systems commissioned before January 1, 2006: 5.67CZK/kWh (0.200 €/kWh). From 2007 onwards the annual price decrease for new installations should be 5 percent maximum.
Denmark	No specific PV program, but settlement price for green electricity 60 Øre/kWh (0.08 €/kWh) for 10 years, then 10 more years 40Øre/kWh.

(Continues)

TABLE 5.2   (*Continued*)

Estonia	No specific PV program, but Renewable Portfolio Standard and tax relief. Feed-in tariff for electricity produced out of RES is 5.1 ct/kWh.
Finland	No PV program, but investment subsidy up to 40 percent, and tax/production subsidy for electricity from renewable energy sources (6.9 €/MWh).
France	New feed-in tariff since 26 July 2006: (only valid for new installations) 0.30 €/kWh (0.40 €/kWh in Overseas Departments and Corsica) for 20 years.
	For building integrated PV installations there is a supplement of 0.25 €/kWh (0.15 €/kWh in Overseas Departments and Corsica).
	50 percent of the investment costs are tax deductible. Lower VAT of 5.5 percent on system costs (without labor). Accelerated depreciation of PV systems for enterprises. Regional support still possible.
	The 5 percent tariff degression for new installations was cancelled. All tariffs (old and new) will be adjusted annually in accordance to the inflation during their duration.
Germany	Feed-in tariff for 20 years with built-in annual decrease of 5 percent from 2005 onward. For plants, neither on building nor sound barriers, the annual decrease is 6.5 percent from 2006 onward.
	Tariffs for new installations in 2006: Free-standing systems: 0.406 €/kWh; Systems on buildings and sound barriers: 0.518 €/kWh < 30 kWp,0.4928 €/kWh >30 kWp, and 0.4874 €/kWh > 100 kWp. For façade integration there is an additional bonus of 0.05 €/kWh.
Greece	New feed-in tariff since June 2006: 0.45 €/kWh (0.50 €/kWh on islands) for systems <100 KWp; 0.45 €/kWh (0.45 €/kWh on islands) for systems > 100 KWp. Guaranteed for 20 years.
	Commercial installations are eligible to grants (30 percent to 55 percent of total system costs) while small domestic systems are eligible for a 20 percent tax deduction capped at €500 per system (€700 in 2007).
	For 2020 a target to reach at least 700 MWp (500 MWp mainland, 200 MWp islands) has been set.
Hungary	No PV specific measure, but feed-in tariffs for RES were set through the Electricity Act, which entered into force on January 1, 2003. According to Regulation No. 105/2003 (XII.29) GKM, the Electricity Suppliers are obliged to purchase electricity from producers utilizing RES, if their capacity is over 100kW. However, in the case of smaller plants, individual arrangements are possible. There is no differentiation between the renewable sources. The current feed-in tariffs are: Peak: 25.30 HUF/kWh (€0.1); Off-Peak: 15.80 HUF/kWh (€0.063); Average: 19.36 HUF/kWh (€0.077).

TABLE 5.2	*(Continued)*
Ireland	The Alternative Energy Requirement (AER) tender scheme was replaced by a new Renewable Energy Feed-in Tariff (ReFIT) scheme in 2006. PV is not included.
Italy	Feed-in tariff: guaranteed for 20 years. The tariffs for 2005 and 2006 are listed below, after that there is a 5 percent decrease for new systems each year, but tariffs and degression will be corrected according to inflation (ISTAT). The original cap of 100 MW to be reached in 2012 was raised to 500 MW (Ministerial Decree, February 6, 2006).
	1) Up to 20 kW: 0.445 €/kWh + "net metering," i.e., each kWh used at home is deducted from the electricity bill. (1 and 2 together have a cap of 60 annually).
	2) Between 20 kW and 50 kW: 0.46 €/kW.
	3) Between 50 kW and 1 MW: 49 €/kWh (cap of 25 MW annually).
Latvia	Feed-in tariff but not PV specific:
	• Licensed before June 1, 2001: double the average sales price (~0.101 €/kWh).
	for eight years, then reduction to normal sales price.
	• Licensed after June 1, 2001: regulators set price.
	A national investment program for RES has been running since 2002.
Lithuania	No specific PV support. National Control Commission for Prices and Energy approves long-term purchase prices for renewable electricity, and grid operators must give priority to its transport.
Luxembourg	A support scheme was set with a Règlement Grand Ducal in September 2005. The Règlement has a cap of 3 MW by 2007. The new feed-in tariff is 0.56 €/kWh for 20 years, but due to the fact that this is a Règlement and not a law, it is not binding.
	In addition, grants up to 15 percent are available, but limited to €900 per each member of a household (only the head of the household can receive double that amount).
Malta	Net metering for electricity from PV systems: 0.126 €/kWh
	Surplus exported to the grid: 0.063€/kWh, but there is a one-off charge of €46 for the extra meter.
	20 percent grant for rooftop PV installations
Netherlands	Feed-in tariff: 0.097 €/kWh for 10 years and net metering up to 3,000 kWh/year for existing systems.
	On August 25, 2006, the Minister of Economy announced the immediate suspension of support for new electricity generation plants using renewable energy sources.

(Continues)

TABLE 5.2 *(Continued)*	
Poland	Tax incentives: no customs duty on PV and reduced VAT (7 percent) for complete PV systems, but 22 percent for modules and components. Some soft loans and subsidies. A new law passed in April 2004 required that tariffs for all renewable energies have to be approved by the regulator. (Until now that was only for projects larger than 5 MW).
Portugal	Revision of feed-in tariff in 2005 with cap of 150 MW (2010). The tariff is guaranteed for the first 15 years or 21 GWh/MW whichever is reached first: 0.45 €/kWh < 5 kWp; 0.28 €/kWh > 5 kWp.
	Reduction of VAT rate from 21 percent to 12 percent on renewable equipment, custom duties exemption and income tax reductions up to €730 for solar equipment.
	Grants up to 40 percent of the total eligible cost (max. €150,000 per application) are available under the PRIME program (2000–2006).
Slovakia	Feed-in tariff set by regulator each year. 8 SKK/kWh (ca. 0.206 €/kWh) for 2006.
	Tax reduction on income earned. RES feed-in tariff in 2005: ~3 ct/kWh.
Slovenia	Feed-in tariff: either fixed price or electricity price (8 SIT/kWh) + premium.
	The plant size limit was removed in June 2006.
Spain	Feed-in tariff with cap of 150 MW: • 0.44 €/kWh < 100 kWp for 25 years (575 percent of average electricity price).
	After 25 years 460 percent of average electricity price. • 0.23 €kWh > 100 kWp for 25 years (300 percent of average electricity price)
	After 25 years 240 percent of average electricity price.
Sweden	70 percent tax deduction on investment and installation cost for systems on public buildings from May 2005 until end of 2007, with maximum limit per building of €550,000 and covers both material and labor costs. Electricity certificates for wind, solar, biomass, geothermal, and small hydro. Energy tax exemption.
Switzerland	Net metering with feed-in tariff of min. 0.15 CHF/kWh (0.10 €/kWh); investment subsidies in some cantons; promotion of voluntary measures (solar stock exchanges, green power marketing).
United Kingdom	Investment subsidies in the framework of a PV demonstration program. Reduced VAT.
China	A Renewable Energy Law went into effect in January 2006 to provide the legal framework for the development of renewable energy in China. However, bidding for wind power feed-in has been in effect for several years and the National Development and Reform Commission (NDRC) said that the bidding system would continue under the new law.

TABLE 5.2   (Continued)

Most of the wind power projects were awarded bids of 0.4 to 0.5 yuan (5.1 to 6.4 U.S. cents)/kWh. In addition, the five big power companies benefited from some preferential tax policies that gave them refunds of 0.1 yuan (1.2 U.S. cents)/kWh.

There is much lobbying by the Chinese solar power companies for the government to adopt a feed-in tariff policy for solar power, but there is little expectation of that happening in the near future. Most use of solar power so far has been in rural areas with no connection to the power grid.

Source: Arnulf Jager-Waldau, *PV Status Report 2006: Research, Solar Cell Production and Market Implementation of Photovoltaics*, European Commission Joint Research Centre, Institute for Environment and Sustainability, August 2006, Table 5, http://www.epia.org/documents/PV_Status_Report_2006.pdf.

incentives for solar PV is likely to grow even further in coming years, thus providing strong support for the solar PV industry as it moves towards parity with fossil fuels.

SOLAR POWER PRICING AND COMPETITIVENESS

Solar power is still expensive relative to other methods of electricity production. Solar power currently costs about 25 cents per kilowatt-hour on average across the world according to Photon Consulting's calculations, a figure that loads in all costs and does not include any subsidies or government support measures.[38] Solar research group Solarbuzz puts U.S. solar PV electricity prices lower at 21 cents/kilowatt-hour.[39] In any case, the actual cost of solar power for any particular user varies quite widely depending on differences in solar equipment and the intensity of the sun at a customer's location.

In any case, the world average cost of solar power of 25 cents per kilowatt-hour is well above the traditional U.S. power generation methods of coal (4 cents), nuclear (6 cents), or natural gas (7 cents), as displayed in Figure 5.13. However, that 25 cent solar power cost is already within the retail price of electricity for some residential and commercial users, which ranges widely throughout the world from about 4 to 30 cents per kilowatt-hour (see Figure 5.14).

It is important to emphasize that solar power does not have to compete against the cheapest utility generation costs to be competitive. Solar PV systems that are installed at residential and commercial buildings have to

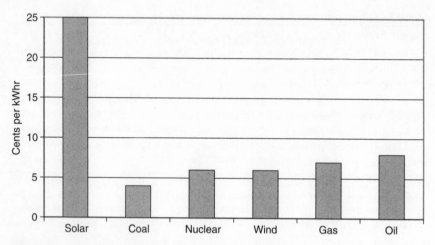

FIGURE 5.13 Average U.S. Electricity Generation Costs
Source: U.S. Department of Energy.

compete only with the retail price of electricity provided by the local utility, not with the utility's generation cost. However, when solar PV power costs drop to or below utility generation costs without subsidies, then utilities will have an economic incentive to build large solar parks as an alternative to coal- and natural-gas-fired power plants and nuclear power plants.

It is also important to emphasize that solar power does not necessarily have to compete against the lowest *flat-rate* retail electricity prices in the world to be competitive. In a variable-rate pricing system, electricity

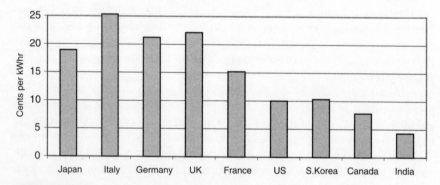

FIGURE 5.14 Global Residential Electricity Prices
Source: International Energy Agency, Key World Energy Statistics 2007, p. 43. http://www.iea.org/textbase/nppdf/free/2007/key_stats_2007.pdf.

prices are higher during the day when electricity demand is high and lower at night when electricity demand is low. In a variable-rate pricing environment, solar power only needs to compete against the peak electricity rates that utilities charge during the day (when solar power is available), which can be as high as 20 to 30 cents per kilowatt-hour in the United States versus the 10 cent per kilowatt-hour average flat-rate seen in the United States. Variable-priced electricity pricing is already the norm for commercial customers and is becoming more popular at the residential level in Europe and the United States as a means to increase overall grid efficiency. As consumers face peak utility electricity pricing of 20 to 30 cents per kilowatt-hour in some areas in the United States, solar PV starts to look attractive even without subsidies.

The conventional wisdom among the public at large is that solar PV power is not even close to being competitive with existing electricity prices worldwide. However, Photon Consulting estimates that solar power is already competitive with residential grid electricity prices in 5 to 10 percent of the developed OECD countries, representing a hefty 150 to 300 gigawatt-hours of electricity.[40] Much of that competitive area is in Japan, where retail electricity prices are high.

Going further, Photon Consulting in its report, *The True Cost of Solar: 10 Cents/kWh by 2010*, makes the aggressive forecast that the cost of solar PV power, excluding subsidies, will fall to 10 to 15 cents per kilowatt-hour by 2010 and will be competitive with 50 percent of OECD residential demand and 10 percent of commercial customers in the OECD countries.[41] Photon Consulting based its estimates on a bottom-up analysis of the cost structures of 75 solar power companies and the figures were peer-reviewed by several senior executives in the solar power industry.

The U.S. Department of Energy's (DOE) Solar America Initiative (SAI) has provided forecasts for how the downward cost curve for solar PV may develop in the United States (see www.eere.energy.gov/solar/solar_america/).[42] Solar America Initiative's cost projections are shown in Figure 5.15 and Table 5.3. The SAI data show that the current cost range of solar power (without subsidies) is above residential and commercial electricity rates in the United States. However, the chart shows how SAI expects solar costs to move progressively lower to compete with retail electricity prices over the 2008–2012 time frame and with grid-generated power by 2012 to 2015 without subsidies.

The DOE's Solar America Initiative program has ambitious goals. By 2015, SAI wants solar PV electricity to be cost-competitive in all sectors without government support and to provide 5 to 10 gigawatts of electricity generating capacity (which is enough to power 750,000 to 1.5 million households). By 2030, SAI wants solar PV to provide 70–100 GW of

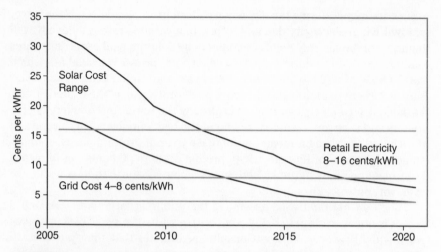

FIGURE 5.15 Solar America Initiative (SAI): Projected Cost Reductions for Solar PV with SAI program
Source: U.S. Department of Energy, Office of Energy Efficiency and Renewable Energy, *Solar American Initiative: A Plan for the Integrated Research, Development, and Market Transformation of Solar Energy Technologies*, 5 February 2007, p. 8, http://www1.eere.energy.gov/solar/solar_america/pdfs/sai_draft_plan_Feb5_07.

electrical generating capacity (10 to 15 million households) and for solar PV to provide 40 percent of all new electric capacity in the United States. SAI envisions that the U.S. solar market value will grow to $30 billion by 2030 and that some 150 million metric tons of CO_2 emissions will be avoided.

How is the solar PV industry going to actually cut its costs? Renewable Energy Corp. (REC) (Oslo: REC NO), the world's largest integrated solar

TABLE 5.3 Current U.S. Electricity Costs vs. Future Solar Costs

	Current Electricity	**Solar PV Costs (cents/kWh)**		
	Cost Range 2005	**Benchmark 2005**	**Target 2010**	**Target 2015**
Residential	5.8–16.7	23–32	13–18	8–10
Commercial	5.4–15.0	16–22	9–12	6–8
Utility Generation	4.0–7.6	13–22	10–15	5–7

Source: U.S. Department of Energy, Office of Energy Efficiency and Renewable Energy, *Solar American Initiative: A Plan for the Integrated Research, Development, and Market Transformation of Solar Energy Technologies*, 5 February 2007, p. 8, http://www1.eere.energy.gov/solar/solar_america/pdfs/sai_draft_plan_Feb5_07.

PV company has a specific *2010 Cost Reduction Roadmap* that illustrates how REC plans to cut its costs.[43] REC has an explicit target of cutting the price per watt for solar PV by 50 percent by 2010 from the baseline in 2005. REC has identified further cost savings beyond its 2010 Road Map. REC's 2010 Road Map includes the following efforts:

- 60 percent reduction in polysilicon costs through REC's fluidized bed reactor (FBR) technology, which is a continuous batch process that uses much less electricity than the industry-standard Siemens process and produces granular polysilicon (rather than rods), which is more efficient for use in the wafer stage of production.
- 50 percent reduction in wafer production costs through improved production line processes and reduced wastage.
- Cost reductions at the cell and module production stages though advanced technologies to be installed in new production lines.

UPSTREAM SOLAR PLAYERS: POLYSILICON AND WAFER PRODUCERS

Polysilicon has been in short supply since about 2004 due to strong demand from the solar industry. The shortage has led to high polysilicon prices and high profit margins for the handful of companies that produce polysilicon. Renewable Energy Corp (Oslo: REC NO), for example, produced an operating profit margin in 2006 of 37.2 percent, which for reference purposes was more than double Intel's 2006 operating profit margin of 17.5 percent and even beat Google's 2006 operating margin of 33.5 percent, according to figures on Bloomberg.

Silicon is indeed the second most plentiful element in the earth's crust, but there is limited global plant capacity for converting raw silicon into the pure polysilicon that is suitable for manufacturing solar cells. Polysilicon is the feedstock for the crystalline silicon wafer solar cell technology that is used in about 94 percent of solar modules (the other 6 percent of modules use various thin film technologies). The polysilicon shortage has been caused by the emergence of strong demand for polysilicon from the solar industry. In fact, the solar industry in 2006 used more polysilicon than the semiconductor electronics industry. Figure 5.16 illustrates how Photon International expects solar demand for polysilicon to grow sharply and gain share against the semiconductor electronics industry where annual growth in demand is fairly steady at about 10 percent.

The world's five largest polysilicon producers are Hemlock Semiconductor Corp. (privately owned: 63 percent by Dow Corning Corp,

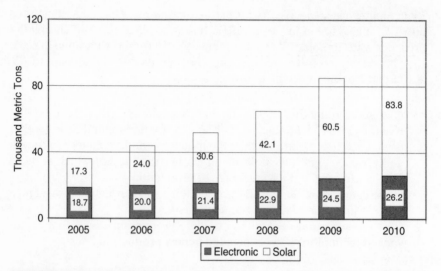

FIGURE 5.16 Polysilicon Supply—PV vs. Electronic (in thousands of metric tons)
Source: Photon International.

25 percent by Shin-Etsu Handotai Co., and 12 percent by Mitshubishi
Materials Corporation), Wacker Chemie (German Xetra: WCH GR), Renewable Energy Corp.(Oslo: REC NO), Tokuyama (Tokyo: 4043 JP), and
MEMC Electronics (NYSE: WFR). The top global polysilicon producers
are ranked in Figure 5.17, according to their 2006 production. A detailed
list of companies involved in polysilicon production is shown in Table 5.4.

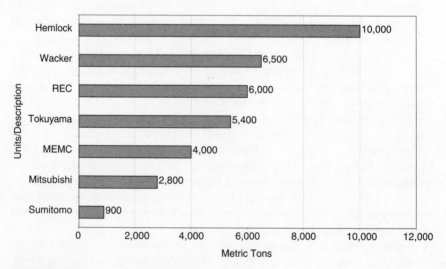

FIGURE 5.17 Top Global Polysilicon Producers
Source: Marketbuzz 2006, www.solarbuzz.com.

TABLE 5.4 Polysilicon Established Producers and Startups

Established Players	Location	Ticker	Web Site
Hemlock Semiconductor	United States	Private	www.hscpoly.com/
Renewable Energy Corp	Norway/United States	REC NO	www.recgroup.com
Tokuyama	Japan	4043 JP	www.tokuyama.co.jp/eng/
Wacker Chemie AG	Germany	WCH GR	www.wacker.com
MEMC Electronics	US/Italy	WFR US	www.memc.com/
Mitsubishi	Japan/United States	5711 JP	www.mmc.co.jp/english/ product/electronics/01. html, www.mpsac.com

New Entrants with Traditional Techniques (Siemens Process)

Arise	Canada	APV CN	www.arisetech.com
CSG Holdings	Hubei Province	200012 CH	www.csgholding.com/en/
DC Chemical Co	Korea	010060 KS	www.dcchem.co.kr/ english/index.asp
Emei Semiconductor Material Factory	China	Private	www.emb739.com/ ehome.htm
GiraSolar	Holland	GRSR US	www.girasolar.com
Hoku Scientific	United States	HOKU US	www.hokuscientific.com
Isofoton/Endesa	Spain	Private (Grupo Berge)	www.isofoton.es/ lanzadera.asp?idioma= _ing
JFE Steel	Japan	Private	www.jfe-steel.co.jp/en/
Jiangsu Sunshine	China	600220 CH	www.sunshine.com.cn
Joint Solar Silicon GmbH & Co (JSSI)	Germany	Private (JV of Degussa AG 51% and SolarWorld AG)	www.degussa.com and www.solarworld.de
Luoyang	China	Private	na
M.Setek	Japan	Private	www.msetek.com/en/ index.html
Mitol	Russia	Private	na
Nanyang Bulk	China	Private	na
Nippon Steel	Japan	5401 JP	www0.nsc.co.jp/ shinnihon_english/

(Continues)

TABLE 5.4 *(Continued)*

Established Players	Location	Ticker	Web Site
Norsun (SCATEC Group), Econcern, & Photon Power Technologies (PPT)	France	Private (Norsk Hydro, et al.)	www.econcern.nl
Photowatt/Total	France	Private	www.photowatt.com/
Sichuan Xinguang Silicon	China	Private	na
SolarWorld	Germany	SWV GR	www.solarworld.de/ sw-eng/
Swiss Wafer	Switzerland	Private	www.swisswafers.ch/
Yunnan Qujing Aixin Silicon Tech Project	China	Private	na

New Entrants with MG-Si or other novel technologies

City Solar	Germany	Private	www.city-solar-ag.com/ index.php?id=51
Dow Corning	Brazil	Private (Corning Intl, Dow Chemical)	www.dowcorning.com/ content/solar/
Elkem Solar	Norway	ELK NO	www.elkem.com/solar
Ferroatlantica/ Apollon	France	Private	www.ferroatlantica.es/ english.html
JFE Steel	Japan	5403 JP	www.jfe-steel.co.jp/en/
Photowatt/ATS	France	Private	www.photowatt.com/
SolarValue AG	Slovenia	SV7 GR	www.solarvalue.com/

Source: Renewable Energy Corp. presentation and Photon International.

Some of these companies sell the majority of their polysilicon to the semi-conductor/electronics industry but Renewable Energy Corp. and some of the newer players are selling the majority of their output to the solar industry.

Moving onto the next stage of solar cell production, a polysilicon wafer manufacturer either produces polysilicon in-house or buys polysilicon from one of the polysilicon producers just mentioned. The wafer manufacturer then melts down the polysilicon, allows it to solidify into a block, and then slices the block into wafers. Figure 5.18 shows the world's largest polysilicon wafer manufacturers, with Renewable Energy Corp. having one-quarter—the largest—market share.

The shortage in polysilicon caused by strong demand from the solar industry has caused polysilicon prices to rise sharply over the past several

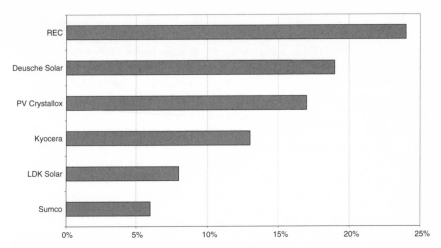

FIGURE 5.18 Global Market Shares Multicrystalline PV Wafers
Source: Renewable Energy Corp presentation, Photon International.

years to recent levels near $60 per kilogram (long-term contract) and $120 to $150 per kilogram (spot). Very little polysilicon trades in the spot market, which means that the contract market rather than the spot market best represents polysilicon prices.

Polysilicon prices rose from $24 per kilogram in 2003 to $32 per kilogram in 2004 to $45 per kilogram in 2005, and $55 per kilogram in 2006, according to *PV News*.[44] Polysilicon prices prior to about 2004 were heavily dependent on cycles in the semiconductor industry and were very volatile. Polysilicon prices were as high as $60 per kilogram in 1980 but then fell below $40 per kilogram by 1989. Polysilicon prices saw renewed strength in the latter half of the 1990s and rallied as high as $55 per kilogram in 1999 but then fell sharply after the post-2000 IT bust and fell as low as $24 per kilogram in 2004, as mentioned earlier.

The polysilicon industry's production for 2008 is already sold out at prices averaging about $60 per kilogram, except for small portions that some polysilicon producers are holding back to sell in the spot market. Polysilicon prices for delivery in 2009–2010 time frame are averaging around $50 per kilogram, which is moderately lower than the average contract price for 2008 of $60 per kilogram.

An important caveat on polysilicon pricing is that polysilicon prices are considered to be highly proprietary by buyers and sellers and are not publicly reported in any organized manner. In addition, there is not much polysilicon trading at present because many long-term contracts have already been locked in, meaning there is not much fresh pricing information.

Due to the tight supply of polysilicon, polysilicon companies and silicon wafer producers such as Renewable Energy Corp. and MEMC Electronic Materials (NYSE: WFR) have been able to extract very favorable long-term contracts from solar cell companies. Recent contracts have featured rising polysilicon prices over the course of the multiyear agreement as well as unusual benefits for the polysilicon companies of up-front, interest-free loan deposits and even warrants on the stock of the solar cell/module company. Polysilicon companies also have the luxury of dealing with only the larger and more financially secure solar cell/module manufacturing companies, meaning the odds are low for any defaults on the long-term contracts. Mid- and lower-level solar cell companies are left to scramble for silicon supplies on the spot market and from short-term contracts.

Renewable Energy Corp.'s recent multiyear contracts show the strong pricing situation for wafers. REC's customers have been willing to sign multiyear contracts with rising wafer prices due to their expectation for a continuation of the polysilicon shortage. From summer 2006 through early 2007, REC signed a $330 million five-year contract with Motech, a $515 million six-year contract with Sharp, a $450 million six-year agreement with BP Solar, and a $200 million five-year contract with Suntech.

The polysilicon shortage has led to a flurry of announcements from established players, as well as new entrants, about their intentions to build new polysilicon production capacity. This new capacity is good for the solar industry as a whole since the polysilicon is needed to support the industry's growth rate of 30 percent to 40 percent. There were concerns in 2006 that growth in the solar cell industry would be restricted by the polysilicon shortage, but the solar cell industry managed to find enough polysilicon to support a growth rate near 40 percent, partially through a drawdown of small existing inventories and through reclamation of scrap. Increased polysilicon capacity is also necessary so that polysilicon and solar cell/module prices can fall in coming years, thus getting solar power closer to the fulcrum where it becomes cost-competitive with fossil fuels without subsidies.

Industry forecasts for polysilicon production growth over the next few years vary widely, although two leading solar research groups happen to have a similar forecast (see Figure 5.19). Prometheus Institute is forecasting 2010 polysilicon production of 110,535 metric tons.[45] Meanwhile, Photon International in October 2006 raised its forecast for polysilicon production in the 2007 to 2010 period. For 2010, Photon International raised its forecast for 2010 production to 110,000 metric tons from 85,000 metric tons, which was very close to Prometheus Institute's 2010 forecast.[46] Both Prometheus Institute and Photon International support their forecasts with

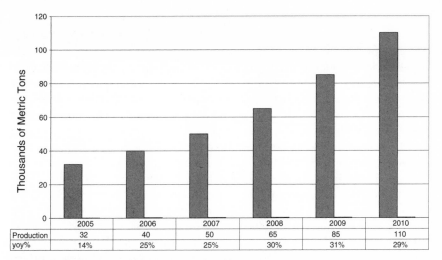

	2005	2006	2007	2008	2009	2010
Production	32	40	50	65	85	110
yoy%	14%	25%	25%	30%	31%	29%

FIGURE 5.19 Polysilicon Production Forecast, 2005–2010
Source: Photon International, "Silicon Sprint," October 2006, p. 110, www.photon-magazine.com.

project-by-project company analyses combined with interviews of companies and industry leaders.

The consensus in the solar module industry in 2006 was that the polysilicon shortage would ease by 2007–2008. However, solar module growth and polysilicon demand has been stronger than the earlier market consensus and new polysilicon production capacity has been slow to come onto the market, thus causing the industry to delay its expectations about when the shortage may ease. The current industry consensus is that the shortage will last until late 2008 or 2009. The reality is that the shortage may last longer than the market consensus because of very strong demand combined with the likelihood that many producers will have trouble following through with their announced polysilicon production plans due to the global shortage of chemical plant building assets, delays in ordering critical plant equipment items, and problems in implementing technology that is not off-the-shelf.

The polysilicon industry in the past has been a boom-bust industry because its only customer was the semiconductor industry, which is notoriously cyclical. In fact, the current shortage of polysilicon arose because the incumbent players in the polysilicon industry, which were burned in the past by overproduction, were reluctant to build new polysilicon plants despite forecasts for strong new demand from the solar industry. The polysilicon industry is now building those new plants, but they are still being cautious by securing up-front deposits and multiyear contracts that ensure they will be able to at least pay off their plant investment costs. The new and inexperienced entrants to the polysilicon industry are the ones who are introducing a wildcard element into the polysilicon supply picture. The marketplace is well aware of the possibility that these new entrants could upset the supply/demand balance and cause a glut of polysilicon down the road. However, Photon Consulting, in its *Solar Annual 2006*, addressed the issue of a possible polysilicon glut by saying, "After months of research, we have come to the conclusion that there is much, much more demand than capacity, and that demand is growing faster than supply."[47]

On the topic of solar industry supply/demand structure, it is important to note that demand for modules appears to be fairly elastic, based on recent experience in Germany where there was a temporary backup of module inventories in early 2006 due to higher prices. The price elasticity of solar modules means that as module prices rise, demand tends to slack off, and by the same token demand increases when module prices fall. This means that if a glut of polysilicon does emerge in coming years, the resulting decline in prices should be effective in reviving demand fairly quickly, thus bringing the market back into balance much more easily than if demand was inelastic (in which case market balance could be achieved only through a sharp drop in supply). It can be argued that the healthiest long-run condition for the solar market is actually a small supply surplus situation, which would allow solar module prices to trend downward and thus reach the point more quickly where solar power becomes competitive with grid power without subsidies, at which point demand would rapidly increase.

Renewable Energy Corp. held a two-day meeting for institutional equity analysts in March 2007 with plant visits to REC's Moses Lake polysilicon plant in Washington state and its polysilicon plant in Butte, Montana. REC management at that meeting specifically addressed the issue of a possible polysilicon glut by making the following points.

1. *Future polysilicon prices are strong.* REC management noted that multiyear contract polysilicon prices remain strong at present, which indicates that buyers are concerned about a lasting silicon shortage and want to lock in prices on multiyear contracts. REC expects its average silicon selling price in 2007 to be up about +15 percent from 2006, reflecting the tight market for silicon. REC notes that the strength in future silicon prices was demonstrated by the fact that two-thirds of its seven-year agreement with Sumco/Komatsu (which was announced March 21, 2007), worth about $780 million, involved take-or-pay terms with predefined and increasing prices (take-or-pay means the buyer must pay for the product regardless of whether they take delivery).

2. *Long industry lead times on building new silicon plants.* REC noted that building and operating a silicon plant is more difficult than some new players may suspect and that REC believes future supply will not be as high as recent announcements indicate. REC noted that the new $600 million plant that it is building next to its existing plant in Moses Lake, Washington will take three years and 3 million man-hours to build and that most of the key equipment is not off-the-shelf equipment that is easily acquired. REC also noted that companies that intend to build a silicon plant are in competition with companies in other industries (such as petroleum or chemical producers) that are also trying to build new chemical refineries. A silicon plant is similar to a chemical plant or petroleum refinery in terms of equipment, processes, and construction assets. REC noted that global demand for chemical refinery construction is strong and that there are currently delays in obtaining engineering and construction talent and critical equipment.

3. *Companies with lower production costs will better survive any glut.* New industry capacity announcements involve mostly the old and expensive Siemens technology, whereas REC's new production is the new *fluidized bed reactor* (FBR) technology, which REC says has a 30 percent lower cost relative to the existing Siemens process. REC is confident that its substantially lower FBR costs will support its financial results even if a supply glut eventually pressures higher-cost suppliers that rely on older technologies. Siemens-based suppliers will probably be the first players that are driven out of the market in any long-term glut, not firms like REC.

4. *Scale is critical.* REC management stressed that scale is critical in driving down a company's polysilicon production costs. REC, as the industry's largest solar polysilicon producer, believes that its large scale (along with its fluidized bed reactor technology) will contribute to its ability to be the lowest-cost producer, again supporting its financial viability in the event of an industry shake-out. Falling polysilicon production costs are critical for preserving profit margins in an industry where module prices typically fall by about 5 percent per year.

The bottom line is that the polysilicon producers, which have recently enjoyed extremely favorable profit margins, will see a more challenging environment in the next few years. During 2009, the polysilicon supply situation will loosen up considerably, with the extent of that loosing depending on the strength of demand and the extent to which new entrants can actually get their production plans executed. Polysilicon pricing is likely to soften as the situation loosens up in 2008–2009. That will likely put some downward pressure on margins for 2009 and beyond. However, it is important to remember that the large polysilicon players are signing multi-year contracts that extend out as far as 2012. These players have therefore already protected their margins to some extent even out as far as 2012. In addition, the large polysilicon players with low-cost polysilicon production technology will be in a much better position than the high-cost producers in the 2010–2012 period.

Due to the uncertain polysilicon supply/demand situation in coming years, the following investment guidelines are offered regarding an investment decision in polysilicon suppliers:

1. Avoid investing in the polysilicon players that are building new capacity with the old Siemens technology since their high costs mean they will be the first companies that will experience a shakeout if there is a polysilicon bust and a sharp drop in polysilicon prices.

2. Focus on investing in polysilicon companies with low polysilicon production costs stemming from manufacturing scale and advanced technology.

3. Focus on investing in polysilicon companies that are capable of establishing long-term contracts with financially secure solar module manufacturers to protect revenues and margins out through at least a three-to-five-year time frame.

THIN FILM THREATS TO CRYSTALLINE SILICON SOLAR CELLS

The traditional silicon solar cell industry is being shaken up at present by the fast emergence of thin film solar players. Crystalline silicon solar cells currently account for about 94 percent of solar module production, versus about 6 percent for thin film. However, the industry consensus is that thin film solar will rise to a 20 percent market share over the next few years.

Applied Materials (NYSE: AMAT) is selling turn-key factory production line equipment that solar module companies can use to manufacture solar modules with thin film silicon. Applied Material's sales have exceeded management's expectations. There will be numerous companies over the next few years producing solar modules with the Applied Materials' production line equipment. First Solar (Nasdaq: FSLR), which produces thin film solar modules using its own cadmium telluride production process, has seen its sales skyrocket because of its low costs and competitive prices.

The main thin film technologies in use today are amorphous silicon (a-Si), cadmium telluride (CdTe or CadTel), and copper indium gallium selenide (CIGS). Other thin film PV technologies include gallium arsenide and organic thin film. The CadTel, CIGS and gallium arsenide technologies

TABLE 5.5 Solar PV Company Breakdown by Technology

Technology		Companies
Siemens Silicon	Silane	REC Silicon
	Trichlorosilane	Hemlock, Wacker, Tokuyama, MEMC, numerous new entrants
Fluid Bed Silicon	Silane	REC Silicon, MEMC (building full scale plant)
	Trichlorosilane	Hemlock, Wacker (older technology; status uncertain)
Upgraded Metallurgical Silicon (uMGS)		Elkem, Dow Corning, JFE, Nippon Steel, Becancour, Ferro Atlantica, Scheuten, Solar Value, others
Thin Films	Silane-Base amorphous silicon (a-SI) thin film module mfgs	Applied Materials, Oerlikon, UniSolar, Kaneka, Mitsubishi Heavy Industries, CSG Solar, others
	Cadmium Telluride (CadTel or CdTe) thin film	First Solar, AntecSolar
	Copper Indium Gallium diSelenide (CIGS) thin film	DayStar Technologies, Shell Solar, Global Solar, Nanosolar, Heliovolt, others
	Organic thin film	Laboratory stage

Source: Renewable Energy Corp. presentation. www.recgroup.com.

have the advantage of not being subject to the current shortage of silicon, although they do have some of their own supply issues. For example, indium is a limited resource and indium prices have risen from $60/kg to $1,000/kg in the last three years. Telluride is a rare metal.

Thin film PV technologies have substantially lower production costs than silicon crystalline technologies, but they also have lower efficiencies of only about 6 to 10 percent, which is well below the efficiencies for crystalline silicon solar cells of 15 to 20 percent. Still, thin film is typically cheaper on a per-watt basis as compared with crystalline silicon technologies. In addition, thin film solar has a wider range of applications since it can be applied to backings of different shapes and sizes, making it ideal for example for *building integrated photovoltaics* (BIPV) where the coating is placed on office windows or roofing shingles.

Figure 5.20 lays out how the DOE Solar America Initiative believes solar PV technologies may play out. The first stage on that time line is currently in progress.

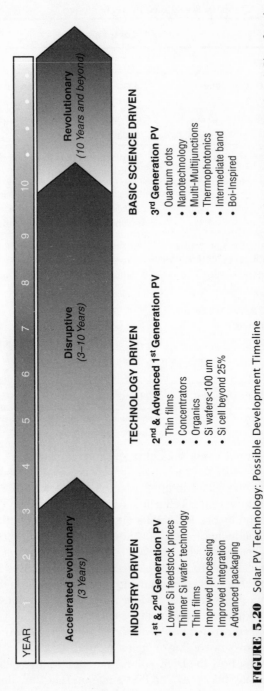

FIGURE 5.20 Solar PV Technology: Possible Development Timeline

Source: U.S. Department of Energy, Office of Energy Efficiency and Renewable Energy, *Solar American Initiative: A Plan for the Integrated Research, Development, and Market Transformation of Solar Energy Technologies,* 5 February 2007, p. 21, http:// www1.eere.energy.gov/solar/solar.america/pdfs/sai.draft.plan.Feb5_07.pdf.

In the present state of the solar industry, current demand for PV modules is so strong that virtually all technologies can thrive over the short-term. In this demand-driven market, buyers of solar modules are snapping up solar modules of all technologies. Over the longer run, however, it is likely that the market will be segmented so that different PV technologies will win within particular PV application markets. It is not necessarily the case that one solar PV technology with the lowest price/watt will win the entire solar PV marketplace.

For example, in the residential and commercial building market, crystalline silicon wafers will likely retain a large market share because there is often a premium on minimizing the space required for the solar installation, thus favoring the higher efficiency solutions. However, in commercial applications where there is plenty of room available for solar modules, thin films may win over the long-run. For building integrated PV (BIPV), thin film applications will clearly win since only thin film can be applied to windows and building materials. For solar parks that produce electricity for the grid, the ultimate winner is unclear at this point. Thin film has the advantage of being cheaper per watt, but the installation area needs to be much larger, thus raising land requirements and increasing installation costs. Traditional crystalline silicon cells will likely still be strong players in the solar power plant applications where the system design puts a premium on higher efficiencies and lower land usage.

The incumbent technology of crystalline silicon wafers is likely to dominate the industry for at least the next 5–10 years, but thin film will grow faster than crystalline silicon and will gain market share. As mentioned earlier, the market consensus is that thin film will grow to a 20 percent market share from 6 percent at present, although with the extraordinary growth rates seen in the solar industry, a setback in market share does not mean sales are going to be weak.

Another important point to make regarding solar PV technology is the importance of the large knowledge base for silicon-based technology, which is shared with the semiconductor industry. The large knowledge base gives silicon-based technologies a large and potentially sustainable advantage over newer, nonsilicon technologies. Some nonsilicon technologies may have attractive attributes in the laboratory but then fail to receive sufficient R&D investment to come to fruition on a mass scale. This point is made in the *Handbook of Photovoltaic Science and Engineering*: "Technically astute investors know that other factors can be more important than efficiency in selecting a technology for development."[48]

The *Handbook of Photovoltaic Science and Engineering* goes on to point out that thin-film silicon has always had a lower efficiency than Cad-Tel and CIGS, but that thin-film silicon has nevertheless been commercialized much earlier and more widely because of the huge knowledge base and capital investment behind silicon from its history in semiconductor industry. By contrast, the CadTel and CIGS technologies, despite their attractive PV properties, are trying to overcome their "orphan" technology status since they have no applications outside photovoltaics and have not attracted big research and investment dollars. The *Handbook of Photovoltaic Science and Engineering* says, "The highest efficiency technology is not always going to be the best choice for a low-cost, high-yield process, at least not until much of the technical background is in place."[49] According to this view, crystalline silicon wafers and thin film silicon can fend off challengers for some time to come.

The bottom line is that there are clearly technology risks in investing in the solar PV sector. There is no way to completely avoid these risks, but several investment guidelines may be helpful in considering the role of PV technology in making a solar industry investment decision:

- Choose companies that can be flexible in shifting course as technology changes.
- Choose leadership companies with aggressive R&D programs that can quickly capitalize on breakthroughs in efficiency and costs.
- Stay away from companies that are stuck using old or high-cost PV technologies.
- Be leery of companies that are using completely new technologies that may not have sufficient time or research dollars to bring the technology to mass production.
- Pay close attention to PV technology developments going forward so that investment shifts can be made as fortunes shift among the various PV technologies.

UPGRADED METALLURGICAL SILICON (uMGS): A THREAT TO TRADITIONAL POLYSILICON PRODUCERS?

Several companies are experimenting with a shortcut method for producing solar-grade (SoG) silicon by using a metallurgical smelting process to transform metallurgical silicon (MGS) directly into solar-grade polysilicon. This process bypasses the Siemens or fluidized bed reactor process of gasifying metallurgical silicon and then growing pure polysilicon rods or granules. This direct-to-polysilicon technique is called "upgraded metallurgical silicon" (or uMGS) and is just getting off the ground. The uMGS process can reduce power consumption by 60 to 80 percent relative to the current Siemens process and overall production costs can be cut to less than $20 per kilogram versus $25 to 35 per kilogram for the traditional Siemens and near $17 per kilogram for Renewable Energy Corp.'s fluidized bed reactor process.[50] The uMGS process therefore appears to be about 20 percent lower than Siemens-based production costs but not as low as REC's claim of a cost reduction of more than 30 percent for FBR technology.

Technical details are sparse on uMGS technology at this point because the companies involved in the research are protecting their trade secrets. However, uMGS so far does not appear to be a disruptive technology that will upend traditional polysilicon producers. Rather, uMGS is simply another source of solar-grade silicon capacity that will be coming on line in coming years. Renewable Energy Corp., in a presentation, forecasted annual uMGS production of 5,000 metric tons by mid-2008, growing to 35,000 metric tons by 2011.[51]

While uMGS production costs are relatively low, the polysilicon that comes from uMGS production is not as pure as the polysilicon that is produced with the Siemens or fluidized bed reactor process (where impurities are measured in parts per billion). In some cases, uMGS needs to be mixed with pure polysilicon to get the quality up to solar-grade. In addition, uMGS currently appears to be capable of producing solar cells with efficiencies of only about 15 percent, which is below the 18 to 20 percent that can be produced with pure polysilicon. That means that the price of uMGS will have to be lower than the price of polysilicon in order to maintain equality on a price/watt basis.

The development of uMGS needs to be watched very carefully going forward because uMGS producers will be direct competitors with traditional polysilicon producers and will contribute to the available supply of polysilicon. Polysilicon supply from uMGS will be on the market as soon as mid-2008 when Elkem Solar finishes its plant that uses the uMGS process. Companies working on uMGS include Nippon Steel (Japan), JFE (Japan), Arise (Canada), Global PV Specialists (United States), and Gira-Solar (Netherlands). In addition, the following companies have already announced actual production plans for uMGS production:

- *Dow Corning.* Dow Corning, which is a part owner of Hemlock Semiconductor, announced in September 2006 that it had produced solar-grade (SoG) silicon derived from metallurgical processes.[52] The product is called PV 1101 SoG Silicon. The PV 1101 SoG Silicon can be mixed with traditional 100 percent pure silicon to produce a silicon mix that is good enough to manufacture solar cells, though at a lower efficiency than pure polysilicon. Dow Corning is producing SoG Silicon in bulk and began bulk customer shipments in August 2006. Dow Corning is a 50–50 joint venture established in 1943 between Corning Inc (NYSE: GLW) and The Dow Chemical Company (NYSE: DOW).

- *Elkem Solar.* Elkem Solar has announced plans to build a $450 million plant in Norway to produce Elkem Solar Silicon®, which is solar-grade silicon manufactured through a metallurgical process. The plant will have an initial annual capacity of 5,000 metric tons. The plant is scheduled to start production by mid-2008. Elkem says that its planned production is already sold out through 2012. Elkem said that production "requires less energy and production costs will compare favorably with the costs of using existing technology." Elkem Solar is a division of Elkem, which is a Norwegian metals and materials company with about $300 million in revenues. Elkem is owned by Orkla (Oslo: ORK NO), which is a Norwegian conglomerate with about $8.8 billion in revenues in 2006. Details are available on Elkem's silicon effort at the News section on its Web site at www.elkem.com.
- *SolarWorld.* SolarWorld AG (German Xetra: SWV GR) announced in July 2006 that it had entered a 50–50 joint venture named "Scheuten SolarWorld Solizium GmbH" with Dutch company Scheuten Solarholding VB to produce solar-grade silicon through a metallurgical process.[53] The joint venture plans to build a plant with annual capacity of 1,000 metric tons. However, the company gave no timeline about when construction on the plant will begin or when production will start.

SOLAR PV CELL AND MODULE PRODUCERS

There are a large number of companies that manufacture solar PV cells and modules. Some of these companies focus on manufacturing just solar cells, but the majority focus on manufacturing solar modules, which is the final product of the PV manufacturing process. Some of the module producers manufacture their own solar cells in-house, making them vertically integrated in the cell/module phase of the solar PV value chain. The output from these companies is measured in terms of the electrical output from their product measured in megawatts.

Table 5.6 ranks the global cell/module players in 2006 by output, according to data collected by *PV News*.[54] As seen in the graph, the large Japanese conglomerate, Sharp, was the largest producer of solar cells/modules in 2006 with 434 megawatts of output. Large industrial conglomerates such as Sharp, Kyocera and Sanyo were big players in 2005, but a variety of pure-play solar manufacturers such as Suntech and other firms gained market share in 2006 due to their intense focus on building new production capacity. As far as pure-play independent solar companies, the largest players are Germany-based Q-Cells (German Xetra: QCE GR),

TABLE 5.6 Top Global Solar PV Cell/Module Producers in 2006 Ranked by Shipments (in megawatts)

Rank	Company	Shipments (MW)	yr-yr %	2005 rank	Ticker	Base Country	Web Site
1	Sharp	434	1%	1	6753 JP	Japan	solar.sharpusa.com
2	Q-Cells	253	53%	2	QCE GR	Germany	www.qcells.de
3	Kyocera	180	27%	3	6971 JP	Japan	www.kyocerasolar.com/
4	Suntech	158	92%	8	STP	China	www.suntech-power.com/
5	Sanyo Electric	155	24%	4	6764 JP	Japan	www.sanyo.com/industrial/solar/
6	Mitsubishi Electric	111	11%	5	6503 JP	Japan	global.mitsubishielectric.com/bu/solar/
7	Motech	110	83%	9	6244 TT	Taiwan	www.motechind.com
8	Schott Solar	96	1%	6	private	Germany	www.us.schott.com
9	Deutsche Solar/Shell	86	−11%	10/12	private	Germany	www.deutschesolar.de/ds-eng/
10	BP Solar	86	−3%	7	BP LN	United Kingdom	www.bp.com/solar
11	SunPower	63	173%	nr	SPWR US	United States	www.sunpowercorp.com
12	Isofoton	61	15%	11	private	Spain	www.isofoton.es
13	First Solar	60	200%	nr	FSLR US	United States	www.firstsolar.com/
14	CEEG Nanjing PV-Tech	60	500%	nr	private	China	www.n-pv.com/
15	Ersol Solar Energy AG	40	100%	nr	private	Germany	www.ersol.de/en

Source: *PV News*, April 2007, Prometheus Institute, Cambridge MA, www.prometheus.org.

China-based Suntech (NYSE: STP), and Taiwan-based Motech Industries (Taiwan: 6244 TT).

The larger solar PV companies that are listed on U.S. exchanges are shown in Table 5.7, ranked by market cap. The U.S.-listed solar sector was very thin prior to 2005 with only a few U.S.-based public solar companies such as Evergreen Solar and EMCORE. However, the U.S.-listed solar sector now has a healthy 13 companies with market caps over $100 million and more IPOs are on the way.

The most notable feature of the U.S.-listed solar sector is that the majority of the companies are based in China. Suntech Power Holdings (NYSE: STP) was the first Chinese company to go public in the United States in December 2005 with a $400 million IPO. Since then, seven more companies with China-based operations have gone public in large IPOs ranging from about $100 million to $470 million. These IPO's included LDK Solar (NYSE: LDK), Yingli Green Energy (NYSE: YGE), Trina Solar (NYSE: TSL), JA Solar Holdings (Nasdaq: JASO), SolarFun (Nasdaq: SOLF), China Sunergy (Nasdaq: CSUN), and Canadian Solar (Nasdaq: CSIQ). Canadian Solar has its headquarters in Canada but its operations are in China.

The Chinese IPOs from December 2005 through June 2007 raised a total of $2.1 billion. That illustrates how the global solar industry has hit the big-time and is attracting substantial amounts of investor capital. The Chinese IPOs illustrate how China is becoming the main manufacturing hub of the world's global solar module industry, although there are still numerous key players outside China that can thrive as well since in the long-run technology is more important than cheap labor in further cutting solar costs.

The two largest U.S.-based solar companies are SunPower Corp (Nasdaq: SPWR) and First Solar (Nasdaq: FSLR). Both companies have seen their respective stock prices soar through mid-2007. SunPower sells premium, high-efficiency solar panels. Sunpower not only has an inside track on sales inside the United States but also made a smart acquisition by acquiring PowerLight Corporation in January 2007, which is the largest U.S. installer of solar power systems on customer sites. SunPower is a spin-off of Cypress Semiconductor (NYSE: CY), which is still the majority shareholder of SunPower.

First Solar has done extremely well because it manufactures low-cost thin film solar panels based on cadmium-telluride. Those low-costs solar modules are being snapped up by solar park operators. First Solar has a huge backlog of orders and is in the process of expanding capacity as quickly as it can. Another U.S.-based solar company, Evergreen Solar (Nasdaq: ESLR) has an innovative "string ribbon" technology for manufacturing solar cells, but the company has been unable to ramp up production fast enough and is still mired in losses.

TABLE 5.7 U.S.-Listed Solar PV Players Ranked by Market Cap (as of July 2007) with 2006 Financial Data

Company Name	Ticker Symbol	Market Cap ($ mln)	Revenues ($ mln)	Net Income (Loss) ($ mln)	Net Income Margin	Web site
First Solar	Nasdaq: FSLR	$8,314	$135	$4.0	2.9%	www.firstsolar.com
Suntech Power Holdings	NYSE: STP	$5,845	$599	$106.0	17.7%	www.suntech-power.com
SunPower	Nasdaq: SPWR	$5,143	$237	$26.5	11.2%	www.sunpowercorp.com
LDK Solar Co	NYSE: LDK	$3,850	$105	$25.9	24.5%	www.ldksolar.com
Yingli Green Energy	NYSE: YGE	$2,367	$1,639	$216.2	13.2%	www.yinglisolar.com
Trina Solar	NYSE: TSL	$1,813	$115	$12.4	10.8%	www.trinasolar.com
Energy Conversion Devices	Nasdaq: ENER	$1,265	$102	($18.6)	–18.2%	www.ovonic.com
JA Solar Holdings	Nasdaq: JASO	$1,077	$72	$11.1	15.3%	www.jasolar.com
Evergreen Solar	Nasdaq: ESLR	$998	$103	($26.7)	–25.9%	www.evergreensolar.com
SolarFun	Nasdaq: SOLF	$604	$81	$13.6	16.8%	www.solarfun.com
China Sunergy	Nasdaq: CSUN	$449	$150	$11.8	7.9%	na
EMCORE Corp	Nasdaq: EMKR	$305	$144	$58.7	40.9%	www.emcore.com
Canadian Solar	Nasdaq: CSIQ	$279	$68	($9.4)	–13.8%	www.csisolar.com

Source: Company financial statements.

121

THE INVESTMENT OUTLOOK FOR SOLAR CELL/MODULE MANUFACTURERS

As mentioned in a previous section on solar industry growth rates, the solar PV industry is growing at a breakneck speed of 40-50 percent per year and will likely more than quintuple in size between 2006 and 2010. Because of strong demand, solar module prices have risen in the past several years, which is unusual since solar module prices typically fall by about 5 percent a year as manufacturers pass through lower production costs. Relatively high solar module prices have undercut solar module demand in some areas of the world. However, the quick expansion of module production in the next several years stemming from an easier polysilicon supply situation and increased thin film production should satisfy demand and help prices to start falling again. As module prices fall, this should stimulate fresh demand, thus keeping the market close to balance, in theory at least.

As seen in Figure 5.21, the retail price for U.S. solar PV modules fell sharply by a total of about 20 percent in the two and a half years from January 2002 through May 2004, according to Solarbuzz's solar price survey.[55] However, module prices started to climb in mid-2004 when demand surged and when module supply was restricted by the polysilicon shortage and the lagging startup of new module production capacity. As the chart shows, solar module prices have been relatively flat since

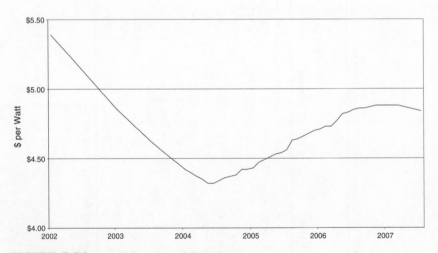

FIGURE 5.21 U.S. Solar PV Module Prices
Source: Solarbuzz LLC Survey, www.solarbuzz.com. http://www.solarbuzz.com/
ModulePrices.htm.

mid-2006, suggesting that supply is catching up with demand. Logic would suggest that module prices should move lower in coming months and years due to the industry's fast ramp-up of module production capacity and due to falling production costs. As mentioned earlier, this would be good news for the solar PV industry in the big picture because lower module prices will bring solar PV closer to grid parity and will stimulate fresh demand.

The question for solar module companies, however, is the extent to which a drop in solar module prices in coming years will pressure profit margins. The challenge for solar cell/module manufacturers is to cut their production costs faster than module prices fall. To the extent that manufacturers can cut their production costs as fast as prices, they will be able to preserve their profit margins. However, with the surge in production capacity coming on line, there remains a significant risk that solar module manufacturers are going to see some profit margin compression in coming years until the industry can get to more of a long-term steady-state situation. The producers with the highest costs are the ones that will be hurt the most by any fast drop in module prices.

In summary, the global solar PV industry has a huge amount of room to grow on the upside with strong demand caused by government mandates and incentives and also from areas that have high retail electricity prices where solar PV is already competitive. The challenge for the solar PV industry is to cut production costs and prices quickly so that solar PV becomes more fully competitive with retail residential and commercial electricity prices throughout the world and eventually with grid-based electricity production without subsidies. This effort is likely to be successful given the progress that has already been made and the huge amount of R&D capital that is flowing into the industry to find scientific and production improvements.

Although the solar industry has a huge amount of upside, there will periodically be bumps in the road when stock prices become overvalued and when profit margins decline to possibly push the weaker players out of the market. It is therefore important to focus investment dollars on the high-technology players that have strategically defensible positions in the industry and that will be the leaders in driving the production cost reductions. The following investment criteria are offered to help in an investment decision on the solar cell/module players:

- Focus on solar PV companies with the best technologies and most aggressive R&D efforts since those companies will be leaders in being able to cut prices and yet maintain profit margins.
- Choose companies with the lowest production input costs (labor, materials).

- Ensure the company has no raw material input constraints. Polysilicon cell-based solar module companies need unfettered access to silicon wafers and thin film producers need access to their input materials.
- Choose companies with high-quality or differentiated products and stay away from low-end commodity-type solar module producers.
- Choose companies with world-class global sales/marketing channels and strong marketing partner relationships.

CHAPTER 6

Wind Power

The Dutch Windmill Gets a Technology Makeover

T he global wind turbine industry is a $23 billion industry with an av-
erage annual growth rate of 20 percent over the period of 2002 to
2006 and annual growth of +41 percent in 2005 and +32 percent in
2006.[1] Wind power provides a significant portion of total electricity in some
European countries such as Denmark, Spain, Portugal, and Germany. In
the United States, wind power is the fastest growing utility-scale electricity
resource, with an annual growth rate of 27 percent in 2006.[2]

Investing in the wind power sector poses some challenges for U.S.-
based investors. Publicly traded pure-play companies are mostly based
in Europe and are traded on European exchanges. Two of the largest
wind companies, GE and Siemens, are large conglomerates and cannot be
considered pure plays on wind power. Still, wind power is growing very
quickly, and there are investment opportunities for investors that are willing to venture into stocks outside the United States.

The main advantage of wind power is that it produces renewable electricity with zero pollution or greenhouse gas emissions. On the other hand,
disadvantages include the intermittent production of electricity, the fact
that some regions do not have enough wind to make a wind turbine economical, and the fact that technology improvements still need to be made
to drive the costs of wind power even lower to parity with fossil fuels. A
detailed list of advantages and disadvantages is presented and discussed in
the next section.

ADVANTAGES AND DISADVANTAGES OF WIND POWER

Advantages

- *Inexhaustible source of power with no pollution or greenhouse gas emissions.* Wind turbines are a completely renewable source of energy, running exclusively on wind. This resource will never run out since wind is produced by atmospheric temperature variations, the rotation of the earth, land and sea effects, and pressure differentials between weather systems. Wind turbines do not pollute because they produce electricity through a purely mechanical process, with no chemicals or combustion involved.

- *Low operation and maintenance costs.* Since no fuels are required, total operating costs for a wind farm are significantly lower than those for a fossil fuel power plant. Costs vary in practice, but the average operating and maintenance cost for projects installed between 2000 and 2005 was only 0.8 cents per kilowatt-hour.[3] This is similar to the operations and maintenance costs for fossil fuel power plants of 0.81 cents per kilowatt-hour (not including fossil fuel purchase costs).[4]

- *Onshore or offshore.* The strongest winds are at sea, making this an ideal spot for wind power. However, building offshore wind turbines is more expensive, both from the standpoint of initial capital expenditure and maintenance. At present, most wind power comes from onshore installations, with only a few turbines installed at sea in Europe.

- *Surrounding land is usable.* Wind turbines are large, tall structures that need lots of space between one another and wind farms therefore occupy extensive geographical areas. However, the land between them can be used for other purposes, such as farming or livestock grazing. Farmers can lease their lands to wind energy operators, obtaining an extra annual income estimated at $55 per acre. For a 250-acre farm, with turbine installations occupying no more than 2 acres, this represents an annual leasing payment of $14,000.[5] Many farms in Texas are already looking to wind towers as a substitute income for depleted oil wells.[6]

- *Creates jobs.* The European Wind Energy Association (EWEA) estimates that every megawatt of installed wind capacity creates 15 to 19 jobs directly or indirectly, and 60 person-years of employment.[7]

- *Diversifies energy sources.* Wind power increases a country's diversification of power generation resources, which has economic and political advantages.

Disadvantages

- *Intermittent power.* The availability of electricity depends on wind speed. If the speed is too low, then the turbines will not turn. If the speed is too high, it might cause damage and the turbines are therefore turned off. These problems can be reduced significantly by simultaneously using power from wind farms located in several regions, which results in smoother energy production. There is also the possibility of adding an electricity storage system (e.g., batteries), which would allow relatively constant output.
- *Operation at less than full capacity.* Since wind turbines depend on wind speed, wind turbines operate only 65 percent to 80 percent of the time[8] and operate at full capacity only 10 percent of the time.[9] A wind turbine on average during a year achieves 25 percent to 40 percent of nameplate capacity, depending on the average wind speed for the location.[10]
- *High cost.* Wind power today still costs more than most conventional power sources when government incentives are excluded. There are three reasons for this:
  - *High installation costs.* Wind towers are tall structures, with total heights including the rotor blades currently exceeding 440 feet.[11] They require solid foundations and towers, and the rotor blades must be made with specialized materials to ensure strength.
  - *Power transmission line costs.* Wind farms are usually more efficient in remote, windy locations, which often require the construction of long transmission lines. These transmission lines raise the cost of the project and can cause an issue in the allocation of costs between electricity producers and consumers.
  - *Intermittency increases costs for the power grid.* The intermittency of wind power generation presents an additional cost to grid operators that need to plug the gaps with backup power plants or the purchase of wholesale power.[12] These costs are small when the grid's reliance on wind power is less than 10 percent. However, costs increase as reliance on wind power increases and some industry observers believe that wind reliance should be capped at 20 percent.[13] Denmark's reliance on wind power is the highest in the world at 21.4 percent of total electricity consumption.[14]
- *Location determines output.* Power output is very sensitive to wind speed. Some regions are good for wind power while others will never be suitable. Locations must be studied extensively before deciding whether the site is suitable for a wind farm. In the United States, the five states with the highest potential for on-shore wind power production are North Dakota, Texas, Kansas, South Dakota, and Montana.[15]

- *A danger to wildlife.* Birds and bats are periodically caught in the blades of wind turbines. However, studies say that the number of birds that have died from wind turbine blades is negligible when compared with the number of birds that have died crashing against windows and buildings. One study says that less than 1 in 30,000 human-induced bird deaths are due to wind turbines.[16] Newer wind turbine systems are addressing the issue of trying to avoid contact with birds and bats.

- *Noise and visual nuisance to communities.* Wind turbines used to be noisy. This problem has been addressed over the years and modern turbines are quiet and have been compared to a kitchen refrigerator from a distance of 750 to 1,000 feet.[17] Shadow flicker is another problem. Shadows from the rotor can be an inconvenience when these turbines are placed close to buildings. The areas covered by these shadows, however, can be calculated precisely and turbines can be placed accordingly. Wind turbines can have a negative effect on local land valuation. Some people consider wind turbines to be visual eyesores akin to high-tension power lines. The only real answer to these objections is to place wind farms in remote locations outside the visible range of towns and cities.

HOW DO WIND TURBINES WORK?

Windmills have been used for centuries to obtain mechanical power to pump water, grind grain, and perform other tasks. The ancient idea of using the wind to create power has migrated today into modern wind turbines, which are enormous structures that can supply large amounts of electricity to a country's power grid. Current models exceed 440 feet tall (including the rotor blades) and the power output can be 3 megawatts or higher. For reference, each 3-megawatt wind tower provides enough electricity to power about 825 homes.[18] Wind turbines need to be constructed using specialize materials so they can endure strong winds and harsh climatic conditions.

Wind turbines can be classified into small and large units, depending on their size and application. Small turbines are used for residential use in remote locations or for communities to produce electricity for themselves or to sell to grid operators. Large wind turbines are utility-grade units that are typically grouped together in wind farms. Large wind turbines have capacities of more than 50 kilowatts according to a definition provided by the U.S. Department of Energy.[19] The largest wind turbines are currently above 3 megawatts. (See Figure 6.1 for a picture of GE's massive 3.6 megawatt prototype.)[20]

FIGURE 6.1 GE's Massive 3.6-Megawatt Wind Turbine
Source: U.S. Department of Energy, http://www1.eere.energy.gov/windandhydro/wind_how.html.

Wind speed is an important factor in considering the location of a wind farm since small variations in wind speed can produce relatively large variations in electricity production. In fact, the electricity output from a wind turbine is a function of the cube of the wind speed. That means that doubling the wind speed, for example, actually increases electricity output by eight times.[21]

TECHNOLOGICAL DEVELOPMENTS

The cost of wind power has dropped by over 80 percent in the past 20 years and is likely to decline further with technological advances producing lighter and larger turbine blades and more efficient generators. The tower height, from the ground to the hub, has increased consistently in the past 10 years, from an average of 130 feet in 1996 to 275 feet in 2006.[22] Taller towers and larger rotor blades mean that more area is exposed to the wind, thus producing more electricity. In general, the "hub height" (which is the height of the center of the rotor from the ground) is almost equal to the rotor blade diameter.[23] This means that a 275-foot hub height and rotor blade diameter will typically add up to a total height of 412 feet for the tower plus the highest reach of the rotor blade.

The average power capacity of wind turbines has been increasing as well. From 1998 to 2006, the average turbine nameplate capacity has increased by a total of 124 percent from 0.71 megawatts to 1.60 megawatts.[24] In 2006, about 17 percent of all installed turbines had a capacity of more than 2 megawatts (up to a maximum capacity of 3 megawatts).[25] The size of wind turbines will continue to increase. Engineers today are in the process of designing models with nameplate capacity of 5 megawatts and total heights of over 700 feet.[26]

The construction of wind turbines requires particularly strong materials. Towers are currently made of steel, while rotor blades are carbon-fiber in an epoxy resin matrix or glass-reinforced plastic (GRP) with an epoxy or polyester resin matrix.[27] To ensure strength, the blades need to be constructed in one piece by specialized manufacturers. This book's companion Web site at www.ProfitingFromCleanEnergy.com has links to video tours of some large wind parks.

OFFSHORE WIND

Offshore wind can be much stronger than the wind on land because there are no buildings, trees, or mountains to slow it down. In addition, installing wind farms offshore beyond the site of land tends to eliminate NIMBY objections ("not in my backyard"). Offshore wind farms typically mean higher efficiency and electricity production because of the higher winds and also because rotor blades can be larger since it is easier to transport large blades by ship than by land. Offshore blades with diameters of 360 feet are currently being designed.[28] The main downside for offshore wind farms is that overall construction costs can be substantially higher than on land and there are also potential problems with corrosion due to the salty ocean air. In addition, electrical cables have to be laid underneath the ocean floor to transport the electricity to shore.

Offshore wind power capacity in Europe by the end of 2006 reached nearly 900 megawatts (which is enough electricity to power 250,000 homes). Most of these wind farms were in shallow waters with depths of less than 82 feet.[29] As of the end of 2006, no offshore wind farms existed in the United States, but 2.5 gigawatts of offshore wind projects were in the planning stage at that time.[30]

INDUSTRY GROWTH RATES AND PROSPECTS FOR FUTURE GROWTH

As mentioned earlier, the global wind industry grew at an average annual growth rate of 20 percent over the period of 2002 to 2006 and at annual growth rate of +41 percent in 2005 and +32 percent in 2006.[31] The Global Wind Energy Council (GWEC) is forecasting that the global wind industry will grow at an average annual rate of 19.1 percent during the 2006–2010 period.[32]

In 2006, $23 billion worth of wind power capacity (15.2 gigawatts) was installed globally, which brought the total installed capacity worldwide to 74 gigawatts (see Figures 6.2 and 6.3).[33] That is enough electricity to power about 20 million homes. GWEC is forecasting that the world's cumulative total capacity will roughly double by 2010 to 149.5 gigawatts, which is enough electricity to power about 41 million homes.

The European market has grown the fastest and in 2006 represented 51 percent of the annual market[34] and 65 percent of cumulative installed global capacity.[35] However, its global market share is expected to settle back in the future as other markets catch up. By 2010, Europe is

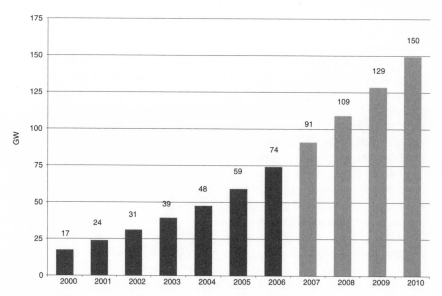

FIGURE 6.2 Forecasted Global *Cumulative* Installed Wind Capacity (in gigawatts) *Source:* Global Wind Energy Counci, *Global Wind 2006 Report*, 2006, p. 8 and 13, http://www.gwec.net/uploads/media/gwec-2006_final.pdf.

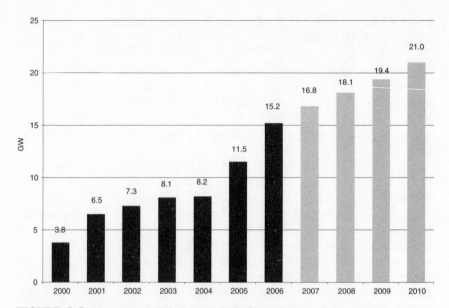

FIGURE 6.3   Forecasted Global *Annual* Wind Installations (in gigawatts)
Source: Global Wind Energy Counci, *Global Wind 2006 Report*, 2006, p. 8 and 13,
http://www.gwec.net/uploads/media/gwec-2006_final.pdf.

expected to account for 44 percent (9.3 gigawatts) of the annual market
and 55 percent of installed capacity.[36] In Europe, Germany and Spain represent 50 percent of new investments and are the countries with the most
installed capacity, together representing 43.4 percent of global installed
capacity.[37]

The region with the second largest installed capacity is North America, with a forecasted average annual growth rate of 24.6 percent for 2006
to 2010 according to the Global Wind Energy Council.[38] The United States
will be the largest national market in the world during this period, with
an average of 3.5 gigawatts of wind power installed each year.[39] More than
$3.7 billion was invested in wind installations in the United States in 2006,[40]
and income from landowners amounted to an additional $5 million to
$9 million.[41] Canada is also expected to show high growth rates, installing
4.5 gigawatts of capacity during 2007 to 2010.[42]

Asian markets have shown spectacular growth rates in recent years,
driven mainly by India and China. India and China are expected to continue
to lead the region and are each expected to install 8 gigawatts of capacity
during 2007 to 2010.[43] Asia will have an average annual growth rate of 28.3
percent for the period, making it the fastest growing region in the world

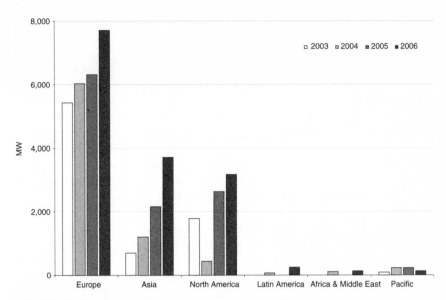

FIGURE 6.4 Installed Wind Capacity by Region (2003–2006)
Source: Global Wind Energy Counci, *Global Wind 2006 Report,* 2006, p. 8 and 13,
http://www.gwec.net/uploads/media/gwec-2006_final.pdf.

according to the Global Wind Energy Council.[44] Figure 6.4 illustrates how
new capacity has evolved in recent years for each regional market.

THE ECONOMICS OF WIND POWER

While wind turbines require a high initial investment, ongoing operations
and maintenance costs are low since no fuel needs to be purchased. The
cost of electricity produced by wind power is calculated by adding up all
the costs of the project (land, construction, operating costs, etc.) and dividing those costs by the expected electricity output over the lifetime of the
equipment. This produces the expected cost of the electricity produced by
the wind farm in terms of cents per kilowatt-hour.

In 1980, wind turbines cost 80 cents per kilowatt-hour generated.[45]
Since then, much research has been done, and today's turbines are more ef-
ficient and have lower costs of about 3 to 5 cents per kilowatt-hour (includ-
ing both the construction and maintenance costs). A study by the Berkley
Lab measured the price of electricity sold by wind projects in the United
States for 1998 to 2006.[46] The study found that wind power costs were

6.1 cents per kilowatt-hour in 1999 (measured in 2006 dollars) and then fell to 3.6 cents per kilowatt-hour in 2006, with a majority of installations falling between 2.3 cents and 4.9 cents per kilowatt-hour.[47]

The study also showed, however, that wind power costs have actually risen in the past several years due to the rising costs of raw materials and component shortages. For projects started in 2002–2003, average wind power costs fell as low as 3.1 cents per kilowatt-hour. However, prices have since increased and reached 4.9 cents per kilowatt-hour in 2006.[48] These prices include the benefit from the U.S. federal government's Production Tax Credit (PTC), explained later, which significantly reduced wind power costs. Without these credits, the prices for projects started in 2006 would have risen to an average of 7 cents per kilowatt-hour, with a range of 5.0 to 8.5 cents.[49]

The prices in this study included transmission costs. Regarding transmission costs, there is an industry problem worth noting that involves interconnection congestion and "rate pancaking."[50] When electricity from wind power needs to travel over long transmission distances, as it usually does, it can pass through various operators' transmission systems. Access charges are billed every time a new operator is involved. By the time the power reaches its destination, several charges may have been added into the price, which is referred to as "rate pancaking" because the various charges have stacked up. The American Wind Energy Association (AWEA) is working to solve this problem by proposing pricing modifications to existing transmission policies.[51]

Regarding the more general issue of wind power costs, wind power produces an additional cost for the utility stemming from the intermittent supply of electricity since the utility company must get power from somewhere else quickly if the wind power system is not operating due to lack of wind. The utility will need to quickly start a backup power plant or buy power on the wholesale market. The overall amount of this cost depends on the percentage of power that the operator gets from wind power. For systems with less than 10 percent reliance on wind power, costs are raised by an average of 0.2 cents per kilowatt-hour. This cost increases to 0.3 to 0.6 cents per kilowatt-hour for systems with a 20 percent or more reliance on wind.[52]

Figure 6.5 illustrates that wind power has become a very significant source of power in a number of countries, primarily Denmark, Spain, Portugal, and Germany. Figure 6.5 shows the percentage of overall power that a country receives from wind power. Critics of wind power point to its intermittency as a fatal flaw, but Denmark has proven that a grid can function well even if more than 20 percent of the country's power is derived from wind power. This graph also illustrates the upside potential for wind power if large countries such as the United States, India, China, France, the

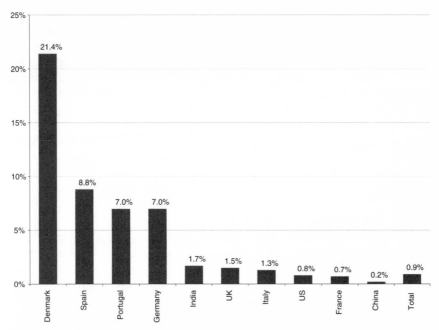

FIGURE 6.5 Percent of Total Electricity Derived from Wind (2006)
Source: U.S. Department of Energy, National Renewable Energy Laboratory, *Annual Report on U.S. Wind Power Installation, Cost, and Performance Trends: 2006,* May 2007, p. 5, http://www.nrel.gov/docs/fy07osti/41435.pdf. The chart takes into account that energy output is less than nameplate capacity, and is a rough approximation, which ignores transmission losses.

United Kingdom, and Italy were to boost their wind power usage up to 20 percent or more of overall electricity usage.

GOVERNMENT-SPONSORED INCENTIVES

The wind power industry still depends heavily on subsidies for its growth. The U.S. federal government provides wind operators with (1) a 10-year production tax credit (PTC) that is indexed to inflation and is currently set at 1.9 cents per kilowatt-hour; and (2) a five-year accelerated depreciation schedule for wind turbines (normally, the useful life of a wind turbine is 20 years). The current production tax credit will benefit projects that become operational by December 31, 2008.

The wind industry expects the U.S. federal government to renew the production tax credit, but there is no guarantee this will occur. The production tax credit for wind power was first implemented in 1992. Since then, Congress has usually allowed the production tax credit to expire before finally getting around to rolling it over again. This resulted in a hit to U.S. wind turbine production in 2000, 2002, and 2004. For the first time, Congress and President Bush in 2005 rolled over the production tax credit until 2007 before it expired, thus boosting U.S. wind power sales in 2005 and 2006. It was rolled over once again in 2006, extending it for an additional year, so that the current expiration date is December 31, 2008.[53]

The wind power industry is pushing for a long-term extension of the credit of more than five years to give the industry some stability and prevent the stop-go government policies of the past.

Another policy designed to grant U.S. wind power an economic advantage is the Renewable Energy Certificates (REC) program. These RECs can be used by utilities to meet their state Renewable Portfolio Standards (RPS), which require utilities to obtain a certain percentage of their electricity from renewable sources. The wind RECs can also be sold on a voluntary basis in the open market, thus improving the project economics for the wind farm operator.[54] Similar programs exist outside the United States.

The U.S. government also provides additional support by funding research and by partnering with manufacturers and universities to conduct research. These wind research programs are administered by the National Renewable Energy Laboratory (NREL), and the Sandia National Laboratories (SNL).[55]

In Europe, feed-in tariffs have been popular in Denmark, Germany, Italy and Spain. With feed-in tariffs, a wind farm operator is guaranteed a fixed price for electricity generated by the wind farm, thus guaranteeing a minimum return on investment for the project and making it easier for the project owner to obtain financing.[56]

China was slow to enter the wind market but wind power there is now gathering momentum. China started out with a feed-in tariff system, but then shifted to a tendering, or competitive bidding, process. Tendering has worked well in some European countries. However, a potential problem with tendering is that a wind operator may bid too low to get the contract and then lose money on the project, eventually going bankrupt and shutting down the wind farm.[57]

While wind power currently depends on government incentives to be competitive with fossil fuel technologies, wind power costs continue to fall. The U.S. Department of Energy has set a goal of lowering costs to 3.6 cents per kilowatt-hour by 2012 for large (Class 4) sites without government incentives.[58] The International Energy Agency estimates that costs can be lowered by 2020 to around 3.4 cents per kilowatt-hour.[59] That pricing would be competitive with even the cheapest coal-fired power plants, particularly if the cost of building *new* coal-fired power plants is considered and if fossil fuel plants see a rise in costs due to a carbon tax or cap-and-trade system. In the meantime, strong government support for wind power is likely to continue and help the wind power industry to expand rapidly in coming years.

WIND INDUSTRY ISSUE: COMPONENT SHORTAGES

The wind power industry is experiencing such tremendous growth that the industry is facing a serious shortage of various components. The component shortages mainly involve gearboxes and bearings.[60] The component shortage has limited the industry's overall growth rate and resulted in large backorders for wind turbine and system manufacturers. At the end of 2006, wind farm developers had to wait 12 months for turbines to be delivered and this delay may grow to 18 to 24 months.[61] Demand in 2007 is expected to be 20 gigawatts and supply is only expected to be 17 gigawatts, resulting in a 3-gigawatt shortage according to the Global Wind Energy Council.[62] The industry consensus is that these component shortages will last until at least 2009.[63]

There are three reasons for the component shortages: political, technological, and economic. From a political standpoint, the unreliability of some government-sponsored wind support programs, such as the U.S. production tax credit, makes component manufacturers reluctant to spend the capital that is needed to permanently expand their manufacturing capacity. From a technology perspective, there is strong demand for technologically improved products and not all manufacturers can keep up with these improvements. From an economic standpoint, raw materials costs (e.g., steel, copper, and carbon) have risen sharply and have made it difficult for component manufacturers to plan production and pricing.

WIND INDUSTRY PLAYERS

The wind power industry can be separated into three types of players: (1) wind turbine manufacturers, (2) component manufacturers, and (3) wind power operators. The following sections describe each in detail.

Wind Turbine Manufacturers

The wind turbine industry has seen a large number of mergers and acquisitions (M&A) in the past few years. The M&A activity has been driven by wind turbine manufacturers trying to (1) grab geographical territory and market share from other turbine manufacturers (horizontal acquisitions); and (2) acquire control of component suppliers to ensure component availability and R&D improvements (vertical acquisitions).

In 2006, 13 M&A transactions took place totaling 35 gigawatts of capacity. That was up from nine transactions in 2005 (12 gigawatts) and four transactions in 2002–2004 (under 4 gigawatts).[64] Acquisition activity has sometimes caused market shares to change quickly. For example, Siemens was only a minor player in the United States in 2005, but after acquiring Bonus Energy A/S, a Danish wind turbine manufacturer, Siemens quickly jumped to second place in the United States in 2006 with a market share of 23.0 percent.[65] Market shares for the top wind turbine manufacturers are shown in Figure 6.6 for the global market and in Figure 6.7 for the U.S. market.

There are three large global conglomerates that are actively involved in wind power: General Electric (NYSE: GE), Siemens (German Xetra: SIE GR), and Mitsubishi Power Systems, a subsidiary of Mitsubishi Heavy Industries (Tokyo: 7011 JP). Wind power represents a very small portion of these conglomerate's revenues and profits, so it doesn't make much sense to buy stock in these companies to gain exposure to the growth in wind power. GE Wind, a subsidiary of GE, has a large market share

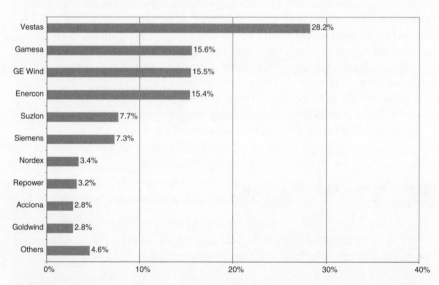

FIGURE 6.6 Wind Turbine Manufacturer Global Market Shares in Percent for 2006 (Total Market Size: 15.016 GW) *Note:* The market shares added together equal 107 percent—this is caused by the fact that 7 percent more capacity was supplied during 2006 than was recorded as installed in the market.
Source: BTM Consult ApS, "Press Release: International Wind Energy Development," March 26, 2007, http://www.btm.dk/documents/pressrelease.pdf.

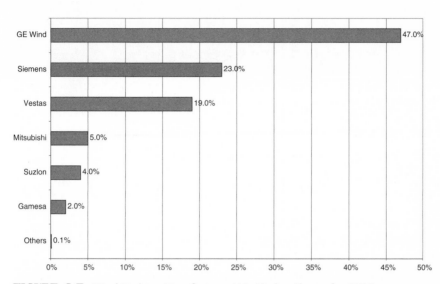

FIGURE 6.7 Wind Turbine Manufacturer U.S. Market Shares for 2006
Source: Depart of Energy, National Renewable Energy Laboratory, *Annual Report on U.S. Wind Power Installation, Cost, and Performance Trends: 2006,*" May 2007, p. 7, http://www.nrel.gov/docs/fy07osti/41435.pdf.

globally and in the United States and GE's 1.5-megawatt wind turbine in 2006 was the world's best-selling model.[66] As mentioned earlier, Siemens grew in the wind industry by the acquisition of Bonus Energy A/S in 2004, the oldest wind company and the pioneer of offshore wind farms and arctic turbines.[67] Siemens recently entered into an agreement to produce floating offshore wind turbines with Hydro,[68] a Norwegian energy company with little experience in the wind industry, but with approved construction licenses.[69]

There are only a handful of pure-play publicly traded wind turbine manufacturers in the world at present, most of which trade outside U.S. markets. Table 6.1 shows the largest pure-play companies, ranked by market capitalization. For easy comparison, the monetary quantities in this table have been converted from local currencies into dollars at current exchange rates. All of the companies are wind turbine/system manufacturers and installers, except Zoltek and American Superconductor, which are wind power component suppliers.

Vestas Wind Systems (Copenhagen: VWS DC). Vestas Wind (www.vestas .com) started making wind turbines in 1979 and has grown to be the largest wind turbine manufacturer in the world. It is a leading player in Europe and the Americas and consolidated its leading market share position by acquiring its rival NEG Micon in 2004.[70] Vestas Wind has

TABLE 6.1 Global Pure-Play Wind Power Manufacturers (for FY 2006, in millions of U.S.$)

Company	Country	Ticker	Market Cap	Revenues	EBITDA	Net Profit (Loss)
Vestas Wind Systems	Denmark	VWS DC	$12,550	$5,241	$446	$151
Suzlon Energy Ltd	India	SUEL IN	$10,350	$933	$209	$185
Gamesa Corporacion Tecnologica	Spain	GAM SM	$9,350	$3,250	$559	$269
Nordex AG	Germany	NDX1 GR	$2,750	$751	$40	$17
Clipper Windpower Plc	United Kingdom	CWP LN	$2,000	$7	($20)	($21)
REpower Systems AG	Germany	RPW GR	$1,750	$628	$23	$10
Zoltek Companies	United States	ZOLT US	$1,400	$92	($10)	($66)
American Superconductor*	United States	AMSC US	$750	$52	($32)	($35)

Source: Company filings and Bloomberg.

*American Superconductor fiscal year ends March 31, 2007.

recently been expanding its business in China, with the installation of a blade factory in 2006. Even before this factory was completed, Vestas decided to double its capacity due to increased demand.[71] Vestas Wind is currently in the process of trying to deal with component shortages and improve its profit margins.

Suzlon Energy Ltd (Mumbai: SUEL IN)—Suzlon (www.suzlon.com) is based in India but targets the European and American markets. The company's manufacturing plants are in India, which results in significantly lower costs and higher profit margins than its Europe-based competitors.[72] In 2007, it signed one of the largest contracts in U.S. wind-power history, agreeing to provide PPM Energy, a subsidiary of Iberdrola, with 700 megawatts of wind capacity over two years.[73] Suzlon acquired 33.85 percent of REpower Systems AG shares in June 2007 and through voting agreements controls 87.1 percent of voting control.[74] REpower is a German company that is developing a prototype 5-megawatt wind turbine. Its business is concentrated in Europe and in Asia/Pacific through subsidiaries and affiliated companies.[75]

Gamesa Corporacion Tecnologica (Madrid: GAM SM). Gamesa (www .gamesa.es/index.php/en/) is a Spanish company with over three-quarters of its revenues coming from wind turbine sales. It has sales commitments with Iberdrola and Babcock & Brown to install 4.5 gigawatts of wind power capacity worldwide during 2007–2009, 60 percent of which will be installed in Europe and the remainder in the United States and China.[76] In 2006, Gamesa started the construction of seven new wind power parks in various locations including the United States, Spain, and China.[77]

Nordex AG (German Xetra: NDX1 GR). Nordex AG (www.nordex-online.com/en/) focuses on larger turbines, constructing 2.3 to 2.5 megawatt wind turbines. Its business is mostly in Europe and it is growing quickly in America and Asia/Pacific. It leads the French wind industry with a 33 percent market share, the largest in that country.[78]

Clipper Windpower (London: CWP LN). Clipper Windpower (www .clipperwind.com) is a relatively new company that produced 2.5 megawatts of wind turbines in 2006. The company currently has firm agreements to deliver over 1 gigawatt of wind turbines through 2011 and has about 4.5 gigawatts worth of contingent or joint development sales.[79] Clipper Windpower has formed a long-term strategic partnership with BP Alternative Energy[80] to supply turbines and wind power capacity to BP. BP intends to become one of the world's leading wind developers by 2015 with help from Clipper Windpower and other partners.

Wind Turbine Component Manufacturers

Wind power component manufacturing involves a complex web of companies, with few pure-play stock opportunities. Most of the component manufacturers are large companies where wind power represents a small portion of their total revenues. Many turbine manufacturers have responded to component shortages by producing their own components or by acquiring companies that manufacture these components. The table in Table 6.2 lists the primary component manufacturers for each of the major turbine manufacturers.

- *Rotor blades.* LM Glasfiber, a private company, had a market share of about 27 percent of the rotor blade market in 2006.[81] Most of the large turbine players manufacture their own turbine blades since that is a complex and proprietary process.
- *Gearboxes and bearings.* The gearbox market is controlled mainly by Winergy (40 percent market share) and Hansen Transmissions (30 percent market share).[82] Those companies were acquired by Siemens Wind and Suzlon, respectively.[83] The bearings market for wind turbines has two main suppliers: SKF AB and FAG Kugelfischer AG.[84] SKF AB (Stockholm: SKFB SS) is a Swedish bearing and seal specialist that also trades in the U.S. over-the-counter market as an American Depositary Receipt (ADR) under the symbol SKFRY. Although only 2 percent of its business comes from wind power, it is their fastest growing segment.[85] FAG Kugelfischer AG (www.fag.com) was acquired by Schaeffler Group (www.schaefflergroup.com) in 2001, which is a privately held German company.

    Generators. The major wind turbine players generally manufacture the generators in-house due to importance of the generator to the overall operation of the wind unit and the need for R&D improvements. The independent producers of generators used in the wind industry include ABB Ltd (NYSE: ABB) and Loher GmbH. ABB is a large Swiss-based company (www.abb.com) that provides the wind industry with many components for turbines, including generators, and with grid connection components as well. Loher (www.loher.de) is a private German company, which also supplies generators to the wind turbine industry.

    Towers. Regarding wind tower manufacturers, NEG Micon was bought by Vestas in 2004. Another wind tower player, DMI Industries, is exclusively dedicated to wind tower manufacturing and is owned by the Otter Tail Corporation (Nasdaq: OTTR). Otter Tail owns several companies in diverse industries, including plastic and food ingredient

TABLE 6.2 Major Wind Turbine Manufacturers and Their Component Suppliers

Turbine maker	Rotor blades	Gearboxes	Generators	Towers	Controllers
Vestas	**Vestas**, LM	Bosch Rexroth, Hansen, Winergy, Moventas	**Weier**, Elin, ABB, LeroySomer	**Vestas**, NEG, DMI	**Cotas (Vestas)**, NEG (Dancontrol)
GE Energy	LM, Tecsis	Winergy, Bosch, Rexroth, Eickhoff, **GE**	Loher, **GE**	DMI, Omnical, SIAG	**GE**
Gamesa	**Gamesa**, LM	**Echesa (Gamesa)**, Winergy, Hansen	**Indar (Gamesa)**, Cantarey	**Gamesa**	**Ingeletric (Gamesa)**
Enercon	**Enercon**	Direct drive	**Enercon**	KGW, SAM	**Enercon**
Siemens Wind	**Siemens**, LM	**Winergy**	ABB	Roug, KGW	**Siemens**, KK Electronic
Suzlon	**Suzlon**	**Hansen**, Winergy	**Suzlon**, Siemens	**Suzlon**	**Suzlon**, Mita Teknik
REpower	LM	Winergy, Renk, Eickhoff	N/A	N/A	Mita Teknik, ReGuard
Nordex	**Nordex**	Winergy, Eickhoff, Maag	Loher	**Nordex**, Omnical	**Nordex**, Mita Teknik

Source: BTM Consult ApS via European Wind Energy, "Focus on Supply Chain: Supply Chain: The Race to Meet Demand," *Wind Directions*, January–February 2007, p. 28, http://www.ewea.org/fileadmin/ewea.documents/documents/publications/WD/2007_january/0701-WD26-focus.pdf.

Table notes:
1. Towers are often produced locally where projects are built.
2. Names in bold indicate in-house supply or ownership of supplier by turbine manufacturer.

processing. The wind tower division of Roug A/S was acquired by Hendricks Industries ApS, a private holding company.

Control systems. Mika Teknik is a private Danish company that supplies specialized control systems for wind turbines.

There are two U.S.-listed companies that are suppliers to the wind power industry: American Superconductor and Zoltek Companies. A brief profile of those two companies follows.

- *American Superconductor* (Nasdaq: AMSC). American Superconductor does not construct or install wind turbines, but instead designs and develops wind systems. American Superconductor also manufactures electrical components for wind power systems. The company is focused on high-temperature superconductor wires and stabilizers for power grids but recently expanded its product offerings for the fast-growing wind power business. In early 2007, American Superconductor acquired Windtec, an Austrian company that develops complete electrical systems for wind turbines. American Superconductor is therefore involved in several parts of the wind power industry: It designs and develops wind turbines; offers consulting services for project development; manufactures electrical systems for wind turbines including voltage and power regulation; and manufactures other electrical components, such as power grid interconnection systems to cope with wind power fluctuations.[86]
- *Zoltek Companies* (Nasdaq: ZOLT). Zoltek (www.zoltek.com) is a specialist in manufacturing materials and products based on carbon fiber and composite materials. Zoltek supplies carbon fiber materials to the companies that manufacture the huge wind rotor blades.[87] For example, Zoltek has a long-term supply agreement to supply Vestas Wind with carbon fiber and carbon fiber materials worth $300 million over the first five years of the agreement according to Zoltek.[88]

Wind Power Operators

There are two types of wind power operators: power utilities and *independent power producers* (IPPs). Independent power producers have been responsible for developing most wind farms worldwide.[89] Independent power producers own wind farms and sell the electricity output from those wind farms to local utilities, usually on long-term power purchase agreements. The top global wind power operators for 2006 are shown in Figure 6.8. Several of these are detailed as follows:

- *FPL Energy.* FPL Energy (www.fplenergy.com), a subsidiary of FPL Group (NYSE: FPL), is an unregulated wholesale power merchant that

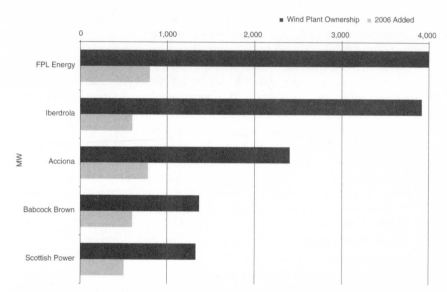

FIGURE 6.8 Top Global Wind Operators by Capacity in 2006 (in Megawatts)
Source: European Wind Energy Association, "Focus on Industry: New Players on Board," *Wind Directions,* March–April 2007, p. 44, http://www.ewea.org/fileadmin/ewea_documents/documents/publications/WD/2007_march/WD0703-focus.pdf.

specializes in low-emissions power generation. As of the end of 2006, FPL Energy was the world's largest owner/operator of wind power capacity. As of mid-2007, FPL Energy had 14 wind power farms in various areas of the United States.[90] Wind constitutes 30 percent of FPL's total power production portfolio, second only to natural gas (49 percent of the portfolio).[91] FPL Energy also happens to be the largest generator of solar power in the United States using trough-based thermal concentrating solar power.[92] FPL Energy's parent company, FPL Group, also owns Florida Power and Light.

- *Iberdrola SA* (Madrid: IBE SM). Iberdrola (www.Iberdrola.es) is Spain's second largest power company and operates elsewhere in Europe and in the Americas. Iberdrola recently made two big acquisitions that allowed Iberdrola to leapfrog FPL Energy into the position as the world's largest wind power producer for 2007. In early 2007, Iberdrola acquired Scottish Power (formerly London: SPW LN) for $24 billion, which was the world's fifth largest wind power producer before the acquisition. Scottish Power in turn owned PPM Energy (www.ppmenergy.com), a large power utility based in Portland, Oregon that is the second largest wind operator in the United States. Iberdrola in 2007 also announced the acquisition of Energy East, an

American power and gas company with about 3 million customers in the northeastern United States, for \$4.5 billion.[93]

- *Acciona SA* (Madrid: ANA SM). Acciona (www.acciona.com) is a large Spanish infrastructure construction company that also has holdings in real estate and energy. Acciona operates in 10 countries across Europe and North America.[94] The company is the world's largest wind power construction company, having built over 163 wind parks for itself and customers.[95] The company itself owns 126 wind parks, representing 3.133 gigawatts of capacity. Acciona, at the end of 2006, had 700 megawatts of wind park projects under construction and another 8 gigawatts in development. Recently, Acciona acquired 1.3 gigawatts of wind energy assets from EcoEnergy, LLC, a unit of the Morse Group, to increase its operations in the U.S. market.[96]
- *Babcock & Brown Ltd* (Australia: BNB AU). Babcock & Brown (www.babcockbrown.com) is an Australian global investment and advisory firm that finances and operates renewable energy projects under its infrastructure division. In 2005, it acquired Enersis, a European renewable energy company. Babcock & Brown has plans to develop around 3 gigawatts of wind energy capacity for 2007–2011.[97]

CHAPTER 7

Fuel Cells

Present and Accounted for in Some Applications Already

The "hydrogen economy" based on fuel cells has been promised for many years as the answer to the world's energy problems. However, it is taking so long for fuel cells to get to an economical and mass-market stage that many people have become disillusioned with them. In fact, the stock prices for fuel cell companies have been in the doldrums over the past several years, reflecting this disillusionment.

While the viability is questionable for some fuel cell applications such as vehicles, fuel cells are already competing in the power backup market every day with incumbent battery technologies. It is therefore important to explain the different types of fuel cell technologies and applications in order to better assess the prospects for investing in fuel cell companies.

A fuel cell is simply an electricity generation device that uses hydrogen as a feedstock, along with oxygen from the air, to produce electricity. The fuel cell releases only water and heat as byproducts and releases no gases, greenhouse or otherwise. Fuel cells possess many key advantages, including high efficiency, quiet operation, and clean operation with no greenhouse gas emissions. In addition, fuel cells can be used in a wide range of applications, including small electronic devices, vehicle transportation, building power and backup, and utility-grade power generation. The main disadvantages are cost and how to supply the hydrogen fuel. The following is a summary of the advantages and disadvantages of fuel cells.

ADVANTAGES AND DISADVANTAGES OF FUEL CELLS

Advantages

- *No pollution.* Fuel cells use only hydrogen and oxygen as inputs and dispel only water and heat, which are all natural elements. No pollution means that fuel cells are not only good for the environment but also that it can be safely used indoors—for example, to power forklifts in warehouses or to power computer rooms.
- *Greater efficiency.* Energy efficiency is defined as the percentage of energy that can be extracted from a given fuel source and turned into electricity.[1] High temperature fuel cells have efficiencies ranging from 32 percent to 47 percent.[2] Low temperature fuel cells have a much wider range of efficiencies, from 25 percent to 60 percent,[3] depending on the specific variety and application.
- *Backup and distributed power.* A building owner can install a fuel cell at a building site (outside or inside), thus providing an electricity generation source that is independent of the grid. This protects the fuel cell owner from grid fluctuations and blackouts and also from the rising price of electricity.
- *Cogeneration as an enhancement to efficiency.* High temperature fuel cells generate a lot of heat as a byproduct. Cogeneration refers to capturing and using this heat. This greatly increases the energy efficiencies associated with high temperature fuel cells, which can achieve efficiency rates of nearly 85 percent.[4]
- *Silent technology.* Fuel cells operate silently, which means they do not cause noise pollution and that they are suitable for use indoors and in residential areas outdoors.
- *Remote operation.* Fuel cells can run independently in remote locations off-grid with only hydrogen provided as a fuel, which provides a source of electricity where the grid may not be available.
- *Electricity can be stored.* Fuel cells allow for energy to be stored and reserved for later use. Excess electricity can be used to create hydrogen through electrolysis, and that hydrogen can then be stored and used later by the fuel cell when the electricity is needed again.

Disadvantages

- *High cost.* Fuel cell technology for some applications (though not all) is still in the developmental stage. Production costs at various stages need to be significantly reduced before large-scale manufacturing can occur. In addition, the construction of a fuel cell can use expensive materials, some of which, such as platinum, are actually getting more expensive.[5]

- *Hydrogen production, delivery and storage.* Hydrogen is not easy or inexpensive to produce, store, or transport. Hydrogen gas in its pure form is flammable and requires special handling. Hydrogen gas is also very light and must be compressed for transportation and storage.
- *Production of hydrogen can pollute.* Hydrogen used in fuel cells can be produced through two processes: electrolysis (splitting of water into hydrogen and oxygen) or reformation of hydrocarbons such as natural gas. Electrolysis is pollution-free, but is still prohibitively expensive today. Reformation of hydrocarbons such as natural gas, which is the main technology used at present, pollutes the environment through the release of CO_2, although the pollution is less than burning the hydrocarbons since hydrogen reformation is a more efficient process.
- *Perceptions on reliability, durability and safety.* Fuel cells are a new technology so their reliability and durability have not been statistically proven, though some claim 99.9999 percent reliability.[6] Long-term reliability records are limited to the relatively few devices currently in operation, which are mostly in controlled environments and not exposed to real world problems.[7] There are also questions regarding the safety of hydrogen as a fuel, since it can be extremely flammable when produced at high purity and concentration levels.

WHAT IS A FUEL CELL? OVERVIEW OF THE TECHNOLOGY

As mentioned earlier, a fuel cell converts hydrogen and oxygen into electricity, releasing only water and heat as byproducts. There are no moving parts in a fuel cell and nothing is burned. As can be seen in Figure 7.1, an anode is used to split hydrogen atoms into positively and negatively charged parts, which are then sent across to the cathode through different paths. The negatively charged electrons generate electricity, and when the hydrogen molecules are combined with oxygen at the cathode, water and heat are produced. This book's companion Web site at www.ProfitingFromCleanEnergy.com has a link to a video from Ballard Energy demonstrating how a fuel cell works.

Types of Fuel Cells

The different types of fuel cells can be classified by two attributes: (1) the temperature at which the fuel cell operates; and (2) whether the fuel cell

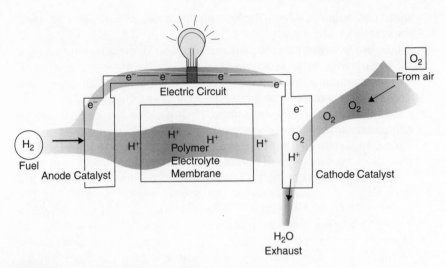

FIGURE 7.1 The internal working of a Fuel Cell
Source: Reprinted by permission and courtesy of Fuel Cells 2000 (www.fuelcells.org) and the U.S. Department of Energy.

is supplied directly with hydrogen or with an intermediate fuel supply that contains hydrogen.

Operating Temperature: A Tradeoff   Fuel cells operate in a range of temperatures, which can be classified as low (under 300°F) or high (from 300°F to over 1,800°F). Low temperature fuel cells are suitable for microelectronic devices, vehicles, and *uninterruptible power supplies* (UPS). High-temperature cells are suitable for stationary energy production, auxiliary power units (APU), megawatt and multimegawatt power production such as power grid support or wastewater treatment plants.

High temperature cells typically have lower operating costs because they operate with higher fuel efficiency and because they can take advantage of cogeneration (use of waste heat) to produce even more electricity. Low temperature fuel cells cannot take advantage of cogeneration, but they can still achieve higher energy efficiencies than conventional energy sources. High temperature fuel cells also require less stringent hydrogen purity requirements, which reduce their operating costs. Low temperature cells, by contrast, contain more sensitive materials that need very pure hydrogen, and very pure oxygen as well in some cases, so as not to damage the equipment. High temperature fuel cells can also be manufactured with cheaper metals such as nickel. On the other hand, low temperature fuel cells, due to their sensitivity, need to be manufactured with more expensive components such as platinum.

While high temperature fuel cells have lower operating costs, they are far more expensive to manufacture in total and they have several practical limitations to their use. First, exposure to extreme temperature variations causes damage to the equipment, meaning it is not practical to turn high-temperature fuel cells on and off. This renders high temperature fuel cells unusable for certain applications, such as vehicles. In general, high temperature fuel cells can only be used for utility or industrial purposes. Second, high temperatures may speed up corrosion of the fuel cells, which means they have a shorter life span than low temperature fuel cells.

Hydrogen: Internal Production or External Reformer? Hydrogen is the main input fuel for fuel cells. Hydrogen is the most abundant element on earth, but hydrogen does not exist alone in nature and needs to be extracted from other compounds such as water (H_2O) or hydrocarbons like natural gas (CH_4) or methanol (CH_3OH). In a fuel cell, the hydrogen can be delivered in a pure form from an external source straight into the fuel cell's external reformer. The other approach is to have a hydrogen extraction device (internal reformer) attached to the fuel cell unit. That allows the unit to use natural gas or methanol (rather than pure hydrogen), which the fuel cell's internal reformer then turns into the necessary hydrogen. The choice of which delivery system to use depends on a variety of factors.

Classification of Fuel Cells

Table 7.1 classifies the various types of fuel cell technologies by the two characteristics explained in the previous section, that is, temperature and hydrogen reformer type. As mentioned, the "external reformer" fuel cells require the delivery of hydrogen, while "internal reformers" use intermediate products such as natural gas or methanol.

TABLE 7.1 Classification of Fuel Cell Types

	High Temperature	Low Temperature
Internal Production of Hydrogen	MCFC (Molten Carbonate Fuel Cell)	DMFC (Direct Methanol Fuel Cell)
	SOFC (Solid Oxide Fuel Cell)	DLFC (Direct Liquid Fuel Cell)
	PCFC (Protonic Ceramic Fuel Cell)	ZAFC (Zinc-Air Fuel Cell)
		RFC (Regenerative Fuel Cell)
External Reformer of Hydrogen	PAFC (Phosphoric Acid Fuel Cell)	PEM (Proton Exchange Membrane)
		AFC (Alkaline Fuel Cell)

FIGURE 7.2   PEM Fuel Cell: Remote Application
Source: Plug Power, "Fuel Cell Systems," http://www.plugpower.com/technology/
overview.cfm.

PEM Fuel Cells

PEM stands for *proton exchange membrane* or *polymer electrolyte membrane*. The PEM fuel cell is typically used for smaller scale *uninterruptible power supplies* (UPS) and for remote power for instruments or lighting (see Figure 7.2). The UPS systems based on PEM fuel cells have higher reliability than other types of UPS systems, but the PEM-based UPS systems are also a bit more expensive than competing battery technologies.

PEM-based fuel cells are also the type of fuel cell that is usually placed in vehicles. The commercialization of fuel-cell powered vehicles is still a long way away, after 2015 according to the Department of Energy (DOE).[8] Furthermore, PEM cells require an external reformer of hydrogen, meaning that a suitable hydrogen delivery and refueling system needs to be present to provide fuel for the vehicles.

Ballard Power Systems (Nasdaq: BLDP) is involved in the development of PEM cells for transportation, while Plug Power (Nasdaq: PLUG)

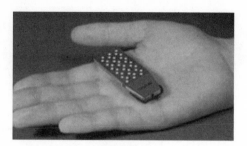

FIGURE 7.3 Direct Methanol Fuel Cell
Source: Toshiba, "Toshiba's Direct Methanol Fuel Cell Officially Certified as World's Smallest by Guinness World Records", Press Releases 28 February 2005, http://www.toshiba.co.jp/about/press/2005_02/pr2801.htm.

and Hydrogenics (Nasdaq: HYGS) lead the development of using PEM-based fuel cells for the UPS power backup market.

DMFC and DLFC Fuel Cells

Direct methanol and *direct liquid* fuel cells, as pictured in Figure 7.3, are small, low-temperature fuel cells that are on the verge of being commercialized for use in microelectronic devices and portable power supplies that can supply electricity for a camping trip, to recharge cell phones on-the-go, or to be carried by the military to power their increasing amount of electrical equipment. These fuel cells are ideal candidates for built-in, long-lasting "batteries" for small electronic devices such as cell phones, personal digital assistants (PDAs), or laptop computers. They can be disposable or rechargeable. They can be rechargeable with the replacement of the methanol or fueling liquid, although this presents somewhat of a challenge in terms of design and consumer usage. Toshiba (Tokyo: 6502 JP), Medis Technologies (Nasdaq: MDTL) and Mechanical Technology (Nasdaq: MKTY) work with these types of fuel cells.

MCFC Fuel Cells

Molten carbonate fuel cells operate at temperatures ranging from 1,100 degrees Fahrenheit to 1,300 degrees Fahrenheit (see Figure 7.4). They contain an internal reformer of hydrogen, thus they can work with almost any hydrogen-based fuel, including natural gas, propane, landfill gas (methane), and synthetic coal gasification products.[9] Due to their high efficiency and large output capacity, they are used as backup power for the megawatt market, which comprises large hotels,

FIGURE 7.4 Molten Carbonate Fuel Cell
Source: FuelCell Energy, "Direct Fuel Cells—About the Technology," Webhttp://
www.fce.com/site/products/about.html.

hospitals, and wastewater treatment facilities. These fuel cells are the
main candidates to supply the multimegawatt market, which includes
backup power for central-station power grids. They are still expensive
to produce, but research continues on trying to cut costs to more competitive levels. FuelCell Energy (Nasdaq: FCEL) is the main company
that works with molten carbonate fuel cells.

FUEL CELL INDUSTRY ANALYSIS: INDUSTRY PLAYERS

Table 7.2 presents a table with the larger U.S.-listed fuel cell companies,
ranked by market capitalization. A quick glance at the table shows that
all of the fuel cell companies are burning large amounts of cash. Most of
the companies have partnerships or agreements with other companies to
develop fuel cell technology toward specific applications, such as telecommunications or transportation, and U.S. government subsidies and tax
breaks are critical for them to be cost-competitive.

- *Plug Power* (Nasdaq: PLUG): The fuel cell industry is moving into the
  commercialization stage in some niche markets. For example, Plug

TABLE 7.2 U.S. Fuel Cell Companies: Selected Financial Data, 2006 (in USD millions)

Company	Symbol	Market Cap	Revenues	EBITDA	Net Income (Loss)	Cash Flow from Operations
Ballard Power Systems	Nasdaq: BLDP	$560	$49.8	($37.4)	($181.1)	($42.7)
FuelCell Energy	Nasdaq: FCEL	$530	$33.3	($72.4)	($76.1)	($48.4)
Medis Technologies	Nasdaq: MDTL	$490	$0.2	($24.0)	($33.0)	($22.9)
Plug Power	Nasdaq: PLUG	$265	$7.8	($55.3)	($50.3)	($46.1)
Hydrogenics	Nasdaq: HYGS	$115	$30.1	($32.6)	($130.8)	($24.5)
Mechanical Technology	Nasdaq: MKTY	$55	$7.7	($11.9)	($13.7)	($12.7)
Distributed Energy Systems	Nasdaq: DESC	$35	$45.1	($52.5)	($53.4)	($21.8)

Source: Company financial statements (data as of June 2007).

Power has already delivered over 650 PEM-based fuel-cell power systems worldwide that have logged some 2.6 million operating hours, according to the company. Plug Power's GenCore system is a UPS backup system that is targeted at large telecom and utility customers. GenCore can be customized, and has already been evaluated and purchased by companies including Verizon Communications. Plug Power's fuel-cell-based UPS system is competing with legacy battery and generator UPS technologies. The company has development agreements with many firms, including General Electric and Honda.

Plug Power burned $46 million in cash on operations in 2006 on revenues of only $7.8 million.[10] However, Plug Power in June 2006 received a $270 million cash infusion from Smart Hydrogen, a partnership between the world's largest nickel-and-palladium-producer Norilsk Nickel and the Russian private investment firm Interros. Smart Hydrogen made the investment after carefully reviewing all players in the fuel cell industry. This cash infusion reduced Plug Power's financing risk and allowed it to accelerate its path to profitability and broaden its product lines and target customer base.

- *Medis Technologies* (Nasdaq: MDTL): Micro fuel cells for use with portable electronic devices are another application that has a path to mass commercialization. Medis Technologies focuses on this sector with its disposable Power Pack charging device, which is based on direct liquid fuel cell (DLFC) technology. The company plans to ramp up production from a few hundred Power Packs per month in 2006 to 1.5 million per month by 2008. While the firm has big plans, it remains in start-up mode and hence the risks are high. The company has virtually no revenue and yet has a market cap near $500 million.
- *Mechanical Technology* (Nasdaq: MKTY): Mechanical Technology is another startup firm targeting the micro fuel cell sector for portable electronic applications, which uses direct methanol fuel cells (DMFC). Though small, the company has partnerships with large firms, including Samsung, DuPont, and Gillette/Duracell.
- *Ballard Power Systems* (Nasdaq: BLDP): Ballard Power Systems, based in Canada, was an early mover in the transportation PEM fuel cell industry and has perhaps the most recognized brand name in the fuel cell industry. Ballard has partnerships with large auto companies such as DaimlerChrysler and Ford. Ballard is a member of the California Fuel Cell Partnership (CaFCP), which is an industry research collaboration group focused on fuel cell vehicles. Ballard is also involved in the cogeneration possibilities that fuel cells have to offer. It is cautiously entering the Japanese residential cogeneration market through partnerships with EBARA, Tokyo Gas, and Nippon Oil. Nevertheless,

Ballard is still heavily involved in research and development and has a long road to commercialization and profitability.

FuelCell Energy (Nasdaq: FCEL): FuelCell Energy tackles a different market and builds large, stationary, high temperature MCFC systems designed to produce electricity for the megawatt market. It has already installed over 60 power stations, generating a total of over 150 million kilowatt-hours of electricity. There are significant cost issues associated with this technology and FuelCell Energy relies on U.S. government subsidies to be competitive. However, economies of scale due to increasing order volume, together with ongoing research, are reducing costs each year.

Hydrogenics Corp (Nasdaq: HYGS): Hydrogenics Corp, also based in Canada, is taking a broader view of the fuel cell product market. Hydrogenics sells (1) PEM fuel cells; (2) onsite hydrogen generation systems to provide the hydrogen that fuel cells need to operate (via electrolysis); and (3) fuel cell testing systems to manufacturers and customers who are testing fuel cell prototypes. Hydrogenics has been working on experimental projects with Chevron, Toyota, and the CUTE Project (Clean Urban Transport Europe),[11] including prototypes for fuel cell powered forklifts and buses. It has a close relationship with GM, which in turn owns around one-eighth of the company. Like most fuel cell companies, Hydrogenics has a high cash burn rate and little visibility for a path to profitability.

Distributed Energy Systems (Nasdaq: DESC): Distributed Energy Systems operates in several divisions, producing conventional power, fuel cells, and hydrogen (for fuel cell power as well as for laboratory and industrial uses). The company's fuel cell division produces PEM fuel cells for backup power systems, with an emphasis on compatibility with renewable sources of energy. It has also been developing regenerative fuel cells (RFCs)[12] for applications within the military and aerospace industries (e.g., for satellites). Developing hydrogen fueling systems, which are a necessary complement for many fuel cell varieties, is an important area of research for the company.

GrafTech International (NYSE: GTI): There is a large market for supplying fuel cell manufacturers with specialized materials, and GrafTech International (GTI) has taken the lead in that area. GrafTech manufactures graphite products for several industrial uses, and has recently begun to make parts for portable, stationary, and transportation-oriented fuel cells, including PEM cells. The company's products are used in 70 percent of fuel cell vehicles and in over 50 percent of fuel cell bus programs worldwide.[13] Ballard Power Systems is one of the company's main customers.

FUEL CELL INDUSTRY TARGET MARKETS

Fuel cells are on the verge of entering mass production in some niche markets, mainly in the uninterruptible power supply (UPS) market. Large quantities of fuel cells are already being sold into the power backup market for the telecommunications industry, which is estimated to be a $1.9 billion market.[14] Motive power, which mainly involves powering forklift and similar material handling trucks, is another niche target market for fuel cells. The motive market is a $1.5 billion market.[15] Ballard is already selling prototype units to various customers in the motive power market, with commercialization in view for 2009–2010.

Residential cogeneration is a potentially large market, although for now fuel cell companies are only considering the market in Japan. Ballard's estimate for Japan's residential market size is $9 billion a year for 2009–2010, taking into account 1.8 million homes.[16] However, the commercialization of residential generation is a long way off and intensive research is still needed to lower costs.

Fuel cell production for automotives and fleet vehicles is a potentially huge market. However, the path for its mass production has been agonizingly slow and mass commercialization is not expected until at least 2015–2020. The industry still faces significant challenges in terms of technology and cost, including the problems of building a nationwide hydrogen delivery network. This book's companion Web site at www.ProfitingFromCleanEnergy.com has links to video demonstrations of various fuel cell vehicles.

COMMERCIALIZATION CHALLENGES

How to Obtain Hydrogen

Hydrogen needs to be separated from other compounds since it does not normally exist on its own in nature. There are two main types of processes: (1) electrolysis, and (2) reforming of hydrocarbon fuels.

Electrolysis is the ideal scenario, where hydrogen is obtained from water in a process that is essentially the reverse from what a fuel cell does. Using electricity, electrolysis separates water into its two parts, hydrogen and oxygen. However, electrolysis cannot be considered completely clean unless the electricity used for the electrolysis process comes from a zero-carbon renewable electricity generation source such as wind or solar power. The reality today is that electrolysis is expensive and years of research are still necessary to make electrolysis commercially viable as a means for producing hydrogen.

Even though electrolysis is currently expensive, it is still necessary for some applications where customers need pure hydrogen onsite in quantity. There are at least two key companies that manufacture electrolysis machines. Distributed Energy Systems (Nasdaq: DESC) has a HOGEN® electrolysis product line that allows users to produce hydrogen at their own location with just water and electricity as inputs.[17] Teledyne Energy Systems, a subsidiary of Teledyne Technologies (NYSE: TDY), also sells an electrolysis-based hydrogen generation unit as well as a PEM-based fuel cell product line.[18]

The alternative process for obtaining hydrogen is the reforming of fuels that contain hydrogen through thermochemical processes. These fuels include fossil fuels (e.g., natural gas, coal), alcohol fuels (e.g., methanol, ethanol), carbon-free hydrogen compounds (e.g., ammonia, borohydride), biomass, methane, landfill gas, and anaerobic digester gas from wastewater treatment plants.[19] Fuel reforming uses a chemical reaction to extract hydrogen from fuels, but then produces waste products similar to those dispelled by current fuel burning techniques. Nevertheless, even if hydrogen is obtained through reforming and is then used in a fuel cell, the overall process is still a more environmentally friendly method than burning fossil fuels. Cars can reduce greenhouse gas emissions by 60 percent when powered by hydrogen obtained from natural gas reforming, compared with internal combustion engine vehicles using gasoline.[20]

Steam reforming of natural gas accounts for 95 percent of the hydrogen that is currently produced in the United States.[21] The U.S. Department of Energy set a goal, which has already been reached, of producing hydrogen for $2.00 to 3.00 per gasoline gallon equivalent (gge)[22] for delivered, untaxed hydrogen fuel, measured in 2005 dollars.[23] This goal was met in 2006 for high scale production, with hydrogen costs in the range of $2.75 to $3.50 gge.[24] This is a comparable cost to U.S. gasoline prices, which are currently near $3 per gallon.[25]

Hydrogen Delivery Costs

As mentioned earlier, some types of fuel cells require pure hydrogen to be delivered and loaded into a fuel cell. This is not a big problem for industrial and commercial applications in the backup power and motive markets since there is already a sales and distribution network for industrial gases. This network can also be expanded to deliver hydrogen to fleet vehicle users that bring their trucks or buses back to a central location each night.

However, the problem of distributing hydrogen throughout the country for use in automobiles on a mass scale will be a huge and perhaps even insurmountable challenge. The United States right now is struggling with trying to get E85 ethanol-gasoline mix distributed widely around the country, which is proving to be a big challenge even though E85 is very similar to gasoline and can use the same types of tanks and pumps. Hydrogen, by contrast, is much more difficult to transport and store and it would take a huge effort to get hydrogen into a large number of fuel stations around the country.

The delivery process for fuel cells that use internal reformers and that can use natural gas or methanol is not as big of a stretch. Again, there is already an industrial gas and chemical sales and distribution network around the world and delivery costs would not differ much from current costs. Large industrial gas companies such as Air Liquide SA (Paris: AI FP) and Air Products & Chemicals Inc (NYSE: APD) already deliver huge quantities of various industrial gases every day. There is also a large natural gas and propane sales and delivery network in operation throughout the world. Moreover, some small hand-held devices in development need no fuel to be delivered since they are disposable and are used like common batteries.

Fuel Cell Costs and Feasibility

Fuel cells have many advantages, but remain expensive to manufacture. Manufacturing costs have been steadily falling over the years due to intensive R&D efforts, reductions in material costs, improvements in the manufacturing process, and increased scale of production. Different applications are in different stages of cost reduction and some are already commercially viable. However, other applications are still in the R&D stage with no assurance that costs will fall far enough or that their practical limitations will be resolved in a cost-efficient way.

The U.S. Department of Energy has a variety of programs in place to promote the development of fuel cells. One program is FutureGen, which grants subsidies to fund the research and development of fuel cells, among other types of clean energy. In 2006, the program spent over $300 million in Fuels and Power Systems, of which almost $60 million (20 percent) was spent on developing fuel cells.[26] Budget projections for fuel cell funding are for $63 million in 2007 and $62 million in 2008.[27] Recently, through the Advanced Energy Initiative, the U.S. government granted an additional $100 million for fuel cell research in October 2006 to be distributed among 25 projects over the next four years.[28]

In the beginning, fuel cell technology was so expensive that only the NASA space program could afford it. During the space program in the 1960s and 1970s, fuel cells cost around $600,000 per kilowatt (kW).[29] This cost has been lowered dramatically over the years and depending on the type of fuel cells, the costs are now around $3,000/kW. This is still far more expensive than a diesel generator (which costs $800 to $1,500/kW) or a natural gas turbine (less than $400/kW).[30] However, fuel cell costs continue to fall due to technology improvements and larger production scale.

PEM fuel cells used as uninterruptible power supply systems are already competitive with incumbent battery technologies. The price of PEM fuel cell UPS systems (such as those sold by Plug Power) are still higher than competing technologies, but the UPS market is willing to pay a premium for the higher reliability of the fuel cell systems. According to the Department of Energy, PEM fuel cells currently cost between $3,000 and $5,500/kW when manufactured in small scales.[31] The U.S. government has a target cost for high production scale of $300/kW by 2015, which represents a tenfold cut.

Another commercially viable use for PEM fuel cells is the forklift market, although costs are still high at around $1,000/kW.[32] Fuel cells can easily enter and compete in this market, given their practical advantages such as the high efficiency and reliability.

PEM cell costs are expected to drop significantly over the next few years for all applications. Ballard Power Systems provides their own cost estimates, taking into account sales volume predictions, as can be seen in Table 7.3.

For the mass vehicle market, PEM cells are still a long way off. The U.S. Department of Energy estimates that commercialization of transportation PEM fuel cells will be feasible only after 2015.[33] Transportation presents a variety of problems such as the need for a powerful and yet compact fuel cell system, along with the difficulties of setting up a nationwide refueling system. Investing in this sector is a shot in the dark even though active R&D efforts continue.

High temperature fuel cells are much more expensive. For example, *solid oxide fuel cells* (SOFC), which are used for large-scale power generation, currently cost about $4,500/kW. The U.S. government's Solid State Energy Conversion Alliance (SECA) Cost Reduction Program aims to reduce costs for SOFCs from $4,500/kW to about $400/kW by 2010.[34] The DOE has "strong confidence" they will achieve their 2010 cost target.[35]

TABLE 7.3 Ballard Projections for Fuel Cell System Costs (per kilowatt)

	2006	2007 (target)	2009–2010 (potential)
Materials Handling (forklifts)	<$1,000	$700–$900	$500–$600
Backup Power	-	$2,000–$3,000	$1,000–$1,800

Source: Ballard Power Systems, *Ballard Power Systems: Making Fuel Cells a Commercial Reality,* http://www.ballard.com/resources/documents/General %20IR%20PPT_May%2010%202007.pdf.

Small, portable fuel cells for hand-held devices are being developed by a number of companies. For instance, Toshiba (Tokyo: 6502 JP) has already developed a direct methanol fuel cell for use in electronic equipment, which they are currently integrating into several electronic prototypes, including digital music players and laptop computers.[36] The main concerns today are related to practical issues for consumers rather than costs pertaining to the refueling systems and to the overall design.

The following guidelines are offered for investing in the fuel cell sector:

- Focus on fuel cell companies that are close to, or are already at, the stage of commercialization and mass production. These companies will be closest to the fulcrum of accelerated revenue and earnings.
- Focus on fuel cell companies that have the clearest path to profitability. By contrast, companies that have years to profitability will need to sell more stock to raise cash, thus diluting current shareholders and dampening the stock price.
- Stay away from fuel cell companies that are still in an early development stage, or at least recognize that investing in these companies may be a long shot.

CHAPTER 8

Geothermal Power

Dante's Contribution to Clean Energy

G eothermal power involves the use of geothermal heat from below the earth's surface to generate electricity or heat. Giovanni Conti first discovered the process of generating electricity with geothermal heat in 1904 in Larderello, Italy, but geothermal energy has been used for heating and cooling as far back as early Roman times.

Heat from the earth can be used in many ways, from utility-grade power stations to simple heat pumps for residential applications. This heat energy, known as *geothermal energy*, is a renewable source that can be found almost anywhere worldwide. The heat continuously flowing from the earth's interior is estimated to be the equivalent of 42 million megawatts of power (which is equivalent to the electricity that would be used by 31.5 billion homes).[1] Tapping geothermal energy is a clean and affordable way to generate electricity and heat and avoid the use of fossil fuels. Figure 8.1 shows a geothermal power plant in the Sierra Nevada mountains in California.

ADVANTAGES AND DISADVANTAGES OF GEOTHERMAL POWER

Advantages
- Low electricity generation costs; competitive with fossil fuel power plant costs.
- Cost of geothermal power is constant over the lifetime of the facility since no fuel is purchased and facility costs are largely fixed.

FIGURE 8.1 Mammoth Pacific Geothermal Power Plant located in the Sierra Nevada Mountains, California, 28 megawatts
Source: Geothermal Resources Council and National Renewable Energy Laboratory, Pix Number 10991, http://www.nrel.gov/.

- Continuous source of power 24/7 (i.e., not intermittent like wind and solar).
- Renewable source of energy since the heat source is the earth's core and since fluids are recirculated back into the earth.
- Newer binary-cycle geothermal plants, which are described later, produce no greenhouse gas emissions and no pollution. Older geothermal fields produce about one-sixth of the carbon dioxide of a natural-gas-fueled power plant and produce only minute emissions of nitrous oxide or sulfur-bearing gasses.
- Geothermal plants are domestic sources of power and reduce dependence on foreign oil.

Disadvantages
- Geothermal power plants are economically viable only in active geothermal areas, for example, in the western United States (although geothermal heat pumps can be used in a wide variety of areas).
- Geothermal power generation involves high levels of capital investment for exploration, drilling wells, and construction of the plant.
- Some geothermal plants do produce toxic solid materials, or sludges, that require disposal in approved sites.

- Construction of a geothermal plant can adversely affect land stability in the surrounding region and seismic activity can occur because of well drilling. Land subsidence can become a problem as older wells begin to cool down.
- Heat sources for geothermal plants can be depleted if they are not carefully managed. At the Geysers geothermal site in California, operators have had to retire at least half a dozen generating plants, even though most of the fields were developed as recently as the 1970s and 1980s.

GEOTHERMAL RESOURCES

Under the earth's crust is a layer of hot and molten rock called *magma*. Heat is continuously produced there, mostly from stored heat, friction, and the decay of naturally radioactive elements such as uranium and potassium. The amount of heat within 33,000 feet of the earth's surface contains 50,000 times more energy than all of the oil and natural gas resources in the world.[2]

The areas in the world with the highest underground temperatures are regions with active volcanoes or geologically young (under 1 million years) volcanic events. These "hot spots" occur at tectonic plate boundaries or where the earth's crust is thin enough to let the heat through. The Pacific Rim, with its many active volcanoes, has many hot spots, along with Alaska, Hawaii, and much of the western United States. These regions are also seismically active with earthquakes and magma movement, which breaks up rock structures and allows water to circulate. As the water rises to the surface, natural hot springs and geysers occur. The water coming from these natural occurrences can have temperatures above 430 degrees Fahrenheit.

The Geothermal Resource map of the United States, shown in Figure 8.2, illustrates the "hot spots" in the United States that make the best areas for geothermal power. The best U.S. geothermal resources are west of the Mississippi River, but the map shows there are also some attractive geothermal resources in West Virginia, Pennsylvania, in a strip of land near the Atlantic seaboard from Virginia to North Carolina, and in the south around Louisiana and east Texas. Figure 8.3 shows a map of the world's geological hot spots where geothermal energy tends to be the best. There is a good interactive map of the world's main geothermal locations at the Geothermal Education Office Web site (geothermal.marin.org).[3]

A 2006 report on geothermal energy by the Massachusetts Institute of Technology (MIT) found that *enhanced geothermal systems* (EGS) could be used to affordably produce at least 100 gigawatts of electricity in the

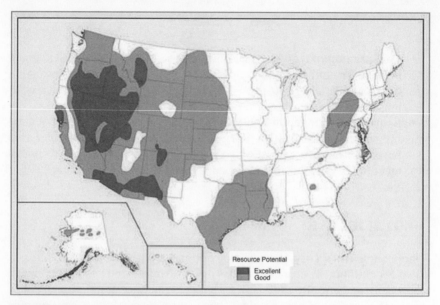

FIGURE 8.2 U.S. Geothermal Resource Map
Source: Union of Concerned Scientists, "Geothermal Resource," http://www.ucsusa
.org/assets/images/renewable_energy/GeothermalMap-Big.jpg. See also U.S. Department of Energy, Office of Energy Efficiency and Renewable Energy, "U.S. Geothermal Resource Map," *Geothermal Technologies Program,* http://www1.eere.energy
.gov/geothermal/geomap.html.

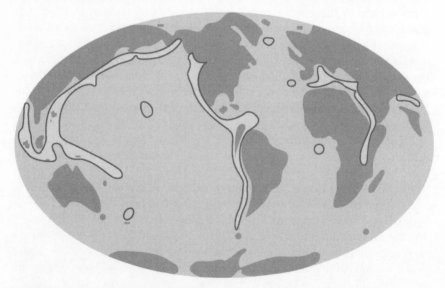

FIGURE 8.3 Global Geothermal Hot Spots
Source: Chevron Corp, "Geothermal Energy," *2005 Corporate Responsibility Report*
Web, http://chevron.com/GlobalIssues/CorporateResponsibility/2005/priorities_
progress_plans/climate_change/supplemental/geothermal_energy.asp.

United States by the year 2050, which would be enough electricity to power 75 million homes.[4] The MIT report estimated there is enough energy in hard rocks 10 kilometers below the United States to supply all of the world's current energy needs for 30,000 years. Enhanced geothermal systems involve drilling down at least 10 kilometers into the ground. Drilling down 10 kilometers is routine today for the oil industry but is more of a challenge for the geothermal industry because the holes need to be larger to extract more steam for energy. At a typical EGS site, two holes are drilled and the rock between them at the bottom of the holes is broken up. Water is then pumped down one hole and steam comes up from the other.

THE EXTRACTION OF GEOTHERMAL ENERGY

The most common way of extracting energy from geothermal sources is to tap into naturally occurring *hydrothermal convection* systems where cooler water seeps into the earth's crust and is heated up before rising to the surface. Geothermal power plants drill holes into this heated rock to capture this naturally created steam and then use the steam to drive a traditional turbine/generator system to create electricity. Geothermal fluid temperatures should be at least 300 degrees Fahrenheit, although geothermal plants are operating on fluid temperatures as low as 210 degrees Fahrenheit. This book's companion Web site at www. ProfitingFromCleanEnergy.com has a link to a video providing a tour and explanation of a geothermal plant.

There are three main designs for geothermal power plants: dry steam, flash, and binary cycle. The ideal type of system for any particular site depends on temperature, depth, and the quality of the water and steam in the area. All three systems take hot water and steam from the ground, use the steam to generate electricity, and then return the warm water into the ground to prolong the life of the heat source.

Dry steam. The dry steam power plant uses hot steam taken directly from the geothermal reservoir (usually above 455 degrees Fahrenheit) to directly run a turbine that powers a generator. This is the oldest type of power plant and is still in use today. See Figure 8.4.

Flash steam. The flash steam power plant uses hot water (above 360 degrees Fahrenheit) from geothermal reservoirs. As the water is pumped from the reservoir to the power plant, the drop in pressure causes the water to vaporize into steam and it runs the turbine that powers the generator. Any water not flashed into steam is pumped back into the reservoir for reuse. See Figure 8.5.

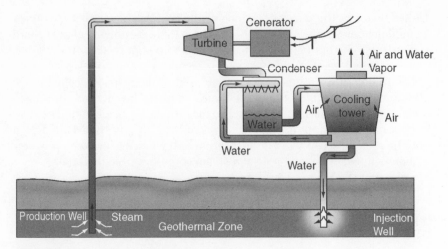

FIGURE 8.4 Dry Steam Geothermal Plant
Source: U.S. Department of Energy, Idaho National Laboratory, "Geothermal Energy:
What Is Geothermal Energy?" http://geothermal.id.doe.gov/what-is.shtml.

Binary cycle. The binary cycle power plant uses water that is cooler than
that of a flash steam power plant. The hot water from the geothermal reservoir is passed through a heat exchanger that transfers heat
to a separate pipe containing a fluid with a much lower boiling point.
These fluids (usually Iso-butane or Iso-pentane) are vaporized to run a
turbine that powers a generator. The main advantage of binary-cycle

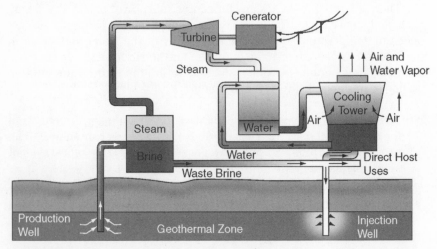

FIGURE 8.5 Flash Steam Geothermal Power Plant
Source: U.S. Department of Energy, Idaho National Laboratory, "Geothermal Energy:
What Is Geothermal Energy?" http://geothermal.id.doe.gov/what-is.shtml.

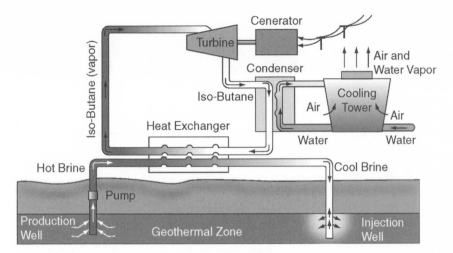

FIGURE 8.6 Binary Cycle Geothermal Power Plant
Source: U.S. Department of Energy, Idaho National Laboratory, "Geothermal Energy: What Is Geothermal Energy?" http://geothermal.id.doe.gov/what-is.shtml.

power plants is their low cost and increased efficiency since these plants do not emit any excess gas and are able to utilize lower temperature geothermal reservoirs, which are the most common. Most new geothermal power plants today are the binary cycle type. See Figure 8.6.

GEOTHERMAL POWER PLANT SYSTEMS UNDER DEVELOPMENT

There are three other advanced geothermal power plant systems that are under development, but are not yet commercially feasible: Hot dry rock, Kalina system, and the Rankine cycle system.

- *Hot dry rock system.* Geothermal heat occurs everywhere under the earth's surface, but the conditions that make water circulate to the surface happen in less than 10 percent of the earth's land area. A way to capture this energy is the hot dry rock system. This procedure produces electricity from hot dry rock by breaking up the hot rock by pumping high-pressured water through the rocks. Water is then pumped from the surface down through the broken hot rocks. After the water is heated, it is brought back to the surface to run a turbine that powers an electrical generator or provides heat. Research applications of this technology are being pursued by many countries, including the United States, to make hot dry rock technology commercially feasible.

- *Kalina system.* The Kalina system uses an ammonia-water fluid mix that claims higher efficiency. A small demonstration power plant using the Kalina system is in operation as part of Iceland's Husavik GeoHeat Project.[5] This system is not yet commercially viable.
- *Rankine Cycle.* The Rankine Cycle System seeks to create geothermal energy from cooler geothermal reservoirs to run a turbine and generator. The U.S. Department of Energy is using the Rankine Cycle system technology to run a remote geothermal power system at the Chena Hot Springs in Alaska. This is a demonstration project and is not yet commercially feasible.

GEOTHERMAL HEAT PUMPS

Geothermal heat pumps (GHP's) are simple pumps that take advantage of the relatively constant temperature of the earth's interior and use it as a source of both heat and cooling. In the summer, the ground is cooler than the air and a geothermal pump can be used for cooling. In the winter, the ground is warmer than the air and the geothermal pump can be used for heating. A simple water pump and underground pipe system operate to circulate the fluids from the surface to the ground in a continuous cycle.

Geothermal pumps can be used anywhere on the planet and are used most often in residential settings. In regions with temperature extremes, such as the northern United States in the winter and the southern United States in the summer, geothermal heat pumps are the most energy efficient and environmentally clean heating and cooling systems available. A study by the U.S. Environmental Protection Agency found that geothermal heat pumps are 72 percent more efficient than standard electrical heating and air conditioning systems.[6] The U.S. Department of Energy found that geothermal heat pumps could save a typical homeowner hundreds of dollars a year in energy costs, with the system paying for itself in 2 to 10 years depending on a variety of factors.[7]

The advantages of geothermal heat pumps include attractive economics compared to natural gas or electrical heating/cooling, and clean operation with no waste products. Drawbacks include high up-front costs, the need for space to install the pipelines in the ground, and the fact that the system only works well when temperature differences between the ground and the air are large. Geothermal heat pumps are particularly economical in rural areas that do not have access to natural gas pipelines and must use propane or electricity for heating and cooling. Geothermal heat pumps are most easily installed when a building is being constructed since the underground pipe system can be installed at the same time as the foundation is being dug.

ECONOMICS OF GEOTHERMAL POWER

Geothermal power plants are currently generating electricity in over 24 countries worldwide with a total output of about 8.9 gigawatts (which is enough electricity to power about 6.7 million homes).[8] The United States is the world's largest geothermal energy producer with output of about 2.8 gigawatts. However, on a percentage basis, Iceland in 2006 produced 26.5 percent of its electricity from geothermal sources compared to just 0.36 percent for the United States.[9]

Geothermal energy is a capital-intensive technology that is characterized by high costs for exploration, drilling wells, and plant installation, but low costs for operation and maintenance. The initial cost for constructing a geothermal power plant is about $2,500 per installed kilowatt, which is higher than a comparably sized natural gas plant, according to the U.S. Department of Energy.[10] However, a natural gas plant has a high operations cost since it must buy natural gas on an ongoing basis. Geothermal power plants are already competitive with fossil fuel plants and will become even cheaper on a relative basis if CO_2 emissions costs are eventually added to fossil fuel plants.

At current market prices, new projects for natural gas power plants cost 8 to 9 cents per kilowatt-hour, compared to just 4.5 to 7.5 cents per kilowatt-hour for a new geothermal power plant.[11] In fact, analysis by the U.S. Energy Information Administration places geothermal energy at a lower levelized cost (i.e., total facility costs including construction cost, operation costs, and fuel costs, divided by the estimated lifetime electricity output) than new facilities for natural gas combined-cycle, wind, open-loop biomass, nuclear, solar thermal, or solar photovoltaic energy.[12]

It is important to note that geothermal electricity generation costs are stable and will show little increase over time because of the low operating costs and the fact that the fuel source is free and renewable. The cost of electricity powered by natural gas power plants, by contrast, can rise sharply if natural gas prices rise.

The cost of building a new geothermal power plant depends on a variety of factors, including (1) the temperature of the heat resources (higher temperature, lower costs); (2) the chemistry of the geothermal water that comes to the surface (high scaling or corrosive properties increase costs); (3) the depth and permeability of the well being drilled (a shallow well with a porous rock formations would be cheaper to build); and (4) labor and construction costs in the local area. Geothermal plants that use higher temperature resources can cost 25 percent less than a plant that uses lower temperature resources. In a typical binary-cycle geothermal plant (which is the most common plant being built today), the equipment can cost 10 percent less if the geothermal resource temperature is higher at 300 degrees versus 250 degrees Fahrenheit.[13] Another cost for geothermal power is running transmission lines from the plant to the grid since most geothermal plants are located in remote areas, although sometimes the local utility will bear the costs of transmission.

Most geothermal power plants use Power Purchase Agreements (PPAs) to sell power on a long-term contract to the local utility, thus giving the geothermal power plant operator a guaranteed source of stable revenue. A geothermal power plant operator can enter a power purchase agreement with the local utility before the geothermal plant is even built, thus allowing the operator to obtain financing based on the collateral of the power purchase agreement, which represents a virtually guaranteed source of revenue.

THE FUTURE OF GEOTHERMAL ENERGY

Geothermal energy has the potential to play a major role in satisfying new electricity demand worldwide and in replacing aging fossil fuel facilities. Geothermal is one of the few renewable energy technologies that can supply continuous base load power. The cost of geothermal power has dropped sharply by 50 percent from costs back in the 1980s, and new geothermal facilities can now produce electricity for between 4.5 and 7.5 cents per kilowatt-hour.[14]

The U.S. Geological Survey estimates that the geothermal resource base in the United States is between 95 to 150 gigawatts, of which 22 gigawatts has been identified as suitable for electric power generation (22 gigawatts is enough electricity to power 16.5 million homes).[15] As of today, only a small part of this resource is currently utilized, with an installed capacity of 2.8 gigawatts. However, geothermal development is likely to develop fairly rapidly due to the low costs and utilities' need for clean power to satisfy renewable energy mandates. Over the next decade, new geothermal projects are expected to cause U.S. capacity to more than triple to 8 to 15 gigawatts.[16] In addition to electric power generation, which is primarily focused in the western United States, there is a bright future for the residential and commercial use of geothermal pumps as a heating and cooling source for homes and businesses everywhere.

Major Players in the Geothermal Energy Market

- *Calpine Corporation* (Pink Sheets: CPNLQ). Calpine Corporation (www.calpine.com) is the world's largest producer of geothermal power and operates approximately 50 percent of the geothermal plant capacity in the United States. Calpine is a large, unregulated wholesale power company that had 25 gigawatts of electricity generating capacity as of December 31, 2006, and produced $6.7 billion in revenue in 2006. Calpine was still operating under bankruptcy protection as of mid-2007 (which is why the company is quoted on the Pink Sheets). Calpine filed for Chapter 11 bankruptcy protection in December 2005 due to heavy losses tied to a high debt load, the overbuilding of merchant power assets in some areas in the 1990s, and volatile natural gas prices (which caused losses at its natural gas power plants).

  Calpine owns and operates 19 of the 21 geothermal power plants in the "Geysers" area of California with generating capacity of 750 megawatts of electricity, which is enough to power about 560,000 homes. The Geysers, comprising 30 square miles along the Sonoma and Lake County borders in California, is the largest complex of geothermal power plants in the world. The Geysers are a "dry steam field," as opposed to most other geothermal reservoirs, which are liquid-dominated and recharge naturally. No water flows naturally in the Geysers geothermal system. The Geysers facility therefore pumps 11 million gallons of treated wastewater daily from nearby Santa Rosa, California for injection into the Geysers geothermal system, thereby increasing its sustainability. The Geysers have produced electricity for 47 years and geothermal facilities at the Geysers are expected to be economically profitable for at least several more decades. Calpine is currently developing new geothermal projects in northern California near the California-Oregon border.
- *Ormat Technologies Inc.* (NYSE: ORA). Ormat Technologies (www.ormat.com) operates approximately 15 percent of geothermal power plant capacity in the United States. In addition, its Ormat Energy Converter (OEC) geothermal system is patented and licensed for commercial use in 71 countries around the world. Ormat's OEC technology supplies over 800 megawatts of geothermal power, which enables geothermal developers to use a wide range of geothermal resources, from low temperature geothermal water to high-pressure steam.

In the United States, Ormat operates the geothermal facility at Puna, Hawaii, that supplies the city with 25 percent of its electrical needs. Ormat owns several facilities in Nevada and California and 50 percent of the Mammoth Pacific geothermal plant in California. In addition to its existing projects, Ormat has signed two power purchase agreements with the Southern California Public Power Authority for the purchase of electrical power from its geothermal projects at the Ormesa and Heber geothermal facilities. In May 2007, Ormat signed a 20-year power purchase agreement with the Nevada Power Company, a unit of Sierra Pacific Resources, to construct a geothermal power plant in northern Nevada and resell 30 megawatts of power to Sierra Pacific Resources. Ormat currently has four new geothermal projects under construction in Nevada, four in California, one in Hawaii, one in Kenya, and one in Guatemala.

- *Caithness Energy, LLC* (privately held). Caithness Energy (caithnessenergy.com) operates approximately 13 percent of geothermal power plant capacity in the United States with over 360 megawatts of geothermal projects located in California and Nevada. It is a privately-held company that specializes in power generation.

- *CalEnergy Generation* (privately held). CalEnergy Generation (calenergy.com) operates approximately 11 percent of geothermal power plant capacity in the United States. It was founded in 1971 to provide consulting and developmental services for geothermal power production facilities in North America. In the 1980s and 1990s it developed its own projects and acquired the assets of several U.S. geothermal companies. It now operates ten geothermal power plants near the Salton Sea in southern California with a combined 340 megawatts of generating capacity. It is currently developing new projects in the Salton Sea geothermal area with a 215-megawatt facility under construction and has 200 megawatts of other projects under development. In addition to its U.S. projects, CalEnergy owns three geothermal facilities in the Philippines with combined capacity of 490 megawatts.

- *Northern California Power Agency* (municipal entity). Northern California Power Agency (www.ncpa.com) operates approximately 8 percent of geothermal capacity in the United States. It was established in 1968 as a California Joint Action Agency with membership open to municipalities, rural electric cooperatives, irrigation districts, and other publicly owned entities interested in the purchase, aggregation, scheduling and management of electricity. NCPA operates two geothermal power plants of 110 megawatts each at the Geysers geothermal field in California.

- *Enel SpA* (NYSE: EN). Enel (www.enel.it) is a worldwide leader in geothermal power generation with geothermal plants in Italy, Canada,

United States, South America, Spain and Slovakia. Enel operates a small percentage of geothermal power plant capacity in the United States. With the acquisition in 2007 of AMP Resources, LLC, Enel is currently working on developing additional geothermal projects throughout the world. Enel is a large electricity operator based in Italy with 58,000 employees, 34 billion euros of 2006 revenues, and a $66 billion market cap.

- *U.S. Geothermal* (OTCBB: UGTH)—U.S. Geothermal (www. usgeothermal.com) is a small renewable energy development company that is in the process of constructing a geothermal plant at Raft River, Idaho and developing Neal Hot Springs in eastern Oregon. U.S. Geothermal has signed a power sales contract for one 10-megawatt power plant with the Idaho Power Company and is currently in negotiations for additional output with Idaho Power Company and other customers. U.S. Geothermal has secured transmission capacity for up to 36 megawatts with the Bonneville Power Association.
- *Polaris Geothermal* (Toronto: GEO CN). Polaris Geothermal (www.polarisgeothermal.com) began trading on the Toronto Stock Exchange in January of 2007. The company was established as a combination of Polaris Geothermal and Iriana Resources Corporation. In 2006, Polaris acquired an 87.6 percent controlling stake in a Panamanian company, which through its wholly owned Nicaraguan subsidiary, San Jacinto Power S.A., controls the San Jacinto-Tizate geothermal fields in Nicaragua. Polaris is developing a 75-megawatt geothermal power project in Nicaragua.
- *Nevada Geothermal Power* (OTCBB: NGLPF). Nevada Geothermal Power (www.continentalridge.com) is a Canadian-based company that develops geothermal power for energy projects in Nevada. It has a 20-year power purchase agreement with Nevada Power and Light for up to 35 megawatts of geothermal power and has plans to develop an initial 30-megawatt geothermal power plant in Blue Mountain, Nevada.

CHAPTER 9

Cleaner Utilities

Teaching an Old Dog New Tricks

E lectricity power plants using fossil fuels produce about one-third of the world's total emissions of CO_2, according to the International Energy Agency.[1] Those fossil fuel power plants and utilities also spew a large amount of pollution into the world's atmosphere, which in turn produces acid rain. The problems caused by fossil fuel power plants have been well documented, but the real problem is what to do about them, particularly since the world needs a huge amount of new electricity generating capacity in coming decades.

Power companies, left to their own devices, will typically choose the cheapest way to generate electricity regardless of environmental impact because the impact is not a cost to their bottom line. Instead, it is an "external cost" borne by society at large. The CO_2 cap-and-trade system is designed to address this problem by capping CO_2 emissions and by putting a price on the CO_2 emissions that exceed the cap. Another approach is to put a so-called "carbon tax" on CO_2 emissions. With either method, placing a price on CO_2 emissions increases the cost of using fossil fuels by including the environmental costs, thus placing renewable energy on a more equal footing with fossil fuels.

While changing the economics of fossil fuel usage is part of the solution, many national and state governments are not relying solely on this tactic. Instead, a large number of countries and states have imposed "Renewable Portfolio Standards" on utilities. These standards require a utility to generate or buy a certain amount of renewable electricity based on a percentage of its total electricity output. As discussed in Chapter 3, there are a large number of states in the United States that have already imposed renewable electricity targets or standards, although the U.S. federal government had yet to take that step as of mid 2007. Renewable energy mandates in the U.S. and elsewhere in the world, along with feed-in tariffs, have had a big impact on forcing utilities to buy into clean energy.

GREEN POWER MARKETING PROGRAMS

Some utility companies have recognized that they have a serious public relations problem and have decided to be proactive in "going green." Utilities have also realized that some consumers are willing to pay a premium to get their electricity from renewable sources. *Green power marketing* is therefore blooming at many utilities.

To encourage electric utilities to use more clean energy, the U.S. Environmental Protection Agency (EPA) set up the Green Power Partnership program (www.epa.gov/greenpower/). In this voluntary program, the EPA works as a partner with hundreds of organizations such as local, state and federal agencies, manufacturers, retailers, and other businesses.

To become a partner, an organization agrees to encourage its local electric utility to get more of its electrical power from green power sources such as wind, solar, geothermal, biomass, or low-impact hydro. To encourage the local utility to use more green energy sources, electricity customers can sign a contract with the local utility in which the customers agree to pay more for their electricity and the utility agrees to get more of its electric power from renewable sources. The utility can either buy the renewable power from a third-party electricity generator or the utility can build its own renewable energy plant. In either case, more renewable power is added to the national grid somewhere when a customer signs up for a renewable power program. The utility cannot just pocket the money and continue to do what it did before. Furthermore, the new green power must be in addition to any federal, state or local mandates the utility may be under to use more renewable energy.

The electricity customer can benefit by becoming an environmental leader and becoming part of the solution instead of the problem. There may also be a public relations benefit for businesses that go green. The utility benefits since it gets extra revenue to cover the higher costs of renewable power and doesn't have to take a hit to its profits. The biggest benefit, however, is to the environment in that the program causes an incremental increase in the use of renewable power.

There is a similar program at the U.S. Department of Energy, the *Green Pricing Program*, for smaller users. Over 600 utilities in most of the states are participating. Under this program, smaller users, including residential customers, can pay a little extra for their electric power to buy what are called energy credits. In return, the local utility agrees to increase its use of green power, either by buying it from a third party or by building its own renewable energy plant. There is a list of state-level Green Pricing Programs at the U.S. Department of Energy Web site.[2] By purchasing the energy credit, smaller users can offset the negative impact caused by their electricity usage.

Vail Resorts provides a good example of how the Green Pricing Program works. Vail Resorts decided to be "responsible stewards of our mountain environments" and effectively buy all of its electricity from wind generation.[3] To do that, it purchased enough renewable energy credits from its local utility to equal all the electric power used at its five ski resorts, its lodging properties, all 125 of its retail locations, and its corporate headquarters. The energy credits it purchased required Vail's local utility to purchase the equivalent amount of electricity from wind-power electricity suppliers. The deal was estimated to keep about 211 million pounds of CO_2 out of the atmosphere each year. That is equivalent to taking about 18,000 cars off the road. Vail Resorts purchased nearly 152 gigawatt-hours of wind power and became the second largest corporate user of wind power in the United States. Vail Resorts used this information extensively in its ad campaigns to generate good will among customers.[4]

A good example of how a utility can encourage its smaller customers to use the Green Pricing program can be found at Florida Power and Light Company (parent company is FPL Group, NYSE: FPL), which serves more than 8.5 million customers. FPL is one the greenest utilities in the United States. The company already has over 23,000 customers signed up for its Sunshine Energy program. To participate in the program, customers add $9.75 to their electric bills each month. In return, FPL commits itself to building solar projects to supply pollution-free energy to its customers. FPL also ensures that for each month that a customer participates in the program, FPL will buy or generate 1,000 kilowatt-hours of clean power from sources such as wind, biomass, or solar. This program is one of the largest in the southeastern part of the United States.[5]

Many energy conscious electric utilities also participate in the federal government's "Energy Star" program. This program certifies that certain electrical products are "energy-efficient." The local utility then periodically gives special rebates to customers who buy those products. There is a list of such programs at the Energy Star Web site.[6] These rebates cover the purchase of Energy Star certified appliances, heating and cooling equipment, fans, electronic equipment, lighting equipment, CFL bulbs, and other items.

TABLE 9.1 Top 10 U.S. Utilities for Renewable Energy Sales (as of December 2006)

Rank	Utility	Resources Used	Sales (GWh/yr)
1	Austin Energy	Wind, landfill gas	581
2	Portland General Electric (NYSE: POR)	Existing geothermal and hydro, wind	433
3	Florida Power & Light (NYSE: FPL)	Landfill gas, biomass, wind, solar	303
4	PacifiCorp (unit of Iberdrola SA (Madrid: IBE SM))	Wind, biomass, solar	300
5	Xcel Energy (NYSE: XEL)	Wind	237
6	Basin Electric Power Cooperative	Wind	217
7	Sacramento Municipal Utility District	Wind, landfill gas, small hydro	216
8	National Grid (formerly named New England Electric System)	Biomass, wind, small hydro, solar	156
9	OG&E Electric Services	Wind	135
10	Puget Sound Energy (NYSE: PSD)	Wind, solar, biogas	132

Source: U.S. Department of Energy, Office of Energy Efficiency and Renewable Energy, "Top Ten Utility Green Power Programs," http://www.eere.energy.gov/greenpower/resources/tables/topten.shtml.

The National Renewable Energy Laboratory (NREL) monitors green power usage at U.S. power utilities. Each year the NREL issues a report on green power programs and ranks the top 10 utilities in terms of the green programs they offer. In its 2006 report, the NREL found that nationwide utility green power sales in 2006 rose sharply by 30 percent over 2005 to 3,500 gigawatt-hours.[7] The study also found that there were more than 500,000 customers participating in green energy programs in the United States in 2006, up more than 10 percent from 2005. Table 9.1 shows the top 10 U.S. utilities for green power sales in 2006, as ranked by NREL.

RENEWABLE ENERGY CERTIFICATES

As mentioned earlier, a Renewable Portfolio Standard (RPS) requires that a power utility must obtain a certain percentage of its power from clean sources, either from its own generating plants or from third party suppliers.

More than 20 states have implemented mandatory RPS programs so far. Other states have implemented voluntary programs.

An important feature of an RPS program is that each clean energy generating plant is awarded one Renewable Energy Certificate (REC) for each unit of clean energy produced, usually one megawatt. Once that amount of clean energy power has been generated and delivered, the REC may be sold to a third party. The environmental value of the REC is equal to the contribution that one megawatt of clean power makes to improve the environment. The monetary value of the certificate, however, is determined by the marketplace, that is, how much a buyer of a REC is willing to pay and how much a seller is willing to accept.

The seller of the REC is the company that generated the clean power. The buyer of the certificate is usually a company or individual that wants to offset CO_2 emissions, either voluntarily or in order to comply with a mandated renewable energy use requirement. Once the buyer purchases the REC certificate, it cannot be resold and is effectively retired. The money the seller received for the REC helps offset the cost of constructing or operating the renewable energy facility, or buying more renewable energy.

The REC program mainly comes into play among utilities that are subject to the state-level Renewable Portfolio Standards, which require a certain percentage of electricity to be derived from renewable sources. Suppose a utility that is subject to an RPS is not in a position to construct a renewable power plant, either because the plant cannot physically or economically be located in its district or because the utility does not want to make the capital expenditure. That utility can simply buy REC credits from another power generator that did construct a renewable power plant somewhere in the country, thus ensuring that the renewable power was delivered into the national grid somewhere. This program helps to ensure that renewable power is being added to the national grid at the lowest possible cost, which of course is a benefit to power consumers.[8]

The REC program is monitored by Green-e, which the leading independent certification and verification company for renewable energy in the United States (see www.green-e.org).[9] Because each REC certificate carries an individual identification number, Green-e is able to track each certificate so that it is not double counted or used in an inappropriate manner. The buying and selling of RECs has become large enough that there are now brokerage companies that facilitate the purchase and sale of RECs.[10]

SOURCES OF RENEWABLE ENERGY

Utilities can increase their use of renewable electricity by building power plants that use solar, wind, or geothermal power. Those methods were discussed in previous chapters. We will discuss three other methods here: biomass, methane gas extraction, and tide/wave power.

Biomass Power Plants

Biomass power plants have been in operation for many years considering that some power plants burn wood or wood products, which is a biomass product. *Biomass* is defined as organic matter that was once a living plant or tree. Biomass power typically involves burning paper mill residue, lumber mill scrap, municipal solid waste, and other waste. In the near future, with new technology, corn stalks and wheat straw will be used. Longer-term plans are to use "energy" crops such as fast-growing trees and grasses that can be grown on land that will not support food crops. Dried animal manure, which typically contains a substantial amount of leftover plant material, can also be used as a feedstock for biomass power plants. Biomass is not a particularly clean source of power since it involves burning waste products and releases CO_2 and other pollution into the air, but it is at least cleaner than burning fossil fuels and is also a homegrown source of energy.

Although biomass power receives little attention, it is currently the largest domestic source of renewable energy in the United States. In 2003, biomass accounted for about 4 percent of total U.S. energy production, according to the Department of Energy.[11] Biomass is also a large source of power generation worldwide.

There are three major technologies for using biomass as a power generation fuel: (1) direct fired, (2) cofired, and (3) gasification. Most biomass power plants today use a direct-fired system, which means the biomass feedstock is burned in a boiler system to produce high-pressure steam that in turn drives a steam turbine to generate electricity. In a co-fired system, biomass material is combined with coal to burn in a power plant. In a gasification system, the biomass is first converted into a flammable gas using heat and steam, and the resulting biogas is burned to run the steam turbine and generator system.

Unfortunately, biomass fuel releases about as much CO_2 into the atmosphere as burning fossil fuels. There is a difference, however. Biomass feedstock generally comes from tree or plant matter that was recently alive (as opposed to coal and petroleum, which formed from organic matter millions of years ago). When that tree or plant was alive, it converted CO_2 into oxygen during its life as a tree or a plant. The CO_2 that the tree or plant absorbed during its lifetime can therefore be treated as an offset to the CO_2 that is emitted when the tree or plant material is burned. Thus, when looking at the net CO_2 situation, burning biomass is more neutral on CO_2 emissions than it might seem.

METHANE GAS EXTRACTION

There are two other technologies for converting biomass-related material into fuel that can be used to generate electrical power. One process is to capture the gas that is emitted naturally from municipal waste landfills as organic matter decomposes. Landfill gas is about 50 percent methane (CH_4) and 50 percent CO_2. The gas is extracted from the landfills using a series of wells and pipes to collect the gas and bring it to a central point where it can be processed and treated. As of December 2006, there were approximately 425 *landfill gas* (LFG) energy projects in operation in the United States. These 425 projects generate approximately 10 billion kilowatt-hours of electricity per year. The Environmental Protection Agency estimates that there are about 560 more landfills that could be developed.[12]

The second process is called anaerobic digestion. In this biochemical process, microbes starved of oxygen are used to break down animal and food industry waste into inorganic compounds. A principal product of the anaerobic digestion process is a biogas that is 60 percent to 70 percent methane (CH_4). One of the major advantages of this process is that it captures methane from animal waste that would otherwise be emitted into the air. This is especially important at large cattle and pig farms where manure disposal is becoming a serious problem due to environmental and regulatory issues. The problem is compounded by the trend toward trying to concentrate the process of raising livestock on the minimum amount of land.

With varying degrees of treatment, the methane from landfills and anaerobic digestion gas can be used as a replacement wherever natural gas is used to create electricity since methane is actually the principal component of natural gas. Methane can be burned to run an electricity generator, or can even cleaned to reach natural gas standards and placed into the natural gas distribution pipeline.[13]

It is true that burning biogas to generate electricity also generates CO_2. However, the amount of CO_2 put into the atmosphere by burning biogas in a steam boiler is far less harmful to the environment than releasing the methane. In fact, according to EarthSave, methane is responsible for nearly as much global warming as all other non-CO_2 greenhouse gases put together. Methane is 21 times more harmful as a greenhouse gas than CO_2.[14] Therefore, it is better to burn the methane to create electricity than it is to just let the methane be released into the atmosphere.

Companies that collect or produce biogas not only receive the revenue from the sale of the biogas or the generation of electricity but can also earn revenue by acquiring and selling greenhouse gas credits. An operation that prevents methane from being released into the atmosphere qualifies for greenhouse gas credits, since, as mentioned earlier, methane is

21 times worse than CO_2. This makes it more worthwhile for companies to extract methane from landfills or install anaerobic digestive plants at livestock farms.

COMPANIES OPERATING IN BIOMASS AND BIOGAS

There are a number of companies that are working in the biomass and biogas power area.

- *Covanta Holding Corp* (NYSE: CVA). Covanta's subsidiary, Covanta Energy Corporation, considers itself to be mainly a waste disposal company for municipal clients. However, Covanta receives additional revenue by operating biomass power plants that burn the municipal waste, produce electricity, and sell the electricity to the municipality, the local utility, or industrial customers. The company currently owns and operates biomass power plants in 15 states. Covanta also owns and operates 10 other renewable power plants using a variety of energy sources including water (hydroelectric), waste wood (biomass), and landfill gas (methane).
- *Environmental Power Corp.* (Amex: EPG). Environmental Power Corp. was founded in 1982 and operates renewable energy facilities. The company's subsidiary, Microgy, Inc., is a large-scale producer of methane-rich biogas from agricultural and food industry wastes using a licensed Danish biogas production process. The technology has been in use for 15 years in Europe where there are dozens of plants in operation. Here in the United States, Microgy has already developed three anaerobic digester plants, seven hydroelectric plants, two municipal waste projects, and three waste coal-fired generating facilities. The company owns and operates these facilities and earns income from either the biogas or the electricity generated. As part of its income, the company also earns greenhouse gas credits that it can sell. In 2006. the company's total revenue was $51.7 million.
- *Schmack Biogas AG* (German Xetra: SB1 GR). German-based Schmack Biogas is the world's largest biogas plant manufacturer. The company was founded in 1995 and since then has built 179 plants to generate biogas from animal and agricultural waste for a combined nominal electricity output of 45 megawatts. Recently, the company formed a subsidiary to operate its own biogas plants. The company's revenue for 2006 was €90 million, up 164 percent from 2005. In March 2007, Schmack received the "Cleantech Emerging Enterprise of the Year" award from the Cleantech Venture Network in the United States.[15]

WAVE AND TIDE POWER

Another source of renewable power involves the use of moving water, either by wave or tidal action to generate electricity. There are three main types of systems involved in wave and tidal power: tide level, tide current, and wave motion.

- *Tide level.* In locations where there is a large difference in ocean levels between low and high tide (16 feet is considered the minimum required difference), a dam with gates is used to seal off a large tidal basin. When the tide is rising the gates are opened to allow the rising tide to fill the basin. At the point of the highest tide level, the gates are closed, thus trapping the water in the basin. When the tide begins to fall, the trapped water is allowed to flow back out to the ocean through turbines that power electricity generators. A large 240-megawatt tidal dam has been in operation in France since 1966, a 100-megawatt system has been in operation in China since 1987, and a 100-megawatt system has been in operation in Canada since 1984.[16]
- *Tide current.* Tidal current systems capture energy from fast-moving tidal currents that flow in and out of harbors, or between offshore islands and the mainland. As tides rise and fall, water can flow at speeds of six to nine miles per hour through the channels. A set of turnstiles can be installed near the surface of the channel to rotate as the current flows by, thus driving generators and creating electricity. Underwater turbines can also be used to drive a generator.[17] These systems can also be placed in rivers that have strong currents. The first major tidal project in the United States is being installed in New York's East River off Manhattan Island. A privately owned company named Verdant Power is installing the system and several turbines were in place as of the end of 2006.[18]
- *Wave motion.* Wave motion is another type of energy that can be harnessed from the ocean. Wave action can generate electricity by using floating buoys or platforms that move with wave action. That movement can be converted into electricity. A Portuguese company ordered several wave energy converters in 2005. Wave energy systems have already been installed in Norway, Scotland, Japan, Australia, and Indonesia.[19] Wave motion is also being used to generate electricity for lighted navigation buoys.

While the oceans of the world contain a huge amount of energy, systems to harness that energy and convert it into power are still in the early stages of development. The capital costs for these systems are high and a large amount of additional research needs to be done to make this type of power feasible on a large scale.

The following companies are involved with using wave and tidal power to generate electricity.

- *Ocean Power Technologies* (Nasdaq: OPTT). Ocean Power Technologies went public in a $90 million IPO in May 2007. The company is using the proceeds to construct demonstration wave power stations and to continue the research and commercialization of their PowerBuoy systems (see www.oceanpowertechnologies). Ocean Power Technologies has installed a wave energy system for the U.S. Navy off the coast of Oahu, Hawaii.
- *Finavera Renewables* (Toronto: FVR CN). Finavera Renewables, based in Canada, focuses on wind and wave power (see www.finavera.com). The company is working a number of renewable energy projects. Finavera, through its subsidiary AquaEnergy Ltd in Seattle, is working on a floating buoy system that produces electricity.
- *Verdant Power* (privately held). Verdant Power (see www.verdantpower.com) has an underwater propeller system that generates electricity as water tides and currents turn the propellers. Verdant Power is the company that is installing an underwater turbine system in New York's East River near Roosevelt Island. The company is currently privately held and is being funded in part by a $15 million investment from well-known hedge fund manager Paul Tudor Jones of Tudor Investment Corp. The company may be headed for an eventual IPO.[20]

CHAPTER 10

Power Efficiency

"The Cheapest and Most Available Source of Energy Is the Energy We Waste"

"The cheapest and most available source of energy is the energy we waste."[1] This quote by U.S. Department of Energy Secretary Samuel Bodman aptly summarizes why efficiency and conservation should be the first place to look to solve the world's energy problems. To the extent that power is not used, that is power and fuel that does not need to be produced, thus saving pollution, greenhouse gas emissions and enormous capital costs.

Rising global electricity demand and the need for an improved electricity transmission infrastructure will require a major global building effort over the next several decades. The International Energy Agency estimates that investment in the generation, transmission and distribution assets required to meet electricity demand worldwide will be $10 trillion in the 30-year period from 2003 to 2033.[2]

The U.S. Energy Information Administration estimates that 292 gigawatts of new power-generating capacity will be needed in the United States by 2030 to meet the "growth in electricity demand and to replace inefficient, older generating plants that are retired."[3] For reference, that would require the equivalent of 584 new 500-megawatt power plants. In addition to new power plants, the Electric Power Research Institute estimates that another $50 to 100 billion will be required over the next 10 years just to bring the North American transmission and distribution grid up to the standards set by the Energy Policy Act of 2005.[4]

The United States certainly has enough financial resources to build the new power plants and the transmission infrastructure to meet the increased demand. However, the costs would be huge since they would include capital costs, additional electricity costs for consumers, and increased environmental costs because fossil-fuel power plants would almost surely be the primary means for generating the additional electricity. Rather than building new power plants, the more rational course is to focus on power efficiency as a way to make our existing power base go farther and thus reduce the need for new power plants.

Power efficiency programs are already delivering annual energy savings of about 1 percent of total electricity and natural gas sales and "are helping to offset the 20–50 percent of expected growth in energy demand in some areas without compromising the end users' activities and economic well-being," according to the National Action Plan for Energy Efficiency.[5]

The National Action Plan for Energy Efficiency, citing various studies, states that energy efficiency programs could (1) yield more than 20 percent savings in total electricity demand nationwide by 2025; (2) create $20 billion per year in energy bill savings; (3) create net societal benefits of more than $250 billion over the next 10 to 15 years; (4) defer the need for 20 gigawatts of power (40 new 500-megawatt power plants); and (5) reduce U.S. emissions from energy production by more than 200 million tons of CO_2, 50,000 tons of sulphur-dioxide, and 40,000 tons of nitrous-oxide annually.[6]

California provides the best example of the substantial impact that power efficiency programs can have in reducing power demand and costs. Remarkably, California's per-capita electricity consumption has been flat since 1970 at about 7,000 kilowatt-hours per person. That stable electricity consumption usage is directly attributable to the power efficiency programs that California has implemented over the past 30 years. This remarkable achievement stands in contrast to the doubling of the overall U.S. electricity consumption from about 6,000 kilowatt-hours per person in 1970 to the current level of about 12,000 kilowatt-hours per person. California, through its energy efficiency efforts, has saved an estimated 40,000 gigawatt-hours of electricity a year (which amounts to 15 percent of consumption), has reduced the state's peak demand requirements by 22 percent, and has deferred 12 gigawatts of peaking capacity over the past 30 years, according to the Electric Power Research Institute.[7]

The benefits of power efficiency, as identified by the National Action Plan for Energy Efficiency,[8] include:

- Lower energy bills, greater customer control, and greater customer satisfaction.
- Lower cost than supplying new generation from new power plants.
- Modular and quick to deploy (as opposed to building new power plants).
- Environmental benefits.
- Economic development.
- Energy security.

Power efficiency clearly has an important role in solving the United States's energy problems by reducing electricity demand, reducing the need for more U.S. fossil-fuel power plants (thus reducing pollution and greenhouse gas emissions), improving the grid transmission infrastructure, and alleviating problems such as brownouts and blackouts. In the remainder of this chapter, we will discuss three areas that are ripe for improvement in power efficiency: efficient appliances, efficient lighting, and efficient buildings. In the next chapter, we discuss how to improve efficiency at the grid level through demand-response systems and smart meters.

EFFICIENT APPLIANCES

There is huge potential for improving efficiency nationwide by requiring that manufacturers build more efficient appliances in the first place. Based on data from the Energy Information Administration, kitchen and laundry appliances by themselves account for about one-third of all household electricity usage.[9] Appliances are a fertile area for power conservation.

The federal government has been very active in pushing manufacturers to produce appliances that are more energy efficient. In 1992, the U.S. Environmental Protection Agency (EPA) and the U.S. Department of Energy (DOE) set up "Energy Star," a voluntary labeling program designed to identify and promote energy-efficient products in order to reduce electricity usage, save money, and reduce greenhouse gas emissions.[10]

Through its partnership with more than 9,000 private and public organizations, Energy Star provides technical information to the public to help them choose energy-efficient appliances. Energy Star provides recommendations for products in over 50 categories for homes and businesses. In the home appliance category, for example, there are recommendations for refrigerators, freezers, dishwashers, clothes washers, and room air conditioners.

When buying a new appliance, or even a light bulb, it is important to look for the Energy Star label because it identifies an energy efficient product. Energy Star estimates that with their help, consumers saved enough energy in 2006 to avoid greenhouse gas emissions equivalent to 25 million cars and at the same time saved $14 billion on their utility bills.[11] Furthermore, the Energy Star label may also mean that the manufacturer will provide the consumer with a rebate for buying the product, and that generates additional savings for the consumer.[12] When an investor is considering an appliance manufacturer as a stock investment, it would be wise to see if the company's appliances are Energy Star compliant since those products are likely to grow in popularity as electricity prices rise and as the public becomes more conscious of the importance of saving electricity as a contribution to lower greenhouse gas emissions.

EFFICIENT LIGHTING

Incandescent Bulbs

Efficient lighting is a very important area for capturing power savings since 22 percent of all the electricity used in the United States is for lighting.[13] About 42 percent of lighting in the United States involves incandescent bulbs, which means that incandescent bulbs consume about 9 percent of all electricity used in the United States.

Unfortunately, the incandescent bulb is a very inefficient source of light because about 90 percent of the electricity used by the bulb is radiated away as heat rather than as light. The incandescent bulb has been around since Thomas Edison invented the first practical bulb back in 1879. Since then, the fundamental design of the incandescent bulb has not changed. An incandescent bulb creates light by passing an electrical current through a thin filament mounted inside an evacuated glass globe. The electricity causes the filament to heat up so that it glows and produces light. The sealed globe prevents oxygen from reaching the hot filament because that would destroy the filament.

Halogen Bulbs

The halogen light bulb was a step forward, but it is still an incandescent bulb. In a halogen bulb, the filament is also sealed inside a globe, but the globe is filled with a halogen gas such as iodine or bromine. This makes the halogen bulb a little more efficient than a regular incandescent bulb and therefore a little cheaper to operate. In addition, a halogen bulb lasts longer than a regular incandescent bulb. However, a major disadvantage of a halogen bulb is that it operates at a very high temperature and special precautions are therefore necessary to prevent a fire, such as a protective grille or a glass or metal housing.

Compact Fluorescent Bulbs

A more recent improvement in lighting is the compact fluorescent bulb, which is a twist on the long, tubular-shaped fluorescent bulbs that have been around for years. Fluorescent bulbs have two major advantages: longer life and significantly lower electricity consumption. Up until the

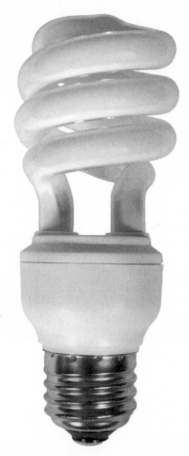

FIGURE 10.1   Compact Fluorescent Lamp (CFL)
Photo Credit: Rob Banks.

1980s, fluorescent bulbs were in the shape of long tubes. These bulbs are mainly used in commercial and industrial locations because many people consider the light to be too harsh for personal or home use and because the fixtures are not particularly attractive. Over the years, however, the color of fluorescent light has been changed to make it softer and more like the color of the incandescent bulb. Other improvements were the elimination of the annoying flicker of the bulbs and their slow start.

In the 1990s the *compact fluorescent lamp* (CFL) was introduced to the market (see Figure 10.1). In addition to its new globular shape, manufacturers were able to improve the color of the light to make it even softer and thus more appealing for home use. They were also able to eliminate or reduce the problem of slow start. They were also able to reduce the size of the bulbs so they would fit into most existing light fixtures. Furthermore, the CFL bulb was made with either a screw or bayonet fitting so it could be used as a direct replacement for an incandescent bulb in most existing light fixtures. As a result of the improvements, the new CFL type bulb became far more acceptable as a replacement for the incandescent bulb.

Still, it is taking a long time for CFLs to gain wide acceptance by the general public. When they were first introduced, the price of a CFL was in the $15 to $20 range. Furthermore, the early bulbs had many of the old fluorescent problems like flicker and harsh light. Since then, however, the prices have dropped into the $5 to $10 range and even lower at some of the big retailers. Wal-Mart recently announced a huge campaign to get CFLs out into widespread public use. GE tripled its manufacturing capacity in 2005 and then tripled it again in 2006.[14]

The compact fluorescent bulb has two very important advantages over the incandescent bulb. One is that it uses much less electricity. A CFL uses only about 20 percent to 25 percent of the electricity consumed by an equivalent incandescent bulb. For example, a CFL bulb that provides about as much light as a regular 150-watt incandescent bulb (i.e., about 2,700 lumens) uses only 42 watts of electricity instead of 150 watts. That is a 72 percent reduction in energy consumption for the same light output.

The second big advantage of the compact fluorescent bulb is that it has a life span of between 8,000 and 15,000 hours of use. That is far longer than the life span of a typical incandescent bulb, which is between 750 and 1,000 hours. With normal usage, that gives a CFL bulb a life of about 7 to 8 years versus a life span of less than a year for an incandescent bulb. As a result, the total cost of ownership for a CFL is dramatically lower.

There are a few disadvantages of CFL bulbs but they are not serious enough to limit their use. Disadvantages of a CFL bulb include difficulty in operating at low temperatures, possible interference with electronic devices if it is place too close, a short warm-up period to get to full brightness, and incompatibility with some dimmer or three-way switches. Some of these disadvantages will be reduced or eliminated with further research and development.

Changing to CFLs can have a significant impact on electricity usage. According to the U.S. government's Energy Star program, if every American home replaced just one incandescent light bulb with a CFL, America could save enough total energy to light more than 3 million homes for a full year, saving more than $600 million in annual energy costs and preventing greenhouse gases equivalent to the emissions of 800,000 cars.[15]

The advantages of CFL bulbs over incandescent bulbs have become so obvious, both for the consumer and for national electricity conservation, that a number of countries and other governmental jurisdictions around the world are banning the use of incandescent bulbs and are effectively mandating the use of CFL bulbs. In early 2007, for example, Australia announced plans to ban incandescent bulbs by the year 2010 and replace them with fluorescent bulbs.[16] Ontario, Canada, in April 2007 announced a plan to ban inefficient light bulbs (i.e., incandescent bulbs) by 2012. The government said that banning inefficient lighting would reduce greenhouse emissions by the equivalent of removing 250,000 cars from the road.[17] California is also considering such a ban. The movement to ban incandescent bulbs and move to CFL's is likely to accelerate in coming years.

The world's three biggest light bulb manufacturers are all big players in CFLs: General Electric (NYSE: GE), Philips Electronics (NYSE: PHG), and Sylvania through its Siemens parent (NYSE: SI). Unfortunately, there are no smaller publicly traded companies that can be considered as stock plays on CFLs.

Light Emitting Diode (LED)

The light emitting diode (LED) is another new form of lighting. An LED involves applying electricity to a solid piece of semiconductor material in order to produce light. Often the broad area of LED technology is referred to as "solid-state lighting."

LED technology was first demonstrated in the early 1900s when Henry Round of Marconi Laboratories discovered that semiconductor diodes could produce light. At that time, however, there was no practical use for that discovery. Since then, numerous scientists have experimented with how to make that phenomenon useful. In the late 1950s, working at Texas Instruments, two men, Dr. Robert Biard and Gary E. Pittmann, invented a gallium arsenide phosphide semiconductor diode that glowed red when an electrical current was applied. They received a patent for the device in 1961. Unfortunately, since the red light was actually infrared, it was invisible to the human eye. The following year in 1962 Nick Holonyak Jr., of General Electric, invented the first visible red LED.[18]

In the early days, LEDs could emit only red, yellow, or green light. Then a blue LED was developed and it became possible to create white light by combining red, green, and blue LEDs. Later in 1993, a Japanese inventor by the name Shuji Nakamura developed a blue indium gallium chip that was able to emit white light from a single LED.[19]

A light emitting diode is made of a semiconductor material, typically aluminum-gallium-arsenide, which has the ability to conduct an electrical current. The material can be molded into different shapes and sizes, but an LED is generally no larger than about one-quarter inch in diameter, about the size of the eraser on a pencil.

The material is called a *semiconductor* because it is a poor conductor of electricity in its pure form. To make it a better conductor, impurities are added to create "holes" through which the electricity can flow. This process is called *doping*. When electricity then flows through the material, light is given off. The device is called a *diode* because it made of two layers of material that force the electricity to flow in one direction from one layer to the other.

LEDs at first could produce only very low levels of light, which meant they could be used only for things like indicator lamps in laboratory and electronic test equipment. Later they were used in TVs, radios, telephones, and calculators. As development continued, the LEDs became bright enough to be used in relatively low-level illumination devices like traffic signals, exit signs, and other specialty purposes. LEDs are now finding applications in automobiles for taillights and in airplanes for interior lighting. Since LEDs are small, to make a larger light source, it is necessary to assemble a number of LEDs into an array.

LEDs are not yet broadly used for general lighting purposes because they generally cannot compete with more traditional light sources like incandescent or fluorescent bulbs on the basis of either performance or cost. More research is needed to improve the performance and decrease the cost of LEDs. The Department of Energy says that while recent research has increased the output of LEDs to produce as much light as 50 to 150 watt incandescent bulbs, the cost of the LED light itself is much higher. For comparison, the cost of an LED light in 2006 was about $50 for a 1,000 lumen bulb (about the illumination of an incandescent 75 watt bulb), while the cost of an incandescent bulb of the same illumination was about $1.

There are, however, several big advantages to using LEDs in many applications. One big advantage is that they use much less electrical power than conventional incandescent bulbs. The usual measure of a bulb's efficiency is the number of lumens (the amount of light) emitted by the bulb for each watt of electricity used. That measure is usually quoted as the number of lumens per watt (lpw). For comparison, the Department of Energy says that an incandescent bulb produces 12 to 15 lpw, whereas the newer LEDs are producing almost 50 lpw. That makes an LED three to four times more efficient than an incandescent bulb.

Another big advantage of an LED is that it lasts much longer than an incandescent bulb. While some manufacturers may make claims of as many as 50,000 to 100,000 hours of use, there is still no industry standard defining the actual life of an LED. However, the Department of Energy estimates that the practical useful life of an LED is at least 35,000 hours. That is about four years of constant use. LEDs do not actually burn out but instead just become dimmer. The 35,000-hour lifetime estimate assumes that the bulb is no longer useful after it has degraded to about 70 percent of its original output.

An LED's long life makes it a good candidate to use when an incandescent bulb would be difficult or expensive to replace. For example, an LED in a traffic light will last about four years whereas an incandescent bulb will last only a matter of months. Using an LED in a traffic light produces big savings on the costs of replacing traffic light bulbs and reducing traffic congestion. An LED in a traffic signal also improves safety since an LED does not ever really burn out. In addition, there is a big savings in electricity consumption. Furthermore, the lower energy consumption of LEDs makes it possible to use solar power for traffic signals in remote locations, thus saving the cost of running a power line to the signal. All these factors justify paying a higher price for an LED light.

Another advantage of an LED is that it can often appear much brighter than an incandescent bulb. That is because an incandescent bulb puts out light in all directions whereas an LED focuses the light more in one direction. This tends to make an LED appear brighter overall when viewed from one direction. This makes an LED ideal for traffic lights, focused reading lights, and other directional light applications.

It is also possible to combine a number of LEDs into various size panels. For example, there are big LED screens or signs in use in Las Vegas, at the Razorback Stadium at the University of Arkansas, and in Chicago's new Millennium Park. In addition, Samsung has introduced a 56-inch TV screen that uses LEDs and is said to rival a plasma TV in terms of contrast and brightness.

A new LED area that is generating a lot of excitement is the development of the *organic LED* (OLED). An OLED is an LED that is constructed on a base made of organic materials rather than on a base made of liquid crystals. This new technology will make it possible to have a television screen that is as thin as a piece of heavy-weight paper. There are even TV screens being developed using OLED technology that will roll up like a projector screen. In other research, whole room ceilings may be turned into one huge overall light source.[20] Applied Materials (Nasdaq: AMAT), a specialist in working with thin film semiconductor materials, is currently involved with Philips (NYSE: PHG) in an organic LED development project.

To encourage the R&D in the lighting area, the U.S. Department of Energy has a program called *solid state lighting* (SSL), which focuses on ensuring the development of energy-efficient solid state lighting technologies (see www.netl.doe.gov/ssl/). The goal of the program is "to ensure that solid state lighting reaches its full energy savings potential, significantly reducing building energy use and costs, and contributing to our nation's energy security."

The following companies are involved in the LED light industry.

- *Philips Electronics NV* (NYSE: PHG). Philips Electronics is currently the world's largest LED manufacturer thanks to its acquisition of Lumileds (www.lumileds.com) in 2005. In June 2007, Philips extended its lead by buying Color Kinetics (formerly, Nasdaq: CLRK) for €592 million in cash. Color Kinetics was an attractive acquisition target because of its heavy R&D work in LED lighting and its patent and licensing portfolio.
- *Cree, Inc* (Nasdaq: CREE). Cree produces semiconductor materials and devices based on silicon carbide, gallium nitride and related compounds. The company focuses on the LED market and provides colored LEDs for use in gaming equipment, consumer products, and other electronic equipment. The majority of the company's sales come from its LED chips that are sold to other manufacturers to assemble into LED packages using industry standard processes. The company also provides high-power products including power switching, radio frequency and microwave devices. The company's LED products produced 81 percent of their total revenue of $423 million in fiscal 2006.
- *Nexxus Lighting, Inc.* (Nasdaq: NEXS). Nexxus Lighting, formerly Super Vision International, Inc., is now concentrating on the emerging market for advanced lighting systems and controls using LED technology. Until the strategic shift, the company derived much of its revenue from commercial architectural and swimming pool lighting products and from fiber optic lighting cables. The company says that it will now focus on designing and manufacturing a new line of LED light bulbs to replace conventional incandescent and halogen light bulbs for commercial white light applications. The company began operation in 1993 and in 2006 had revenue of $11.0 million.

Solar Lighting

Many buildings are designed to allow sunlight to enter the building through windows and skylights to help light the building and thereby reduce the number of lighting fixtures that are needed. However, new technology, Hybrid Solar Lighting (HSL), is providing a much more sophisticated way of directing sunlight into a building.[21] This technology is currently in the research stage and has yet to be commercialized.

In a Hybrid Solar Lighting system, sunlight collectors are placed on the roof of a building so that visible sunlight is directed into flexible optical cables that are strung into the building and connected to special light fixtures. The light fixtures can contain a regular electric bulb as well that can automatically adjust its output up or down depending on how much solar light is being delivered, thus maintaining a constant amount of overall light from the fixture. The Hybrid Solar Lighting system can provide substantial electricity savings by substituting sunlight for electric bulbs.

In addition to providing light, the Hybrid Solar Lighting system can also direct infrared light from the sun into a concentrating thermo-photovoltaic cell that converts infrared radiation directly into electricity. The electricity can then be fed into the building's electricity system to be used wherever it is needed.

There is a second, completely different application for Hybrid Solar Lighting Systems that involves the operation of a photobioreactor, the purpose of which is to absorb CO_2 being emitted from a power plant or other industrial plant. This will be covered in the Chapter 16, which discusses cleaner coal.

EFFICIENT BUILDINGS—GREEN BUILDINGS

Improving building efficiency is another key solution to reducing the need for electricity and reducing greenhouse gas emissions. According to the U.S. Environmental Protection Agency (EPA), commercial and industrial buildings in the United States account for a hefty 39 percent of total primary energy use, 70 percent of total electricity consumption, and 12 percent of total water consumption.[22] The term *green building* is now used to refer to the whole area of reducing the environmental footprint of buildings. The EPA defines "green building" as "the practice of creating healthier and more resource-efficient models of construction, renovation, operation, maintenance, and demolition."[23] Green building refers not only to the efficient use of electricity, but also to the efficient use of heating/cooling, natural gas, and water. The term also includes measures to reduce exposure of humans in buildings to toxic materials and fumes.

The green building movement officially began with the founding of the U.S. Green Building Council in 1993. In 2000, the Council published a set of building standards, *Leadership in Energy and Environmental Design* (LEED). The standards were designed so that architects and builders would have a standardized set of tools to use for designing new buildings and renovating existing buildings. The standards have been widely accepted and a number of cities have incorporated them into their building codes for new and renovated buildings.

Buildings that meet the LEED standards are designated as *LEED certified*. The standards are based on a point system and buildings fall into one of four categories: certified, silver, gold, or platinum. Since the program started, the number of LEED-certified buildings has gone up every year.

There are LEED projects in all 50 states and 24 foreign countries. In 2007, the value of all "green building" construction, including the buildings that meet LEED standards, is expected to exceed $12 billion, according to the U.S. Green Building Council.[24]

The main goal of the fast-growing green-building movement is to increase the efficiency of electricity usage for lighting and *heating/ ventilating/air conditioning* (HVAC) in new and existing buildings. Building owners are well aware of the rising cost of electricity and are eager to cut their electricity and HVAC expenses.

Awareness is growing about the importance of building efficiency as a solution to power efficiency and climate change. Former President Bill Clinton raised the visibility of building efficiency with his "Clinton Climate Initiative" (see www.clintonfoundation.org). Part of the Initiative is to work with the C40 Large Cities Climate Leadership Group (www.c40cities. org) in finding ways to help the world's largest cities reduce greenhouse gas emissions. An important part of the Clinton Climate Initiative is to form a partnership of large building efficiency companies and banks to finance projects with the goal of carrying out major building retrofits in the major cities of the world to boost HVAC and electrical efficiency and reduce a city's overall power needs and greenhouse gas emissions.

COMPANIES INVOLVED IN BUILDING EFFICIENCY

The following companies are involved in building efficiency.

- *Johnson Controls, Inc.* (NYSE: JCI)—Johnson Controls is the largest player in the area of building efficiency. Johnson Controls can be considered the world's *first* building efficiency company since Professor Warren Johnson started the company in 1885 to commercialize his invention, the room thermostat. Johnson Controls has a building efficiency division that will account for about 38 percent of its revenue in fiscal 2007 (fiscal 2006 revenues were $32 billion). Johnson Controls' other two segments are automotive interiors and the automotive battery market (including hybrid batteries).

    Johnson Controls acquired York International Corp. in December 2005 for $3.1 billion to build its lead in the HVAC and building control and management space. Johnson Controls, with its building efficiency programs, can reduce energy consumption for building customers by 10 percent to 50 percent depending mainly on the extent of previous improvements. JCI has saved customers over $32.7 billion in energy cost savings from 1990 to 2005, according to company information.

At an equity analyst meeting in June 2007, Johnson Controls stressed the following strategic goals: (1) maintain and extend its lead in the complex building market (i.e., skyscrapers, hospitals, arenas, etc; (2) focus on developing products for mid-market buildings (e.g., buildings of less than 10 stories); (3) roll out its "Metasys" building management software which provides building management with the ability to integrate and optimize various building systems including electricity usage, HVAC, fire monitoring, and video security surveillance; and (4) extend its lead in emerging markets such as China (where Johnson Controls already has 3,600 employees).

• *Lime Energy* (OTCBB: LMEC)—Lime Energy (www.lime-energy.com), with 2006 sales of $8.1 million, is an emerging technology, engineering and installation company that focuses on improving lighting and HVAC (heating, ventilating, air conditioning) efficiency for existing commercial, industrial and office buildings. Energy efficient lighting upgrades by Lime typically involve retrofitting older-model light fixtures with state-of-the-art lamps, fixtures, ballasts and lighting controls, that provide customers with substantial savings in electricity, maintenance, and cooling costs. Typical retrofit projects improve lighting levels by 10–50 percent while reducing energy costs by up to 70 percent resulting in project paybacks of 1–3 years depending on hours of use, location, utility rates and rebates, according to Lime. Customers can also claim various federal tax breaks and cash rebates in states such as California, which further reduce the payback period. Lime Energy also has proprietary HVAC control equipment called the "eMac," which can substantially reduce heating and cooling costs.

As a sample case study, Lime completed an energy efficient lighting upgrade for the Associated Food Stores' Distribution Center in Farr West, Utah.[25] The project reduced the Center's electricity consumption by 4.7 million kilowatt-hours and saved the company about $260,000 per year in electricity costs, according to Lime. The payback period for the project was less than 1.2 years. The upgrade project reduced electricity consumption for lighting by well over 50 percent and at the same time increased light levels by 10 percent to 20 percent.

To illustrate the amount of environmental benefit that a single lighting retrofit can provide, Lime Energy's lighting upgrade at Associated Foods prevented the emission annually of 5,060 tons of CO_2, 12 tons of sulfur dioxide (the leading cause of acid rain), and 13 tons of nitrogen oxides (the leading cause of smog and acid precipitation).[26] The retrofit also eliminated the need to burn 2,300 tons of coal per year.[27]

Lime Energy estimates the size of the market for products and services that produce electricity savings in lighting and HVAC at over $200 billion. Lime also estimates that there are approximately 3 billion light fixtures in the United States that could benefit from energy efficient upgrades and retrofits.[28]

- *Echelon Corporation* (Nasdaq: ELON)—Echelon (www.echelon.com), with 2006 sales of $57.3 million, specializes in getting various components and equipment to work together on a network under a centralized control system. The company has control and automation products for a variety of applications including commercial, industrial, residential, utility, and transportation. The company has a building automation product, LonWorks, that allows all of a building's various functions (lighting, security, HVAC and others) to be tied into a single control and automation system. The company has NES, a two-way smart meter product that it has sold to European utility customers and is now in the process of introducing it to U.S. customers.

CHAPTER 11

Smart Meters

Getting Smart on Grid Efficiency and Reliability

T he issue of power efficiency clearly needs to be addressed at the electricity consumer level through increased efficiency of appliances, lights, and heating/air conditioning, as detailed in the previous chapter. However, power efficiency also needs to be addressed at the utility level, where inbalances between supply and demand cause excess power generation capacity, wasted capital, and unnecessary greenhouse gas emissions. Another key problem that needs to be tackled at the grid and utility level is to modernize the entire electricity delivery system to make it more reliable. Smart electric meters, which are installed by the utility at its customers' locations, are an important way to achieve the goals of both power efficiency and improved reliability of the grid.

SMART GRID

The American electric power infrastructure is extraordinarily complex, and it is a major challenge to get everything working together without any hitches. A quote from a report by the Center for Smart Energy illustrates the scope of the problem:

> *The North American electric power industry comprises more than 3,000 electric utilities, 2,000 independent power producers, and hundreds of related organizations. Together, they serve 120 million residential customers, 16 million commercial customers, and*

201

700,000 industrial customers. With about $275 billion in annual sales, the industry is one of the continent's largest—30% larger than the automobile industry and 100% larger than telecommunications. North American utilities own assets with a book value of nearly $1 trillion, roughly 70% in power plants and 30% in the grid. The continent has 700,000 miles of high-voltage transmission lines, owned by about 200 different organizations and valued at more than $160 billion. It has about 5 million miles of medium-voltage distribution lines and 22,000 substations, owned by more than 3,200 organizations and valued at $140 billion. The North American electric power industry will purchase more than $20 billion in grid infrastructure equipment in 2005, nearly one quarter of the worldwide total of $81 billion.[1]

The "grid" can be defined as the entire system involved in generating and delivering electricity to customers. Table 11.1 illustrates the dramatic improvements that need to be made to get a 20th century grid to the smart grid that is needed now—for the 21st century. The major blackouts and transmission disruptions that have been seen in the United States in recent years demonstrate that the North American grid is in bad shape and that

TABLE 11.1   The Smart Grid of the Future

20th Century Grid	21st Century Smart Grid
Electromechanical	Digital
One-way communications (if any)	Two-way communications
Built for centralized generation	Accommodates distributed generation
Radial topology	Network topology
Few sensors	Monitors and sensors throughout
"Blind"	Self-monitoring
Manual restoration	Semi-automated restoration and, eventually, self-healing
Prone to failures and blackouts	Adaptive protection and islanding
Check equipment manually	Monitor equipment remotely
Emergency decisions by committee and phone	Decision support systems, predictive reliability
Limited control over power flows	Pervasive control systems
Limited price information	Full price information
Few customer choices	Many customer choices

Source: Global Environment Fund, Center for Smart Energy, *The Emerging Smart Grid: Investment and Entrepreneurial Potential in the Electric Power Grid of the Future,* October 2005, p. 2, http://www.globalenvironmentfund.com/GEF%20white%20paper_Electric%20Power%20Grid.pdf.

there is a huge amount of work that needs to be done to move to the smart grid of the future. This process has barely started.

The Center for Smart Energy lists the key elements of grid modernization based on recommendations from the U.S. National Energy Technology Laboratory:

1. *Self-healing.* A grid able to rapidly detect, analyze, respond and restore itself from perturbations.

2. *Empowers and incorporates the consumer.* The ability to incorporate consumer equipment and behavior in the design and operation of the grid.

3. *Tolerant of attack.* A grid that mitigates and stands resilient to physical and cyber security attacks.

4. *Provides power quality needed by 21st century users.* A grid that provides a quality of power consistent with consumer and industry needs.

5. *Accommodates a wide variety of generation options.* A grid that accommodates a wide variety of local and regional generation technologies (including green power).

6. *Fully enables maturing electricity markets.* Allows competitive markets for those who want them.

7. *Optimizes assets.* A grid that uses IT and monitoring to continually optimize its capital assets while minimizing operations and maintenance costs.

Smart meters are a key element of grid modernization because they allow a utility to gather data from customer locations and allow grid managers to see the entire picture of electric generation, transmission, and consumption. Smart meters can not only make the entire grid system more robust and reliable, they can also help to more accurately match supply and demand and reduce the need for excess electricity generation capacity.

DEMAND RESPONSE AS A POWER EFFICIENCY SOLUTION

Creating a better balance of supply and demand of electricity in the overall power system would be a big step forward in improving efficiency and lowering electricity costs. Electricity cannot be stored and power utilities, therefore, face a peculiar and volatile market in which supply has to be continually ramped up and down to match demand, which is typically high during the day and low at night.

One solution is to make demand responsive to price, which is called "demand response." The Federal Energy Regulatory Commission defines "demand response" as follows: "Changes in electric usage by end-use customers from their normal consumption patterns in response to changes in the price of electricity over time, or to incentive payments designed to induce lower electricity use at times of high wholesale market prices or when system reliability is jeopardized."[2] The goal of demand response is to flatten out demand by making electricity more expensive during times of high demand and less expensive during times of low demand.

Demand for electricity from household end-users, which account for about 40 percent of overall electricity demand in the United States, is currently unresponsive to the variations in wholesale power costs because most household electricity consumers have flat pricing. Consumers have no economic incentive to shift their discretionary electricity usage from periods of high grid demand (day time) to periods of low grid demand (night time) because the retail price of electricity is the same for household electricity consumers across all periods.

Meanwhile, utilities are forced to maintain power generation capacity that can more than meet the peak demand seen during the day and on a few hot days during the summer, even though that capacity goes to waste during periods of normal or low demand. This represents a very high cost for the utilities, which need to build extra power plants or buy expensive wholesale electricity from other utilities on peak days, just to meet the extraordinary demand seen a few days a year.

Utilities are extremely interested in creating a flatter power demand curve and "shaving" the peak electricity usage seen during the day and seasonally on particularly hot days. One of the best ways to create a flatter demand curve is to introduce "time-of-use pricing," where electricity consumers pay an electricity rate as much as three times higher during the few peak hours of the day and then pay a lower rate during the other non-peak hours of the day. This encourages consumers to shift their discretionary electricity usage to non-peak hours of the day, reducing overall grid demand during peak hours of the day and "shaving the peak" of the demand curve (see Figure 11.1). Consumers can turn down their heating/cooling during peak hours and can also shift electricity usage for clothes washers, clothes dryers, dishwashers, and other power-intensive appliances to evening nonpeak hours.

Utilities can also implement "critical use" pricing that imposes very high electricity prices during the few days of the year when power demand is very high and utilities are bumping up against their reserves. Consumers are typically notified when critical use pricing goes into effect, thus giving them a chance to cut their power usage and avoid the higher costs. The

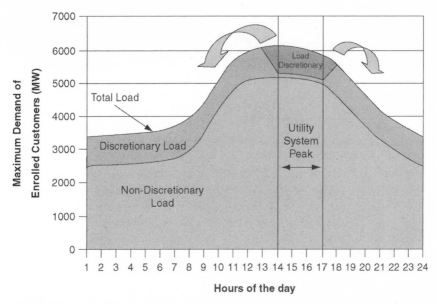

FIGURE 11.1 Schematic of Peak Shaving from Demand Response
Source: Federal Energy Regulatory Commission, *Assessment of Demand Response and Advanced Metering,* August 2006, p. 80, http://www.ferc.gov/legal/staff-reports/demand-response.pdf.

advantage to the utility is that the high critical use pricing will encourage cut-backs in power usage by price-sensitive consumers, thus cutting the overall power load on the utility's power generation system.

The flatter demand curve that results from variable pricing allows the utility to maintain lower generating capacity and reduce their overall costs, which is a cost savings that can be passed on to electricity consumers. Variable pricing also reduces the spikes in wholesale electricity prices that typically occur on particularly hot days when reserve electricity is in short supply, thus providing another source of cost savings to utilities.

Time-based pricing has already been introduced to most commercial and industrial electricity customers in the United States. However, the next step is to introduce time-based pricing at the household level on a widespread basis, thus further smoothing power demand and reducing the overall cost of providing power. Studies of existing retail demand response programs have shown that these programs have potential savings of as much as 10 percent to 20 percent of peak load.

Another program that utilities can use to reduce discretionary power demand during critical periods is "curtailment programs." Under a curtailment program, the electricity consumer agrees to cut power usage during times of stress on the system in return for a payment from the utility. The utility has a self-interest in paying to curtail demand because of the money that the utility saves by reducing the peak generation assets that it must have on hand to cover a few hot days of the year. There are a variety of ways that the utility can notify the customer when the curtailment program is activated, including automated systems or by telephone or email.

THE ROLE OF SMART METERS

In order to introduce variable pricing, advanced electricity meters are necessary that can measure *when* electricity is used, not just the total amount of electricity used. The old electromechanical meters that have turning wheels are typically physically read by a meter reader once a month. The old meters only give a read-out on the total amount of electricity used during the month, not the day and time when the electricity was used. Thus, variable pricing cannot be introduced with the old electromechanical meters.

A modern electricity meter, on the other hand, is a digital meter with an integrated electronic solid-state circuit board that collects data on the amount and time of electricity usage. The utility can then retrieve the data saved inside the meter whenever the utility wishes—continual, every 15 minutes, hourly, daily, or monthly. Figure 11.2 shows an old electromechanical meter that has turning wheels. Figure 11.3 shows a newer digital electricity meter that collects and saves detailed electricity usage data.

A utility can retrieve the data from a smart meter using four different network transmission methods:

1. *Public wireless.* Public wireless operates like the public wireless Internet, using public wireless frequencies for the base unit to communicate with the meters at customer locations.

2. *Radio frequency (RF).* Radio frequency also involves wireless technology but uses special frequencies (either licensed or unlicensed) that are typically more reliable than public wireless Internet frequencies. The collection methods for wireless transmission include handheld units, mobile systems, or fixed network collection towers.

3. *Broadband over power line (BPL).* Broadband over power line involves the use of the Internet over electricity power lines (as opposed to normal broadband usage over cable or DSL telecom lines).

4. *Power line carrier (PLC).* Power line carrier is a slower system that involves installing modem-type gear at both the customer and the utility ends of the power lines to transmit communication messages.

FIGURE 11.2 Old Electromechanical Electric Meter
Photo credit: Greg Niemi.

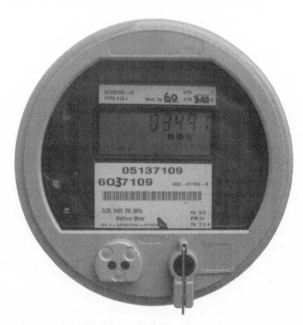

FIGURE 11.3 New Solid-State Digital Electric Meter
Photo credit: Norman Morin.

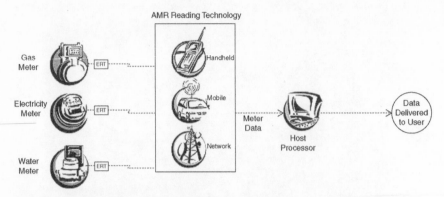

FIGURE 11.4 Automatic Meter Reading (AMR) One-Way System
Source: Itron Inc., *2005 Annual Report,* p. 4.

The most obvious benefit of a smart meter is that it eliminates the cost of having a utility employee visit every household each month to visually read the meter, which reduces costs and eliminates safety problems. The much larger benefits from smart meters come from the utility being able to provide better customer service, size its transmission assets more efficiently, and flatten the demand curve to reduce the amount of excess electricity generating reserves that must be available to meet peak demand.

The process of reading meters automatically is called *automatic meter reading* (AMR). Figure 11.4 shows a schematic diagram of how AMR works with data from an electricity meter being collected via a handheld, mobile unit, or fixed communication network, and then being funneled into a database/software system.

However, smart meters can also be set up to communicate on a two-way basis, i.e., where the utility can both receive a meter reading of electricity usage *from* the meter and also transmit various signals *to* the meter. Two-way meter systems are typically referred to as *advanced metering infrastructure* (AMI). An AMI system includes the meters, the transmission assets, and the software to run the system and analyze the data. Figure 11.5 shows a schematic diagram of an AMI system.

The two-way meter communication available through AMI allows the utility to send information to the meter to input variable electricity pricing schedules, transmit automatic connect/disconnects, test for outages or theft, implement curtailment programs, or interface with smart thermostats and smart appliances (lighting, water heaters, dryers, dishwashers, etc) in order to minimize a consumer's electricity usage and overall electricity bill. The smart meter then becomes part of a more efficient power system that can benefit both producers and consumers of electricity.

System involves multiple communication paths to link the utility to meters to customer

- **Home Area Network** (HAN) links Utility & Meter to Customer through 2-way open standards based wireless communications (ZigBee).

- **Local Area Network** (LAN) links meters together in a 2-way wireless mesh network for reliability through an aggregator (one meter may act as the aggregator).

- **Wide Area Network** (WAN) links utility back office systems through 2-way public or private network to the meter aggregators in the field.

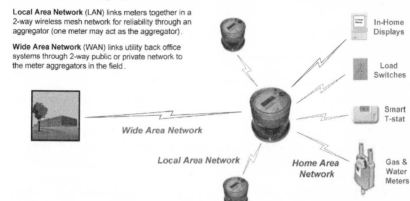

FIGURE 11.5 Advanced Metering Infrastructure (AMI) Two-Way Communication System
Source: Southern California Edison, "AMI Program Overview," 9 October 2006.

A homeowner, for example, can use a *smart thermostat* that communicates with the smart meter via wireless. The smart thermostat is capable of retrieving real-time pricing data from the utility and then automatically calculating how to minimize electricity costs while staying within heating/cooling parameters set by the homeowner. Figure 11.6 shows a photo

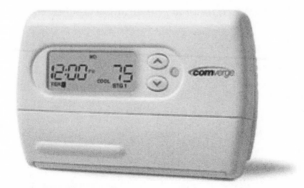

FIGURE 11.6 Smart Thermostat
Source: Converge Inc. SuperStat smart meter, www.comverge.com.

of the smart thermostat marketed by Converge Inc (Nasdaq: COMV) and manufactured by Emerson Electric (NYSE: EMR).

DEMAND RESPONSE AND ADVANCED METERING

The Energy Policy Act of 2005 made demand response an explicit policy goal of the United States federal government. More specifically, Congress recognized that the increased usage of advanced metering is important for the future development of electric demand responsiveness in the United States. Congress instructed the Federal Energy Regulatory Commission (FERC) to assess demand response resources and conduct a comprehensive survey of electric demand response and advanced metering. FERC issued its report, entitled *Assessment of Demand Response and Advanced Metering*, in August 2006.[3]

FERC estimated that the potential peak reduction from existing demand response systems is about 37.5 gigawatts, which is equivalent to the amount of electricity used by about 28 million homes. The report confirmed the importance of implementing demand response systems as a way to reduce U.S. electricity usage, thus reducing the need for new power plants and cutting the overall cost of the U.S. power system.

BENEFITS OF SMART METERS

One of the main goals of smart meters is to allow utilities to implement variable pricing. However, there are other important benefits of smart metering as noted by FERC:

- Enhanced customer service including more accurate billing.
- Automated meter reading, which eliminates manual meter reading costs.
- Remote connect/disconnect and reduction of service calls.
- Tamper detection and theft reduction.
- Load forecasting and reduction of excess capacity.
- Outage management and lower outage repair costs.
- Asset management including transformer sizing.
- Premise device/load control interface or capability, e.g., with smart thermostats or appliances.[4]

CURRENT SMART METER USAGE

FERC's survey found that advanced meters currently account for only about 6 percent of the total 144 million electric meters in the United States.[5] Smart meter usage varied considerably by region and by type of power company entity. The states with the highest usage of smart meters are Pennsylvania and Wisconsin, as seen in Figure 11.7. The survey found that 42 states have usage rates of less than 10 percent.

By utility type, the FERC survey found that the highest usage rate for advanced metering is found among smaller rural power companies. This makes sense since rural utilities can save more money by eliminating the need for utility employees to travel long distances to read meters at customer premises every month.

Table 11.2 shows some of the large advanced metering deployments in the United States. The deployments mainly used fixed *RF* (radio frequency) as the meter reading collection method, although *power line carrier* (PLC) and *broadband over powerline* (BPL) have started appearing in the past 2 years. Most of the projects included in this list are automatic meter reading projects and not the new two-way advanced metering infrastructure systems.

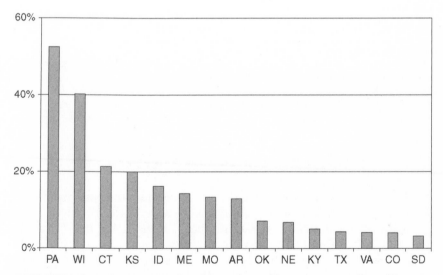

FIGURE 11.7 Smart Electric Meters as Percent of Total—Top 15 U.S. States
Source: Federal Energy Regulatory Commission, *Assessment of Demand Response and Advanced Metering*, August 2006, p. 30, http://www.ferc.gov/legal/staff-reports/demand-response.pdf.

TABLE 11.2 Announced Large Advanced Metering Deployments in the United States

Utility	Commodity	AMI type	Units	Year Started
Kansas City Power & Light (MO)	Electric	Fixed RF	450,000	1994
Ameren (MO)	Electric & Gas	Fixed RF	1,400,000	1995
Duquesne Light (PA)	Electric	Fixed RF	550,000	1995
Xcel Energy (MN)	Electric & Gas	Fixed RF	1,900,000	1996
Indianapolis Power & Light (IN)	Electric	Fixed RF	415,000	1997
Puget Sound Energy (WA)	Electric & Gas	Fixed RF	1,325,000	1997
Virginia Power	Electric	Fixed RF	450,000	1997
Exelon (PA)	Electric & Gas	Fixed RF	2,100,000	1999
United Illuminating (CT)	Electric	Fixed RF	320,000	1999
Wisconsin Public Service (WI)	Electric	PLC	650,000	1999
Wisconsin Public Service (WI)	Gas	Fixed RF	200,000	2000
JEA (FL)	Electric	Fixed RF	450,000	2001
PPL (PA)	Electric	PLC	1,300,000	2002
WE Energies (WI)	Electric & Gas	Fixed RF	1,000,000	2002
Bangor Hydro	Electric	PLC	125,000	2004
Colorado Springs	Electric	Fixed RF	400,000	2005
Laclede	Gas	Fixed RF	650,000	2005
TXU	Electric	BPL	2,000,000	2005
Ameren (IL)	Electric & Gas	Fixed RF	1,000,000	2006
PG&E (CA)	Electric	PLC	5,100,000	2006
PG&E (CA)	Gas	Fixed RF	4,100,000	2006
Hundreds of Small Utilities	Electric & Gas	Various	5,000,000	na

Source: Federal Energy Regulatory Commission, *Assessment of Demand Response and Advanced Metering,* August 2006, Table III-3, p. 32, http://www.ferc.gov/legal/staff-reports/demand-response.pdf.

AMI types: Fixed Radio Frequency (RF), PLC (power line communication), BPL (broadband over powerline)

ADVANCED METERING COSTS AND BENEFITS

The FERC Demand Response and Advanced Metering study provided some useful cost benchmark information. Specifically, FERC noted that the average cost for a meter has recently been in the range of $75 to $85 per meter (see Table 11.3). However, the meter typically represents only 45 percent of the total system cost, with other costs including network hardware (20 percent), installation (15 percent), project management (11 percent) and IT (9 percent). The total capital cost per meter system has recently been in the $135 to $150 area, according to information collected by InteliPoint International.

TABLE 11.3 Advanced Metering Cost Benchmarks

Utility	Year	Meters (mlns)	Hardware ($mln)	Total Capital ($mln)	Hardware Cost per meter	Total Capital Cost per meter
DLCo	1996	0.6	$60	—	$99	—
Virginia Power	1997	0.5	$44	—	$98	—
PREPA	1998	1.3	$130	—	$100	—
ENEL	2000	30	$2,673	—	$89	—
JEA	2001	0.7	—	—	$150	$214
PPL	2002	1.3	$112	$160	$86	$123
Bangor Hydro	2004	0.1	$7.50	$15	$68	$136
TXU	2005	0.3	$19	$38	$76	$150
PG&E	2005	9.8	$721	$1,328	$74	$135
SDG&E	2006	2.3	$199	$329	dollar;86	$143

Source: Federal Energy Regulatory Commission, *Assessment of Demand Response and Advanced Metering,* August 2006, Table III-4, p. 35, http://www.ferc.gov/legal/staff-reports/demand-response.pdf.

There are a variety of financial benefits for a utility that offset the capital cost of the meters. These cost savings include reduced meter reading costs, the elimination of estimated bills, the ability to better size electric generation and transmission assets, reduced outage management costs since crews can more accurately determine the scope of a problem, reduced invoicing time (thus reducing receivables), among others. As the buyers of the smart meters, utilities must see a positive return from their capital investment through cost savings and/or by a pass-through of the costs to customers before they will decide to proceed with smart metering programs. This book's companion Web site at www.ProfitingFromCleanEnergy.com has a link to a video that explains the benefits of the smart meter project at Hydro One in Ontario, Canada.

The business case for AMR depends on the circumstances at a particular utility. No single economic analysis applies across the board. However, a study by Gary Fauth and Michael Wiebe came to the following conclusions about the cost benefits from advanced metering:

Properly measured, advanced meter reading benefits can amount to between $1.35 and $3.00 per customer per month, over the useful life of the hardware. In contrast, advanced meter reading in many situations can cost $1.25 to $1.75 per customer per month, measured over the useful life of the hardware and including both capital and

*operating costs. These cost and benefit numbers by themselves pro-
duce a positive business case outcome in most cases. Business cases
for advanced meter reading can produce internal rates of return
ranging from 15–20% and payback periods of less than six years.*[6]

SOUTHERN CALIFORNIA EDISON'S BUSINESS CASE EXPERIENCE FOR ADVANCED METERING

Southern California Edison, a subsidiary of Edison International (NYSE: EIX), is currently in the midst of implementing a 5-million-unit smart meter program that provides valuable data for analyzing the future of smart meters. After the California power crisis of 2001–2003, the California Public Utilities Commission (CPUC) ordered major California utilities to develop a cost analysis for implementing advanced metering. Southern California Edison in its first go-around found that an automated meter reading system based on existing technologies would create a net loss of $500 million for the utility.[7]

However, Southern California Edison went back to the drawing board and looked at a more sophisticated advanced metering infrastructure that would provide two-way communications to allow the use of automatic connects/reconnects, time-of-use pricing, load control, and other benefits. With the additional benefits from a more sophisticated AMI system, the business case analysis changed from a $500 million net loss to a $514 million net gain. The net gain resulted from estimated benefits of $761 million (i.e., demand response worth $315 million, remote connect/disconnect capabilities worth $298 million, improved communication system coverage worth $45 million, reduced meter failure rates worth $33 million, and various other smaller benefits worth a total of $70 million), minus the $247 million cost of the meters and infrastructure. Further details on the Southern California Edison AMI program are available at www.sce.com/ami. Southern California Edison is moving ahead with the most sophisticated AMI project yet conceived in the United States.

INTEROPERABILITY AND INDUSTRY STANDARDS

Utilities have an important concern that current advanced metering equipment may become a stranded asset because of rapid technology improvements or because a particular vendor of proprietary equipment may go out of business and not support the equipment. In order to address this problem, there is a strong movement toward adopting industrywide interoperability standards, thus giving utilities more assurance that they will have a wider choice of vendors and a longer shelf life for their advanced metering assets.

The American National Standards Institute (ANSI), in conjunction with the Automated Meter Reading Association (AMRA), has already issued standards for meter communications and meter data storage. The next standard (ANSI C12.22) covers meter communications over a network. Some of the leading smart meter vendors have already announced that their products are compatible with the new standards, thus placing pressure on other AMI vendors to conform as well.[8]

There is some concern that the movement toward standards and interoperability could be a negative factor for advanced metering vendors because it may commoditize the product, increase competition, and reduce profit margins. On the other hand, standards and interoperability may overcome a major concern of utilities about stranded equipment and lead to much wider adoption of advanced metering systems and much higher unit sales for advanced metering vendors. On balance, the move toward standards and interoperability will likely be a net negative factor for smaller vendors that have limited and propriety systems, but will be a net positive factor for the larger advanced metering vendors that can meet the standards and take advantage of larger unit volume sales.

GLOBAL DEMAND RESPONSE

The focus on energy efficiency and demand-side management is a global movement, as seen by the activities of the International Energy Agency (IEA). The IEA in its 2006 annual report *Implementing Agreement on Demand-Side Management Technologies and Programmes* provides a wealth of information on various initiatives on efficiency and demand-side management in the United States, Canada, Europe, Japan, and elsewhere.[9] The IEA's report notes that energy efficiency has reduced global energy needs by some 50 percent since 1973, but that energy efficiency improvements have progressively slowed in the last two decades. However, the IEA's report notes that the "past year was a remarkable one from the point of view of energy efficiency awareness. Never before have we seen so many initiatives from world leaders to put energy efficiency at the top of the agenda and to really back the rhetoric with action.... world leaders have sensed that sustainability begins with energy efficiency."[10] The report makes clear the extent of global interest in demand response solutions involving products such as smart meters.

U.S. REGULATORS—GENERALLY POSITIVE TOWARD ADVANCED METERING

U.S. National Energy Policy requires that utilities in the United States evaluate advanced metering and report to their respective Public Utility Commissions (PUCs) by the end of 2007. The majority of utilities have already taken a close look at advanced metering and many utilities are currently in various stages of evaluation, pilot programs, or implementation.

The attitude of Public Utility Commissions (PUCs) is critical for the future of advanced metering since PUC regulators typically decide whether a utility can recover its capital costs for advanced meters by passing through the cost to customers through higher electricity prices. A survey by Utili-Point International found that the attitude among PUC regulators was positive toward advanced metering, with 35 percent of respondents saying they would allow full recovery of advanced metering capital costs, 39 percent saying they would allow partial recovery, and only 9 percent saying they would not allow rate increases (17 percent of the responses were "no reply").[11]

WHAT IS AHEAD FOR THE SMART METER INDUSTRY?

Now that utilities are getting a good look at the emerging smart meter products, their demands for even more sophisticated capabilities is rapidly expanding. The Director of AMR and Demand Response at UtiliPoint International, Patti Harper-Slaboszewicz, lists the requirements that utilities are now generally asking for in smart meters:

- Interval or real-time meter data collection.
- Low-cost, universal remote connect/disconnect under-the-glass.
- Remote updating of firmware and all metering parameters.
- Positive notification of outage detection/restoration.
- Support for a home area network, including sharing price signals/load control messages to customer premise (ZigBee is often mentioned in this regard).
- Voltage alerts and logs.
- Significant memory storage on endpoint (7 to 35 days is typical).
- Robust provision of interval data (hourly or 15-minute are typically required).
- Sufficient bandwidth to handle communications to and from the endpoints.

- Net metering capability to enable consumers to put power back into the grid.
- Open standard protocols preferred.[12]

Many utilities have quickly recognized the benefits that smart meters can provide, as seen by the list above. Ms. Harper-Slaboszewicz notes in her article that the following utilities are actively considering AMI smart meter projects: Pacific Gas & Electric (PGE), Southern California Edison (SCE), San Diego Gas and Electric (SDG&E), DTE Energy, Baltimore Gas and Electric (BGE), Consolidated Edison (ConEd), TXU, CenterPoint, Energy East, Northeast Utilities, and many others.[13]

The advanced metering industry is currently on the cusp of moving from the one-way AMR phase to a much more sophisticated phase involving two-way AMI communications systems. The move to AMI will pick up steam going into 2008. Automatic meter reading sales in 2007 will continue to be relatively strong but there may be some slowdown in overall industry growth as utilities take time to investigate and conduct pilot programs for AMI. The meter industry is likely to see a decent year in 2007 and will then start to see a significant ramp-up in growth in 2008 and beyond as the more sophisticated AMI systems start to take off.

There is every reason to be optimistic about the growth prospects for advanced metering overseas where efficiency is being pushed even harder than in the United States and where countries such as China and India are in the process of a huge build-out of new power plants and transmission system assets to meet the demands of their fast-growing economies.

The specific catalysts for the smart meter industry include (1) larger AMI pilot programs; (2) the roll-out of full AMI installations that are currently in the pilot stage; (3) demand for advanced metering solutions in Europe, Asia, and South America; (4) increased pressure for power efficiency from new government regulations such as higher renewable energy standards (which can typically be met in part with efficiency programs); and (5) the possibility that Congress may provide a tax break for smart meters through accelerated depreciation for the utilities purchasing smart meters.

INDUSTRY METER PENETRATION RATES AND UPGRADE OPPORTUNITIES

There is a significant opportunity for growth in the United States, but even more so globally, for solid-state digital electricity meters, one-way automated meter reading (AMR) systems, and two-way advanced metering infrastructure (AMI) systems.

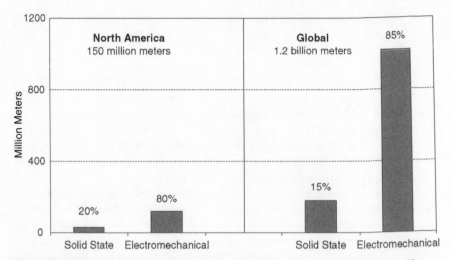

FIGURE 11.8 Potential for Electricity Meter Upgrades to Solid State from Electromechanical
Sources: The Scott Report, ABS Energy Research, and Itron, Inc. management estimates.

Of the 150 million electricity meters in the United States-Canada, about 80 percent (120 million) are the old electromechanical meters and only 20 percent (30 million) are the newer solid-state electricity meters (see Figure 11.8). This leaves an upgrade base of 120 million old electromechanical electricity meters in the United States-Canada that could be replaced with the new solid-state electricity meters. Globally, the penetration rate for the newer solid-state meters is even lower at 15 percent, meaning there are some 1 billion of the old electromechanical electricity meters that could be replaced by the new solid-state electricity meters.

SMART METER INDUSTRY GROWTH RATES

The annual growth rate for the new solid-state electricity meters was very rapid at +50 percent over the 2000–2005 time frame in the United States and Canada.[14] At the same time, sales of the older electromechanical electric meters fell by an annual rate of –15 percent during the same time frame since those meters are becoming obsolete. The annual growth rate for both types of meters combined was 9 percent. This data is illustrated in Figure 11.9. Unit sales in the United States and Canada for solid-state

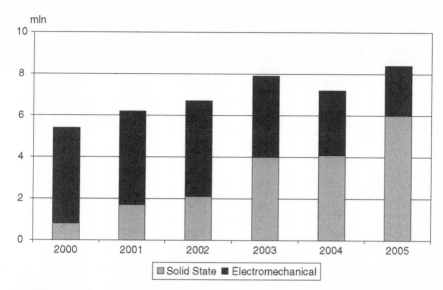

FIGURE 11.9 Electricity Meter United States-Canada Shipments
Source: Itron Inc. 10k annual report, management presentations, 2006.

electricity meters that had embedded AMR functionality grew at an annual rate of +17 percent during the 2000–2005 period.

ELECTRICITY METER MARKET SHARES

In the United States-Canadian market for electric meters that are capable of automatic meter reading, Itron has a leading share with about 53 percent of the market, followed by Cellnet (19 percent), ESCO Technologies (16 percent) and Hunt (9 percent), as illustrated in Figure 11.10. In the global electric AMR meter market, Itron/Actaris has a leading market share with 16 percent followed by Landis & Gyr with 14 percent, as illustrated in Figure 11.11.

- *Itron Inc* (Nasdaq: ITRI). Itron (www.itron.com) has a leading market share in North America and globally in the automatic meter reading electric meter segment. Itron's new OpenWay product is an advanced metering infrastructure system that provides two-way communications between a utility and its customers' meters. Itron also sells natural gas and water meters and provides various software and

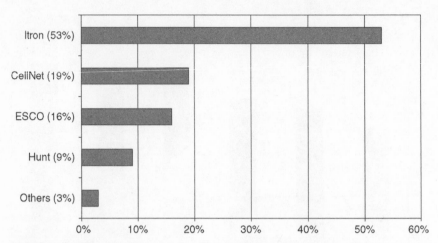

FIGURE 11.10 United States-Canada AMR Electric Meter Market Shares
Source: Itron, Inc. management presentation and *The Scott Report on AMR Deployments in North America,* 10th ed.

data management services for large utilities. In April 2007, Itron completed the $1.7 billion acquisition of European-based Actaris Metering Systems. Itron-Actaris had combined 2006 revenues of $1.659 billion. The acquisition reunited the former Schlumberger North American and European meter divisions that were sold separately in previous years.

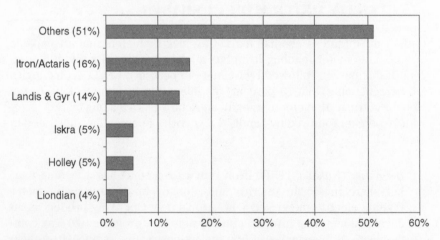

FIGURE 11.11 Global AMR Electric Meter Market Shares
Source: Itron, Inc. management presentation and *The Scott Report on AMR Deployments in North America,* 10th ed.

- *Elster Metering* (privately held). Elster Metering (www.elstermetering. com), a subsidiary of Ruhrgas Industries Group, had 9,000 employees and 1.3 billion euros of revenues in 2005, according to company information. Ruhrgas Industries Group is a private company that was bought by British firm CVC Capital Partners in 2005. In North America, Elster has three business units: Elster Electricity, which focuses on providing metering and metering system technology to electric utilities, AMCO Water Metering Systems, which provides metering products and meter reading solutions to water utilities, and Elster Integrated Solutions (EIS), which provides an AMR)/AMI system solutions across gas, electricity and water to multiutility customers.
- *Bayard Group* (privately held). Bayard Group (see www.bayard. com.au) is a private equity investment group based in Australia that has spent more than $2 billion to acquire several companies focused in the power efficiency and smart meter sector. These companies include Landis & Gyr, Hunt Technologies, CellNet, and Enermet. The combined group has 700 million of annual sales and more than 4,000 employees, according to company information. Bayard Group says on its Web site that it intends to list on a public stock exchange in the next two to three years. The principal shareholders of Bayard Group, according to company information, include DB Capital Partners (the private equity arm of Deutsche Asset Management in Australia), Allianz Capital Partners, Dubai International Capital, and various other private investors. The Bayard Group has acquired the following companies:
  - *Landis & Gyr.* Landis & Gyr (www.landisgyr.net) is a private company owned by Bayard Group. Landis & Gyr is based in Switzerland and operates in 29 countries with about 4,000 employees. Landis & Gyr had sales in 2005 of 496 million euros. Products include electricity, gas and water meters and automated meter reading systems.
  - *CellNet.* CellNet (www.cellnet.com) was recently acquired by Bayard Group for $705 million from major shareholder GTCR Golder Rauner LLC (a Chicago-based private equity firm with $8 billion in capital) on November 30, 2006. CellNet provides equipment and managed services for the electricity, water and gas industries. CellNet, with its 10-year operating history, has an installed base of some 11 million meters in the United States, according to company information.
  - *Hunt Technologies.* Hunt Technologies (huntechnologies.com), based in Pequot Lakes, Minnesota, has 330 employees and provides advanced metering hardware and software products to electric, gas and water utilities.
- *ESCO Technologies* (NYSE: ESE). ESCO Technologies (www.esco technologies.com) operates in three segments: (1) the *Filtration/Fluid*

segment, which provides a range of fluid filtration products and accounted for 38 percent of ESCO's revenue in fiscal 2006 (ending September 30, 2006); (2) the *Test* segment, which provides products to measure and contain electromagnetic and acoustic energy and accounted for 28 percent of ESCO's revenue in fiscal-2006; and (3) the *Communications* segment, which is the segment that provides AMR electric meter reading technologies and accounted for 34 percent of ESCO's sales in fiscal 2006. ESCO's subsidiary, Distribution Control Systems Inc (DCSI), provides the TWACS® fixed-network AMI communication system that provides two-way communications between utilities and their electricity and gas customers with smart meters.

ESCO was originally a subsidiary of Emerson Electric and was subsequently spun-off and migrated through a series of acquisitions and divestitures. ESCO acquired Nexus Energy Software on November 29, 2005, which provides software for energy meter applications. ESCO acquired Hexagram on February 1, 2006, which produces radio frequency fixed network automatic meter reading systems for gas and water utilities. ESCO Technologies in fiscal 2006 (ended September 30, 2006) had $459 million in revenues.

- *Cannon Technologies* (subsidiary of Cooper Power Systems NYSE: CBE). Cannon Technologies (www.cannontech.com), headquartered in Minneapolis, Minnesota, provides load management and automated distribution solutions to electric utilities. Cannon has over 400 electric utilities as clients and provides them with solutions to manage peak load, improve system power factor, read meters remotely, and improve substation reliability. Cannon Technologies was acquired by Cooper Industries Ltd (NYSE: CBE) in August 2006 and was folded in the Cooper Power Systems division. The Cooper Power Systems division, with about $900 million in revenues, manufacturers electric equipment (e.g., transformers, distribution switchgear, capacitors, protective relays, voltage regulators, etc.) and also provides engineering services for the electrical and industrial markets.

- *Sensus Metering Systems Inc* (privately held). Sensus Metering Systems (www.sensus.com) is the largest global manufacturer of water meters and has a 16 percent market share of the automatic water meter reading market in North America. The company is headquartered in Raleigh, North Carolina, and operates globally with 35 facilities in the United States and other countries. The company is a leading global manufacturer of gas and heat meters and is an emerging participant in the North American electric metering market with its iCon® solid-state electric meter. The company also produces pipe joining and repair products for water and natural gas utilities and is a supplier of aluminum die castings.

Sensus Metering Systems was formed in 2003 when a private equity group bought the Invensys Metering Systems Group from Invensys PLC (London: ISYS LN). The primary shareholders in the company are The Resolute Fund (65.9 percent ownership) and GS Capital Partners (32.9 percent ownership). Sensus Metering Systems can trace its history back more than 100 years to the founding of the National Meter Company in 1870 and the Pittsburgh Meter Company in 1886. Sensus Metering Systems is a private company but publicly reports its financial statements to the SEC. The company has about 3,800 employees. Sensus Metering Systems in the fiscal year ended March 31, 2006, reported annual net sales of $613.9 million.

- *Comverge Inc* (Nasdaq: COMV). Comverge, Inc. (www.comverge.com) provides demand response solutions to electric utilities, using a combination of systems including wireless communications, software, and hardware devices installed at utility customer locations such as smart meters and smart thermostats. Comverge can sell a physical demand response system to a utility, or Comverge can provide its Virtual Peaking Capacity program to a utility, which is an outsourced peak management service on a pay-for-performance basis. Through its demand response systems, Comverge can save electric utilities money by reducing peak power requirements and cutting operational costs. Comverge also has a Virtual SCADA System, which allows electric utilities to monitor and control distribution equipment and systems such as substations, grid equipment and remote generators. Comverge estimates that its products have been installed in 3.3 percent of homes in the United States. Comverge in 2006 had revenues of $33.9 million. Converge went public in a $95 million IPO in April 2007.

EnerNOC Inc (Nasdaq: ENOC). EnerNOC (www.enernoc.com), with 2006 sales of $26 million, provides demand response services to utilities and commercial/industrial electricity customers. EnerNOC enters long-term contracts with utilities to reduce the utility's peak by interfacing with utility customers and shedding electricity load during times of peak demand. EnerNOC went public in a $97.5 million IPO in May 2007.

CHAPTER 12

Power Storage and Backup Systems

When the Grid Just Won't Do

A t first glance, electricity storage systems may not seem to come under the heading of clean energy. However, electricity storage systems are an important part of clean energy because they improve the quality and usefulness of electricity to consumers. Electricity storage systems can also improve the overall efficiency of the grid, thus reducing the need for new power plants. Moreover, if electricity storage systems (e.g., batteries) can be used for transportation vehicles on a mass scale, then we avoid the need to burn fuel in internal combustion engines, thus reducing greenhouse gas emissions and pollution (assuming the original electricity use came from renewable sources). Electricity storage systems by themselves don't make electricity clean, but they do make a very important contribution to the usefulness and efficiency of the overall electricity system.

There are number of ways that electricity storage systems are used. The first comes in powering the remarkable array of electronic equipment and instruments that have been developed in recent decades. Computer equipment, medical equipment, scientific instruments, video equipment, and many other types of electronic equipment are very sensitive to variations in voltage or power spikes. In addition, businesses are now highly dependent on electricity to keep their operations running and any downtime from a power failure can quickly cost businesses a lot of lost revenue. There are also critical care facilities such as hospitals that cannot afford to have power spikes or blackouts since human lives are literally at stake. The bottom line is that few people can trust the grid anymore and many homes and businesses need to take matters into their own hands to provide regulated and backup electricity for their facilities.

The need for electricity storage solutions also comes from new electricity generation sources such as wind and solar power, which are hampered by being intermittent and running only when the wind blows or the sun shines. Large-scale electricity storage solutions would allow wind and solar parks to use the excess electricity they generate during the day to charge up a storage system. The storage system could then provide electricity to maintain a continuous flow of electricity from the overall facility even when the wind or solar resource is offline. This would be a huge step forward in bringing solar and wind power up to the 24/7 scale that is needed for a complete and long-term renewable electricity solution.

Large-scale electricity storage solutions would also be very useful for utilities. One of the properties of electricity is that it cannot easily be stored on a large-scale basis, which means that utility power companies when they generate electricity either "use it or lose it." As a result, utilities spend a lot of extra money bringing power generation facilities up during the day and down at night in order to match generation with demand. Utilities would greatly benefit from having large-scale multimegawatt electric storage facilities that are charged at night when electricity demand is low and then provide the extra electricity during the day when electricity demand is high. This would allow utilities to generate electricity at a relatively constant rate 24 hours a day, taking care of peak requirements with stored electricity and thus reducing the overall power generating capacity that the utility must have available. That reduced capacity would have a substantial impact on cutting the utility's power generation costs, a cost savings that could be passed through to consumers with lower electricity rates.

Advanced electricity storage solutions would also be useful in the transportation market. To the extent that electricity for a vehicle can be stored in an advanced battery or some other storage system, the vehicle would not need to burn fuel in an internal combustion engine. That would be a big step forward in reducing pollution and greenhouse gas emissions from the transportation sector. Of course, the electricity that charges the vehicle's batteries must be generated in a clean and renewable manner or else we would just be swapping transportation emissions for coal-fired plant emissions.

One of the interesting things about electricity is that it does not necessarily need to be stored as electricity in order to be retrieved later. It can be stored in the form of water, compressed air, hydrogen, or mechanical energy. For example, many hydroelectric dams around the world already use a power storage system whereby excess electricity at night can be used to pump water into large tanks, which can then be drained to drive turbines and generate extra electricity when the electricity is needed during peak periods during the day. This is just one example of how electricity can be transferred into another type of energy, and then turned back into electricity later. This topic will be discussed in more depth later in the chapter.

There are basically three ways to store electricity directly: batteries, supercapacitors, and superconducting magnetic energy storage. There are four ways to store electricity in other energy forms to turn back into electricity later: pumped-hydro, compressed air, hydrogen for a fuel cell, or mechanical energy in a flywheel.

TYPES OF DIRECT ELECTRICITY STORAGE SYSTEMS

Rechargeable Batteries

The earliest storage of electricity was accomplished in 1745 when Ewald Georg von Kleist invented what came to be known as the *Leyden Jar*. It stored electricity between two metal plates positioned close to each other. Then, in 1800, Alessandro Volta invented the first practical electrical storage battery using alternating discs of zinc, copper, and pieces of cardboard soaked in brine. The term "volt" was derived from Mr. Volta's name.[1]

Today, the global battery market is worth about $30 billion per year. About 90 percent of the batteries sold are nonrechargeable disposable batteries. These are called primary batteries. Only about 10 percent of the batteries sold are rechargeable, but they account for about 63 percent of the revenue because they are more expensive. The rechargeable batteries, called secondary batteries, are divided into three main categories: transportation, industrial, and portable.

There are seven different types of rechargeable chemical batteries. The fundamental principle of these batteries is the same, with the differences coming in the types of materials that are used inside the battery.

1. *Lead acid.* The lead-acid battery is 130 years old and is still the battery with the largest use today. The lead-acid battery is the familiar battery used in most automobiles. The lead-acid battery can be made in many sizes and can also be linked in chains so that the total system can be used as backup storage for large-scale industrial applications where uninterrupted power is critical. About 73 percent of lead-acid batteries are used in the automotive market with the remaining 27 percent in the industrial market. The lead-acid battery is the least expensive battery made.

Lower-end lead-acid batteries are called "flooded batteries" because the liquid acid in the battery periodically requires topping off with distilled water. The more advanced *valve-regulated lead-acid* (VRLA) batteries contain the acid in the form of a gel and the battery requires no maintenance. A lead-acid battery can be used in almost any position without leakage. Typical uses for lead-acid gel batteries are wheel chairs, hospital equipment, emergency lighting, computer power backup, and burglar alarm backups. Another big user is the motive market that includes electric vehicles like forklifts.

2. *Nickel cadmium.* The nickel cadmium battery is another type of rechargeable battery that also has been around a long time. It requires less maintenance than the lead-acid battery, but it is environmentally unfriendly because of the cadmium. The battery was used for a long time in portable electronic devices like mobile phones and laptop computers but it has lost ground in those applications to newer types of batteries. Nickel cadmium batteries are generally used where long life, high discharge rate, and low price are important.

3. *Nickel-metal-hydride.* The nickel-metal-hydride battery stores somewhat more energy that nickel cadmium but for a shorter period of time. A big advantage is that it is nontoxic. This type battery is used in many hybrid electric cars. It is also used for telecom backup power and for consumer electronics.

4. *Reusable alkaline.* The reusable alkaline battery provides fewer charge/discharge cycles than other rechargeable batteries but it holds its charge longer. These batteries are a relatively small part of the total market since most alkaline batteries are nonrechargeable. Typical uses are for portable radios and flashlights.

5. *Lithium-ion.* The lithium-ion battery is a newer technology. It can store much more energy for its weight than most other types of batteries, but it is also more expensive. Typical applications include laptop computers and cellular phones. There is some controversy over the safety of the lithium-ion battery because it can be unstable and there have been some incidents where one has exploded or caught fire causing some injuries. Lithium-ion batteries with special safety arrangements are already showing up in hybrid gasoline-electricity vehicles due to superior performance characteristics as compared with the nickel-metal-hydride batteries that have been used in hybrid vehicles for the past several years.

6. *Lithium-polymer.* The lithium-polymer battery is the next generation lithium battery and is an improvement over the lithium-ion version because of its potentially lower cost. The lithium polymer battery is a

solid polymer composite and does not need a metal case around it. As a result it can be shaped to fit into whatever device is being powered. While it is safer than the lithium-ion battery, it is still subject to explosion or fire if it is recharged incorrectly.

7. *Sodium sulfur.* The sodium sulfur battery is in wide use in Japan for storing power during low usage periods for release during peak usage. The battery is also used to store power that is generated intermittently, such as in wind and solar power generation systems. The battery uses a beta alumina electrolyte that separates the positive sulfur and negative sodium electrodes. The electrons move back and forth between the two electrodes depending on whether the battery is charging or discharging. The advantages of this technology are that the battery has large energy density, high efficiency, and long-term reliability. The battery was designed for both long discharge durations, up to eight hours, but also has the capability to discharge rapidly with seconds to minutes of discharge duration.[2] American Electric Power will be adding this battery technology to their systems in Ohio and Virginia in 2008.[3]

Supercapacitors

A capacitor stores electricity in an electrostatic field rather than in chemical form. A capacitor consists of two electrodes, or plates, of opposite polarity separated by an electrolyte. The capacitor is charged by applying a voltage across the terminals and that causes the ions in the electrolyte to move to the electrode of the opposite polarity. Since the charge is only collected on the surface of the electrodes, a capacitor generally has very low electrical storage capacity. Two big advantages of a capacitor, however, are that (1) it can be charged or discharged very quickly; and (2) it can be charged and discharged almost an unlimited number of times without causing degradation in the equipment.

A supercapacitor works just like a regular capacitor except that it is made with electrodes that have extremely high surface areas so that they can store greater amounts of electricity. Supercapacitors are being used as temporary backup power to provide power briefly until the main backup power system can come on line. Supercapacitors are also being used in hybrid and electric cars to provide a quick burst of energy for quick acceleration. Larger supercapacitors of over 20 kilowatt-hours per square meter are still under development.

One particularly interesting potential application for supercapacitors is the possibility of using them as the main power source to propel an electric vehicle, rather than just as a small power booster as they are used now.

A large-scale supercapacitor would allow a vehicle's electrical propulsion system to be charged very quickly in a few minutes and the stored electricity would then allow the vehicle to operate on the roads for a matter of hours. This raises the possibility of having an electrical charge plug at the average service station where the vehicle owner can stop to get a quick charge, taking no more time than filling a vehicle with gasoline. This would eliminate the problem of the plug-in electric vehicles that are in operation now that require a relatively long period of time to charge, longer than a person would want to wait at a service station. Vehicles powered by large super capacitors would provide a way to bring electric-only vehicles to the road in mass quantities, thus eliminating altogether the need for vehicles with internal combustion engines that require gasoline or ethanol and that emit CO_2 and other contaminants.

Maxwell Technologies, Inc (Nasdaq: MXWL) is a company that specializes in producing capacitors for power storage and delivery systems. The company focuses on three lines of products: supercapacitors, high-voltage capacitors, and radiation-mitigated microelectronic products. Supercapacitors are used in electric and hybrid-electric vehicles to provide some extra stored electricity that can be used when there is a need for a burst of power for passing or climbing hills. High voltage capacitors are used mainly in the electric utility industry for protecting the grid. The radiation-mitigation technology is used mainly in the space and satellite industry. The company had annual revenue of $53.9 million in 2006.

Superconducting Magnetic Energy Storage

Superconducting magnetic energy storage systems store electrical energy in the magnetic field generated by a DC current flowing through a superconducting coil. The direct current stored in the magnet field can be converted back into alternating current as needed. These systems operate at over 90 percent efficiency. While today's technology allows for very high bursts of energy, the bursts are very short.

Superconductivity occurs in the coil when the wire in the coil is cooled to temperatures as low as –452 degrees Fahrenheit. At that temperature, materials lose all their resistance and electricity flows without loss. To reach this low temperature, the system must be cooled by liquid helium. Extensive research is being done to make superconductivity take place at a higher (but still very cold) temperature of about 216 degree Fahrenheit, which would greatly reduce the cost. Despite this low temperature, the new superconductors are called *high temperature superconductors*.[4] This is not a technology that will be commercialized anytime soon, but is nevertheless a technology to watch for the future.

TYPES OF POWER STORAGE SYSTEMS

As mentioned earlier, in these next types of power systems, electricity is converted into a different type of power, which can then be converted back to electricity when it is needed. The intermediate form of power can be pumped-hydro, compressed air, hydrogen for a fuel cell, or mechanical energy in a flywheel.

Pumped-Hydro Storage

As mentioned earlier in this chapter, pumped-hydro refers to pumping water into a tank so it can drain out later to drive a turbine/generator system to produce electricity. Conventional pumped-hydro storage uses two water reservoirs, one above the other. During periods when electricity demand is low, surplus electricity is used to pump water into the upper reservoir. Then when the electricity is needed again, the water in the upper reservoir is allowed to flow via gravity through water turbines to generate electrical power. About 70 percent to 85 percent of the electrical energy used to pump the water up into the upper reservoir can be recovered, meaning there is a loss of 15 percent to 30 percent. Pumped-hydro was first used in the 1890s in Italy and Switzerland. Today over 90 gigawatts of pumped-hydro storage is in operation around the world, which equals about 3 percent of total global generation capacity.[5]

Compressed Air Energy Storage

Compressed air energy storage systems use off-peak electrical power to compress and pump air into airtight chambers underground. Then when electricity is needed during peak hours, the air is released from the underground chambers. The air is heated and expanded through a combustion turbine to generate the needed electricity. The underground chambers are generally caverns cut out of impervious rock formations, salt caverns, or depleted gas or oil fields.

There are at least two such systems currently in operation. One is located in Huntorf, Germany, and the other is at McIntosh, Alabama. The $65 million McIntosh plant in Alabama was funded primarily by the Alabama Electric Co-operative. The system has a rated capacity of 100 megawatts and uses a deep limestone mine as the storage chamber. Two other compressed air systems are planned for Norton, Ohio, and Markham, Texas.[6]

Fuel Cells

A fuel cell is typically thought of as a primary electricity generation method that converts hydrogen into electricity. However, a fuel cell can also be used as an electricity storage device and may in fact eventually play a big role in that regard. For example, the U.S. National Renewable Energy Laboratory and Xcel Energy just unveiled a wind-to-hydrogen demonstration project.[7] The project will use a wind turbine to produce electricity to power an electrolysis machine that in turn produces the hydrogen. The hydrogen can then be used for any purpose, but the main eventual goal would be to use the hydrogen to drive a fuel cell to produce electricity.

Combining a wind turbine or solar power system with a fuel cell is a way to overcome the disadvantage that the wind and sun are only intermittent sources of power. When the wind is blowing or the sun is shining, some of the electricity from the wind or solar power system would be diverted to drive an electrolysis machine to produce hydrogen. (See the discussion on fuel cells in Chapter 7 for more information on hydrolysis, which uses electricity to split water into oxygen and hydrogen.) The hydrogen can then be stored and used to power the fuel cell when the wind or solar power system is offline. In this way, the overall system can produce power 24 hours a day, 7 days a week. The overall system would be a 24/7 electricity generation system with zero greenhouse gas or waste emissions.

Flywheels

Most modern flywheel systems consist of a rotating drum that is mounted on a vertical shaft. The shaft is supported on a stator by an electromagnetic bearing that virtually eliminates friction and wear. The stator is connected to a motor/generator. When surplus power is applied to the motor during off-peak periods, it causes the flywheel to spin faster. During peak load periods, when extra electricity is needed, the spinning flywheel turns the generator and generates electricity. To minimize the drag on the spinning drum, the drum is housed in a vacuum chamber. Flywheels can be up to 98 percent efficient, which means that 98 percent of the electricity used to cause the flywheel to spin can be recovered as usable electricity. Only 2 percent is lost in the storage process. Figure 12.1 shows a schematic diagram of a flywheel.

One of the problems with a flywheel is that it spins at such a high rate of speed, up to 100,000 rpm, that the rotating drum can literally fly apart. Modern drums are made of carbon-fiber materials to avoid this problem. However, since there is still a danger of the rotor breaking up, the entire

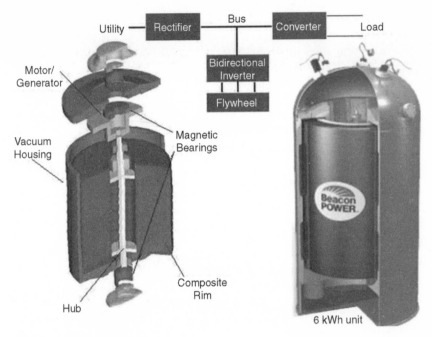

FIGURE 12.1 Flywheel Schematic
Source: Reprinted by permission and courtesy of Beacon Power Corp. (www.beacon power.com).

unit is housed in a strong container to prevent any release of debris in the event of failure.

TARGET MARKET SIZES

The storage and backup of electricity is big business. The size of the market is a bit difficult to estimate because of the wide variety of electricity storage methods. The market in any case is destined to grow much larger due to increased electricity usage in general and the increased need for power protection and backup for businesses and sensitive electronic equipment.

The global market for large battery systems is about $15 billion per year, according to the Electricity Storage Association (ESA), which represents electric utilities and researchers in advanced storage technology.[6] The ESA estimates that the industrial battery market, which is more limited and services motive applications (forklifts, materials handling trucks), uninterruptible power supplies, power quality applications, standby, and reserve batteries, amounts to $5 billion per year.[8] The industrial battery market as of mid-2007 was growing at an annual rate of about 7–8 percent in terms of units, according to EnerSys.[9] The main companies involved in the industrial battery market are Enersys (NYSE: ENS), Exide Technologies (Nasdaq: XIDE), and C&D Technologies Inc (NYSE: CHP).

The global market for small batteries used in portable electronic devices like cameras, phones, laptop computers, etc. is about $50 billion, of which about $5.5 billion is for secondary (rechargeable) batteries, according to the Battery University.[10] The small battery market is growing at a rate of about 6 percent per year.[11]

For the advanced power storage technologies, BCC Research says that the market for super capacitors, flywheels, and superconducting magnetic storage systems was $9.1 billion in 2005 and estimates that it will grow to $12.2 billion by 2010.[12]

Companies with Advanced Power Storage Products

- *Active Power, Inc.* (Nasdaq: ACPW). Active Power (www.activepower .com) designs and manufactures uninterrupted power supply (UPS) products. One of its products is a flywheel UPS system that is marketed under the name of CleanSource UPS. That product produces about 40 percent of the company's revenue. This system is also marketed by Caterpillar, Inc. under the name of Cat UPS. Another Active Power product for UPS systems uses thermal and compressed air storage and is marketed under the name of CoolAir UPS. Active Power is based in Austin, Texas, and produced $25.0 million in sales in 2006.

- *American Superconductor Corp.* (Nasdaq: AMSC). American Superconductor Corp, (www.amsuper.com) has two main product lines: (1) power converters that are used as electronic components by wind farms to regulate and convert the DC power generated by a wind farm; and (2) *high-temperature superconductor* (HTS) wires that carry up to 150 times as much electricity as a comparably sized copper wire. The HTS wires are sold mostly to the utility transmission market. American Superconductor recently received a major contract from the city of New York to lay new superconductor wires between power substations in the city to improve the robustness of the city's power network. The company has other products for the utility grid market that switch, control, and modulate power. In the 2007, fiscal year ended March 31, 2007, the company had total revenue of $52.2 million.

- *Beacon Power Corp.* (Nasdaq: BCON). Beacon Power Corp. (www. beaconpower.com) was founded in 1997 as a spinoff of SatCon's Energy Systems Division to develop flywheel-based energy storage. The company designs and develops products and services to support stable, reliable and efficient electrical grid operation. Beacon successfully demonstrated a prototype for a megawatt-level, utility-grade flywheel-based system to provide sustainable frequency regulation service. In late 2006, the company was awarded a contract by the Department of Energy to design a large-scale power plant based on the demonstrated technology. In 2006, the company had total revenue of $969,000.

- *C&D Technologies, Inc.* (NYSE: CHP). C&D Technologies (www. cdtechno.com) is a manufacturer of electrical power storage systems. The Standby Power division manufactures lead-acid batteries for backup and standby power. The Power Electronics division manufactures the control equipment that is used in the company's other products. The Motive Power division manufactures the lead-acid batteries used in the motive market, which includes forklift trucks and other material handling equipment. The company is headquartered in Blue Bell, Pennsylvania, and has manufacturing plants in several locations around the country. The company has been in operation since 1906 and had revenues in the fiscal year 2007, which ended on January 31, 2007, of $525 million.
- *Capstone Turbine Corp.* (Nasdaq: CPST). Capstone Turbine (www. capstoneturbine.com) develops and manufactures microturbine technology solutions for use in stationary distributive power generation applications. The microturbines are compact generators of electricity. They operate on the same principles as a jet engine, but can use a variety of fuels including natural gas, diesel oil, kerosene, and propane. The products are designed for producing electrical power for commercial and small industrial users. Capstone's microturbines run on fossil fuels and the turbines therefore emit greenhouse gases and pollutants, but the company is considered by many to be an "alternative energy" company because it provides distributed power generation products that allow users to operate off the grid or have nongrid power backup. The company was founded in 1988 and is headquartered in Chatsworth, California. In the fiscal year 2007 ended March 31, 2007, the company had revenues of $21.0 million.
- *Distributed Energy Systems Corp.* (Nasdaq: DESC). Distributed Energy Systems (www.distributed-energy.com) manufactures distributed electrical power systems that produce and store power at a customer or remote location. The systems are both standalone for power use in remote locations or for connection to the grid. The source of power for the generation can be from wind, solar, oil, natural gas, or biofuels. The company also produces hydrogen gas generating systems that produce hydrogen from water. To complement the hydrogen generators, the company provides hydrogen fuel cell systems to generate electricity.

The small fuel cell/hydrogen generating systems are designed for use in laboratories. The larger systems are designed for industrial use. The company was founded in 1974 and is headquartered in Wallingford, Connecticut. In 2006, the company had revenue of $45.9 million.

- *SatCon Technology Corp.* (Nasdaq: SATC). SatCon Technology (www.satcon.com) manufactures products for electrical power conversion and control. The products are used in areas such as alternative energy, hybrid electric vehicles, and distributed power generation. The Power Systems Division provides UPS systems used for power backup and power quality; inverters to convert the DC power produced by fuel cells, solar power, or wind power into usable AC power; and equipment to permit alternative power sources to be connected with the grid. Both the Electronics and the Applied Technology divisions design and build specialty products for both commercial and military customers. The company was founded in 1986 and is headquartered in Boston. In 2006, SatCon had total revenues of $28.8 million.

CHAPTER 13

Clean Transportation

Electric Hybrids Are Charged Up and Ready to Go

The world has a transportation problem. There are presently about 800 million vehicles on the world's roads, with more than 200 million of those vehicles operating in the United States.[1] There are alarming estimates that there will be some 2 billion vehicles on the world's roads by 2050. Virtually all of the vehicles that are currently on the road are equipped with internal combustion engines that burn fuel and spew various contaminants and greenhouse gases into the air. In fact, about 27 percent of all greenhouse gas emissions in the United States come from the transportation sector, according to the Environmental Protection Agency (EPA).[2] As to specific greenhouse gases, the EPA estimates two thirds of all carbon monoxide and almost one half of all ozone-forming emissions come from motor vehicles.

The transportation sector is clearly a big part of the energy problem, both from the standpoint of greenhouse gas emissions and from the standpoint of energy security since the U.S. imports 60 percent of its oil, which is mostly used to power America's vehicles. Clean energy solutions in the transportation sector would go a long way toward solving the world's overall greenhouse gas emissions problem, as well as America's problem of being addicted to oil.

THE INTERNAL COMBUSTION ENGINE: CAN IT BE SAVED?

The internal combustion engine is the propulsion device that is used in virtually all of the world's vehicles. In the internal combustion engine, gasoline (or some other combustible fuel such as ethanol) is fed into a cylinder where it is ignited. The resulting explosions drive pistons, which turn a crankshaft and ultimately the wheels via the transmission system. The exhaust from the small explosions is expelled through the muffler system into the atmosphere. The bottom line is that the internal combustion engine relies upon the burning of fuel as the propulsion source. The burning of fuel inevitably releases CO_2 and other gases and contaminants into the air.

Aside from the greenhouse gas emission and pollution problem, the internal combustion engine is also very inefficient. The overall efficiency of a gasoline-powered car is only about 20 percent. That means that only 20 percent of the energy contained in the gasoline is actually converted into mechanical energy. Some of the energy is used to run the various fans, pumps, and other devices and the rest is wasted as heat or unused mechanical energy.

Over the years scientists have done many things to make the internal combustion engine more efficient and also less harmful to the environment. Car engines today are much better than even five years ago. However, regardless of what scientists do to make the engine better, it is still an internal combustion engine that burns fuel.

The U.S. federal government got involved in the effort to reduce the environmental impact of the internal combustion engine in 1975 when it passed the Energy Policy Conservation Act. The Act was passed in response to the 1973–1974 Arab oil embargo. The goal was to double new car fuel economy by model year 1985. The Act set mileage standards to force the car manufacturers to get more miles from a gallon of gas. The standards were called the Corporate Average Fuel Economy (CAFE) standards.[3] Since 1975, nothing has been done to raise the standards to more realistic levels. Now, with the growing problem of climate change and higher gasoline prices, some leaders in Congress are mobilizing to raise CAFE standards. Yet, U.S. automakers and their political supporters in Congress are doing everything they can to block or at least water down the increase.

Many consumers are not waiting for Congress to raise fuel standards. They are instead voting with their pocketbooks and are simply buying vehicles that have better gasoline mileage and increasingly, gasoline-electric hybrids. In fact, Toyota officially became the world's largest automaker in April 2007, taking over the position from General Motors. Toyota gained the world's largest market share by focusing on quality and fuel economy.

ALTERNATIVE FUELS FOR THE INTERNAL COMBUSTION ENGINE

There are fuels that can be used in an internal combustion engine that are cleaner than others. Using cleaner fuels would represent a small step forward toward cleaning up transportation sector pollution and emissions.

Cleaner Diesel Fuel

Diesel engines are more efficient than gasoline engines, but their exhaust fumes still expel pollutants and greenhouse gases. To make diesel engines more environmentally friendly, the U.S. Environmental Protection Agency has mandated that *ultra-low sulfur diesel* (ULSD) fuel must be used in the future. The new fuel is 97 percent cleaner than current diesel fuel in terms of the sulfur content. This mandate has implications for refiners and manufacturers alike. Refiners started producing ULSD fuel in 2006 but both diesel fuels will be on sale for the next few years. All diesel fuel sold in the United States must be ULSD by 2010. The new fuel can be used in today's diesel cars and trucks, but the real benefits of the new fuel will not be realized until the new compatible engines are in use. Starting with the 2007 model year, manufacturers can only produce engines that are compatible with ULSD. The new engines using ULSD are expected to meet the same emission standards as gasoline-powered vehicles.[4]

Natural-Gas-Powered Vehicles

Engines that use natural gas as fuel operate like a gasoline combustion engines with only minor differences. Natural gas is still a fossil fuel and releases pollutants and greenhouse gas emissions. However, natural gas burns cleaner than gasoline and releases fewer pollutants. Disadvantages of natural gas vehicles include (1) the gas storage cylinders are so bulky that they take up a lot of trunk and cargo space; (2) the range of a natural gas vehicle is limited to about 200 miles versus a 300-mile range of a gasoline-fueled car; and (3) refueling locations are still limited.

Natural gas has been used as fuel for vehicle fleets for many years, mainly because natural gas is typically cheaper than gasoline. These fleets include taxicabs, transit and school buses, delivery trucks, public works trucks, and the like. What these all have in common is that their daily driving range is within the mileage limit of a single fill-up of fuel so their fuel tanks can be filled at the end of each day at the garage where the vehicles are stored.[5]

LPG Vehicles

Liquid petroleum gas is a fossil fuel that is refined from natural gas or petroleum. It is the same LP gas that is used for heating and cooking in many parts of the country. The technology for using it in cars has been around for decades. There are currently over 9 million vehicles in 38 countries that use LPG for fuel, according to the World Liquefied Petroleum Gas Association. In the United States, there are about 300,000 cars with LPG engines. The advantages are that (1) the harmful emissions are about half those of a gasoline engine; (2) the LPG engine runs much cleaner and therefore needs less maintenance; and (3) LPG is usually cheaper than gasoline.

Many automobile models that have an LPG engine as an option are available from major auto companies like Ford, General Motors, and Chrysler. However, most cars with the LPG option are also equipped with an alternate fuel system for gasoline. The cars can run on either LPG or gasoline and the car can switch from one to the other automatically. The advantage of the dual fuel system is that there is no danger of running out of fuel if an LPG refueling station is not available.[6]

Hydrogen-Boosted Engines

An emerging technology is to add hydrogen to the gasoline mixture to enhance the overall combustion quality. The small amount of hydrogen would be extracted from the gasoline by a reformer device added to the engine. The hydrogen would make it possible to increase the amount of air used in the gasoline ignition, thus making it possible to use less fuel. Scientists believe this technique could create a fuel-economy gain of 20 percent to 30 percent.[7]

Biofuel Vehicles

Ethanol and biodiesel are becoming more popular as transportation fuels. Ethanol, which is simply alcohol, has been added to the U.S. gasoline supply in some regions for years in order to make the gasoline burn cleaner, but usually at levels only up to 10 percent of the mix. *Flex fuel* is the name given to vehicles that can use any mix of gasoline and ethanol, ranging from straight gasoline, to E10 (10 percent ethanol and 90 percent gasoline), to E85 (85 percent ethanol and 15 percent gasoline). There are already about 6 million flex-fuel vehicles on U.S. roads today and looking ahead manufacturers expect to sell about 2 million more flex-fuel vehicles each year. Ethanol reduces the amount of pollutants and the CO_2 emitted from a vehicle, but the fact remains that ethanol is still powering an internal combustion engine. Biofuels will be discussed in more depth in the next chapter.

ELIMINATING THE INTERNAL COMBUSTION ENGINE

These improvements to the internal combustion engine are all helpful, but the fact remains that the internal combustion engine is still burning fuel and is releasing pollutants and CO_2 into the air. The real solution is to use a propulsion method that does not burn fuel and that produces zero pollution and zero CO_2 emissions. There are three main propulsion technologies that fall into this category: compressed air, fuel cells, and electric vehicles. These technologies will now be discussed in more depth.

Compressed-Air-Powered Vehicles

A French company, Moteur Developpment International (MDI), has developed two compressed air cars called the *MiniCAT* and *CityCAT* (see www.theaircar.com).[8] These vehicles will be manufactured first in India by Tata Motors (Mumbai: TTMT IN) and sold there in 2008. According to the developer, the two vehicles are designed for city use. CityCAT, for example, will have top speed of about 68 mph and will be able to travel about 125 miles before needing an air recharge. The air recharge will take only a few minutes when done with a high-pressure pump at specially equipped service stations. The vehicle also has a small built-in compressor that can be plugged into a 220-volt power source to recharge the tank. That recharge takes about six hours.[9]

MDI says that they are also working on an air/gasoline hybrid that uses an onboard gasoline powered compressor to refill the air tanks on the road. With this arrangement, the travel distances are limited only by the amount of fuel needed to run the compressor. The company says the vehicle should be able to travel thousands of miles on a tank of gas.

MDI has signed deals to bring the vehicles to 12 more countries. The three-seater compact MiniCat will sell for about $10,000 and the six-seater CitiCat will sell for about $16,000.[10] The main downside to these particular vehicles is that they use a fiberglass construction and they may not be able to pass U.S. crash tests. Nevertheless, MDI has at least validated the compressed air engine technology.

Fuel-Cell-Powered Vehicles

The fuel cell has been billed by some as the ultimate solution for powering the world's transportation fleet since a fuel cell produces only heat and water as waste. A fuel cell vehicle produces zero emissions, which is a highly attractive attribute. However, as noted in Chapter 7, creating the hydrogen in the first place can be an emission-producing operation. In addition, there is the challenging task of producing, transporting, storing, and delivering mass quantities of hydrogen, which is a highly flammable gas that requires special handling. The United States is having enough trouble trying to get E85 ethanol tanks installed in the nation's service stations let alone building a completely different hydrogen delivery infrastructure. Moreover, fuel cell manufacturers are still a long way away from producing a fuel cell vehicle that comes even close to the cost of current vehicles. Nevertheless, a variety of manufacturers are moving full speed ahead on trying to develop economical and practical fuel cell powered vehicles. This book's companion Web site at www.ProfitingFromCleanEnergy.com has links to videos clips of various fuel cell concept cars.

The most attractive application for fuel cell vehicles over the near to medium term is for fleet vehicles such as buses and delivery trucks. These vehicles return to a home base each night, which allows them to be refueled from a central location. Vehicle fleets powered by fuel cells would represent a step forward, even if the hydrogen is produced by reforming natural gas since the total emission and pollution amounts would still be much less than from a gasoline or diesel powered vehicle.

HYBRID GASOLINE-ELECTRIC VEHICLES

Most consumers have a hard time taking the thought of an all-electric vehicle seriously since the pictures of electric vehicles we usually see in newspapers and magazines look more like an overgrown golf cart than a vehicle someone would want to take out on a highway. However, most consumers are not aware of the rapid advances that are being made in the field of electric vehicles. Moreover, pairing an electric motor and a gasoline engine creates a *gasoline-electric hybrid vehicle* (HEV) that has a greater range than either an electric or a gasoline vehicle alone.

Sales of hybrid electric vehicles are in fact starting to take off. In 2006, sales of hybrids in the United States rose +28 percent from 2005 to 254,545 vehicles, representing 1.5 percent of U.S. auto sales, according to R. L. Polk.[11] U.S. hybrid sales accounted for about two-thirds of total world hybrid sales in 2006. Global hybrid sales in 2006 rose +25 percent to 378,000 vehicles and have shown fairly steady growth in the past three years, as seen in Figure 13.1. Global hybrid sales hit a monthly record of 51,400 in March 2007 and are on track to reach annual sales of nearly 500,000 vehicles in 2007, which would be up 22 percent year-on-year.[12]

Toyota Motor Corp (NYSE: TM) is by far the world's leader in hybrid sales. In the United States, Toyota accounted for 79 percent of hybrid sales

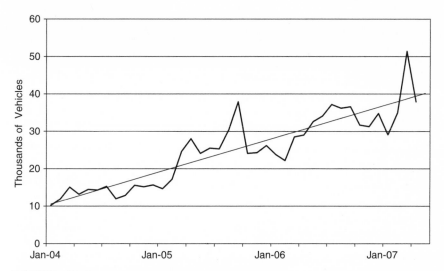

FIGURE 13.1 Global Hybrid Vehicle Monthly Sales
Source: "Worldwide HEV (Hybrid Electric Vehicle) Sales," *MarkLines,* July 2007,
http://www.marklines.com/en/numproduct/index.jsp.

in June 2007, according to HybridCars.com (see Figure 13.2).[13] The next closest competitor is Honda (NYSE: HMC) with a market share of 10 percent. Ford (NYSE: F) weighs in with a market share of 7 percent, and General Motors (NYSE: GM) with a market share of only 2 percent.

Regarding individual hybrid models, as of mid-2007 there were 12 hybrid cars on the market made by six different automakers.[14] The most popular hybrid vehicle by far is the Toyota Prius (www.toyota.com/prius), which accounted for 50.9 percent of hybrid vehicle sales in June 2007, according to HybridCars.com. The next most popular hybrids were the Toyota Camry (15.9 percent market share), Honda Civic (9.3 percent market share), and the Ford Escape (6.3 percent market share).[15]

The gasoline-electric hybrid vehicle has both a gasoline internal combustion engine and an electric motor to provide propulsion for the car. The batteries that drive the electric motor are charged either constantly or when the vehicle is slowing down, depending on the design of the system. The batteries cannot be charged from an external source. The two big advantages of gasoline-electric hybrid vehicles are that they reduce pollution and CO_2 emissions and get better mileage.

Mileage for hybrids is measured in miles per gallon of gasoline, even though the vehicle may run on electricity some or even most of the time depending on the length of the trip and the type of driving. EPA mileage estimates for hybrids run all the way from the lower end of 25 to

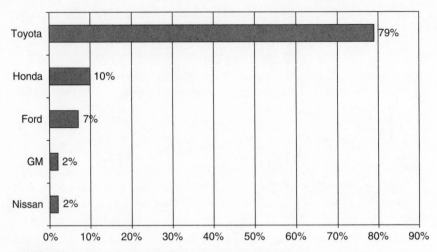

FIGURE 13.2 U.S. Hybrid Market Share (June 2007)
Source: "New Car Pricing: Hybrids: All," *Edmonds.com,* http://www.edmunds.com
/apps/vdpcontainers/do/ViewMarketModels/category=market/attribute=hybrid?
mktcat=hybrid-reviews&kw=hybrid-reviews&mktid=gc28593958.

28 miles/gallon for one of the Lexus models, to the higher end of 49 to 51 mpg for the Honda Civic and 51 to 60 mpg for the Toyota Prius, according to *Consumers Guide.* However, these are EPA figures and the mileage is never as high in real driving conditions.[16]

A hybrid vehicle typically costs a few thousand dollars more than a comparable gasoline vehicle to buy. However, this is offset by the better gasoline mileage and by up to a $2,600 federal tax credit, which brings down the total cost of ownership. In addition, there are sometimes local benefits such as being able to drive in a car pool lane even with only one person in the car and exemptions from sales tax, parking meter fees, and vehicle inspections.

PLUG-IN ELECTRIC HYBRID VEHICLES (PHEVs)

While the current gasoline-electric hybrid vehicles are a step forward, the real improvement will come with the next generation of gasoline-electric hybrid vehicles, which will be the *plug-in hybrid electric vehicle* or PHEV for short. In a plug-in hybrid, the electric motor is the primary source of power and the gasoline engine is used only as a supplemental power source when needed for recharging the battery on the road, accelerating, passing, or going up a hill. The battery is charged by plugging a cord into a conventional 110-volt electrical outlet in the home, garage, or charge station.[17]

The main advantage to a plug-in hybrid is that it will get even better mileage and produce even less pollution and CO_2 emissions than current hybrids. Several auto manufacturers are developing plug-in hybrids for mass production. Two new plug-in hybrid vehicles, the Ford Edge and the Chevrolet Volt, were introduced at the 2007 Detroit Auto Show and should be available in a few years. GM's Saturn division expects to have a plug-in hybrid version of its Saturn Vue SUV available in 2009. The mileage equivalent for these vehicles is very attractive. The Chevrolet Volt, for example, is being designed to go 40 miles without a recharge. If a commuter's daily round trip is 40 miles or less, then no gasoline would be used at all. If the round trip is 60 miles, the car would use gas for only 20 of those miles and the overall mileage calculation would be about 150 miles per gallon, according to GM.

Another big step forward will be hybrids that use ethanol rather than gasoline, making them flex-fuel hybrids that can use E85 ethanol. When hybrids are run on E85 and electricity, then gasoline usage will fall towards the attractive level of zero, which should ring a few alarm bells at OPEC. Ford recently announced that its current Ford Escape hybrid would soon come with the option of being a flex-fuel model that can run on E-85 ethanol. Chevrolet has announced that its Volt plug-in hybrid product line will include models that can run on E85 ethanol or biodiesel.

The delay in getting plug-in hybrids on the road is that they depend on new lithium-ion battery technology. The lithium-ion battery has been used for years for small electronic devices like cell phones, laptops, and power tools. Now they are being adapted for heavy-duty use in automobiles.

The lithium battery is a rechargeable battery like the familiar nickel-cadmium battery used in many electronic devices today. However, the lithium-ion battery has some significant advantages, which include (1) high energy capacity; (2) low self-discharge rate when not being used; (3) no need for a periodic total discharge; (4) high current output when needed; and (5) the ability to form the battery into many different shapes depending on space requirements.

The disadvantages of the lithium-ion battery include (1) the possibility of overheating, which requires protection circuitry to keep voltage and current within safe limits; (2) the battery ages even if it is not in use; and (3) the battery is currently more expensive to manufacture than older battery technologies.

Safety is the biggest concern in using lithium-ion batteries in vehicles. Laptops that use lithium batteries have been known to sometimes overheat and catch fire.[18] However, a great deal of work has been done to make the lithium-ion battery safer and strong enough to power a car and the automobile companies believe that the safety issues have been solved. In fact, lithium-ion battery powered vehicles are already on the road today, though not in mass quantities.

HYBRID AND ELECTRIC VEHICLE PLAYERS

The world's largest auto manufacturers are the companies that are presently selling the vast majority of gasoline-electric hybrid vehicles. The large auto manufacturers are also the companies that will be rolling out next-generation plug-in hybrids and eventually all-electric vehicles on a mass scale. As mentioned earlier, Toyota has a huge head start in producing and selling hybrids.

The size of the hybrid market opportunity demands that the hybrid battery suppliers for these vehicles are also large companies with large R&D budgets and mass production capabilities. One company that is currently heavily involved in developing and selling hybrid batteries is Johnson Controls (NYSE: JCI).[19] Johnson Controls currently has twelve development contracts for lithium-ion plug-in hybrid vehicle batteries and three production contracts for hybrid technology. In addition, Johnson Controls and Saft Advanced Power Solutions (parent: Saft Groupe, Paris: SAFT FP) in January 2006 formed a joint venture to supply advanced-technology batteries for hybrid-electric vehicles and electric vehicles.[20] Other companies involved in hybrid vehicles and batteries include the following:

- *Altair Nanotechnologies Inc.* (Nasdaq: ALTI). Altair (www.altairnano. com), with 2006 sales of $4.3 million, is involved in a variety of businesses having to do with nanomaterials and nanomanufacturing. Regarding batteries, Altair produces its NanoSafe brand of lithium-ion batteries that are used in all-electric vehicles. In January 2007, Altair entered into a multiyear agreement with Phoenix Motorcars to supply more than $2.0 million of lithium-ion batteries, which Phoenix Motorcars will incorporate into its all-electric SUVs.[21]
- *Valence Technology* (Nasdaq: VLNC). Valence Technology (www.valence.com), with 2006 sales of $16.7 million, has developed a phosphate-based lithium-ion technology *Saphion* that is used to produce lithium-ion batteries for the large appliance market including vehicles. The company says that it is close to commercializing its Saphion product line.
- *GM's lithium-ion battery partners.* General Motors in June 2007 announced that it awarded two contracts for the supply of advanced lithium-ion batteries for its upcoming plug-in hybrid electric vehicle, the Chevrolet Volt. The batteries will be more thermally stable and less

expensive than current models. The two suppliers will be: (1) Compact Power, Inc. (www.compactpower.com), which is a subsidiary of Korean battery manufacturer LG Chem (parent company LG Group, South Korea 003550 KS), and (2) Germany-based Continental AG's Automotive Systems division (www.conti-online.com) (German Xetra: CON GR).

ALL-ELECTRIC VEHICLES

Chris Paine's documentary film, *Who Killed the Electric Car?*, released in 2006 at the Sundance Film Festival by Sony Pictures, provides an extremely interesting view of the recent history of the electric vehicle. The film's Web site can be found at www.WhoKilledTheElectricCar.com.

The film documents how U.S. automakers produced a limited number of all-electric vehicles starting in the late 1990s in response to demands of California regulators. General Motors first built its all-electric *EV1* vehicle in 1997 with a production quantity of 650 vehicles. Over the next few years, several hundred more cars were made with some improvements. The car was a two-seater, could accelerate from 0–60 mph in about 8 seconds, had a top speed of about 80 mph, and had a driving range of about 75 miles without a recharge. The vehicle was useful for commuting to work and for quick trips around town. Rather than selling the vehicles outright, GM leased the EV1 vehicles to users and retained the right to repossess the vehicles at the end of the lease term.

In 2003, GM canceled the EV1 program. GM then took back the EV1 vehicles from users and destroyed virtually all of the vehicles in junkyards. The film *Who Killed the Electric Car?* investigates why the electric vehicle program was killed. The film concludes that there was plenty of blame to go around, including consumer ignorance, automobile companies that didn't want a threat to their high-end gasoline-powered vehicles and to the dealer aftermarket for auto maintenance and replacement parts, and California regulators who caved in to heavy pressure from automobile and oil industry officials and lobbyists.

The film actually provides an important cautionary lesson for investors about the ability of legacy companies with strong lobbying forces and political clout to sometimes bury promising technologies and products before they can even get off the ground. Yet the film also documents the surprising popularity of the EV1 among its users. Some EV1 users actually banded together to protest the cancellation of the EV1 program and they documented how GM rounded up the vehicles and destroyed the EV1's, presumably to prevent the electric vehicle from being a threat to their gas-guzzling franchise vehicles. The EV1 was actually based on rather rudimentary battery technology using lead acid batteries, meaning EV1 users would presumably be even happier with the new gasoline-electric and all-electric vehicles that will be emerging in coming years.

While U.S. automakers, with their heads in the sand as usual, refused to move ahead with an all-electric vehicle program, the U.S. government pushed ahead with a research program for gasoline-electric hybrids. U.S. automakers have always assumed that U.S. consumers would not buy all-electric vehicles because of the perception of weak power and limited ranges. However, the U.S. government pushed a program to bring gasoline-electric hybrid vehicles to market with the idea that U.S. consumers would buy an electric/gasoline vehicle with extended ranges and low operating costs. Japanese automakers, which felt threatened by the U.S. government support for a hybrid gasoline-electric vehicle program, embarked on their own aggressive hybrid research programs. The result was that Toyota emerged as the dominant hybrid vehicle manufacturer in the world and U.S. automakers were left playing catch-up as usual.

Full-sized all-electric vehicles with a reasonable range are now starting to be produced by smaller manufacturers. The electric vehicle is really very simple in its operation. The power portion of the vehicle is simply a battery, an electric motor, a foot pedal/controller to regulate the flow of electricity to the motor, and a transmission to transfer the motor's power to the wheels. The battery technology for all-electric vehicles is lithium-ion.

There are three main small U.S. companies that are involved in producing all-electric vehicles:

- *Phoenix Motorcars* (privately held). Phoenix Motorcars (www.phoenixmotorcars.com) is currently in production with its all-electric sport utility truck for a variety of customers including Pacific Power & Light. Phoenix is ramping up production to about 500 vehicles per year. The truck carries up to five people, can go from 0 to 60 mph in 10 seconds, has a top speed of 95 mph, and has the usual features of heat, air-conditioning, power windows and locks, and front airbags. The cost of the vehicle is about $45,000. These trucks use lithium-ion batteries supplied by Altair Nanotechnologies, as discussed in the previous section. The truck has a range of 100 miles per charge and can recharge in six hours, or in as little as 10 minutes with a special charging device.[22] The company says an upgrade will extend the truck's range to 250 miles. An independent review of the vehicle carried in *PC Magazine* gave the truck high marks.[23] This book's companion Web site at www.ProfitingFromCleanEnergy.com has links to some video clips demonstrating the Phoenix all-electric SUV.

- *Tesla Motors* (privately held). Tesla Motors in 2007 will officially start delivering the all-electric Tesla Roadster (www.teslamotors.com).[24] The Tesla Roadster is a high-end sports car that can accelerate from 0–60 mph in about 4 seconds and hit a top speed of over 130 mph. Its driving range on a single charge is over 200 miles. Its rechargeable lithium-ion battery has a life of over 100,000 miles. The company says that the Roadster's mileage performance will be the equivalent of getting 135 miles per gallon in a gasoline-powered car. The first production run of 100 cars is already sold out. The price of the high-performance sports car is about $100,000. The initial model is a two-seater convertible, but the company plans to have a four-door sedan model available in 2008. *Forbes*, in its Best Cars 2006 feature, gave the Tesla Roadster a "New car that lived up to the hype" award:.[25] This book's companion Web site at www.ProfitingFromCleanEnergy.com has links to video clips demonstrating the Tesla Roadster.
- *ZAP, Inc.* (OTCBB: ZAAP). ZAP (www.zapworld.com) is a company that sells small, all-electric vehicles, scooters, motorcycles, and all-terrain vehicles. ZAP was incorporated in 1994 and had 2006 sales of $10.8 million. Most of its products are manufactured in China. The company's vehicles are generally low powered and are designed for local or off-road use. However, ZAP recently announced its new ZAP-X Crossover, which is a full-sized all-electric vehicle that the company says will be able to travel 350 miles per charge (rapid 10 minute recharge) at a cost of only 1 cent per mile. The company in 2006 also started selling rechargeable batteries using lithium-ion and lithium polymer technology for use with devices like cell phones, digital cameras, and laptops.

CLEAN TRANSPORTATION INVESTMENT CONCLUSIONS

We can start from the premise that there is nothing that can save the internal combustion engine over the long haul, assuming that climate change is real and that greenhouse gases and pollution need to be curbed. Regardless of the fuel being burned, even ethanol and biodiesel, internal combustion engines release CO_2 into the atmosphere and other contaminants as well. Moreover, the process for obtaining the fuel (gasoline or biofuels) for the internal combustion engines carries an additional set of environmental issues. Companies that provide solutions for improving the internal combustion engine can be successful for a period of time, but will ultimately fade if they do not migrate into alternative zero-emission propulsion technologies.

Looking at the alternatives to the internal combustion engine, fuel cell vehicles at first glance present an attractive option given that a fuel cell produces zero emissions. However, even if fuel cell vehicles eventually become economically competitive, there is the potentially insurmountable cost and logistics problem of creating and delivering hydrogen (or intermediate hydrogen products such as natural gas) to service stations across the nation. As mentioned earlier, the United States cannot even get E85 ethanol delivered across the nation, let alone hydrogen which is a much more challenging fuel from the standpoint of safety, production, storage, and delivery.

The option that clearly makes the most sense for the long haul is to start with the gasoline-electric hybrid vehicle and eventually move to the all-electric vehicle. Electricity is a "fuel" that is already delivered to every household, business and service station in the United States. Moreover, the economics of hybrid and all-electric vehicles are attractive because electricity is a relatively cheap source of energy. All-electric vehicles can be operated for as little as 1 to 4 cents per mile, which is far less than the fuel cost of a gasoline engine of 10 to 20 cents per mile (depending on mileage and gasoline prices).

Gasoline-electric hybrid sales are currently growing at an annual rate of more than 20 percent and that growth rate is likely to strengthen as plug-in hybrids start to become available. Plug-in hybrids are likely to be far more popular than the marketplace currently believes. U.S. automakers are skeptical about plug-in hybrids because they don't think consumers will be willing to take the extra step of plugging their cars into a socket to recharge them. Indeed, not all consumers park their cars near an electric outlet where they can plug them in.

However, there are already charging stations for plug-in vehicles and many consumers are likely to be attracted to vehicles that allow them to use very little gasoline in return for the minor inconvenience of plugging the car in overnight. U.S. automakers have already seriously underestimated demand for current hybrid-electric vehicles as evidenced by the fact that they are so far behind Toyota in producing and selling hybrid vehicles. In fact, an executive vice president at Toyota has been quoted as saying, "In the future, the cars you will see from Toyota will be 100 percent hybrid."[26]

Is there enough electricity capacity in the American grid to charge up all of America's cars? In fact, a study by the Pacific Northwest National Laboratory found that the current idle off-peak electricity capacity in the United States could power 84 percent of America's 220 million vehicles right now if they were all plug-in hybrid vehicles.[27] That means America could switch overnight to plug-in hybrids and the current power system would be able to handle 84 percent of the extra load.

Sales of advanced batteries and hybrid vehicles are likely to be significantly stronger than the market expects in coming years. Companies that are at the forefront of battery and electric vehicle technology are likely to thrive in coming years and decades.

CHAPTER 14

Ethanol and Biofuels

Long-Term Transportation Solution or Flash in the Pan until More Environmentally Friendly Vehicle Technologies Take Over?

The ethanol boom is the best thing to hit U.S. farmers since the Great Depression brought the farm subsidy system. U.S. farmers have suffered for literally decades under the weight of falling inflation-adjusted crop prices combined with rising production and land costs. Willie Nelson, Neil Young, and John Mellencamp still hold the Farm Aid concerts that these artists started during the farm recession in 1985, when many family farms were forced out of business (www.farmaid.org). But U.S. farmers now have a new spring in their step since a major source of new demand has emerged for their product and has driven farm profits sharply higher.

Ethanol demand has driven not only corn prices sharply higher, but has also boosted the prices of other crops such as soybean, wheat, and cotton prices because less farmland is being planted with those crops and more farmland with corn. The U.S. agricultural sector is now a booming industry, both for farmers themselves and for all the businesses connected with agriculture.

BIOFUELS: WHAT ARE THEY?

Biofuel is a general term that refers to a liquid or gas fuel derived from biomass plant materials such as crops, crop waste, wood and wood products, plant oils, and similar materials. *Ethanol* is alcohol produced by the fermentation of sugars in corn, cane or beet sugar, or other types of plant matter. *Biodiesel* is a flammable oil that is comparable to petroleum-based diesel fuel except that it is manufactured from various types of plant oil or animal fats.

253

Biodiesel

Biodiesel is produced from vegetable oil (e.g., palm oil, soybean oil, corn oil) or from animal fats such as tallow. Biodiesel is popular in Europe where there are more diesel passenger cars, but biodiesel has not caught on yet in the United States. Biodiesel is biodegradable and nontoxic. Pure biodiesel is *B100*. *B20* is 20 percent biodiesel and 80 percent petroleum diesel. B20 can be used in existing diesel engines without any modifications. B100 requires some minor engine modifications such as replacing the engine seals with nonrubber seals and in colder climates a fuel heating system may be necessary to keep the fuel from becoming too thick.

Ethanol

The process of producing ethanol is essentially the same as running a moonshine still. The process involves decomposing the glucose ($C_6H_{12}O_6$) or other sugar contained in plant matter into alcohol (C_2H_5OH) and CO_2 through the process of microbial (yeast) fermentation. The resulting ethanol product is then treated with denaturing ingredients to make it unfit for human consumption and to avoid liquor taxes. For American vehicles, ethanol is typically mixed with gasoline to produce *E10* (10 percent ethanol and 90 percent gasoline) or E85 (85 percent ethanol and 15 percent gasoline). E10 is sometimes called *gasohol*. This book's companion Web site at www.ProfitingFromCleanEnergy.com has a link to a video providing a tour of an ethanol refinery.

Ethanol is certainly not a new fuel for operating internal combustion engines. The first Ford Model T was designed to run on ethanol. Ethanol's image received a boost when the IRL IndyCar Series, starting with the 2007 season, switched to using 100 percent ethanol instead of methanol, illustrating that ethanol is a powerful fuel that can run high performance engines.

ADVANTAGES AND DISADVANTAGES

The big benefit from ethanol is that it is derived from naturally grown crops such as corn and sugar. It is therefore a "renewable" energy source since farmers can simply grow more corn and sugar next year for the next round of ethanol production. This contrasts with an energy source such as petroleum, which is contained in fixed quantities in the earth's crust and is not renewable. Once petroleum is removed and burned, it is gone.

For the United States and other countries such as Brazil that are big agricultural producers, ethanol also provides the advantage of energy security since the crops are grown within a country's borders, thus reducing or even eliminating dependence on foreign sources of fuel. In fact, Brazil does not need to import any foreign oil because of its status as the world's second largest ethanol producer.

Another big advantage of ethanol is that the ethanol industry provides significant economic stimulus to a country's agricultural sector and overall economy. Spending dollars at home on fuel, with economic multiplier effects for other industries, is certainly much better than sending dollars overseas to Middle East oil sheiks. In fact, the U.S. ethanol industry added $17.7 billion to U.S. GDP in 2005, created 153,725 jobs, increased American consumer income by $5.7 billion, and provided $1.9 billion in tax revenue to the federal government and $1.6 billion to state and local governments (thus reducing individual taxpayer contributions), according to the research firm LEGG LLC.[1] Those domestic economic benefits stand in stark contrast to simply shipping dollars overseas to oil producers.

Ethanol also has an advantage in that it burns more cleanly than gasoline, thus producing fewer pollutants. Ethanol produces up to one-third less carbon monoxide and one-quarter less CO_2 than a comparable gallon of gasoline. Ethanol also eliminates the sulfur dioxide emission from gasoline that comes back to earth as acid rain. Nevertheless, ethanol is still a combustion fuel that emits greenhouse gases. The production process for ethanol also releases CO_2 into the atmosphere, although that is offset by the fact that the feedstock plants absorbed CO_2 during their lifetime.

The main disadvantage of ethanol, at least for right now, is that ethanol in the United States is produced almost exclusively from corn, which is a high-value crop that is very important in the human food chain. Strong demand for corn from ethanol producers has driven the price of corn sharply higher, thus also raising the price of food for humans and the cost of feedstock for livestock producers.

Lester Brown, who founded Earthwatch, has gone so far as to predict that the biofuel craze will cause the price of food to skyrocket and will cause food riots.[2] In fact, there have already been street protests in Mexico tied to sharply higher corn tortilla prices, which are a key food staple for the poor in Mexico.

A startling statistic is that the corn used for a single refill of a 25-gallon vehicle tank could feed one person for an entire year, according to Co-op America.[3] The "food versus fuel" debate will continue in coming years, but will become less important over time as ethanol producers eventually switch over to cellulosic feedstocks that are cheaper and are not part of the human food chain.

Ethanol produced from corn also has a disadvantage in that it is not a particularly efficient way to produce fuel. A large effort is required to produce an acre of corn, including human labor, fertilizers, pesticides, and fuel to run farm equipment. There has been a heated debate in the past several years about the net energy balance of corn-based ethanol. The U.S. Department of Energy has tried to settle the issue by citing a net energy balance ratio of 1.34, which means that for every unit of energy that goes into growing corn and converting the corn into ethanol, we get back 1.34 units of energy in the form of transportation fuel.[4] A net energy balance of 1.34 is at least above 1.0 and therefore results in net positive energy output, but that is still not a particularly efficient way to produce energy. This debate will fade as cellulosic ethanol comes on line, because cellulosic ethanol has much higher yields. The U.S. Department of Energy cites a net energy balance of 2.62 for cellulosic ethanol, which means that 2.62 units of energy would be produced for every unit of energy expended in the production effort.[5]

The most damning disadvantage of ethanol produced from corn in the United States, however, is that there is simply not enough farmland in the United States to produce all the ethanol that would be needed to completely replace gasoline. The situation is less severe for sugar-based ethanol, however, because the world's big sugar producers such as Brazil have plenty of extra land that can be cultivated with sugar if ethanol and sugar demand is high enough (although deforestation and loss of CO_2 conversion may be involved in clearing that land). In any case, the land situation in the United States will be alleviated to some extent when cellulosic ethanol comes on line with its higher yield of ethanol per acre of land. In addition, cellulosic-based products are either agricultural waste products or low-value crops such as *switchgrass*, which can be grown on marginal land that may not be able to support a high-value crop such as corn.

The inefficiency of using land and sun energy to produce biofuels is the topic of an interesting article in *Photon International* magazine titled "Organized Wastefulness: Biofuel Is the Most Inefficient Renewable Energy. Why Not Fill the Car's Tank Directly with Solar Electricity?"[6] The author provides calculations indicating that one hectare of land (which is about 2.5 acres) can produce enough ethanol for an automobile to travel 22,500 kilometers, whereas that same amount of land containing a reasonably efficient solar photovoltaic park could produce enough electricity for a plug-in electric vehicle to go 3.25 million kilometers, or 144 times farther. The author's point is that crop-based biofuels do a very poor job of converting the energy contained in sunlight (via photosynthesis) to transportation fuel as compared with solar photovoltaic power. The author's other point is that biofuels represent a very inefficient use of land as compared with an alternative of constructing solar parks. The author makes a cogent argument that crop-based biofuels make no economic sense (or environmental sense) as compared with encouraging the use of utility solar power and plug-in hybrid electric vehicles.

Ethanol: Summary of Advantages and Disadvantages

Advantages

- Ethanol is derived from renewable corn and other plant-based feed-stocks. If the feedstock comes from domestic sources, then a country is insulated from unstable sources of imported oil.
- Ethanol burns more cleanly than gasoline and gives off fewer green-house gases, making it better for the environment (ethanol produces up to one-third less carbon monoxide and one-quarter less CO_2 than a comparable gallon of gasoline).
- Ethanol can be mixed with gasoline as an oxygenate additive to improve combustion efficiency and reduce pollution.
- Ethanol is easy to distribute using the current U.S. and global gasoline retail distribution system (unlike hydrogen for fuel cells).
- Ethanol industry provides an economic stimulus to a country's agriculture sector and overall economy.

Disadvantages

- Ethanol-fueled internal combustion engines still release CO_2 and other pollution into the air.
- Ethanol produces about 25 percent lower mileage than gasoline.[7]
- Ethanol raises a feedstock debate about "food or fuel," although that issue will disappear when cellulosic ethanol becomes more prevalent.
- Corn-based ethanol is not a particularly efficient way to produce fuel because of the large amount of energy and land that goes into producing each gallon of ethanol.
- Ethanol is more expensive to transport than gasoline because ethanol cannot easily be sent through pipelines and is currently transported only by rail car, tanker truck or ship. Ethanol in the United States is produced mostly in the Midwest and transportation costs are high to the east and west coasts.
- Ethanol helps promote internal combustion engines, which from a policy standpoint should be eliminated in favor of more environmentally friendly vehicle propulsion methods such as electric or fuel cell vehicles.

U.S. GOVERNMENT SUPPORT FOR ETHANOL

U.S. ethanol producers are currently receiving strong support from the U.S. federal government, which has helped the U.S. ethanol industry to get on its feet. First, the U.S. federal government has a Renewable Fuels

Standard (RFS), which requires fuel distributors and blenders to use 7.5 million gallons of biofuels per year by 2012. The industry will easily beat that standard and reach the 7.5 million gallon goal by early 2008, four years ahead of schedule. Washington is in the process of raising the RFS.

President Bush has proposed his "Twenty in Ten" plan, which seeks to reduce gasoline usage by 20 percent over the next 10 years. The plan involves raising the Renewable Fuel Standard (RFS) to 35 billion gallons of renewable fuels by 2017, which would reduce the need for gasoline by 15 percent. The remaining 5 percent of gasoline savings would come from reducing gasoline demand by raising the Corporate Average Fuel Economy (CAFE) standards for cars.[8]

In addition, there are two tax provisions that provide strong support for the U.S. ethanol industry. First, the federal government gives fuel blenders a 51-cent per gallon excise tax credit for blending ethanol into gasoline (the credit lasts until 2010). Second, the federal government protects U.S. ethanol producers with a 54-cent per gallon import tariff on imported ethanol, which is enough to make large-scale ethanol imports from Brazil uneconomical. The 54-cent per gallon tariff is currently set to expire on January 1, 2009, although it is likely to be rolled over.

States are also taking action on their own to boost ethanol use. California Governor Schwarzenegger in early 2007, for example, moved to reduce the carbon content of transportation fuels in California by 10 percent by 2020, which would largely be met with increased ethanol usage.

OBSTACLES FOR THE U.S. ETHANOL INDUSTRY

Ethanol is currently used in the United States almost solely as a gasoline additive in E10 (10 percent ethanol and 90 percent gasoline). Ethanol is blended into about 46 percent of the nation's gasoline, according to *Biofuels Journal*.[9] That usage stems mainly from the fact that ethanol is an "oxygenate" that helps the gasoline to burn more completely, thus reducing pollution emissions. Ethanol is used to raise the octane of the fuel mix, thus meeting octane requirements. Demand for ethanol as an oxygenate additive rose sharply in the spring and summer of 2006 when gasoline retailers dropped MTBE (methyl tert-butyl ether) as an additive due to liability and ground water contamination issues, instead substituting ethanol as the oxygenate of choice. Ethanol is also being used as an additive to meet the federal Renewable Fuel Standard, which requires blenders to use 7.5 billion gallons per year of renewable fuels by 2012.

Ethanol as a primary fuel in the form of E85, however, has yet to take off in any significant way. U.S. automakers have been manufacturing a fairly large number of "flex-fuel" vehicles (FFV's) in the past several years because they received credit toward their fuel economy standards for producing those vehicles. There are already about 6 million flex-fuel cars on the road in America. U.S. automakers have announced plans to double production of flex-fuel autos by 2010. Flex-fuel vehicles can use straight gasoline, E10, or E85.

However, many car owners do not even realize that they have a flex-fuel vehicle. Even those that know they have a flex-fuel vehicle would have a hard time finding a service station that carried E85. In California, for example, only one of the state's 10,000 public service stations carried E85 ethanol as of mid-2007, according to U.S. Department of Energy Web site (there were also four private E85 stations in California but those were not open to the public).[10] In the United States as a whole, there were only 1,250 service stations that carry E85 as of mid-2007, which represents only 0.7 percent of the 169,000 service stations in the United States.[11]

There are three main reasons why E85 pumps are not being installed at many service stations in the United States:

1. *E85 pump costs.* First, E85 equipment is a large expense for the service station. A service station usually must install a new underground tank and pump on the service island, a process that can cost as much as $200,000.[12] The federal government provides a tax break for installing the E85 equipment, but there is still a relatively large up-front cost for service stations to install E85 pumps.

2. *E85 obstruction by major oil companies.* The second obstacle for installing E85 pumps is that some major oil companies are blocking the efforts. Ethanol is not a product produced by major U.S. oil companies and instead provides direct competition to gasoline. Oil companies therefore have an interest in blocking E85 from being sold in service stations alongside gasoline. Service stations that are owned by major oil companies will certainly not be installing ethanol pumps any time in the near future, unless they are required to do so by law.

   The oil companies also have a way of blocking independently owned service stations from selling E85 because many of the contracts between major oil company suppliers and independent service stations stipulate that the service station must exclusively sell the products sold by the major oil company, which typically do not include ethanol. Oil companies are using that contract provision to block E85 from being sold at independently owned service stations, although the oil company can provide an exemption if they wish. It is no coincidence that of the stations that have E85 available, 91 percent are independently owned and only 9 percent are owned by the major oil companies, according to the Center for American Progress.[13]

3. *Ethanol economics.* The third obstacle for E85 adoption is simple economics. Many service station owners see little demand from the public for E85. Service station owners may also have about doubts about whether E85 is inexpensive enough to compete with gasoline. A motorist gets about 25 percent less mileage with E85, which means E85 needs to be substantially cheaper than gasoline to compete. According to the U.S. Department of Energy, consumers need to multiply the price of E85 by 1.41 to place it on an equal mileage footing with gasoline.

   There are various efforts being made to expand the availability of E85. VeraSun (NYSE: VSE), for example, which sells its own brand of E85 (called *VE85*), partnered with Ford in order to launch an ethanol corridor in service stations located along Interstate 55 in Illinois and Interstate 70 in Missouri. VeraSun has also partnered with General Motors to bring E85 to the Pittsburgh area. Wal-Mart is considering selling E85 at its service stations around the country as part of its partnership with Murphy Oil. Moreover, many states are considering legislation that would require, or at least make is easier, for service stations to install E85 pumps. That would go a long way towards forcing the availability of E85 to motorists with flex-fuel vehicles.

4. *Underwriters Laboratories E85 certification.* Another hitch for E85 arose when the Underwriter's Laboratories (UL) in late 2006 said that they had not yet certified existing service station tanks and pumps to handle E85, which is more corrosive than gasoline. Existing tanks and pumps have only been certified by UL for a mix to a maximum of 15 percent ethanol. Existing fuel tanks and pumps have already been used for a decade to sell E85 and there have been no reported safety problems. However, the technical issue remains that without UL certification, some existing tanks and pumps may be in violation of state and local fire codes that require certification of an independent tester such as UL. BP responded to the UL news by saying that it will delay the expansion of E85 pumps at its service stations in the United States until the issue is resolved. Underwriters Laboratories in March 2007 said that it expected to publish its certification requirements by the end of the fourth quarter of 2007, which would then allow pump manufacturers to make sure they are UL compliant and eliminate the problem.[14]

BRAZILIAN COMPETITION

Brazil is the world's second largest producer of ethanol behind the United States. In 2006, Brazil produced 4.227 billion gallons of ethanol, which was just slightly behind the U.S. production of 4.264 billion gallons in 2006

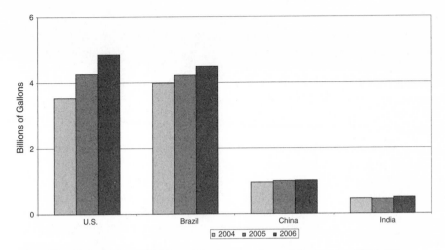

FIGURE 14.1 Top World Ethanol Producers—Annual Production 2004–06
Source: Renewable Fuels Association, "Annual World Ethanol Production by Country,"
July 2007, http://www.ethanolrfa.org/industry/statistics/#E.

(see Figure 14.1).[15] Ethanol accounts for over one-third of Brazil's total fuel usage.

Brazil's government started an energy independence program more than a decade ago and actively pushed for domestic ethanol production to eliminate the need to import foreign petroleum products. Brazil has now achieved that energy independence. About 75 percent of the new cars sold in Brazil are flex-fuel vehicles that can use any mix of gasoline and ethanol. Brazil currently requires its fuel to contain a minimum of 20 percent ethanol, and the government is considering raising that requirement to 25 percent.

The big difference between ethanol production in the United States and Brazil is that the United States uses corn to produce ethanol while Brazil uses sugar. Brazil uses about one-half of its sizeable sugarcane crop to produce ethanol. Brazil's sugar-based ethanol is about 50 cents per gallon cheaper to produce than U.S. corn-based ethanol, mainly because sugarcane produces much higher ethanol yields than corn. In addition, labor and other production costs are generally lower in Brazil. Brazil's lower ethanol production costs make it possible for Brazil to export ethanol and have money left over to cover the transocean shipping fees.

Brazil is the only country in the world that is capable of producing major ethanol exports over the short to medium term. Brazil's president said in April 2007 that Brazil could expand its sugar production and double its ethanol production over the next 10 years.[16] As far as actual export deals, Brazil's state-owned oil company, Petroleo Brasileiro SA (Petrobras) in April 2007 was in an advanced stage of negotiations with Japan to supply up to 800 million gallons of ethanol annually within 4 years.[17] That would amount to about 55 percent of Brazil's projected export capacity by 2012 according to the *Wall Street Journal*.[18] In the same reportage, Petrobas was in talks about long-term ethanol contracts with buyers in China and South Korea.[19]

It is not currently economical for Brazil to export large quantities of ethanol to the United States primarily because of the 54-cent per gallon U.S. import tariff on imported ethanol that the United States imposed starting in 1980 (that tariff is currently due to expire on January 1, 2009). Brazil did, in fact, temporarily export large quantities of ethanol to the United States in the spring and summer of 2006 when the phase-out of MTBE as an oxygenate additive caused a surge in demand for ethanol and an upward spike in prices. That upward spike in ethanol prices temporarily made it economical for U.S. blenders to import Brazilian ethanol. However, ethanol imports dropped back when U.S. ethanol prices normalized later in 2006 and again made Brazilian ethanol uneconomical.

The reality is that Brazil is waiting in the wings to pounce on the U.S. ethanol market, which would happen if the 54-cent U.S. tariff on ethanol were dropped. There are some groups and politicians who believe that the U.S. ethanol import tariff should be dropped. For example, the Interamerican Ethanol Commission co-chaired by Jeb Bush (President Bush's brother) favors dropping the U.S. ethanol import tariff in order to expand U.S. usage of ethanol and to promote U.S. petroleum independence and environmental goals (see www.helpfuelthefuture.org). Former World Bank President Paul Wolfowitz, at a carbon-finance conference in London in March 2007, also argued in favor of ending ethanol tariffs in the interest of creating a healthy and efficient global biofuels market.[20] Dropping the U.S. ethanol import tariff would make ethanol cheaper for U.S. motorists and would result in even greater use of ethanol and reduced used of gasoline.

However, the U.S. farm lobby is very powerful and is fighting hard to retain the 54-cent import tariff. If the 54-cent tariff were to be dropped, then Brazilian ethanol would start flowing to the United States in quantity, thus providing competition for U.S. corn-based ethanol companies and undercutting U.S. ethanol company profits. The U.S. ethanol industry is protected by the 54-cent tariff through January 1, 2009, and another rollover of that tariff is likely. Nevertheless, the politics of the tariff must be watched carefully since any serious attempt to drop the tariff would likely cause a sharp sell-off in U.S. ethanol company stock prices.

HOW FAR CAN ETHANOL GO TO REPLACE GASOLINE IN THE U.S. TRANSPORTATION FUEL SUPPLY?

In the United States, ethanol production has been growing very rapidly in the past several years. As of July 2007, there were 123 operating ethanol distilleries in the United States, 76 plants under construction, and 7 plants being expanded, according to the Renewable Fuels Association.[21] The annual capacity of the plants under construction and expansion totaled 6.374 billion gallons, which is nearly as much as the existing plant capacity of 6.444 billion gallons. That means that when the new capacity comes online over the next 12 to 18 months, U.S. ethanol production will roughly double.

U.S. ethanol production in 2006 totaled 4.855 billion gallons, which was up 24.4 percent from 3.904 billion gallons in 2005 (see Figure 14.2). In March 2007, U.S. ethanol production was 500 million gallons, which equates to an annualized production figure of 6 billion gallons. That means that annualized production in March 2007, in just the third month of the year, was already running 24 percent higher than 2006. Considering the amount of capacity that is in progress, ethanol production in 2007 is likely to show growth on the order of 30 percent or more from 2006.

From a consumption standpoint, the United States used 539.1 million gallons of ethanol in March 2007, which translates to an annualized rate

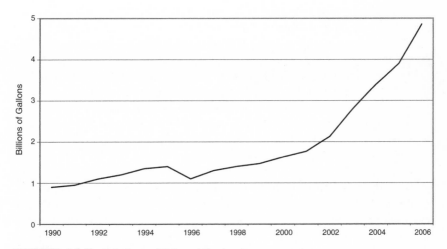

FIGURE 14.2 U.S. Annual Ethanol Production
Source: Renewable Fuels Association, "Industry statistics," www.ethanolrfa.org/industry/statistics/.

of about 6.5 billion gallons.[22] U.S. ethanol usage in March 2007 therefore accounted for about 4.3 percent of total U.S. fuel consumption.

President Bush in his State of the Union Address in January 2007 announced a very ambitious plan for the United States to use 35 billion gallons of alternative fuels annually by 2017. That is about six times current usage and five times the current Renewable Fuel Standard of 7.5 billion gallons per year by 2012.

However, the U.S. corn-based ethanol industry simply cannot produce 35 billion gallons per year of ethanol because (1) there isn't enough farm land in the United States to support that much corn acreage; (2) there would not be enough corn left over for human food consumption and livestock feed (about 55 percent of U.S. corn currently goes for livestock feed); and (3) corn prices would likely soar beyond economical levels for ethanol producers.

The practical limit for corn-based ethanol is probably about 15 billion gallons per year, which is two-and-a-half times current production and about 10 percent of the U.S. fuel supply. Even on that scale, corn-based ethanol producers would need about 3.6 billion bushels of corn, which would represent one-third of the U.S. 2006–2007 corn crop and would require the use of about 12 percent of all U.S. corn/soybean/wheat farmland.[23]

Practically speaking, there are only two ways for a 35 billion gallon goal to be met: (1) open up the United States to ethanol imports from Brazil and other countries by dropping the 54-cent tariff; and/or (2) create 20 billion gallons of cellulosic-based ethanol by 2017 in addition to current corn-based ethanol production. At present, there are no commercial ethanol plants that use cellulosic feedstocks (such as switchgrass, corn stalks, wood chips, etc.) because more research needs to be done to develop economical ways to process that cellulosic material into ethanol. The industry consensus is that it will take another five years before cellulosic-based ethanol can be produced economically on a large scale.

There is a negative aspect to government mandates for increased ethanol usage since the United States can only produce a limited quantity of corn-based ethanol. If the government pushes too hard for corn-based ethanol output, there is a risk that corn prices will be driven to excessively high levels, thus causing negative earnings for ethanol producers and bankruptcies among the smaller and weaker ethanol producers. The U.S. corn-based ethanol industry can only grow as fast as farmers are willing to boost corn production, thus keeping corn prices stable.

The U.S. ethanol industry will be able to produce much larger quantities of ethanol when cellulosic ethanol becomes more feasible and cost effective, but the day of mass production for cellulosic-based ethanol is still about five years away according to most industry estimates. In the meantime, federal and state governments must be careful not to push the ethanol too quickly and cause an upward spike in corn prices and widespread losses among ethanol producers.

THE FUTURE OF ETHANOL: CELLULOSIC-BASED ETHANOL

Ethanol is currently produced using either corn or sugar as the feedstock. However, ethanol can also be produced from *cellulosic* feedstocks such as agricultural plant wastes (corn stalks, corn cobs, leaves, cereal straws, rice straw), wood waste (sawdust, wood chips, and paper pulp), and energy crops grown specifically for fuel production such as switchgrass. Conventional ethanol and cellulosic-based ethanol are exactly the same product, they just come from different processes.[24]

The problem with cellulosic feedstocks is that the sugars are locked in complex carbohydrates and it is difficult to separate out those sugars. As a result, processing cellulosic biomass into ethanol is more difficult than getting ethanol from corn or sugarcane. Two processes can be used to extract the sugar from cellulose. One way is to use acids to break down the carbohydrates. The other way is to first reduce the biomass into small pieces and then use enzymes to convert the biomass into sugars. In both cases, the last step is to use microbe fermentation to convert the sugar into ethanol.

The big advantage of cellulosic ethanol is that it is derived from plant matter that is either waste or is from nonedible crops, meaning it is not taking food away from the nation's food supply or causing a run-up in food prices. In addition, the quantity of ethanol that could theoretically be produced from cellulosic feedstocks is much higher than from corn-based ethanol since there are so many different types of cellulosic feedstocks.

A researcher with the U.S. Department of Energy estimates that there could be as many as 1 billion tons per year of cellulosic biomass available in the United States from agricultural and forest residues, trees, energy crops, and other sources. That would be enough feedstock to produce 65 billion gallons of ethanol at current yields of 65 gallons of ethanol per biomass ton, and enough to produce 90 billion gallons per year of ethanol at the targeted conversion yield of 90 gallons per ton by 2012.[25] Adding 90 billion gallons of ethanol from cellulosic feedstocks to 15 billion gallons of ethanol from corn feedstock (which is near the limit mentioned earlier for corn-based ethanol) would produce a grand total of 105 billion gallons of ethanol. That would be enough ethanol to satisfy about two-thirds of current U.S. fuel consumption and reduce gasoline consumption to one-third of its current level.

However, this theoretical potential would take decades to achieve. A U.S. Department of Energy researcher sets a best-case scenario of 44.8 billion gallons of cellulosic ethanol production by 2030.[26] Adding in 15 billion gallons from corn-based ethanol would produce a grand total of ethanol production of 60 billion gallons, which would be enough to satisfy about 40 percent of current U.S. fuel consumption.

These back-of-the-envelope figures are very tentative because it is not yet known how far production costs can be cut for cellulosic ethanol or how far yields can be increased. The U.S. government is targeting a cut in cellulosic production costs to just over $1.00 by 2012 from about $2.00 in 2005. However, this depends on how well the R&D goes on cutting enzyme costs and plant processing costs. In addition, biomass feedstock costs need to be cut in half.

There are many companies around the world that are working furiously to make cellulosic ethanol commercially attractive. There are currently about 30 pilot and demonstration cellulosic ethanol plants in operation or being built around the world.[27] However, there are no cellulosic ethanol plants at present that are producing ethanol in mass quantity at commercially attractive prices. Yet the companies that achieve the breakthroughs needed for mass production of cellulosic ethanol will be in a highly attractive position of having virtually unlimited and cheap feedstocks available and of being able to push production costs well below those of corn-based ethanol producers. In short, these progressive companies will be in the driver's seat as the low-cost, mass producers, much to the consternation of the legacy ethanol producers who would still be using the old-fashioned method of corn-based ethanol production.

ETHANOL COMPANY INVESTMENT ANALYSIS

A corn-based ethanol company is simply a processing company that buys corn as its raw material and converts it into ethanol, which is then sold as a transportation fuel. An ethanol company's profit margin is highly dependent on the margin that can be earned by buying corn, processing it into ethanol, and then selling the ethanol. In this sense, ethanol producers have a business model that is similar to petroleum refiners that buy crude oil, process it into gasoline, and then sell the gasoline. Corn-based ethanol producers are also similar to food processing companies that buy raw crops (corn, soybeans, etc.) and process them into retail products such as livestock feed, high fructose corn syrup, processed food products, etc.

Corn accounts for about 50 percent of a corn-based ethanol producer's costs (depending on corn, ethanol and other costs at any given time). This

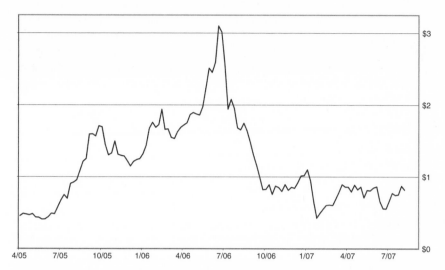

FIGURE 14.3 Ethanol-Corn Crush Profit Margin (in $/gallons of ethanol)
Note: Corn-ethanol crush = CBOT nearby ethanol future prices – CBOT corn nearby future price/2.8 gal./bushel

Source: Corn and Ethanol Prices from Chicago Board of Trade.

means that the largest determinant of an ethanol producer' profit is the spread between ethanol prices and corn prices, that is, the extent to which the ethanol company can buy corn low and sell ethanol high.

The profit margin between ethanol prices and corn prices is the *ethanol-corn crush spread* and is simply defined as the ethanol price minus the corn price. Figure 14.3 shows a recent price history for the ethanol-corn crush spread. Before subtracting corn prices from ethanol prices, however, corn prices need to be converted into dollars per gallon (by dividing the quoted corn price by the 2.8 gallon/bushel yield of the modern ethanol plant).

For example, on July 27, 2007, the last day of data on the price chart in Figure 14.3, front-month futures at the Chicago Board of Trade were trading at $3.21 per bushel for corn and $1.964 per gallon for ethanol. The ethanol-corn crush spread is calculated as follows: $1.964 − ($3.21/2.8 conversion) = 82 cents per gallon. This means that as a very rough estimate, a corn-based ethanol producer could make a profit of about 82 cents per gallon on converting corn to ethanol, minus the producer's other costs such as other raw material inputs, labor, plant operating costs, depreciation of plant construction costs, administrative and selling costs, and any financing or other costs (distiller-dried grain revenue needs to be added back into the profit margin).

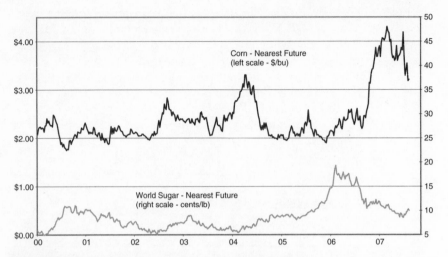

FIGURE 14.4 Ethanol Feedstock Prices: Corn and Sugar
Source: Chicago Board of Trade (corn prices) and New York Board of Trade (sugar prices).

The ethanol-corn crush spread is critical to understanding ethanol industry profits. One can readily see that an ethanol producer's profit margin will improve as ethanol prices rise, but fall as corn prices rise. The reality is that an investor in an ethanol company is betting more on the spread between ethanol and corn prices than on anything else.

As seen in Figure 14.3, the ethanol-corn crush spread can be very volatile, which in turn creates a large amount of volatility in ethanol company profits and stock prices. The volatility in the spread can stem from sharp changes in ethanol prices, corn prices, or both (see Figure 14.4 for corn prices and Figure 15.1 in the next chapter for ethanol prices).

In the first half of 2007, the ethanol-corn crush spread ranged from a low of 43 cents in January 2007 (when corn prices rallied above $4 per bushel) to a high of about 90 cents in July 2007 as corn prices fell back. The big upward spike in the ethanol-corn profit margin in the first half of 2006 was tied to a surge in ethanol prices to over $3 per gallon when ethanol was in extremely high demand as a gasoline additive (oxygenate) to replace MTBE (methyl tertiary butyl ether) which had been phased out because of environmental and liability concerns. Ethanol producers in the first half of 2006 were rolling in profits and ethanol stock prices were high. Ethanol stock prices fell sharply later in 2006, however, when corn prices rallied sharply to over $4 per bushel.

The decision to invest in a corn-based ethanol company depends heavily on an investor's forecast for ethanol and corn prices. If the investor is bullish on ethanol prices and believes that corn prices will stay under control, then an investor could consider buying stock in an ethanol company. But if an investor is concerned that corn prices may rise sharply or that ethanol prices will fall, then an investor should stand aside from ethanol companies because the company's profit margin will be headed lower. Ethanol companies employ a range of pricing and hedging strategies to try to protect their profit margins, but hedging typically only goes out two to three quarters and the ethanol-corn spread will eventually catch up with the company's profit margins.

U.S. ETHANOL INDUSTRY MARKET SHARES

Archer Daniels Midland (NYSE: ADM) is the largest producer of ethanol in the United States with a market share of 16.6 percent as of mid-2007 (see Table 14.1). However, POET Biorefining, formerly named Broin Companies, has been moving very aggressively in the past year to acquire capacity and has now built up to the second largest market share of 15.1 percent. Of the publicly traded ethanol companies, VeraSun Energy (NYSE: VSE) has a market share of 5.3 percent, U.S. BioEnergy (Nasdaq: USBE) has a market share of 2.9 percent, The Andersons (Nasdaq: ANDE) has a market share of 2.6 percent, and Aventine Renewable Energy (NYSE: AVR) has a market share of 1.6 percent. Two other publicly traded producers that are not in the Top 10 list include MGP Ingredients (Nasdaq: MGPI) with a market share of 1.2 percent and Pacific Ethanol (Nasdaq: PEIX) with a market share of 0.5 percent. As a side note, most ethanol companies have new plants coming on line and these market shares are subject to change substantially in coming months and years.

VeraSun (NYSE: VSE) is the largest pure-play publicly traded U.S. ethanol producer and has moved aggressively to expand capacity. In July, VeraSun announced that it planned to acquire three ethanol plants from ASAlliances Biofuels, LLC for $775 million with production capacity of 330 million gallons per year.[28] This production capacity is not included in Table 14.1 because the deal has not yet closed. This acquisition will double VeraSun's present capacity. The cost of acquiring this capacity can be readily calculated at $2.20 per gallon ($725 million divided by 330 million gallons per year of capacity), which the company said is just moderately above its own costs of $1.75 to 1.85 per gallon for building a new plant from scratch. VeraSun also has a productive R&D department and was the first company to announce plans to produce biodiesel from the distiller-dried grain that is a byproduct of the ethanol process that is normally sold as livestock feed.[29] By processing distiller-dried grains into biodiesel, VeraSun

TABLE 14.1 Largest U.S. Ethanol Producers (ranked by capacity)

Largest U.S. Ethanol Producers (by capacity)	Capacity (mln gallons/yr)	Percent market shares	Ticker	Web site
Archer Daniels Midland	1,070	16.6%	ADM	www.admworld.com
POET Biorefining (formerly Broin)	976	15.1%	private	www.poetenergy.com
VeraSun Energy	340	5.3%	VSE	www.verasun.com
Hawkeye Renewables, LLC	200	3.1%	private	www.hawkrenew.com
US BioEnergy	190	2.9%	USBE	www.usbioenergy.net
The Andersons	165	2.6%	ANDE	www.andersonsinc.com
Global Ethanol (formerly Great Lakes Ethanol)	147	2.3%	private	www.greatlakesethanol.com
Cargill	120	1.9%	private	www.cargill.com
Abengoa Bioenergy Corp.	110	1.7%	private	www.abengoabioenergy.com
Aventine Renewable Energy, Inc.	100	1.6%	AVR	www.aventinerei.com

Note: Market shares are calculated using the total industry capacity of 6,444.4 million gallons per year determined by the Renewable Fuels Association as of July 2007. These market shares are subject to change quickly as new plants come on line.

Source: American Coalition for Ethanol (ethanol.org) and Renewable Fuels Association (ethanolrfa.org).

will be able to squeeze more revenue and profit out of each bushel of corn input.

Aventine Renewable Energy Corp (NYSE: AVR) not only produces its own ethanol but also runs a big marketing operation that sells ethanol for many other producers for a commission. Pacific Ethanol (Nasdaq: PEIX) receives a large amount of media attention because Microsoft Chairman Bill Gates's foundation invested in the company in its early stages and because it is based in California and is thought to have the upper hand on supplying ethanol in California and elsewhere on the west coast. The Andersons (Nasdaq: ANDE) in July 2006 entered a partnership with Marathon Oil (NYSE: MRO) to build ethanol plants.[30]

ETHANOL INVESTMENT CONCLUSIONS

The prospects for ethanol as a replacement for gasoline are bright, particularly when cellulosic ethanol becomes commercially viable. Ethanol currently accounts for only about 4 percent of the U.S. fuel supply, meaning that there is plenty of room on the upside. Increased ethanol production helps support U.S. farmers, reduces pollution, and increases America's energy independence.

The attractiveness of ethanol as an alternative to gasoline from a policy and consumer standpoint, however, does not necessarily mean that investing in ethanol stocks is a good idea. As mentioned earlier, ethanol company profits depend mainly on the spread between ethanol and corn prices, which is volatile and difficult to predict. In addition, there are some significant investment risks for the U.S. corn-based ethanol industry that should give investors pause about investing in U.S. corn-based ethanol producers:

- Corn prices may rise sharply in 2008 and 2009 when new ethanol plants will demand even more corn.
- The ethanol industry may overbuild capacity and eventually cause a glut of ethanol.
- The U.S. government may eventually drop or dilute the 54-cent import tariff that protects U.S. farmers from Brazilian competition.
- The U.S. government may eventually drop or dilute 51-cent excise tax credit for ethanol.

An even larger existential risk for the biofuel industry is whether it becomes a popular solution as a gasoline and diesel replacement over the next decade, but then dies out along with the internal combustion engine as more environmentally friendly vehicle technologies such as electric and possibly fuel cell vehicles take over. It is possible to envision a future where

(1) electric vehicles take over as electric vehicle technology improves, and (2) governments across the globe effectively legislate away the internal combustion transportation engine because of its CO_2 emissions and the environmental stress caused by producing its fuel. If the internal combustion engine is indeed effectively legislated away through progressively tighter environmental regulations, there will be no need for any ethanol or biodiesel fuel (or gasoline for that matter). This may not happen for 10 to 20 years, but it is still a very real risk factor for anyone thinking about building a biofuel plant with a 20+ year life or making a long-term investment in a biofuel company.

Having duly noted the risks, some investors may nevertheless be interested in investing in ethanol companies, at least for short or medium term investment purposes. In that regard, it is useful to consider some investment criteria for choosing an ethanol company stock to buy. The top criteria for deciding on an ethanol company should be whether the company has a strong likelihood of making research breakthroughs on cellulosic ethanol and quickly becoming a mass producer of cellulosic-based ethanol. The larger ethanol companies that have more R&D resources and the financial capacity to quickly build production capacity once the lab and pilot plant work are done are the most likely companies to succeed in coming years as the industry migrates from corn-based ethanol to cellulosic-based ethanol. The following list summarizes investment criteria for choosing ethanol stock investments.

Ethanol Company—Investment Criteria

1. Aggressive R&D research that allows the ethanol company to boost yields on existing products and eventually move to cellulosic feedstock.
2. Low production costs through larger scale, access to cheap feedstock, and low transportation costs to market.
3. The ability to use sophisticated hedging and storage techniques to maximize profit margins.
4. A diversified product line that smooths out profits in the event of a plunge in the ethanol-corn profit margin. Global reach and/or involvement in biodiesel is a plus.

COMPANIES SUPPORTING THE U.S. ETHANOL INDUSTRY

Ethanol companies, and investors in ethanol company stocks, face a significant amount of risk because of the volatility of their profit margins and because of the possibility that the industry may overbuild and eventually cause an ethanol glut. However, the old "pick and shovel" analogy is useful in this regard (i.e., that the hardware stores selling picks and shovels during the gold rush made more money than most gold miners).

Suppliers to the U.S. ethanol industry fall into several categories. These companies generally cannot be considered pure-plays on ethanol since revenues tied to the ethanol business are generally a small portion of their total revenues. Nevertheless, these companies can expect to see a continued boost to their revenue and earnings as the ethanol boom continues. The railroads have been big beneficiaries of the ethanol industry because ethanol is generally transported cross-country by rail. Other categories include suppliers to U.S. farmers such as seed and fertilizer companies and companies that sell farm equipment such as Deere & Company and AGCO Corp. There are a host of other companies that could be added to this list, but this provides at least a starting point.

Largest U.S.-Listed Railroads
- Burlington Northern Sante Fe Corp (NYSE: BNI)
- Union Pacific Corp (NYSE: UNP)
- Canadian National Railway (NYSE: CNI)
- Norfolk Southern (NYSE: NSC)
- CSX Corp (NYSE: CSX)
- Trinity Industries (NYSE: TRN)—(largest U.S. manufacturer of tank railcars)
- American Railcar Industries (Nasdaq: ARII)—(manufacturers and repairs tank railcars)

Seed Companies
- Monsanto (NYSE: MON)—a big seller of seed corn
- DuPont (NYSE: DD)—Pioneer-brand seed corn
- Syngenta (Switzerland: SYNN VX)

Fertilizer Products
- Agrium (Toronto: AGU CN)
- Potash Corp of Saskatchewan (Toronto: POT CN)
- Mosaic Co (NYSE: MOS)

Farm Tools & Implements
- Deere & Co (NYSE: DE)
- AGCO Corp (NYSE: AG)
- CNH Global NV, subsidiary of Fiat SpA (Milan: F IM)

CHAPTER 15

Trading Biofuel Markets

Feedstock Frenzy

T he ability to the trade futures markets that are related to biofuels is another way to trade and invest in the clean energy world. Trading the futures market, however, is a risky game considering the high leverage and volatile market conditions. Yet trading biofuel-related markets opens up another playing field for those investors who are looking to profit from clean energy. This chapter focuses on five commodity futures markets: ethanol, corn, sugar, soybean oil, and palm oil. Corn and sugar are feedstocks for ethanol, and soybean oil and palm oil are feedstocks for biodiesel.

ETHANOL

The ethanol futures market is still in its infancy. Most of the ethanol in the United States is currently sold on cash contracts lasting six months or longer, with the contracts entered into directly between a buyer and seller. The buyer is typically a large gasoline/ethanol wholesaler or retailer and the seller is usually a company that produces ethanol. There is a loosely organized over-the-counter spot market in ethanol but it is still relatively small. However, ethanol production is growing very fast and that is boosting demand for spot trading and hedging tools. It is only a matter of time before an actively traded futures market develops for ethanol.

Several U.S. futures exchanges have tried listing ethanol futures, but only the Chicago Board of Trade (CBOT) has made any headway so far. The CBOT's ethanol futures contract as of mid-2007 had very low volume and open interest, which means that the CBOT ethanol futures market has a way to go before it can be considered as a satisfactory investment medium for investors. The CBOT in December 2006 launched over-the-counter ethanol calendar swap contracts, which are reportedly starting to catch on. Those swap contracts provide a mechanism for privately negotiated transactions to clear through the CBOT's clearing system.

The contract size for the CBOT ethanol futures contract is 29,000 gallons or about 1 railcar full of ethanol. There is a futures contract for each month of the year, similar to gasoline futures. The CBOT ethanol contract trades in dollars and cents per gallon with a minimum tick size of 1/10 cent. As far as price movement goes, each 0.001 cent change in the futures contract is worth $29, meaning a 1 cent move is worth $290 and a 10 cent move is worth $2,900. There is obviously a large amount of leverage in the contract, since a small change in the ethanol futures price, say from $2.00 to $2.10 per gallon, would result in a gain/loss of $2,900 for an investor holding just one futures contract. Ethanol futures prices can be found at the Chicago Board of Trade Web site or at a futures-related Web site such as Barchart.com (symbol code: AK).[1]

Figure 15.1 shows the recent price history for ethanol at the wholesale level (not at the retail level at service stations), compared to gasoline prices for reference purposes. The chart shows that ethanol prices have traded in a wide range in the past two years, from as low as $1.10 per gallon to as high as nearly $4.00 per gallon. A price of about $2 per gallon has been a recent equilibrium level.

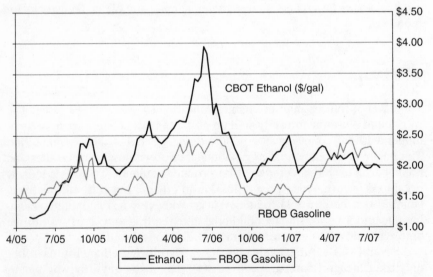

FIGURE 15.1   Ethanol vs. Gasoline Prices ($/gallon)

The single most important market factor that drives ethanol prices is gasoline prices. Ethanol and gasoline are fungible products to a large extent, which means that end-users and wholesale blenders can increase or decrease their usage of ethanol based on its price relative to gasoline. The fungibility of ethanol and gasoline tends to keep ethanol prices roughly in line with a constant spread to gasoline prices, except for special supply/demand factors in the gasoline or ethanol markets that may cause the spread to diverge temporarily.

From 1998 to 2006, ethanol at the wholesale level showed an average 49.2 cent premium to wholesale gasoline prices with a large standard deviation of 28 cents. The 49 cent premium is closely tied to the 51 cent excise tax credit that the U.S. federal government gives to ethanol. If that subsidy is subtracted from ethanol prices, then wholesale ethanol and gasoline prices have been roughly equal over the past 8 years. In reality, aside from the tax credit effect, ethanol prices should trade at a discount to gasoline prices since motorists get about 25 percent less mileage from ethanol versus gasoline.

While gasoline is an important guide for ethanol prices, ethanol also has its own supply/demand dynamics that sometimes cause it to trade at unusual extremes relative to gasoline. For example, during the spring and summer of 2006, ethanol prices skyrocketed because of very strong demand from blenders who needed ethanol to replace MTBE as an oxygenate in their gasoline mix in order to meet clear air regulations. Ethanol prices then fell back later in 2006 as the supply increased and as the ethanol market adjusted to the sharp one-time increase in demand.

Gasoline also has its own dynamics that can cause it to move away from ethanol prices. Figure 15.1 shows how gasoline prices in the first half of 2007 rallied sharply while ethanol prices moved basically sideways near $2 per gallon. Gasoline prices rallied because of strong U.S. gasoline demand, a series of U.S. gasoline refinery breakdowns, and tight gasoline U.S. inventories. At the same time, ethanol prices remained relatively constant as increased ethanol supply easily kept up with demand. As of July 27, 2007, front-month gasoline futures prices (at $2.10 per gallon) were actually trading 14 cents above front-month ethanol futures prices (at $1.96 per gallon). That put ethanol in a very good position since it was cheaper than gasoline at the wholesale level, and even more so after the blenders factored in their 51-cent excise tax credit.

The strip curve for the ethanol futures contracts can provide an interesting perspective on the ethanol market (see Figure 15.2). A futures strip curve presents a time-based graph showing the prices of commodity futures contracts that expire soon as compared with those that expire in the distant future. As seen in Figure 15.2, the ethanol futures strip curve on the day of the data snapshot (July 30, 2007) was sloping

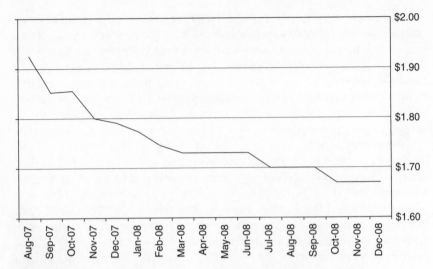

FIGURE 15.2 CBOT Ethanol Futures Strip Curve ($/gallon)
Source: Chicago Board of Trade.

downward. The downward sloping curve indicates that the market expects the huge amount of new ethanol capacity that is currently under construction to depress ethanol prices in the future when those plants start up operations. For example, the longest-dated futures contract for delivery in December 2008 was trading 25.5 cents lower (at $1.67 per gallon) than the nearest futures contract of August 2007 ($1.925 per gallon).

CORN

Corn is the feedstock for more than 40 percent of the world's ethanol production, according to Worldwatch.[2] The United States, the world's largest ethanol producer, uses corn almost exclusively as the feedstock for its ethanol production.

The world's largest corn futures market is at the Chicago Board of Trade. The CBOT offers both full-sized corn futures contracts ($100 per 1 cent move) and mini-contracts as well ($10 per 1 cent move). The size of the full-sized futures contract is 5,000 bushels. The contract is priced in terms of dollars/cents per bushel. Each penny of price movement (e.g., from $3.00 to $3.01 per bushel) represents a $50 change in the value of the futures contract. Corn futures prices can be found at the Chicago Board of Trade's Web site or at a futures-related Web site such as Barchart.com (symbol: C).

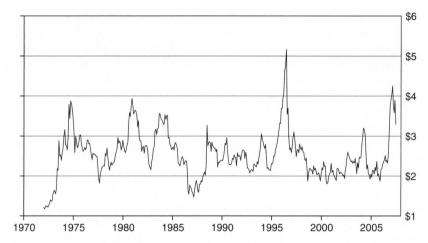

FIGURE 15.3 CBOT Corn Futures Prices ($/bushel)
Source: Chicago Board of Trade.

As seen in Figure 15.3, corn futures prices traded in a relatively narrow range from 1998 until mid-2006. Then, in September 2006, corn prices began a very sharp rally that took the contract all the way up to an 11-year high of $4.37 per bushel by February 2007. That was the highest level seen since 1996 when prices spiked higher on Chinese buying.

The rally in corn prices that started in September 2006 was due almost exclusively to strong demand for corn from ethanol producers. The markets had not yet recognized the extent of the emerging demand from ethanol producers and U.S. farmers planted a normal crop during the summer of 2006, which turned out to barely be enough to satisfy total demand. The level of corn inventories left over from the summer 2006 crop (i.e., the carry-over for the 2006–2007 marketing year) fell sharply by 52 percent from the previous year to a historically low 947 million bushels.[3] That was the lowest level of inventories since the 1995–1996 marketing year when corn prices soared above $5 per bushel.

High corn prices in early 2007 made planting corn appear very profitable, however, so U.S. farmers in the spring of 2007 planted a huge corn crop. U.S. farmers planted 92.9 million acres of corn, up 19 percent from the previous year and the most acres planted with corn in 63 years. Moreover, growing weather during the summer of 2007 was nearly ideal, meaning a record crop would easily be produced. As of July 2007, the U.S. Department of Agriculture was predicting that corn inventories would rise sharply back up to the 1.5 billion bushel area because of the large crop. Corn prices during the first half of the summer responded by falling back sharply to the low $3 per bushel area.

The sharp drop in corn prices in the first half of summer 2007 was a big relief for ethanol producers, whose profits had been threatened by the run-up in corn prices above $4 per bushel. Ethanol producers can make a respectable profit with corn prices at or below $4 per bushel, but they would start to see losses if corn prices were to rally above the low-$5 per bushel area (assuming ethanol prices remain near $2 per gallon).

Looking ahead, the problem is that there is a huge amount of new ethanol production capacity that will be coming on line in the second half of 2007 and all through 2008. That means demand for corn from ethanol producers will continue to ratchet higher through at least 2009. U.S. farmers in 2007 responded by boosting corn acreage by 19 percent, but U.S. farmers are going to have to continue to increase acreage to meet the further increase in demand from ethanol producers.

At some point, since there is a limit on how much corn that U.S. farmers can reasonably produce, the ethanol industry is going to hit a limit on how many new ethanol plants can be built. The ethanol industry is hoping that equilibrium can be reached in a relatively controlled manner. However, there is a danger that the continued rise in corn demand from ethanol producers will eventually force corn prices above the low-$5 per bushel level, at which point ethanol producers will start losing money and will have to start shutting down plants. This would eventually cut ethanol production back to levels that can be sustained by available corn supply. However, in the meantime, there could be some nasty dislocations for the U.S. ethanol industry. The bottom line is that the U.S. ethanol industry going into 2008 and 2009 will be on progressively thinner ice and the risks of a corn price spike will grow, particularly if any significant drought conditions emerge. There will also be increased risks of an ethanol supply glut, particularly if demand for ethanol does not grow fast enough.

SUGAR

Sugar, like corn, is also the feedstock for more than 40 percent of the world's ethanol production.[4] Brazil, the world's second largest ethanol producer, uses sugar almost exclusively for its ethanol production. Brazil uses more than half of its large sugar cane crop for ethanol. Brazil is the world's largest sugar producer with 30.9 million metric tons of production in the 2006–2007 sugar marketing year (October–September).[5] The world's second largest sugar producer is India with 25.1 million metric tons of production in 2006–2007.

Sugar futures trade at the New York Board of Trade (NYBOT), which is a subsidiary of the Intercontinental Exchange Inc. (NYSE: ICE). The

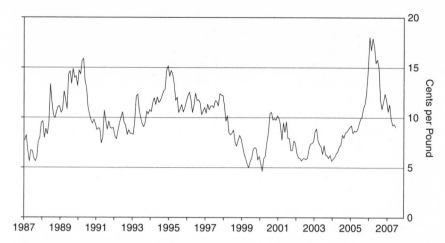

FIGURE 15.4 NYBOT World Sugar (#11) Futures Prices
Source: New York Board of Trade.

NYBOT's world sugar #11 futures contract is quoted in terms of cents per pound. Figure 15.4 shows a chart with the history for the NYBOT sugar futures contract. Sugar futures also trade at other futures exchanges around the world.

Sugar prices rallied sharply in the latter half of 2005 and posted a 24-year high of 19.73 cents/pound in February 2006. Sugar prices on that high were more than triple their 2004 levels. The 2005 rally was mainly due to strong demand for sugar from ethanol producers in Brazil, combined with three straight years of global sugar supply deficits in the marketing years of 2003–2004, 2004–2005, and 2005–2006. However, sugar prices plummeted through the remainder of 2006 and into 2007 because of sharply increased sugar production by both Brazil and India. Sugar producers responded to the high prices seen in 2005 by boosting production, only to see prices fall back quickly. There was a small global surplus of sugar in the 2006–2007 marketing year, indicating that sugar producers were more than keeping up with strong and rising demand from ethanol producers.

SOYBEAN OIL

Biodiesel can be made from a wide variety of vegetable oils and animal fats. Europe produces about 90 percent of the world's biodiesel and rapeseed (canola) oil is the feedstock used for 80 percent of that production.[6] The other feedstocks used include soybean oil and sunflower oil. However, in the U.S., soybean oil is used as the feedstock in about 85 percent of biodiesel production, with other feedstocks including rapeseed oil and other vegetable oils.

Soybean oil is produced on a large scale around the world. Global soybean oil production in the 2006–2007 marketing year was 35.8 million metric tons according to Commodity Research Bureau's *CRB Yearbook*.[7] In the United States, soybean oil accounts for 80 percent of margarine production and for more than 75 percent of total U.S. consumer vegetable fat and oil consumption.[8] Soybean oil comes from processing ("crushing") soybeans, a process that produces both soybean oil and soybean meal. About 19 percent of a soybean's weight is typically extracted as crude soybean oil.[9]

Futures on soybean oil trade at the Chicago Board of Trade (symbol code: BO). Figure 15.5 shows a price history chart for the CBOT soybean oil futures contract. The futures contract is quoted in terms of cents per pound of soybean oil. The chart shows that soybean oil at the end of June 2007 was trading near a record high. The sharp rally in soybean oil prices in 2006 and 2007 was due in large part to the sharp rally in underlying soybean prices, which rose because of the much smaller soybean crop planted during spring 2007. The sharp rally in corn prices caused farmers to plant more land with corn and less land with soybeans, thus cutting the size of the soybean crop. Soybean oil also rallied in 2006 and 2007 because of strong biodiesel demand.

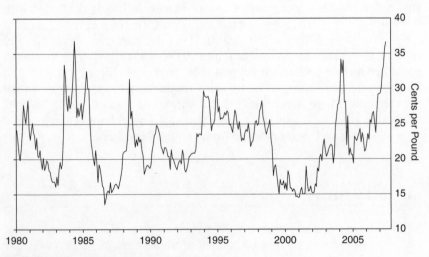

FIGURE 15.5 CBOT Soybean Oil Futures
Source: Chicago Board of Trade.

PALM OIL

Palm oil is becoming a more popular feedstock for biodiesel production in Asia. About 20 percent of palm oil production currently goes toward biodiesel production. The Malaysian and Indonesian governments in August 2006 announced their intention to promote increased production of palm oil and devote 40 percent of supply to biodiesel production.[10] This book's companion Web site at www.ProfitingFromCleanEnergy.com has links to videos discussing palm oil plantations in east Asia.

Palm oil comes from the fruit of the oil palm tree, which is a different type of palm tree from the more familiar tropical coconut palm. Palm oil is used for cooking oil and margarine and also has industrial uses. Malaysia and Indonesia are the world's largest producers and exporters of palm oil. Over the past three decades, the production of palm oil has grown by roughly 17 times from the 1970 production level.[11] Palm oil futures trade at the Malaysian Derivatives Exchange (MDEX), which is a subsidiary of the Bursa Malaysia stock exchange (www.klse.com.my).[12]

Figure 15.6 shows a price history chart for palm oil futures. The futures contract is quoted in terms of Malaysian ringgit per metric ton. The crude palm oil contract closed June 2007 at 2513 Malaysian ringgit, which is equivalent to about $718 per metric ton at the exchange rate on that day of about 3.5 ringgit per U.S. dollar. The chart illustrates that crude palm oil in the latter half of 2006 and the first half of 2007 nearly doubled in price to post record highs, mainly because of strong demand from biodiesel producers.

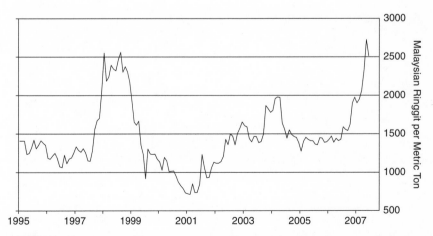

FIGURE 15.6 Malaysian Derivatives Exchange: Crude Palm Oil Futures Prices
Source: Malaysian Derivatives Exchange.

CHAPTER 16

Big Coal—Meet Your New Partners

Cleaner Coal Technology and Carbon Capture

C oal is an inexpensive and abundant source of fuel for power generation that will be with us for some decades to come. Solar and wind power cannot grow fast enough to completely replace coal. Moreover, solar and wind power are intermittent sources of power that only work during the day or when the wind blows. Power utilities need a power generation source that provides a stable base load 24 hours a day and solar and wind power do not fit that bill. For base load power, utilities will be forced to rely on some mix of coal, natural gas, biomass, and nuclear power, with increasing help in the future from geothermal and wave/tide power.

Coal-fired power plants have the advantage of being inexpensive and helping to provide energy security if the coal comes from within the country's borders. The disadvantages of coal are substantial, however, and include environmental damage from coal mining, injuries and deaths of coal miners, and greenhouse gas emissions and pollution when the coal is burned. Coal accounts for 40 percent of the world's CO_2 emissions, which is the same as petroleum at 40 percent, and twice as much as natural gas at 20 percent.[1]

Despite coal's serious disadvantages, there is no practical way to eliminate coal as a significant source of electricity generation for at least the next few decades. Ontario's Liberal government has been trying to go cold turkey and shut down all of the province's coal-fired plants, which provide about 25 percent of the province's electricity. The Liberal government originally promised to close the province's coal-fired plants by 2007, but was forced to delay the shutdown date until 2014.[2] While Ontario's government is making a valiant effort to close coal-fired power plants and reduce emissions, they are running up against the practical barrier of trying to quickly substitute new sources of power generation.

Regulators around the globe are slowly turning up the pressure on utilities to reduce their dependence on coal-fired power plants. Public pressure against building new coal-fired power plants is also growing. The large power utility in Texas, TXU, for example, planned to build eleven new coal-fired power plants. However, there was a public outcry against the coal-fired plants. In response, the two equity firms that are in the process of buying TXU, Kohlberg Kravis Roberts and the Texas Pacific Group, scrapped the plans to build eight of the coal-fired power plants in order to smooth the way for the acquisition.[3] In addition, the private equity buyers announced that two of the coal-fired power plants that remain on the drawing board would be new-style coal-fired plants that burn more cleanly through gasification (i.e., integrated gasification combined cycle).[4]

As a means to plug the gap caused by the eight scrapped coal-fired plants, TXU is looking to natural-gas-fired plants, nuclear power, and renewable energy. Texas already generates 2.8 gigawatts of wind power, which is nearly 5 percent of the state's total capacity. Texas land commissioner, Jerry Paterson told the *New York Times*, "Wind has the potential to help fill the shortfall. Every day that passes, renewables make more economic sense."[5]

GLOBAL COAL USAGE

The United States and many other countries in the world are huge consumers of coal. The United States has been called the "Saudi Arabia of coal" because it has the world's largest coal reserves, as seen in Figure 16.1. As mentioned in Chapter 4, coal in the United States accounts for 23 percent of overall U.S. energy usage and 52 percent of electric power generation.[6] Worldwide, coal accounts for 26 percent of total world energy production and 40 percent of world electricity generation.[7] World coal consumption rose by +4.5 percent in 2006, making it the world's fastest growing fossil fuel, according to the BP Statistical Review.[8]

The United States is not the world's only big player in coal. Russia, China and India are ranked as the world's second, third and fourth largest holders of coal reserves, respectively. This explains why it is extremely tempting for them to build coal-fired power plants to meet sharply increased domestic power demand in their countries, since coal is nearby and inexpensive.

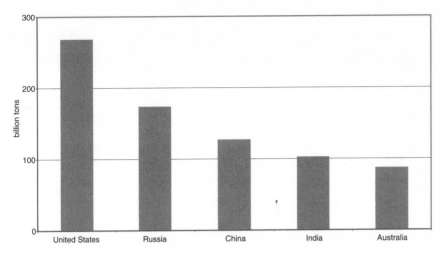

FIGURE 16.1 Top 5 Coal Reserve Countries (2002)
Source: U.S. Department of Energy, Energy Information Administration, *Annual Energy Review 2006,* June 2007, Table 11.13, http://www.eia.doe.gov/emeu/aer/ txt/stb1113.xls.

China relies on coal for 90 percent of its electric power generation. Chinese coal consumption accounted for 39 percent of world coal consumption in 2006.[9] Coal consumption in China in 2006 was up by a dramatic total of 79 percent since 2000 and rose +8.7 percent in 2006, as seen in Figure 16.2. A key element of the world's energy problem involves China's pell-mell use of coal to meet its rapidly expanding electricity demand.

India has also ramped up its use of coal to generate electricity, as seen in Figure 16.3. Coal consumption in India rose +7.1 percent in 2006 and is up by a total of 41 percent from 2000.[10]

It is worth noting that current coal-fired power plants have a top-end efficiency of only about 33 percent to 35 percent.[11] The remainder of the energy content contained in the coal (65 percent to 67 percent) is wasted with the release of heat into the atmosphere. Coal is widely touted as a cheap source of fuel, but its efficiency is not particularly impressive. Top-end solar photovoltaic power efficiencies of 22 percent do not look so low when compared with coal efficiency of only 35 percent.

U.S. COAL COMPANIES

"Big Coal" is an accurate description of the U.S. coal industry, referring not only to the coal companies but also to their associated political

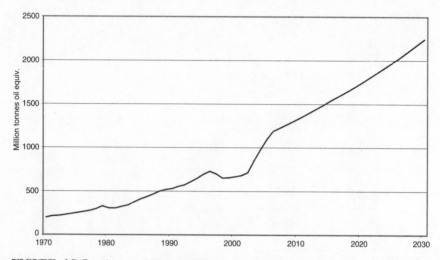

FIGURE 16.2 China Coal Consumption
Source: BP Global, "Global coal consumption increased by 4.5% in 2006," *Statistical Review of World Energy 2007: Coal consumption,* http://www.bp.com/sectiongenericarticle.do?categoryId=9017919&contentId=7033429.

lobbying and public relations firms. U.S. coal companies are particularly adept at operating below the radar and avoiding the harsh public criticism that is often directed at the world's big petroleum companies. Big Coal is able to keep out of the public eye even though coal produces more environmental extraction damage and just as much CO_2 emission as the petroleum industry. The largest publicly traded coal companies in America include Peabody Energy Corp (NYSE: BTU), Consol Energy (NYSE: CNX), Arch Coal (NYSE: ACI), and Massey Energy (NYSE: MEE).

Peabody Energy is by far the largest American coal company with $5.3 billion in revenues and $601 million in net income in 2006. Peabody is very active in Washington, D.C. by lobbying and providing contributions to politicians. According to Jeff Goodell in his book, *Big Coal: The Dirty Secret Behind America's Energy Future,* Peabody Energy during 2000–2004 was the single largest corporate contributor to the Republican Party in terms of percentage of company revenues.[12] The reality is that Big Coal has a lot of political clout and will therefore have an impact on the future direction of energy policy in the United States. The coal industry is likely to survive in some modified form in the future, but only with help from cleaner coal technologies.

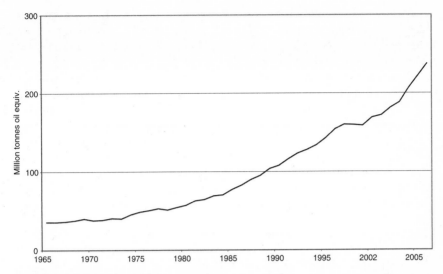

FIGURE 16.3 India Coal Consumption
Source: BP Global, "Global coal consumption increased by 4.5% in 2006," *Statistical Review of World Energy 2007: Coal consumption,* http://www.bp.com/sectiongenericarticle.do?categoryId=9017919&contentId=7033429.

CLEANER COAL TECHNOLOGIES

As mentioned earlier, the United States and the world are so dependent on coal-fired power plants that there is no way to quickly phase out coal as a source of fuel. In spite of that, there is strong pressure to reduce the pollution and greenhouse gas emissions from coal-fired power plants. This squeeze produces a big opportunity for companies that offer solutions for making coal a more environmentally friendly source of power.

These solutions fall into several categories: (1) upgrading the quality of coal so that it burns more cleanly; (2) retrofitting existing coal-fired plants with scrubbers to reduce pollution; (3) coal gasification, which removes many impurities prior to burning; (4) technologies to capture and bury or convert CO_2 gas from the plants; and (5) liquefying coal to be used as motor fuel. These technologies will now be discussed in greater detail.

CLEANER BURNING COAL

Coal comes in many different grades. High-grade coal is a hard coal that has low ballast, meaning it has low ash and water content. It burns hotter and with relatively low emissions and is more expensive. Low-grade coal is less expensive but it has limited uses because of its high ash and moisture content. This soft coal burns less effectively at lower temperatures and with greater harmful emissions.

Technology is now available to improve the quality of low-grade coal to make it burn hotter and emit fewer pollutants. Evergreen Energy (NYSE: EEE), formerly KFx, Inc., has a technology that heats low-grade coal while under pressure and turns it into coal that burns more efficiently. This K-Fuel process removes about 80 percent of the water as well as much of the mercury, sulfur dioxide and nitrogen oxides.[13] Another company, Headwaters (NYSE: HW), has several product lines, including construction materials, but one of its divisions provides solutions for converting coal and heavy oil into higher-value and cleaner products.

COAL-FIRED POWER PLANT POLLUTION CONTROLS

There are many coal-fired power plants in the United States, and particularly overseas, that could be retrofitted with scrubbers so that they emit fewer pollutants. Currently, there are approximately 540 coal plants in the United States and of those only 140 have scrubbers that cleanse coal emissions of harmful pollutants.[14]

In the most common type of coal plant, pulverized coal is blown into a furnace where it burns while it is airborne. The heat converts water that is flowing in pipes through the furnace into steam, which is in turn feed into a turbine that turns an electric generator and produces electricity. As the coal burns, it releases sulfur dioxide, nitrogen oxides, and carbon dioxide, among other gases. The sulfur is partially removed by scrubbers. A scrubber uses a limestone slurry to absorb the sulfur as it passes through. Scrubbers can remove about 90 percent of the sulfur emissions but the rest of the smaller particles go up the smoke stack into the atmosphere. However, the scrubbers do not remove carbon dioxide from the plant's exhaust and it all goes out the smoke stack into the atmosphere.[15] There are two main U.S.-based companies that manufacture and install pollution control equipment:

- *Fuel Tech Inc* (Nasdaq: FTEK). Fuel Tech specializes in pollution-control equipment for power-generation facilities. Fuel Tech notes the size of the pollution-control opportunity, quoting *Industrial Information Resources* as saying that the 87 environmental-compliance projects that began in 2006 were worth about $8 billion. Fuel-Tech is a small company that will only be able to capture a small portion of the target market. However, Fuel-Tech is growing quickly with sales of $75 million in 2006 (+25 percent year-on-year) and a large backlog of orders.

- *Babcock & Wilcox.* Babcock & Wilcox, a unit of McDermott International (NYSE: MDR), is a key player in constructing and retrofitting power plants. Babcock & Wilcox is also the biggest player in cleaning up power plants to meet environmental regulations. Babcock & Wilcox also happens to be a major player in the construction and maintenance of biomass power plants. As a large conglomerate, the parent of Babcock & Wilcox, McDermott International, cannot be considered a pure play in clean energy but the company will nevertheless see significant benefits from effort to clean up U.S. and global coal plants.

COAL GASIFICATION AND CO_2 SEQUESTRATION

A better method of dealing with the pollution problems associated with coal is to use coal gasification technology. Rather than burning coal directly, a gasification process first breaks the coal down into its main chemical constituents of carbon monoxide (CO) and hydrogen (H_2), plus other gases. This gas mixture is called *synthesis gas* or *syngas* for short. The syngas is then fed into a furnace where it is burned to create steam for the turbines. Coal gasification can remove as much as 97 percent of the sulfur and 82 percent of the nitrogen oxides from the emissions. In addition the plant emits 50 percent less mercury and 20 percent less carbon dioxide.[16]

An improvement on simple coal gasification is the use of oxygen in the gasification process rather than just air. This makes the CO_2 easer to extract from the unit before burning the syngas. The syngas, which then has a high concentration of hydrogen and virtually no nitrogen, burns cleaner. In a further boost to efficiency, the exhaust from the hot gas turbine goes into a steam generator to create steam for a steam turbine-generator to generate more electricity. This book's companion Web site at www.ProfitingFromCleanEnergy.com has a link to a video explaining the new coal gasification plant that will be built at Taylorville, Illinois.

An optional addition to the coal gasification process is that the extracted CO_2 from the plant can be pumped into underground caverns or depleted oil wells, or otherwise captured or converted.[17] The process of capturing and containing CO_2 is called *CO_2 sequestration* or *carbon capture.*

CO_2 sequestration is already being used successfully at the Dakota Gasification Company's Great Plains Synfuels Plant in North Dakota. The coal gasification plant, which extracts a form of natural gas from coal, sends its waste CO_2 through a 205-mile-long pipeline northward to Canada. The CO_2 is then injected into a 70 square-mile underground oil field near Weyburn, Saskatchewan, owned by EnCana (Toronto: ECA CN).

The stored CO_2 increases the pressure in the nearly depleted 50-year-old underground oil field and enhances the recovery of the remaining oil. When the oil field is fully depleted, the underground oil field will be capped off, ensuring that the 20 million tons of CO_2 remains underground permanently instead of being released into the atmosphere. Scientific studies have shown that there has been no CO_2 leakage so far from the underground oil field. The success of this project has raised the possibility of developing more CO_2 pipeline projects, which could offer new business opportunities to pipeline operators and pipeline construction companies.

The technology for building power plants that first gasify coal and then burn the gas is called *integrated gasification combined cycle* (IGCC). There are two IGCC plants currently operating in the United States, one plant at Wabash River in Indiana and another plant run by Tampa Electric, which is a subsidiary of TECO Energy (NYSE: TE). Neither plant is currently capturing and sequestering CO_2 but that technology could be added later. Both Duke Energy Corp (NYSE: DUK) and American Electric Power (NYSE: AEP) have announced plans to build IGCC power plants, thus lending further credibility to the technology and economics of coal-gasification power plants.

The U.S. Department of Energy is providing funding for clean coal projects through its Clean Coal Power Initiative.[18] The biggest project on the docket is the $1 billion FutureGen industry consortium that will combine IGCC clean coal gasification technology with the underground sequestration of CO_2 emissions. The FutureGen power plant will have 60 percent efficiency (versus the typical pulverized coal-fired plant efficiency of 35 percent) and extremely low emissions. However, the project is moving slowly and is not due to be completed until 2012, meaning that other companies may beat FutureGen to the goal of producing the world's first IGCC plant combined with CO_2 sequestration.

There are other large-cap companies that will see benefits from clean coal as well. For example, General Electric (NYSE: GE) and Bechtel (privately held) have teamed up to offer turnkey coal gasification power plants to power utilities. GE is developing technologies for CO_2 capture and sequestration, looking ahead to the likelihood of eventual CO_2 emission regulation. Shell and ConocoPhillips also offer coal gasification technologies.

Gasification can also be used to separate hydrogen gas from other feedstocks such as petroleum coke (which is a low grade byproduct of oil refining), biomass materials, and municipal waste. Regarding gasification of petroleum coke, a project is currently underway to build a hydrogen-powered electricity generating plant using petroleum coke near BP's Carson, California petroleum refinery. This is a joint venture between BP (NYSE: BP) and Edison International (NYSE: EIX). For fuel, the plant will use the petroleum-coke residue left over from the BP refinery after all the useful products have been removed. The petroleum coke will be heated to convert it into hydrogen and carbon dioxide. The hydrogen will then be burned in a specially modified gas turbine to make electricity. The main byproduct of this process is water. The CO_2 will be transported by pipeline and pumped thousands of feet down into depleted oil and gas fields for storage and to help flush out gas and oil that would otherwise be left behind. The project was announced in February 2006 and the project is planned for completion by 2011.[19] The same gasification technology that produces hydrogen for the plant could also be used to produce hydrogen for fuel cells.

ALGAE-BASED CO_2 ABSORPTION

Technology to convert CO_2 into oxygen would obviously be a much better solution to stopping global CO_2 emissions than just pumping the CO_2 into the ground and hoping it stays there. In fact, there is photo-bioreactor technology that uses algae to convert CO_2 into oxygen. After the algae have done their job, their mass can be dried and turned into fuel or animal feed. This solution to reducing greenhouse gases is already in the testing stage at a large coal-fired power plant in New Roads, Louisiana.[20] The system was designed and built by Greenfuel Technologies Corp (see below).

Algae are microscopic plants that are familiar to us as pond scum. Since they are plants, they use CO_2 as fuel and use sunlight to convert it to oxygen (photosynthesis). The CO_2 for the conversion process can come straight from the waste gas from a coal-fired power plant. The gaseous emission from the smoke stack is fed directly into a large container filled with algae. The microscopic-sized algae are suspended in water and when exposed to sunlight they multiply and grow rapidly using the CO_2 as food. An algae mass can double in size in less than a day, making algae one of the fastest growing plants on earth. In the growth process, they give off harmless oxygen and nitrogen that is let out into the atmosphere. The process periodically filters out some of the algae, which is then dried into granules. These granules can be used directly as fuel for the electricity generating plant or processed into ethanol fuel, biodiesel fuel, animal food, or many other useful products.[21]

There are many different types of algae that can be used and the strain chosen for a particular system depends in part on the desired end product. Some algae strains have more oil, so their residue is more suited to making bio-diesel fuel. Other algae strains have more sugar content, so their residue is more suited to making ethanol. Still other algae strains have greater protein content so their residue is more suited to making animal feed.

The output from the algae conversion process is remarkable and can provide a much more efficient source of feedstock for biodiesel production than crops such as soybeans. According to the U.S. National Renewable Energy Laboratory, "microalgae are capable of producing 30 times the amount of oil per unit area of land, compared with terrestrial oilseed crops.[22]

Two privately held companies that are involved in algae CO_2 conversion are GreenFuel Technologies Corporation (www.greenfuelonline.com) and Solix Biofuels (www.solixbiofuels.com). GreenFuel Technologies was formed in 1994 and works closely with the Massachusetts Institute of Technology where it built the first field photo-bioreactor system.[23] The company is now in the process of building a test facility for NRG Energy's power plant in Louisiana. Solix Biofuels was started in April 2006 and completed its first generation prototype in August 2006. Since then the company has started work on its second-generation prototype.

Since sunlight is critical to the process, researchers are working on a way to create even larger photo-bioreactor systems using concentrated sunlight brought into the bioreactor with *hybrid solar lighting*.[24] A hybrid solar light system, using optical cables, can deliver the visible sunlight that is needed inside the photo-bioreactor.

Research on algae-based CO_2 conversion is still in the early stages. However, a breakthrough on creating a large-scale algae-based CO_2 conversion system that is economically attractive would have immense importance to the goal of curbing greenhouse gas emissions.

COAL-TO-LIQUID TRANSPORTATION FUEL

The technology for converting coal into liquid fuels has been around since 1925. The basic technology, the *Fischer-Tropsch process*, which uses heat and steam to convert coal to a synthetic gas, is still the technology used today. The synthetic gas is then cleaned by removing the sulfur and CO_2. The synthetic gas then reacts with a catalyst to form synthetic petroleum, which is refined to make diesel fuel. Companies that use this technology include:

- *Sasol Ltd* (Johannesburg: SOL SJ). Sasol is the world's largest producer of coal-based liquid fuel. Sasol, which is based in South Africa, was founded in the 1950s because South Africa's leaders were worried that the country might eventually be subject to a petroleum blockade because of apartheid. The country therefore encouraged the development of synthetic petroleum manufactured from coal. Sasol is currently producing about 150,000 barrels a day of coal-based liquid fuel. Sasol improved the Fisher-Tropsch process in the 1980s by developing a low-temperature slurry phase reactor which uses iron or cobalt based catalysts. This technology allows for the creation of liquid fuels and other chemicals from either coal or natural gas.[25]
- *Rentech Inc* (Amex: RTK). Rentech is a U.S.-based company that has a flexible process (coal-to-liquids or gas-to-liquids) that converts underutilized hydrocarbon resources such as coal, petroleum coke, and remote or stranded natural gas into synthesis gas. The process can also convert biomass into synthesis gas. The process then converts the synthesis gas into diesel fuel, fertilizers, and petrochemical products that are cleaner than standard petroleum products. In May 2007, Rentech announced an agreement with Peabody Energy (NYSE: BTU), the world's largest nongovernment owned coal company, to codevelop two coal-to-liquid projects that will produce cleaner liquid transportation fuel. Through this technology, the United States obtains cleaner burning diesel fuel and petrochemicals directly from U.S.-based coal, thus avoiding the need to import more foreign crude oil.

CLEAN COAL INVESTMENT CONCLUSIONS

Coal as an energy source for electricity generation is clearly under attack from an environmental and policy standpoint. However, coal will still be with us for at least the next several decades simply because it plays such a large role at present in generating the world's electricity. There are a number of interesting investment plays in this sector. However, investors should recognize that coal is likely to play a sharply reduced role in power generation going forward and coal may be completely phased out as an energy source within three to four decades, thus rendering all investments in the sector obsolete on that long-term time horizon.

CHAPTER 17

Carbon Trading

*Poised to Become the World's
Largest Commodity Market?*

C arbon trading is expected by some to become the world's largest commodity market and perhaps even the largest market overall. The carbon trading market is presently centered in Europe since the European Union implemented a cap-and-trade system for CO_2 emissions as part of its compliance with the Kyoto Protocol. Australia is close to setting up a cap-and-trade system and the United States appears to be moving slowly toward adopting a cap-and-trade system. Right now the carbon trading market is about $30 billion, but some industry leaders expect the industry to grow to $1 trillion within a decade according to an article in the *New York Times*.[1]

TRADING EUROPEAN CO2 ALLOWANCES

The largest market for trading CO_2 at present is at the European Climate Exchange (ECX) futures market. The European Climate Exchange was founded in January 2005 and is currently handling about 80 percent of the world's exchange-traded CO_2 futures volume.[2] Since the European Climate Exchange doesn't have an electronic trading network of its own, the trading is actually done on the Intercontinental Exchange's ICE Futures network. ICE Futures is Europe's leading energy exchange for futures and options and the world's largest electronic energy futures exchange.[3] Intercontinental Exchange, Inc. is a publicly traded company (Nasdaq: ICE) with a market cap of about $10 billion.

The European Climate Exchange's CO_2 futures contract is called a Carbon Financial Instrument or CFI. The underlying instrument is the European Union Allowance (EUA), which is an allowance to emit 1 metric ton of CO_2. The CFI futures contract represents 1,000 EUAs and is quoted in terms of euros per metric ton of CO_2 emissions. Thus if the CFI futures contract were trading at 20 euros per metric ton of $C0_2$, the nominal value of the futures contract would be €20,000 (20 euros times 1,000 EUAs). If the futures contract were to rise by €0.10 to €20.10 /ton CO2, then the futures contract would rise in value by 100 euros to €20,100.

The growing popularity of the European Climate Exchange CFI futures contract can be seen from the fact that the average daily volume has doubled in the past year to the current level near 3,500 contracts per day (see Figure 17.1).

Further evidence of the growing popularity of trading CFI futures is the growing level of open interest (see Figure 17.2). Open interest is the total number of futures contracts that have been bought and sold and are still outstanding. The sharp dip in open interest seen around December 2006 occurred when the December 2006 futures contracts expired.

Table 17.1 shows a table provided by the exchange of the settlement prices as of July 13, 2007. Each row represents a different futures expiration month. For example, the first line, which is for December 2007 shows the data related to the CFI futures contract that expires in December 2007.

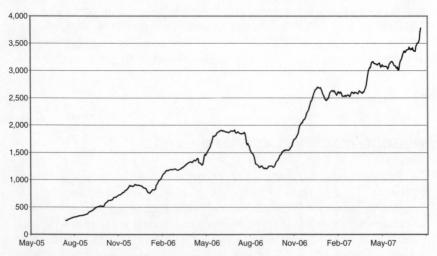

FIGURE 17.1 ECX EFI CO_2 Futures—Average Daily Volume in Contracts (60-day average)
Source: European Climate Exchange, "ECX CFI Futures Contracts: Historic Data 2007," http://www.europeanclimateexchange.com/uploads/documents/ECXCFIFutures Contract-HistoricData-12July2007.xls.

TABLE 17.1 Table of ECX CFI CO$_2$ Futures Settlement Prices

European Climate Exchange CFI CO2 Futures Closes (13-Jul-2007)

Data current at: 13/07/2007 17:00:33 GMT

Month	Open	Last	High	Low	Settle	Exchange for Physicals (EFP)	Exchange for Swaps (EFS)	Block Trades	Volume	Settle	Volume	EFP	Open Interest
										Previous Business Day			
Dec-07	€0.14	€0.14	€0.13	€0.13	€0.13	0	0	0	25	€0.13	500	375	45,758
Jan-08	€0.00	€0.00	€0.00	€0.00	€0.00	0	0	0	0	€0.13	0	0	0
Feb-08	€0.00	€0.00	€0.00	€0.00	€0.00	0	0	0	0	€0.13	0	0	0
Mar-08	€0.00	€0.00	€0.00	€0.00	€0.00	0	0	0	0	€0.13	0	0	20
Dec-08	€20.50	€19.85	€20.00	€19.25	€19.89	1,844	0	0	3177	€19.79	4,795	3,202	50,806
Dec-09	€20.35	€20.21	€20.21	€19.76	€20.21	164	0	0	247	€20.13	1,766	1710	19,293
Dec-10	€20.22	€20.20	€20.63	€20.20	€20.63	416	0	0	433	€20.50	248	248	5,725
Dec-11	€21.20	€21.20	€21.02	€20.45	€21.02	34	0	0	44	€20.88	57	248	1,458
Dec-12	€20.80	€20.90	€21.40	€20.78	€21.40	34	0	0	104	€21.28		50	2,340
Total						2,492	0	0	4,030		7,366	5,585	125,400

Source: European Climate Exchange, http://www.europeanclimateexchange.com/.

There are several notable items on this table. First, the most actively traded futures contract in the complex on that day was the December 2008 futures contract, as seen by the volume figures shown in the third column from the right. The other futures months for 2008 had yet to start trading. Second, the December futures contracts are the benchmark contracts for any given year as seen by the fact that only December contracts are trading for 2009 and beyond. Fourth, trading volume in the December 2007 contract had dried up but the contract still had very high open interest of 45,758 contracts, representing more than one-third of the total open interest.

Looking at the settlement prices for the contracts, the December 2007 futures contract closed at €0.13 per ton on that particular day, whereas the December 2008 contract closed at €19.89 per ton. The December 2007 contract was trading at such a low level because the EU Registries issued too many allowances for the 2005 through 2007 compliance period, which eventually made them practically worthless. However, the National Registry sharply decreased the number of allowances for the 2008 through 2012 compliance period, which accounts for the higher prices for the December 2008 futures contracts and beyond, which were trading in the €20 to €21 area.

CAUSES OF PRICE MOVEMENTS

The price of the CFI futures contract tracks closely with the cash price for the European Union Allowance (EUA) itself. The difference is that the futures price tries to anticipate what the price of an EUA will be in the future.

The price of an EUA and its futures contract usually vary quite a bit as seen in Figure 17.3. The biggest factor affecting the price of an EUA is the total number of allowances issued by the EU Environment Commission. The greater the number of allowances issued (i.e., the more CO_2 emissions that are allowed), the lower is the value of each EUA.

As mentioned earlier, in October 2001, when the European cap-and-trade system got started, the EU Environment Commission allowed the member states to issue too many allowances.[4] One outcome of that decision was that the price of allowances fell sharply. Another outcome of that decision was that the European Union found it difficult to meet their goal of an average 8 percent reduction in CO_2 emissions because they had allowed too many emissions.

In early 2007, regulators began to look forward to the next compliance period and sharply reduced the number of allowances for the second compliance period of January 1, 2008, to December 31, 2012. As a result,

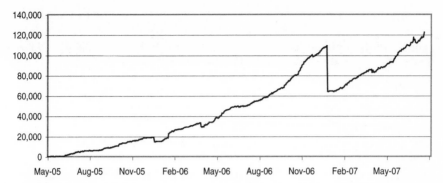

FIGURE 17.2 European Climate Exchange CFI CO_2 Futures – Open Interest (in # of contracts)
Source: European Climate Exchange, "ECX CFI Futures Contracts: Historic Data 2007," http://www.europeanclimateexchange.com/uploads/documents/ECXCFIFutures Contract-HistoricData-12July2007.xls.

the futures price of the EUA went up into the €20 range.[5] Then, in July 2007, the EU backtracked a bit and increased the number of allowances for Ireland and Latvia, which depressed prices somewhat.

Another factor affecting the price of an EUA is the relative price of fuel used by power utilities. In 2005, for example, there was a sharp increase in the price of natural gas and that forced many power utilities to increase power generation from their coal-fired plants and reduce generation from their natural gas plants. The increased burning of coal increased greenhouse gas emissions and caused the price of emission allowances to rally above €30 in April 2006.

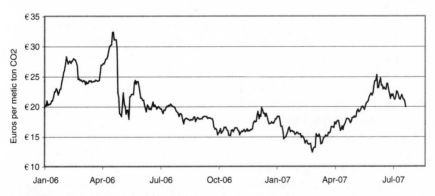

FIGURE 17.3 ECX ECI CO_2 – Futures Prices (Dec-08 Contract)
Source: European Climate Exchange, www.europeanclimateexchange.com.

Another factor affecting the price of an EUA is the world cap-and-trade situation. Prices rose in June 2007 after President Bush proposed a new round of international talks to curb greenhouse emissions. This gave validity to the cap-and-trade systems now operating in many countries. There is also anticipation that sooner or later, the United States will have to begin a cap-and-trade system and that will create an even bigger market for allowances.[6]

Another market factor is whether the European Union will decide to expand its existing Emission Trading System to include transportation. If that happens, there will be many more allowances available from a whole new group of companies. The effect on EUA prices could be either bullish or bearish depending on whether there is an easy or tight supply of the new allowances, but the expansion of the system in any case would sharply increase volume and open interest.[7]

EUROPEAN CAP-AND-TRADE CO2 EMISSIONS BACKGROUND EXPLANATION

The European Union, as part of its agreement to the Kyoto Protocol, committed to reducing its CO_2 emissions by 8 percent. In 2001, the EU set up a National Allocation Plan that set an emission cap for each member state. Then each member state in turn put an emission cap on each major individual company. The cap for each company was set at a level of emission that was lower than the baseline figure calculated from the company's normal level of emissions. The caps covered about 12,000 companies representing over half of all the CO_2 emitted in the EU. All this activity is administered the by the EU Environment Commission and a registry office in each member state.[8]

Under the cap-and-trade system being used by the European Union, the EU Environment Commission issues allowances (or permits) for each company to emit an amount of CO_2 gas equal to its cap. Each European Union Allowance (EUA) permits the holder to emit one metric ton of CO_2 during the compliance period. A total of about 2.2 billion EUAs were issued to the 12,000 companies for the first compliance period of February 16, 2005, to December 31, 2007. At the end of the compliance period, each company must surrender the number of EUAs equal to its total emissions for the period. If a company's total emissions for the period are less than its cap, then the company has extra EUAs to sell. On the other hand, if the company's emissions for the period exceed its cap and the company therefore doesn't have enough EUAs to equal its actual emissions, then it must buy the allowances from a company that has extra ones. If a company by the compliance date doesn't have enough EUAs to equal its total emissions, then the company incurs a penalty of €40 (rising to €100 later on) per metric ton. Under the Kyoto Protocol, a second five-year compliance period will begin on January 1, 2008, and end on December 31, 2012.[9]

The trading part of the EU's cap-and-trade system is called the European Union Emissions Trading Scheme. It started on January 1, 2005, and allowed for trading the European Union Allowances (EUAs). Each EUA equals the right to emit one metric ton of CO_2. Companies can buy and sell EUAs among themselves or they can buy or sell them in the cash market (also called the spot or over-the-counter market) at the prevailing market price. The cash market for the European Union is composed of those companies that are authorized by the EU Environment Commission to trade EUAs.

The EUA futures market is far bigger than the cash market, comprising about 95 percent of the total nominal trading volume in CO_2 emissions.[10] Each futures or options contract is for 1,000 European Union Allowances (EUA) and these contracts can be bought and sold by anyone for investment or hedging purposes.

CHICAGO CLIMATE EXCHANGE

The United States does not yet have a CO_2 cap-and-trade system so there are no mandatory U.S. allowances to trade. There is a voluntary CO_2 allowance system administered by the Chicago Climate Exchange, but there is no derivatives trading on those voluntary allowances as yet because the market is too thin. However, the Chicago Climate Exchange, which is a sister company of the European Climate Exchange, will be in a prime position to start trading futures on mandatory U.S. emissions allowances if and when the United States government adopts a cap-and-trade system for CO_2 emissions.

Both the Chicago Climate Exchange and the European Climate exchange are owned by the Climate Exchange Plc (London: CLE LN), which is a publicly traded company listed in London. The company's market cap as of July 2007 was £700 million. The company was founded in 2003 by Dr. Richard Sandor, a well-known and visionary figure in the Chicago futures markets.

While CO_2 trading has yet to come to the United States in a significant way, there are nevertheless futures trading opportunities at the Chicago Climate Exchange. The Chicago Climate Futures Exchange (CCFX), which a subsidiary of the Chicago Climate Exchange, handles trading of U.S. futures and options contracts on sulfur dioxide emission allowances

(Sulfur Financial Instrument-SFI) and nitrous dioxide emission allowances (Nitrogen Financial Instrument-NFI). The market has expanded to a value of about $2 billion annually.[11]

The first large-scale cap-and-trade program in the United States was introduced in the early 1990s as a result of the Clean Air Act Amendments of 1990. Title 1 of the Amendment set a goal of reducing annual sulfur dioxide (SO_2) emissions by 10 million tons below 1980 levels by the year 1995. It also mandated the reduction of annual nitrous dioxide (NO_2) emissions by 2 million tons by the year 2000. This program was called the Acid Rain Program. The program started with an EPA auction of emission allowances that was held at the Chicago Board of Trade in 1993. Phase I affected 445 coal-burning utility electricity generating plants. The program was expanded in Phase II to include about 2,000 plants. The sulfur-cap-and-trade program was very successful and SO_2 emissions by 1995 had been reduced by almost 40 percent below the target level.[12]

The EPA now allocates emission allowances to participating companies each year. The EPA administers the trading of allowances through its Allowance Management System. The EPA also keeps some allowances in reserve and these are auctioned off each March through the Chicago Board of Trade.[13]

Figure 17.4 shows the price history of the Chicago Climate Futures Exchange's Sulfur Financial Instrument (SFI) futures contract price going

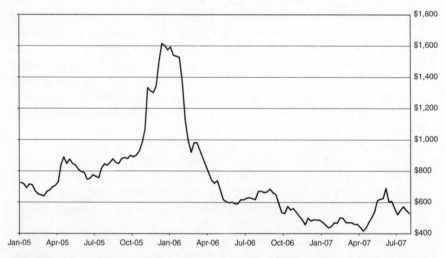

FIGURE 17.4 Chicago Climate Futures Exchange: Sulfur Financial Instrument (SFI) Futures Price (nearest futures price in dollars per U.S. EPA SO2 allowance) *Source:* Chicago Climate Futures Exchange, "Chicago Climate Futures Exchange Market Data," http://www.ccfe.com/mktdata_ccfe/index.jsf.

back to early 2005. The price is quoted in terms of dollars per U.S. EPA SO_2 Emissions Allowance. Each futures contract represents 25 U.S. EPA SO_2 Emissions Allowances, meaning that the nominal value of the contract can be calculated by multiplying the price of the contract by 25. Details on the terms of the contract can be found at the Chicago Climate Exchange's Web site (www.ccfe.com).[14]

Investment Conclusions

A s this book has discussed, clean energy involves an incredibly wide variety of completely different solutions and technologies, each with its own investment opportunities and risks. Perhaps the most interesting thing about clean energy is that there is no silver bullet that provides the complete answer to the world's energy problems. Instead, there are likely to be a wide variety of solutions that will be successful.

The world is at a juncture where there needs to be a transition from fossil fuels to cleaner forms of energy. The demand for new and cleaner forms of energy comes not only from environmental considerations, but also from the sheer amount of new energy generation that will be needed to satisfy the world's fast-growing energy needs. We have the technology, we have the capital, and we are gathering the will.

Fossil fuels helped the world economy get to where it is today, but now it is time to move on to fuels and technologies that can sustain the earth for centuries to come. This transition will cause dislocations in certain legacy industries, but it will also create incredible opportunities for completely new industries. Investors still have plenty of opportunity to get in at the early stages of this transition, which has only just begun. The bulk of the money in this sector has yet to be made.

The following is a summary of some of the investment conclusions offered by this book:

- The world will need 57 percent more energy over the next two decades. Much of this new demand will come from China, India, and the rest of the developing world.

- Fossil fuels do not offer a realistic solution for meeting this huge demand. This is because fossil fuels carry serious negative attributes such as pollution, greenhouse gas emissions, and vulnerability to supply disruptions and prices spikes. Moreover, the United States' dependence on foreign oil makes it vulnerable from a political, military, and economic standpoint. Energy security is a critical goal. Every country in the world could benefit from generating energy from within its own borders.

- World policymakers and the public at large are becoming more convinced that global warming is a serious problem. Government measures to curb the use of fossil fuels are likely to grow. All around the world, support for clean energy solutions and power efficiency is likely to increase. In the United States, action on clean energy at the state and local level is causing increased pressure for action at the federal level. A post-Kyoto CO_2 cap-and-trade system that includes the United States, China, India, and the developing world would provide a huge, additional boost for clean energy solutions that would last for decades.

- The target market for clean energy can be measured in terms of trillions of dollars, first with clean energy used as a supplement and eventually even as a replacement for fossil fuels. With its low starting base, the clean energy industry can easily grow at double-digit annual rates for decades.

- Some clean energy solutions are already commercially viable and don't need government support to thrive. These solutions include power efficiency products and services, smart meters, power backup and storage products, geothermal power, biomass, biogas, and hybrid vehicles. Other solutions such as wind and solar power need further cost reductions, but progress is being made because of technological breakthroughs and the huge amount of capital that is flowing into those areas. Fuel cells are already in commercial sales for some applications such as power backup and motive power, although much more work needs to be done for other fuel cell applications such as transportation and utility/commercial/residential power.

- Solar power has massive potential because both thermal and photovoltaic solar power can be used to generate power at the utility-scale level. Solar photovoltaic power can also be used at the residential and commercial building level as a distributed source of power to protect users from rising electricity prices. Solar power is already competitive with retail electricity prices in parts of the developed world and will become increasingly competitive in coming years due to the huge amount of resources that are being dedicated to cutting manufacturing and balance of system costs.

- Wind power is already a very popular power generation solution worldwide. The wind industry is currently plagued by production capacity shortages and cannot keep up with current demand. However, the industry is addressing component shortages and is quickly ramping up production capacity. Wind power economics will continue to improve due to improvements in technology. Wind power will become competitive with fossil fuel power generation ex-subsidies even more quickly if a CO_2 emission cost is added to fossil fuel power generation costs.

- Fuel cells have disappointed investors in the past due to their slow development. However, the fuel cell industry is making steady progress and is attracting interest from the world's large industrial companies. Fuel cells are likely to become commercially successful slowly and perhaps only in certain markets. Yet fuel cells represent such an attractive zero-emission power generation solution that further development will likely bring them eventually to full fruition.

- Geothermal power is already cost-competitive with fossil fuel power generation without subsidies and presents a highly attractive power generation solution in appropriate geological locations. Geothermal power runs 24 hours and day and contributes to a utility's base load generation portfolio.

- Power efficiency and smart grid solutions are in high demand right now and will only increase in popularity going forward as the world struggles to deal with the huge increase in demand for power and with outdated transmission and distribution systems. Power efficiency solutions make imminent economic sense right now and present excellent investment opportunities.

- Regarding the transportation area, the internal combustion engine is likely to be slowly phased out in coming decades because of pollution and greenhouse gas emissions. The world will literally choke if there are 2 billion vehicles with internal combustion engines on the world's roads by 2050, as some experts forecast. Gasoline-electric hybrid vehicles and eventually plug-in hybrids are likely to be much more popular than most observers currently expect. Battery technology is advancing rapidly and pure electric vehicles are likely to dominate the roads in coming decades since electric power is cheap and widely available. Fuel cell vehicles may provide a solution for fleets but may never be adopted on a mass scale because of the problems and cost of hydrogen production and delivery and because of eventual low-cost competition from electric vehicles.

- In the biofuels industry, the companies that are likely to be successful in the medium term are those that have (1) the R&D capability to make technological breakthroughs in cellulosic ethanol; and (2) the global presence for feedstock acquisition and biofuel production/distribution.

Investing in U.S.-based pure-play ethanol producers is mostly a bet on the corn-ethanol price spread, with the attendant uncertainties and risks. There is also the risk that biofuels may only be a temporary solution until the eventual phase-out of the internal combustion engine.

- Technological superiority, scale, and the ability to drive costs lower are the key attributes of the clean energy companies that will be the most successful in coming years. In choosing individual stocks in the clean energy sector, investors should focus on companies that have the potential for major technological breakthroughs and the ability to quickly commercialize those technologies on a mass scale and drive costs lower.

- In order to participate in the sector, investors can buy stocks of companies that focus on clean energy. A safer strategy is to diversify risk by buying a green exchange-traded fund or mutual fund. Investors should consider green ETFs and mutual funds that are global in nature since many of the world's clean energy companies are outside the U.S.

- While there will certainly be some bumps along with the way, the clean energy sector has all the earmarks of proving to be one of the best investment trends ever due to the sheer size of the task in moving from the legacy fossil fuels of the Industrial Age to the new and clean technologies that are necessary to move into a sustainable future in coming decades.

Information Resources

P lease see this book's companion Web site at www.ProfitingFrom
CleanEnergy.com for an updated resource list and for automatic
click-through links to these sites.

U.S. ENERGY STATISTICS

- Annual Energy Outlook 2007 with Projections to 2030, U.S. Department of Energy, Office of Energy Information Administration, February 2007, annual publication, www.eia.doe.gov/oiaf/aeo/.
- Monthly Energy Review, U.S. Department of Energy, Office of Energy Information Administration, monthly publication, www.eia.doe.gov/mer/.
- Electric Power Monthly, U.S. Department of Energy, Office of Energy Information Administration, monthly publication, www.eia.doe.gov/cneaf/electricity/epm/.
- Short-Term Energy Outlook, U.S. Department of Energy, Office of Energy Information Administration, monthly publication, www.eia.doe.gov/emeu/steo/pub/contents.html.

GLOBAL ENERGY STATISTICS

- International Energy Outlook 2007, U.S. Department of Energy, annual publication, www.eia.doe.gov/oiaf/ieo/.

- Key World Energy Statistics, 2006 Edition, International Energy Agency, www.iea.org/Textbase/stats/index.asp.
- World Energy Investment Outlook, 2003 Insights, International Energy Agency, http://www.iea.org/Textbase/work/2003/beijing/6WEIO.pdf.
- World Energy Outlook, International Energy Agency, www.worldenergyoutlook.org.
- BP Statistical Review of World Energy 2007, BP, www.bp.com/statisticalreview/.

RENEWABLE ENERGY DATA

- Renewable and Alternative Fuels U.S. Data, U.S. Department of Energy, Office of Energy Information Administration, www.eia.doe.gov/fuelrenewable.html.
- Renewable Energy Annual, U.S. Department of Energy, Office of Energy Information Administration, Updated 2006 with preliminary data for 2004, www.eia.doe.gov/cneaf/solar.renewables/page/rea_data/rea_sum.html.
- Renewables, Global Status Report, 2006 Update, Renewable Energy Policy Network for the 21st Century, www.ren21.net.

RENEWABLE ENERGY AND CLIMATE CHANGE PLANS AND REPORTS

- Recommendations to the Nation on Reducing U.S. Oil Dependence, Energy Security Leadership Council, December 2006, www.secureenergy.org/reports.php.
- U.S. Climate Change Technology Program, Strategic Plan, U.S. Climate Change Technology Program, September 2006, www.climatetechnology.gov.
- National Action Plan for Energy Efficiency, U.S. Department of Energy and U.S. Environmental Protection Agency, July 2006, www.epa.gov/cleanrgy/actionplan/eeactionplan.htm.
- American Energy, The Renewable Path to Energy Security, WorldWatch Institute for American Progress, September 2006, americanenergynow.org.
- Carbon Disclosure Project Report 2006, Innovest Strategic Value Advisors, www.cdproject.net.

RENEWABLE ENERGY AND CLIMATE CHANGE WEB SITES

- Union of Concerned Scientists, www.ucsusa.org/clean_energy/.
- Pew Center for Climate Change, www.pewclimate.com.
- Intergovernmental Panel on Climate Change, www.ipcc.ch.
- National Oceanic and Atmospheric Administration, www.noaa.gov/ climate.html.
- United Nations Framework Convention on Climate Change, unfccc.int.
- United Nations Environment Program, grida.no/climate/.
- United States Department of Energy, www.energy.gov/.
- United States Department of State, www.state.gov/g/oes/climate.
- United States Environmental Protection Agency, www.epa.gov/ globalwarming/.
- Global Change Master Directory, NASA Goddard Space Flight Center, globalchange.nasa.gov.
- United States National Assessment, www.gcrio.org/NationalAssessment/.
- The United States Global Change Research Program (U.S.GCRP), www.usgcrp.gov.
- Carbon Dioxide Information Analysis Center, cdiac.esd.ornl.gov.
- Emissions Database for Global Atmospheric Research, www.rivm.nl/ en/milieu/.
- International Institute for Applied Systems Analysis, www.iiasa.ac.at.
- International Energy Agency, Greenhouse Gas Programme, www. ieagreen.org.uk.

RENEWABLE ENERGY LEGISLATION AND INCENTIVES

- Renewable Legislation and Incentives, U.S. Department of Energy, Office of Energy Information Administration, www.eia.doe.gov/cneaf/ solar.renewables/page/legislation/renewleg.html.
- Union of Concerned Scientists, www.ucsusa.org/clean_energy/clean_ energy_policies/.
- International Energy Agency, Global Renewable Energy Policies and Measures Database, renewables.iea.org.
- International Energy Agency, WEO World Energy Policy Database, www.iea.org/textbase/pamsdb/searchweo.aspx.

RENEWABLE ENERGY TECHNOLOGY

- Power Technologies Data Book, National Renewable Energy Laboratory, U.S. Department of Energy, March 2006, www.nrel.gov/analysis/power_databook/.
- National Renewable Energy Laboratory, Dynamic Maps, GIS Data, and Analysis Tools, www.nrel.gov/gis/maps.html.

SOLAR PHOTOVOLTAIC POWER

- Prometheus Institute, PV News, www.Prometheus.org.
- Photon Magazine, www.photon-magazine.com.
- SolarBuzz, www.solarbuzz.com.
- International Energy Agency, Photovoltaic Power Systems Programme, www.iea-pvps.org.
- Solar Energy Technologies Program, U.S. Department of Energy, Energy Efficiency and Renewable Energy, www1.eere.energy.gov/solar/photovoltaics.html.
- Solar America Initiative, www1.eere.energy.gov/solar/solar_america/index.html.
- PV Watts, Performance Calculator for Grid-Connected PV Systems, rredc.nrel.gov/solar/calculators/PVWATTS/.

SOLAR THERMAL POWER

- Solar Heating, U.S. Department of Energy, Office of Energy Efficiency and Renewable Energy, www1.eere.energy.gov/solar/solar_heating.html.

WIND POWER

- National Renewable Energy Laboratory, Wind Research, www.nrel.gov/wind/.
- Wind and Hydropower Technologies Program, U.S. Department of Energy, Office of Energy Efficiency and Renewable Energy, www1.eere.energy.gov/windandhydro/.

FUEL CELLS

- Fuel Cells 2000, www.fuelcells.org/.
- California Air Resources Board, Hydrogen and Fuel Cell Guide, www.arb.ca.gov/h2fuelcell/h2fcguide/h2fcguide.htm.
- Hydrogen, Fuel Cells & Infrastructure Technologies Program, U.S. Department of Energy, Office of Energy Efficiency and Renewable Energy, www1.eere.energy.gov/hydrogenandfuelcells/.
- Wind-to-Hydrogen Project (Wind/Fuel Cell combined system), National Renewable Energy Laboratory, www.nrel.gov/hydrogen/proj_wind_hydrogen.html.

GEOTHERMAL POWER

- Geothermal Energy Association, www.geo-energy.org.
- Union of Concerned Scientists, www.ucusa.org/clean_energy/renewable_energy_basics/offmen-how-geothermal-energy-works.
- International Geothermal Association, iga.igg.cnr.it/geo/geornergy.php.
- U.S. Department of Energy, www1.eere.energy.gov/geothermal/printable_versions/faqs.html.
- Geothermal Technologies Program, National Renewable Energy Laboratory, www.nrel.gov/geothermal/.
- National Renewable Energy Laboratory, Geothermal Resource Information Clearinghouse, rredc.nrel.gov/geothermal/.
- Yale Global Online, yaleglobal.yale.edu/environment.
- Geothermal Heat Pump Consortium, www.geoexchange.org.
- Geothermal Resource Maps, www1.eere.energy.gov/geothermal/maps.html.

GREEN POWER MARKETING PROGRAMS

- Purchasing Renewable Power, U.S. Department of Energy, Office of Energy Efficiency and Renewable Energy, www1.eere.energy.gov/femp/program/utility/utilityman_renew.html.
- Guide to Purchasing Green Power, U.S. Department of Energy, Office of Energy Efficiency and Renewable Energy, www.eere.energy.gov/femp/pdfs/purchase_green_power.pdf.

- Green Power Network (utility green power markets and marketing), U.S. Department of Energy, Office of Energy Efficiency and Renewable Energy, www.eere.energy.gov/greenpower/.
- Library of Green Utility Power Publications, U.S. Department of Energy, Office of Energy Efficiency and Renewable Energy, www.eere.energy.gov/greenpower/resources/publications.shtml.

BIOMASS POWER

- Biomass Program, U.S. Department of Energy, Office of Energy Efficiency and Renewable Energy, www1.eere.energy.gov/biomass/electrical_power.html.
- Biomass Research, National Renewable Energy Laboratory, www.nrel.gov/biomass/.

POWER AND BUILDING EFFICIENCY

- Union of Concerned Scientists, Energy Efficiency, www.ucsusa.org/clean_energy/energy_efficiency/.
- Energy Star program, www.energystar.gov.
- EPA Green Building Site, www.epa.gov/greenbuilding.
- U.S. Green Building Council, www.usgbc.org.

GRID RELIABILITY AND SMART METERS

- Office of Electricity Delivery and Energy Reliability, www.oe.energy.gov/.
- Advanced Meter Reading Association (AMRA), www.amra-intl.org.
- Electric Power Research Institute (EPRI), www.epri.com.
- Smart Grid News, www.smartgridnews.com.

ELECTRICITY STORAGE AND BATTERIES

- Electricity Storage Association, www.electricitystorage.org.
- Battery University, www.batteryuniversity.com.
- Battery Council International, www.batterycouncil.org.

HYBRID ELECTRIC VEHICLES

- Hybrid and Vehicle Systems, U.S. Department of Energy, Energy Efficiency and Renewable Energy, www1.eere.energy.gov/vehiclesandfuels/technologies/systems/index.html.
- Advanced Vehicles and Fuels Research, National Renewable Energy Laboratory, www.nrel.gov/vehiclesandfuels/.

BIOFUELS AND ETHANOL

- Biomass Program, U.S. Department of Energy, www1.eere.energy.gov/biomass/.
- Renewable Fuels Association (RFA), www.ethanolrfa.org.
- Ethanol Promotion and Information Council (EPIC), www.drivingethanol.org.
- American Coalition for Ethanol (ACE), www.ethanol.org.
- Governors' Ethanol Coalition, www.ethanol-gec.org.
- National Ethanol Vehicle Coalition, www.e85fuel.com.
- The National Corn Growers Association (NCGA), www.ncga.com.
- Alternative Fuels Data Center, www.afdc.doe.gov.
- National Biodiesel Board, www.biodiesel.org.

COAL GASIFICATION AND CO2 SEQUESTRATION

- Gasification Technology R&D, U.S. Department of Energy, www.fossil.energy.gov/programs/powersystems/gasification/index.html.
- Pollution Control Innovations for Power Plants, U.S. Department of Energy, www.fossil.energy.gov/programs/powersystems/pollutioncontrols/index.html.
- FutureGen, Tomorrow's Pollution-Free Power Plant, U.S. Department of Energy, www.fossil.energy.gov/programs/powersystems/futuregen/index.html.
- Carbon Sequestration, U.S. Department of Energy, www.fossil.energy.gov/programs/sequestration/index.html.

CARBON CREDITS

- Point Carbon, www.pointcarbon.com/, news and analysis on global power, gas and carbon markets.

CLEAN ENERGY GLOSSARIES

- Renewable Energy Glossary, U.S. Department of Energy, www.eia
  .doe.gov/cneaf/solar.renewables/page/rea_data/gl.html.
- U.S. Renewable Resource Data Center, List of Glossaries, rredc.nrel
  .gov/solar/glossary/otherlinks.html.
- Solar Power Glossary, www1.eere.energy.gov/solar/solar_glossary
  .html.
- Smart Meter Glossary (from Itron), www.itron.com/pages/resources_
  glossary.asp.
- Biomass Feedstock Glossary, U.S. Department Energy, www1.eere
  .energy.gov/biomass/feedstock_glossary.html.

ENERGY CONVERSIONS

- Conversion of Units, en.wikipedia.org/wiki/Conversion_of_units.
- Greenhouse Gas Equivalencies Calculator, www.usctcgateway.net/
  tool/.
- Cleaner and Greener Emission Reduction Calculator, www.cleaner
  andgreener.org/resources/emission_reductions.htm.

Notes

CHAPTER 1

1. Shell Springboard, "Opportunities for Innovation: The Business Opportunities for SMEs in Tackling the Causes of Climate Change," http://www.shellspringboard.org/downloads/news/Q65_Springboard_Doc_V4.pdf.

2. Renewable Fuels Association, "Investment Opportunities," www.ethanolrfa.org/industry/investment.

3. "2006 European and North American Cleantech Venture Investment Totals $3.6 billion," 15 Febuary 2007, Cleantech Network, www.cleantechnetwork.com, press releases at http:// cleantechnetwork.com/index.cfm?pageSRC=PressReleases.

4. Author calculations; company market caps sourced from Bloomberg, www.bloomberg.com] and Reuters, www.reuters.com.

5. Mary Milliken, "GE CEO Sees 'Green" Unit Growing Faster," *Reuters*, 24 May 2007.

6. See GE Energy Financial Services, www.geenergyfinancialservices .com.

7. Robinson, Edward, "VCs Set on Solar, Biofuel Money-Losers in Green Energy Frenzy," *Bloomberg*, 29 June 2006, http://www.bloomberg.com/apps/news?pid=20601109&sid=a9wBJqPgMUT8&refer=home.

8. Ibid.

9. Todd Woody, "Big Solar's Day in the Sun," *Business 2.0 Magazine*, June 2007, http://money.cnn.com/magazines/business2/business2_archive/2007/06/01/100050990/index.htm.

10. For intermittent power such as solar and wind, 1 megawatt of rated capacity can power about 275 homes. This is calculated as ((1 megawatt × 1,000 kilowatts/megawatt × 8,760 hours/year)/(10,656 kilowatt-hours per year usage for average U.S. household)) × (About 1/3

capacity realized). The average annual U.S. household usage of 10,656 kilowatt-hours per year is sourced from Energy Information Administration, Electricity Consumption by End Use in U.S. Households, 2001, Table US-A, www.eia.doe.gov/emeu/reps/endues/er01_us_tab1.html. See also Bob Bellemare, "What Is a Megawatt?," UtiliPoint International, http://www.utilipoint.com/issuealert/print.asp?id=1728; and Johathan G. Koomey, et al., "Sorry, Wrong Number: The Use and Misuse of Numerical Facts in Analysis and Media Reporting of Energy Issues," *Annual Review of Energy and the Environment Journal* 27 (2002):119–158, http://arjournals.annualreviews.org/).

11. See Spectra Fund, http://www.spectrafund.com/sf/appmanager/spectraportal/welcome.

CHAPTER 2

1. Massachusetts Institute of Technology, *The Future of Coal: Options for a Carbon-Constrained World*" (Cambridge, MA: Massachusetts Institute of Technology, 2007), http://Web.mit.edu/coal/.

2. U.S. Department of Energy, Energy Information Administration, *Annual Energy Review 2006*, May 2007, Table 5.1, http://www.eia.doe.gov/emeu/aer/txt/stb0501.xls.

3. Ibid.

4. U.S. Department of Energy, Energy Information Administration, "Persian Gulf Fact Sheet," http://www.eia.doe.gov/emeu/cabs/Persian_Gulf/Background.html.

5. U.S. Department of Energy, Energy Information Administration, "Nigeria Country Brief, April 2007," http://www.eia.doe.gov/emeu/cabs/Nigeria/Oil.html.

6. Ibid.

7. U.S. Department of Energy, Energy Information Administration, International *Energy Outlook 2007*, May 2007, p. 1, www.eia.doe.gov/oiaf/ieo/index.html.

8. The population of China (1.322 billion), India (1.130 billion), and Russia (142 million) combined is 2.6 billion according to the Central Intelligence Agency, *CIA Fact Book*, https://www.cia.gov/library/publications/the-world-factbook/index.html.

9. U.S. Department of Energy, Energy Information Administration, International *Energy Outlook 2007*, p. 8.

10. Ibid.

11. See nation profiles in Central Intelligence Agency, *CIA Fact Book* (June 2007), https://www.cia.gov/library/publications/the-world-factbook/index.html.

12. Ibid.

13. Keith Bradsher and David Barboza, "Pollution from Chinese Coal Casts a Global Shadow," *New York Times*, 11 June 2006, http://www.nytimes.com/2006/06/11/business/worldbusiness/11chinacoal.html?ex=1307678400en=e9ac1f6255a24fd8ei=5088partner=rssnytemc=rss.

14. Ibid.

15. U.S. Department of Energy, Energy Information Administration, *International Energy Outlook 2007*, pp. 19–20.

16. Ibid.

17. John M. Broder and Majorie Connelly, "Poll Finds Majority See Threat in Global Warming," *New York Times*, 26 April 2007, http://www.nytimes.com/2007/04/26/washington/27pollcnd.html?ex=1184472000&en=ab2b53dff4b3b058&ei=5070.

18. Intergovernmental Panel on Climate Change, *Climate Change 2007: The Physical Science Basis, Summary for Policymakers* (February 5, 2007), http://www.ipcc.ch/SPM2feb07.pdf.

19. U.K. Government Economic Service, *Stern Review on the Economics of Climate Change*, October 2006, http://www.hm-treasury.gov.uk/independent_reviews/stern_review_economics_climate_change/sternreview_index.cfm.

20. Ibid.

21. Ibid.

22. E.I. du Pont de Nemours and Company, "Sustainability: Biobutanol Performance Similar to Unleaded Gasoline," *DuPont News* press release, 20 April 2007, http://www2.dupont.com/Media_Center/en_US/daily_news/april/article20070420.html.

23. "List of Power Outages," *Wikipedia: The Free Encyclopedia*, http://en.wikipedia.org/wiki/List_of_power_outages.

24. "Northeast Blackout of 2003," *Wikipedia: The Free Encyclopedia*, http://en.wikipedia.org/wiki/Northeast_Blackout_of_2003.

25. Ibid.

26. Canada-US Power System Outage Task Force, "Causes of the August 14th Blackout in the United States and Canada," 16 April-2006, http://www.nrcan-rncan.gc.ca/media/docs/reports_e.htm.

27. U.S. Department of Energy, Energy Information Administration, *Annual Energy Review 2006*, June 2007, Table 8.10 Average Retail

Prices of Electricity, 1960-2006, http://www.eia.doe.gov/emeu/aer/txt/stb0810.xls.

28. U.S. Department of Energy, Energy Information Administration, *Annual Energy Review 2006*, June 2007, Table 2.1f, http://www.eia.doe.gov/emeu/aer/txt/stb0802a.xls.

CHAPTER 3

1. Thomas Friedman, "The Power of Green," *New York Times Magazine*, 15 April 2007, p. 72.

2. Andrew Batson, "For Chinese tycoon, solar power fuels overnight wealth," *New York Times*, 12 October 2006.

3. "Manhattan Project," Wikipedia, *Wikipedia: The Free Encyclopedia*, http://en.wikipedia.org/wiki/Manhattan_project.

4. United Nations Environmental Programme, "Global Trends in Sustainable Energy Investment 2007," 2007, http://www.ren21.net/pdf/Glob_Sust_Energy_Inv_Report_2007.pdf.

5. Janet L. Sawin and Christopher Flavin, "National Policy Instruments: Policy Lessons for the Advancement and Diffusion of Renewable Energy Technologies Around the World," International Conference for Renewable Energies, Bonn 2004, http://www.renewables2004.de/pdf/tbp/TBP03-policies.pdf.

6. Renewable Energy Policy Network for the 21st Century, "Instruments of Renewable Energy Policies," http://www.ren21.net/REPolicies/policy/instruments.asp.

7. REN21: Renewable Energy Policy Network for the 21st Century, *Renewables Global Status Report, 2006 Update* (Paris: REN21 Secretariat and Washington D.C.: WorldWatch Institute, 2006), p. 23, http://www.ren21.net/pdf/RE_GSR_2006_Update.pdf.

8. Ibid.

9. Zogby International and TechNet, "Green Tech Task Force poll," 18 January 2007, www.technet.org, press releases.

10. Union of Concerned Scientists, "State Renewable Electricity Standards," http://www.ucsusa.org/clean_energy/clean_energy_policies/res-at-work-in-the-states.html.

11. See note 10, Chapter 1.

12. Friedman, "The Power of Green," p. 71.

13. Green Car Congress, "New Jersey becomes third state with greenhouse gas reduction law, 7-Jul-2007. http://www.greencarcongress.com/2007/07/new-jersey-beco.html#more.

14. Ibid.

15. "China's Signals on Warming," New York Times, 16 April 2007, http://www.nytimes.com/2007/04/16/opinion/16mon2.html?_r=1&oref= slogin.

16. Environmental Defense, Press Release: Leading Companies Call for Bold Action on Global Warming, 22 January 2007; 27 February 2007, http://www.environmentaldefense.org/pressrelease.cfm?contentID= 5830.

17. "Bush faces growing dissent from Republicans on climate change," *Bloomberg News*, 24 April 2006.

CHAPTER 4

1. U.S. Department of Energy, Energy Information Administration, *Annual Energy Review 2006*, June 2007, http://www.eia.doe.gov/emeu/ aer/diagram1.html.

2. U.S. Department of Energy, Energy Information Administration, *The International Energy Outlook 2007*, May 2007, Figure 40, http://www.eia.doe.gov/oiaf/ieo/excel/figure_40data.xls. The world consumed 100 trillion cubic feet of natural gas in 2004 and the EIA estimates consumption will be 163 trillion cubic feet in 2030. Using a conversion factor of 1,031 Btu per cubic feet and the recent NYMEX price of $7.00 per million Btu, the 100 trillion cubic feet for 2004 has a value of $722 billion. Likewise, the 163 trillion cubic feet for 2030 has a value of $1.2 trillion.

3. Ibid., Figure 54, http://www.eia.doe.gov/oiaf/ieo/excel/figure_54data.xls. The world consumed 114.5 quadrillion Btus of coal in 2004 and the EIA is forecasting 199.1 quadrillion Btus of coal consumption in 2030. Using a conversion factor of 24 million Btus per ton (the NYMEX contract requires a minimum content of 12,000 Btus per pound of coal) and the recent price of $45 per ton, the 114.5 quadrillion Btus for 2004 has a value of $215 billion. Likewise, the 199.1 Btus for 2030 has a value of $373 billion. Details on the NYMEX coal futures contract and pricing can be found at the www.Nymex.com Web site at http://www.nymex.com/QL_spec.aspx.

4. International Energy Agency, *Renewables in Global Energy Supply: An IEA Fact Sheet*, January 2007, p 12,. http://www.iea.org/textbase/ papers/2006/renewable_factsheet.pdf.

5. Ibid., p. 16.

6. Joel Makower,Ron Pernick, and Clint Wilder, *Clean Energy Trends 2007*, Clean Edge Inc., May 2007, http://www.cleanedge.com/reports/Trends2007.pdf.

CHAPTER 5

The author would like to thank and acknowledge Melvin & Company for permission to use several excerpts and graphics in this chapter that the author originally published in research reports written for Melvin & Company.

1. U.S. Department of Energy, National Renewable Energy Laboratory, Renewable Resource Data Center, "RRDC Energy Tidbits," http://rredc.nrel.gov/tidbits.html.

2. "A Consumer's Guide: Heat Your Water with the Sun," U.S. Department of Energy, Energy Efficiency and Renewable Energy, Dec 2003, p 12. http://www.nrel.gov/docs/fy04osti/34279.pdf.

3. Ibid., p. 12.

4. Solar Energy Technologies Program, U.S. Energy Efficiency and Renewable Energy, http://www1.eere.energy.gov/solar/sh_rd_partnerships.html#nrel.

5. REN21: Renewable Energy Policy Network for the 21st Century, *Renewables Global Status Report, 2006 Update* (Paris: REN21 Secretariat and Washington D.C.: WorldWatch Institute, 2006), p. 5, http://www.ren21.net/pdf/RE_GSR_2006_Update.pdf.

6. Ibid.

7. European Solar Thermal Industry, "Solar Thermal Markets in Europe," June 2006, http://www.estif.org/9.0.html.

8. Concentrating Solar Power, Energy Efficiency Technologies Program, U.S. Dept. of Energy. http://www1.eere.energy.gov/solar/csp.html,

9. Parabolic Trough Solar Field Technology, National Renewable Energy Lab, http://www.nrel.gov/csp/troughnet/solar_field.html.

10. Sterling Energy Systems, http://www.stirlingenergy.com/products.asp?Type=solar.

11. Ibid.

12. U.S. Department of Energy, National Renewable Energy Laboratory, *Power Technologies Energy Data Book*, August 2006, p. 18, http://www.nrel.gov/analysis/power_databook/.

13. Ibid.

14. Ibid., p. 19.

15. Ibid., p. 20. See also Mark S. Mehos, "Overview of the 1000 MW CSP Southwest Initiative," National Renewable Energy Laboratory, 13 July 2004, http://www.nrel.gov/csp/troughnet/pdfs/40027.pdf.

16. See note 10, Chapter 1.

17. Stephen Lacey, "Tracking the Sun: Concentrating Solar Power Faces Bright Future," RenewableEnergyAccess.com, 20 March 2007, http://www.renewableenergyaccess.com/rea/news/printstory;jsessionid=B6 9835CE815F90CFF6807D662E5125F0?id=47803.

18. Schott AG, "Largest Solar Thermal Power Plant Built in 16 Years Goes Online with SCHOTT Receivers," 8 June 2007, http://www.us.schott .com/english/news/archive.html?NID=186. See also Schott AG, "Schott White Paper on Solar Thermal Power Plant Technology," http://www. us.schott.com/solarthermal/english/download/schott_white_paper.pdf.

19. U.S. Department of Energy, National Renewable Energy Laboratory, *Power Technologies Energy Data Book*, August 2006, p. 18. http://www.nrel.gov/analysis/power_databook/.

20. Ibid., p. 20.

21. Ibid.

22. Ibid.

23. U.S. Department of Energy, Office of Energy Efficiency and Renewable Energy, "Solar Myths," *Energy Efficiency and Renewable Energy Information Center*, http://www1.eere.energy.gov/solar/myths.html.

24. Joel Makower, Ron Pernick, and Clint Wilder, "Clean Energy Trends 2007," *CleanEdge*, March 2007, p. 2, www.cleanedge.com.

25. U.S. Geological Service, "Silicon: Statistics and Information," http://minerals.usgs.gov/ minerals/pubs/commodity/silicon/.

26. U.S. Geological Service, *Mineral Commodity Summaries: Silicon*, January 2007, p. 146, http://minerals.usgs.gov/minerals/pubs/ commodity/silicon/silicmcs07.pdf.

27. Kosuke Kurokawa, Keichi Komoto, Peter van der Vleuten, David Faiman (eds.), *Energy from the Desert: Practical Proposals for Very Large Scale Photovoltaic Systems* (London: Earthscan, 2006). A 29-page summary of the book is available from the International Energy Agency at http://www.iea-pvps.org/products/rep8_02s.htm.

28. International Energy Agency, *World Energy Investment Outlook 2003*, p. 346, http://www.iea.org/Textbase/publications/free_new_ Desc.asp?PUBS_ID=1200.

29. International Energy Agency, "Renewables in Global Energy Supply: An IEA Fact Sheet," January 2007, http://www.iea.org/Textbase/ publications/free_new_Desc.asp?PUBS_ID=1596.

30. U.S. Department of Energy, Office of Energy Efficiency and Renewable Energy, *Solar American Initiative: A Plan for the Integrated Research, Development, and Market Transformation of Solar Energy Technologies,* 5 February 2007, p. 9, http://www1.eere.energy. gov/solar/solar_america/pdfs/sai_draft_plan_Feb5_07.pdf. The home page for the Solar American Initiative is http://www1.eere.energy.gov/ solar/solar_america/.

31. "23rd Annual Data Collection—Final," *PV News,* April 2007, p. 8. *PV News* is published by the Prometheus Institute, Cambridge MA, http://www.prometheus.org/.

32. Ibid.

33. Michael Rogol, "Solar Annual 2006: The Gun Has Gone Off," *RenewableEnergyAccess.com,* 4 September 2006, http://www.renewable energyaccess.com/rea/news/story?id=45869. *Solar Annual 2006* can be purchased at www.photon-consulting.com.

34. Ibid.

35. Ibid.

36. Solarbuzz, LLC, "Market Buzz 2007: World PV Industry Report Highlights," *Market Buzz 2007,* www.solarbuzz.com/marketbuzz2007-intro.htm.

37. "PV Market Demand through 2010," PV News, July 2007, pp. 5–7, Promethesus Institute, Cambridge, MA, www.prometheus.org.

38. Photon Consulting, "Executive Summary of *The True Cost of Solar Power: 10 cents/kWh by 2010,*" April 2007. This report summary is available on the company's Web site at www.photon-consulting.com. The report itself can be purchased at the Web site.

39. Solarbuzz LLC, Solar Electricity Price Index verses US Electricity tariff Price Index (U.S. cents per kilowatt hour), July 2007, http://www.solarbuzz.com/SolarPrices.htm.

40. Photon Consulting, "Executive Summary of *The True Cost of Solar Power: 10 cents/kWh by 2010.*"

41. Ibid.

42. U.S. Department of Energy, Office of Energy Efficiency and Renewable Energy, *Solar American Initiative: A Plan for the Integrated Research, Development, and Market Transformation of Solar Energy Technologies,* 5 February 2007, http://www1.eere.energy.gov/ solar/solar_america/pdfs/sai_draft_plan_Feb5_07.

43. *"2010 Cost Reduction Roadmap,"* in "Analyst Silicon Field Trip, March 28, 2007," Renewable Energy Corp, p. 12, See investor relations area of www.recgroup.com web site, http://hugin.info/136555/R/1115224/203491.pdf.

44. PV News, various issues, Prometheus Institute, Cambridge, MA, www.prometheus.org.

45. "Supply and Demand Reconciliation," PV News, August 2007, p. 7, Prometheus Institute, Cambridge, MA, www.prometheus.org.

46. Photon International, "Silicon Sprint," October 2006, p. 110.

47. Michael Rogol, "Solar Annual 2006: The Gun Has Gone Off."

48. Antonio Luque and Steven Hegedus (eds.), Chapter 1: "Status, Trends, Challenges and the Bright Future of Solar Electricity from Photovoltaics," *Handbook of Photovoltaic Science and Engineering* (Hoboken, NJ: John Wiley & Sons, 2003), p. 30.

49. Ibid.

50. Dow Corning, "Dow Corning Solar Solutions Introduces Breakthrough Solar Material," *Silicon Metal,* September 2006, www.dowcorning.com.

51. "Analyst Silicon Field Trip, March 28, 2007," Renewable Energy Corp, p. 30, See investor relations area of www.recgroup.com Web site, http://hugin.info/136555/R/1115224/203491.pdf.

52. Ibid, p. 29.

53. See company press release at http://www.solarworld.de/sw-eng/presse-adhoc/index.php.

54. "23rd Annual Data Collection, Final," *PV News,* April 2007, pp. 8–10, Prometheus Institute, Cambridge, MA, www.prometheus.org.

55. Solarbuzz LLC Module Price Survey, www.solarbuzz.com, www.solarbuzz.com/ModulePrices.htm.

CHAPTER 6

1. Global Wind Energy Council, *Global Wind 2006 Report,* 2006, p. 4, http://www.gwec.net/uploads/media/gwec-2006_final.pdf.

2. U.S. Department of Energy, National Renewabl Energy Laboratory, *Wind Power Today,* May 2007, p. 2, http://www.nrel.gov/docs/fy07osti/41330.pdf.

3. U.S. Department of Energy, Office of Energy Efficiency and Renewable Energy, "Wind and Hydropower Technologies Program: How

Wind Turbines Work," http://www1.eere.energy.gov/windandhydro/wind_how.html.

4. U.S. Department of Energy, National Renewable Energy Laboratory, *Annual Report on U.S. Wind Power Installation, Cost, and Performance Trends: 2006*, May 2007, p. 19, http://www.nrel.gov/docs/fy07osti/41435.pdf.

5. U.S. Department of Energy, National Energy Technology Laboratory, *Cost and Performance Baseline for Fossil Energy Plants*, May 2007, vol. 1, p. 150, http://www.netl.doe.gov/energy-analyses/pubs/Bituminous%20Baseline_Final%20Report.pdf.

6. American Wind Energy Association, "Wind Energy Fact Sheet: Wind Energy and Economic Development: Building Sustainable Jobs and Communities," http://www.awea.org/pubs/factsheets/EconDev.PDF.

7. Ibid.

8. Ibid.

9. American Wind Energy Association, "Wind Energy 101: Basics," http://www.ifnotwind.org/we101/wind-energy-basics.shtml.

10. American Wind Energy Association, "Wind Energy Facts & Myths: Expensive and Unreliable," http://www.ifnotwind.org/myths/myth-expensive.shtml.

11. American Wind Energy Association, "Wind Energy 101: Basics."

12. Ibid.

13. U.S. Department of Energy, National Renewable Energy Laboratory, *Grid Impacts of Wind Power: A Summary of Recent Studies in the United States: Conference Paper*, June 2003, http://www.nrel.gov/docs/fy03osti/34318.pdf.

14. American Wind Energy Association, "Wind Energy 101: Potential," http://www.ifnotwind.org/we101/wind-energy-potential.shtml.

15. U.S. Department of Energy, National Renewable Energy Laboratory, *Annual Report on U.S. Wind Power Installation, Cost, and Performance Trends: 2006*, May 2007, p. 5, http://www.nrel.gov/docs/fy07osti/41435.pdf.

16. American Wind Energy Association, "Wind Energy 101: Potential."

17. U.S. Department of Energy, National Renewable Energy Laboratory, "Wind Powering America Fact Sheet Series: Wind Energy Myths," May 2005, http://www.nrel.gov/docs/fy05osti/37657.pdf.

18. Ibid.

19. See note 10, Chapter 1.

20. U.S. Department of Energy, National Renewable Energy Laboratory, *Annual Report on U.S. Wind Power Installation, Cost, and Performance Trends: 2006*, p. 3.

21. Ibid., p. 7.

22. American Wind Energy Association, "Wind Energy 101 - Basics."

23. U.S. Department of Energy, National Renewable Energy Laboratory, *Wind Power Today*, May 2007, p. 2, http://www.nrel.gov/docs/fy07osti/41330.pdf.

24. American Wind Energy Association, "Wind Energy 101:Basics."

25. U.S. Department of Energy, National Renewable Energy Laboratory, *Annual Report on U.S. Wind Power Installation, Cost, and Performance Trends: 2006*, p. 7 pdf.

26. Ibid.

27. U.S. Department of Energy, National Renewable Energy Laboratory, *Wind Power Today*, p. 2. pdf.

28. American Wind Energy Association, "Wind Energy 101: Basics."

29. Ibid.

30. U.S. Department of Energy, National Renewable Energy Laboratory, *Annual Report on U.S. Wind Power Installation, Cost, and Performance Trends: 2006*, May 2007, p. 5.

31. Ibid.,

32. Global Wind Energy Council, *Global Wind 2006 Report*, 2006, p. 4. pdf.

33. Ibid., p. 12.

34. Ibid., p. 4.

35. Ibid., p. 12.

36. Ibid., p. 4.

37. Ibid., p. 12.

38. Ibid., pp. 4 and 7.

39. Ibid., p. 12.

40. Ibid.

41. U.S. Department of Energy, National Renewable Energy Laboratory, *Annual Report on U.S. Wind Power Installation, Cost, and Performance Trends: 2006*, May 2007, p. 4, pdf.

42. U.S. Department of Energy, National Renewable Energy Laboratory, *Wind Power Today*, May 2007, p. 2, pdf.

43. Global Wind Energy Council, *Global Wind 2006 Report*, p. 12, pdf.

44. Ibid., p. 13.

45. Ibid.

46. U.S. Department of Energy, National Renewable Energy Laboratory, *Wind Power Today*, May 2007, p. 2, pdf.

47. The study, measured in 2006 dollars, took a sample comprising 58 percent of added capacity for the period 1998–2006, and measured the cumulative weighted average costs. Costs include U.S. government sponsored Production Tax Credits (PTCs). They include some interconnection and transmission costs, and in some cases include the Renewable Energy Certificates (REC) program.

48. U.S. Department of Energy, National Renewable Energy Laboratory, *Annual Report on U.S. Wind Power Installation, Cost, and Performance Trends: 2006*, May 2007, p. 10, pdf.

49. Ibid., p. 11.

50. Ibid.

51. Ibid.

52. Ibid.

53. American Wind Energy Association, "Wind Energy 101—Potential."

54. American Wind Energy Association, http://www.awea.org/newsroom/releases/Congress_extends_PTC_121106.html.

55. U.S. Department of Energy, National Renewable Energy Laboratory, *Annual Report on U.S. Wind Power Installation, Cost, and Performance Trends: 2006*, May 2007, p. 12, pdf.

56. U.S. Department of Energy, National Renewable Energy Laboratory, *Wind Power Today*, May 2007, p. 4. http://www.nrel.gov/docs/fy07osti/41330.pdf.

57. Global Energy Network Institute, "Policy Options: Electricity Feedin Laws: Case Study in Germany," http://www.geni.org/globalenergy/policy/renewableenergy/electricityfeed-inlaws/germany/index.shtml.

58. Worldwatch Institute, "Behind the Chilly Air: Impacts of China's New Wind Pricing Regulation," *Worldwatch.org*, 30 March 2006, http://www.worldwatch.org/node/3904.

59. Class 4 refers to the classification of wind sites according to average wind speed, ranging from class 1 through class 6, the higher the class the faster the wind speed and, therefore, the better the location is for wind turbines. See U.S. Department of Energy, National Renewable Energy Laboratory, "Advanced Component Technology," *Wind Research—Advanced Component Technology—Wind Pact*, 10 April 2007, http://www.nrel.gov/wind/advanced_technology.html.

60. International Energy Agency, "Activities and Accomplishments," *Current Activities and Accomplishments*, http://www.ieawind.org/ activities_accomplishments.html.

61. European Wind Energy Association, "Focus on Supply Chain: Supply Chain: The Race to Meet Demand," *Wind Directions*, January–February 2007, p. 28, http://www.ewea.org/fileadmin/ewea_ documents/documents/publications/WD/2007_january/0701-WD26-focus.pdf.

62. Global Wind Energy Council, *Global Wind 2006 Report*, 2006, p. 2. pdf.

63. Ibid.

64. Ibid.

65. Ibid., p. 6.

66. Ibid.

67. Siemens AG, "Wind Turbines for Power Generation," *Siemens Power Generation: Case Studies*, http://www.powergeneration.siemens .com/en/windpower/casestudies/index.cfm.

68. Siemens AG, "Hydro and Siemens cooperate on technology for full-scale demonstration of floating wind turbines," Press Release, 26 June 26 2007, http://www.siemens.com/index.jsp?sdc_p=fmls4uo1452973 ni1165473pcz3&sdc_bcpath=1330815.s_4,1330854.s_4,1305779.s_4,:1328 494.s_4,&sdc_sid=17642218393&.

69. Hydro has only one wind farm in operation with 40 MW capacity. Source: Hydro, "Operating Power Plants," *Operating Power Plants—Hydro*, http://www.hydro.com/en/our_business/oil_energy/ renewable_energy/wind_power/operating_power_plants.html.

70. Hoover's, "Vestas Wind Systems A/S," http://premium.hoovers.com/ subscribe/co/overview.xhtml?ID=fffrtryyyyfjfkhxxx.

71. Vestas Wind Systems, *Vestas Annual Report 2006: Wind, Oil and Gas*," 2006, p. 16, http://www.vestas.com/NR/rdonlyres/01B94D06-8F6B-4443-ABC7-0DAF2C97AA40/0/2006_AR_UK.pdf.

72. Staff, "Going Global," *New Energy: Magazine for Renewable Energy* February 2007, p. 26, http://www.newenergy.info/index.php?id= 1430.

73. Suzlon Energy Ltd., "Suzlon signs one of the largest contracts in the history of US wind power industry," Press Release, 29 June 2007, http://www.suzlon.com/images/you/Suzlon-PPM%20Announcement %20290607.pdf.

74. REpower Systems AG, "Suzlon successfully concludes acquisition bid for REpower and controls 87% of votes in the Hamburg-based

company," Press Release, 1 June 2007, http://www.repower.de/index. php?id=151&backPID=25&tt_news=1363&L=1.

75. REpower Systems AG, "Portrait," *REpower Unternehmen*, http://www.repower.de/index.php?id=38&L=1

76. Gamesa Corporacion Tecnologica, *Gamesa, Resultados 2006*, 20 February 2007. http://www.gamesa.es/files/File/Gamesa_ Resultados_ 2006.pdf.

77. Ibid.

78. Nordex AG, *Annual Report 2006*, 30 April 2007, p. 18, http://www. nordex-online.com/fileadmin/MEDIA/Geschaeftsberichte/Nordex_ GB_2006_GB.pdf.

79. Clipper Windpower, Inc., "Investor Information 2006 Highlights," 2006, http://www.clipperwind.com/2006_highlights.php.

80. For more information on BP's wind business, see BP, Alternative Energy: Wind Power, http://www.bp.com/subsection.do? categoryId= 9013381&contentId=7026158.

81. BTM Consult ApS via European Wind Energy (EWEA), "Focus on Supply Chain: Supply Chain: The race to meet demand," Wind Directions, January/-February 2007, p. 29,. http://www.ewea.org/fileadmin/ ewea_documents/documents/publications/WD/2007_january/0701-WD26-focus.pdf.

82. Ibid.

83. Ibid.

84. Ibid., p. 30.

85. Ibid., p. 31.

86. American Semiconductor, Form 10-K, filed 6/14/2007 for period ending 3/31/2007, pp. 3–5.

87. Zoltek Corp., "Panex: Applications and Uses," http://www.zoltek.com/ products/panexuses.php.

88. Zoltek Corp. "Zoltek reports new expanded carbon fiber supply agreement with Vestas Wind Systems," 22 May 2007, http://ir.zoltek.com/ releases.cfm.

89. European Wind Energy Association, "Focus on Industry: New Players on Board," *Wind Directions*, March–April 2007, p. 41, http://www. ewea.org/fileadmin/ewea_documents/documents/publications/WD/200 7_march/WD0703-focus.pdf.

90. See FPL Energy, "Plant Fact Sheets," http://www.fplenergy.com/ portfolio/wind/plantfactsheet.shtml.

91. FPL Energy, "About Us," http://www.fplenergy.com/about/contents/ about_us.shtml.

92. See FPL Energy, "Solar," http://www.fplenergy.com/portfolio/solar/ index.shtml.

93. Jim Jelter, "Iberdrola to buy Energy East for $4.5 billion," *Market Watch*, June 25, 2007, http://www.marketwatch.com/news/story/ spains-iberdrola-buy-energy-east/story.aspx?guid=%7BB8510E60-B4AE-4F70-BDDD-0E73259C7E57%7D.

94. Acciona Energáia, "Eáolica," http://www.acciona-energia.es/default. asp?x=00020201.

95. Ibid.

96. Staff, "Acciona nets US wind power assets," *Yahoo! News*, 28, June 2007, ttp://news.yahoo.com/s/afp/20070628/bs_afp/spainenergy company_070628171750&printer=1;_ylt=Ap8Wbu1PJ28vbMaqy1ZtbC6 oOrgF.

97. Babcock & Brown, "Business Activities," http://www.babcockbrown. com/bnb-business-groups/infrastructure-/business-activities.aspx.

CHAPTER 7

1. For instance, an energy efficiency rate of 30 percent means that out of all the energy contained within a fuel, only 30 percent can be put to use by means of the technology in question, the rest is lost.

2. U.S. Department of Energy, Office of Energy Efficiency and Renewable Energy, *Comparison of Fuel Cell Technologies*, http://www1. eere.energy.gov/hydrogenandfuelcells/fuelcells/pdfs/fc_comparison_ chart.pdf.

3. Ibid.

4. Fuel Cells 2000, Fuel Cell Basics: Types, *Fuel Cells 2000: The Online Fuel Cell Information Source*, http://www.fuelcells.org/basics/ types.html.

5. For example platinum, whose prices have risen by 129 percent over a five-year period, from June 13, 2002, to June 13, 2007, in U.S. markets for opening prices per troy ounce. See Johnson Matthey, "Current and Historical: PGM Prices,". *Platinum Today*, http://www.platinum.matthey.com/prices/current_historical.html.

6. Fuel Cells 2000 claims that "properly configured fuel cells can achieve up to 99.9999% reliability, less than one minute of down time in a six year period." See Fuel Cells 2000, Fuel Cell Basics: Benefits,

Fuel Cells 2000: The Online Fuel Cell Information Source, http://www.fuelcells.org/basics/benefits.html.

7. U.S. Department of Energy, Office of Energy Efficiency and Renewable Energy, *Technical Plan: Technology Validation*," 27 April 2007, http://www1.eere.energy.gov/hydrogenandfuelcells/mypp/pdfs/tech_valid.pdf.

8. Ibid., p. 3.5-3.

9. Fuel Cells 2000, Fuel Cell Baiscs: Types, *Fuel Cells 2000: The Online Fuel Cell Information Source*, http://www.fuelcells.org/basics/types.html.

10. Plug Power, Form 10-K, Filed 3/16/2007 for period ending 12/31/2006, p. F-5.

11. Hydrogenics Corp., *Delivered HySTAT Hydrogen Stations*, http://www.hydrogenics.com/onsite/pdf/delivered_success.pdf.

12. *Regenerative fuel cells* (RFC) are a closed-loop system in which water is decomposed into hydrogen and oxygen through electrolysis. When the fuel cell is put to work, it reunites them to form water, which is refueled into the system to be put through electrolysis again. A big advantage is that fuel does not occupy much space. The energy for the electrolysis process comes from a renewable source, such as solar or wind, which makes RFCs ideal for satellites with solar panels.

13. GrafTech, "GrafCell: Fuel Cells, http://www.graftechaet.com/Home/Brands/GRAFCELL.aspx.

14. See Frost and Sullivan estimate, Thomas Weisel Partners, *Plug Power: Clean, Reliable On-Site Energy*, 13 June 13, slide 8, http://www.b2i.us/Profiles/Investor/Investor.asp?BzID=604&from=du&ID=39091&myID=1930&L=I&Validate=3&I=.

15. EnerSys, Inc. Corporate Presentation, William Blair Growth Conference, Chicago IL, June 2007.

16. Ballard Power Systems, *Ballard Power Systems: Making Fuel Cells a Commercial Reality*, http://www.ballard.com/resources/documents/General%20IR%20PPT_May%2010%202007.pdf.

17. See Distributed Energy Systems, "Onsite Hydrogen Generation," http://www.distributed-energy.com/hydrogen_generation/onsite.html.

18. For more information, visit the Teledyne Energy Systems, Inc. Web site at http://www.teledyneenergysystems.com/.

19. Fuel Cells 2000, Fuel Cell Basics: Types, *Fuel Cells 2000: The Online Fuel Cell Information Source*, http://www.fuelcells.org/basics/types.html.

20. U.S. Department of Energy, Office of Energy Efficiency and Renewable Energy, "Natural Gas Reforming," *Hydrogen, Fuel Cells & Infrastructure Technologies Program,* 8 November 2006, http://www1.eere. energy.gov/hydrogenandfuelcells/production/natural_gas.html.

21. Ibid.

22. *Gasoline gallon equivalent* is the amount of hydrogen that produces the same amount of energy as a gallon of gasoline.

23. U.S. Department of Energy, Office of Energy Efficiency and Renewable Energy, DOE Announces New Hydrogen Cost Goal," *Hydrogen, Fuel Cells & Infrastructure Technologies Program,* 28 April 2006, http://www1.eere.energy.gov/hydrogenandfuelcells/news_cost_goal. html.

24. U.S. Department of Energy, Office of Energy Efficiency and Renewable Energy, "Hydrogen Production Overview," *FY 2006 Annual Progress Report: DOE Hydrogen Program,* p. 18, http://www.hydrogen. energy.gov/pdfs/progress06/ii_1_introduction.pdf.

25. U.S. Department of Energy, Energy Information Administration, "U.S. Regular All Formulations Retail Gasoline Prices (Cents per Gallon)," http://tonto.eia.doe.gov/dnav/pet/hist/mg_rt_usw.htm.

26. U.S. Department of Energy, *Department of Energy FY 2008 Congressional Budget Request: Fossil Energy and Other,,* February 2007, vol. 7, p. 47, http://www.mbe.doe.gov/budget/08budget/Content/Volumes/ Vol_7_FE.pdf.

27. Ibid.

28. U.S. Department of Energy, "U.S. Department of Energy Awards $100 million in Fuel Cell R&D," 24 October 2006, http://www. energy.gov/news/4401.htm.

29. U.S. Department of Energy, "Future Fuel Cells R&D," 10 May 2007, http://www.fossil.energy.gov/programs/powersystems/fuelcells/.

30. Ibid.

31. U.S. Department of Energy, Office of Energy Efficiency and Renewable Energy, "Preliminary draft research topics subject to revision prior to a solicitation being issued May 18, 2007," http://www1. eere.energy.gov/hydrogenandfuelcells/pdfs/preliminary_solicitation_ topics.pdf.

32. Ballard Power Systems, *Ballard Power Systems: Making Fuel Cells a Commercial Reality.*

33. U.S. Department of Energy, Office of Energy Efficiency and Renewable Energy, *Technical Plan: Technology Validation* p. 3.5.

34. U.S. Department of Energy, Office of Energy Efficiency and Renewable Energy, "U.S. Department of Energy Awards $100 million in Fuel Cell R&D," 24 October 2006, http://www.energy.gov/news/4401.htm.

35. U.S. Department of Energy, Office of Fossil Energy, *2006 Office of Fossil Energy Fuel Cell Program Annual Report*, September 2006, p. 6, http://www.fossil.energy.gov/programs/powersystems/fuelcells/FY06_Fuel_Cell_Program_Report.pdf.

CHAPTER 8

1. Energy and Geosciences Institute, University of Utah, *Briefing on Geothermal Energy*, prepared by the U.S. Geothermal Institute Industry Renewable Energy Task Force, 1997, Washington, D.C. *Note:* This book uses the figure that 1 megawatt of power can supply 750 homes when discussing traditional power plants or geothermal power plants (as opposed to wind and solar plants which are intermittent), as recommended by the California Independent System Operator after consultations with California utilities. This is calculated as ((1 megawatt × 1000 kilowatts/megawatt × 8760 hours/year)/(10,656 kilowatt-hours per year usage for average U.S. household)) × (about 90% capacity realized). The average annual U.S. household usage of 10,656 kilowatt-hours per year is sourced from Energy Information Administration, Electricity Consumption by End Use in U.S. Households, 2001, Table US-A, www.eia.doe.gov/emeu/reps/endues/er01_us_tab1.html. See also Bob Bellemare, "What is a Megawatt?," UtiliPoint International, http://www.utilipoint.com/issuealert/print.asp?id=1728; and Jonathan G. Koomey, et al., "Sorry, Wrong Number: The Use and Misuse of Numerical Facts in Analysis and Media Reporting of Energy Issues," *Annual Review of Energy and the Environment Journal* 27 (2002):119–158, http://arjournals.annualreviews.org/).

2. Union of Concerned Scientists "How Geothermal Energy Works," http://www.ucsusa.org/clean_energy/renewable_energy_basics/offmen-how-geothermal-energy-works.html.

3. See Geothermal Education Office, "Geothermal Energy—Worldwide," geothermal.marin.org/geomap_1.html.

4. Massachusetts Institute of Technology, *The Future of Geothermal Energy Impact of Enhanced Geothermal Systems (EGS) on the United States in the 21st Century*," 22 January 2007, http:// geothermal.inel.gov. *Note:* A geothermal energy plant running at about 90 percent capacity could supply 750 homes for each megawatt of power. See note 1.

5. Hreinn Hjaratarson, "Husavik Energy:- Multiple Use of Geothermal Energy," *GHC Bulletin*, June 2005, http://geoheat.oit.edu/bulletin/bull26-2/art3.pdf.

6. U.S. Department of Energy, Office of Energy Efficiency and Renewable Energy, "Geothermal heat pumps make sense for homeowners," DOE/GO-10098-651, 1999, http://www1.eere.energy.gov/geothermal/pdfs/2616b.pdf.

7. Ibid.

8. Geothermal Energy Association, "All About Geothermal Energy: Current Use," http://geo-energy.org/aboutGE/currentUse.asp. *Note:* A geothermal energy plant running at about 90 percent capacity could supply 750 homes for each megawatt of power. See notes 1 and 4.

9. "Geothermal power," *Answers.com*, http://www.answers.com/topic/geothermal-power?cat=technology.

10. U.S. Department of Energy, Office of Energy Efficiency and Renewable Energy, "Geothermal FAQs," http://www1.eere.energy.gov/geothermal/printable_versions/faqs.html.

11. California Energy Commission, *Comparative Cost of California Central Station Electricity Generation Technologies: Final Staff Report*, June 2003, http:www.energt.ca.gov/reports/2003-06-06 100-03-001f.pdf.

12. J. Brugman, M. Hattar, K. Nichols, and Y. Esaki, *Next Generation Geothermal Power Plants*, (Pasadena, CA: CE Holt Co. 1996).

13. California Energy Commission, *Comparative Cost of California Central Station Electricity Generation Technologies: Final Staff Report*.

14. Ibid.

15. Environmental and Energy Study Institute, *Energy: Tapping into the Earth's Core*, 2006, http://www.eesi.org/publications/fact%20sheets/ec_fact_sheets/geothermal.pdf.

16. Ibid.

CHAPTER 9

1. International Energy Agency, "The Utilization of CO2," http://jobfunctions.bnet.com/whitepaper.aspx?docid=111159).

2. See U.S. Department of Energy, Office of Energy Efficiency and Renewable Energy, "Green Pricing," *The Green Power Network*, http://www.eere.energy.gov/greenpower/markets/pricing.shtml?page=1.

3. See Vail Resorts Management Company, "Ski with the Wind," http://www.snow.com/ info/windpower.asp.

4. Joanne Kelley, "Vail casts its fate to wind power," *Rocky Mountain News*, 2 August 2006, http://www.rockymountainnews.com/ drmn/other_business/article/0,2777,DRMN_23916_4887201,00.html.

5. Florida Power and Light, "Sunshine Energy," http://www.fpl.com/ residential/electric/sunshine_energy.shtml.

6. See Energy Star, "Special Offers and Rebates from Energy Star Partners," http://www.energystar.gov/index.cfm?fuseaction=rebate. rebate_locator.

7. National Renewable Energy Laboratory, "NREL Ranks Leading Utility Green Power Programs: Pricing programs give consumers clean power choices," *NREL Newsroom*, 3 April 2007, http:// www.nrel.gov/news/press/2007/506.html.

8. Anna Giovinetto, "On the Track of Green Certificates," *Environmental Finance*, 15 September, 2003, http://www.evomarkets.com/assets/ articles/ef9RECs_rep.pdf.

9. The Green-e Web site is located at http://www.green-e.org/about.shtml.

10. U.S. Department of Energy, Office of Energy Efficiency and Renewable Energy, "Renewable Energy Certificates: Commercial &/or wholesale Marketers, *The Green Power Network*, http://www.eere.energy.gov/ greenpower/markets/certificates.shtml?page=4.

11. U.S. Department of Energy, Office of Energy Efficiency and Renewable Energy. Biomass Today, *Biomass Program*, http://www1.eere. energy.gov/biomass/biomass_today.html.

12. U.S. Environmental Protection Agency, "Energy Projects and Landfill Candidates," http://www.epa.gov/lmop/proj/index.htm.

13. Environmental Power Corp., "Frequently Asked Questions," http:// www.environmentalpower.com/about/faq.php4.

14. Noam Mohr, "A New Global Warming Strategy: How Environmentalists are Overlooking Vegetarianism as the Most Effective Tool Against Climate Change in Our Lifetimes," *EarthSave.org*, August 2005, http://www.earthsave.org/news/earthsave_global_warming_report.pdf.

15. Schmack BioGas AG, "References," http://www.schmack-biogas. de/wEnglisch/referenzen/index.php?navid=80.

16. Environmental and Energy Study Institute, "Renewable Energy Fact Sheet," http://www.eesi.org/publications/Fact%20Sheets/EC_Fact_ Sheets/Ocean_Energy.pdf.

17. Ibid.

18. Peter Fairley, "Tidal Turbines Help Light Up Manhattan," *Technology Review*, 23 April 2007, http://www.technologyreview.com/Energy/18567/.

19. Environmental and Energy Study Institute, "Renewable Energy Fact Sheet."

20. Anthony Effinger, "War of the Tides," *Bloomberg Magazine*, June 2007, http://www.bloomberg.com/apps/news?pid=newsarchive&sid=a3vW Dlqcl6sU.

CHAPTER 10

1. U.S. Department of Energy, "Johnson Controls Energy Efficiency Forum: Remarks for Energy Secretary Samuel Bodman," 13 June 2007, http://www.doe.gov/print/5129.htm.

2. International Energy Agency, *World Energy Investment Outlook: 2003 Insights*, 2003, p. 341.

3. U.S. Department of Energy, Energy Information Administration, *Annual Energy Outlook 2007 with Projections to 2030*, February 2007, http://www.eia.doe.gov/oiaf/aeo/pdf/trend_3.pdf.

4. More information about the Electric Power Research Institute (EPRI) can be found at its Web site, www.epri.com.

5. U.S. Environmental Protection Agency, *National Action Plan for Energy Efficiency: Executive Summary*, July 2006, p. ES-4, http://www.epa.gov/cleanrgy/pdf/napee/napee_exsum.pdf.

6. Ibid., p. ES-5.

7. Electric Power Research Institute, "Turning on Energy Efficiency", *EPRI Journal*, Summer 2006, p. 11, http://mydocs.epri.com/docs/CorporateDocuments/EPRI_Journal/2006-Summer/1013720_EnergyEff.pdf.

8. U.S. Environmental Protection Agency, *National Action Plan for Energy Efficiency: Executive Summary*, July 2006.

9. U.S. Department of Energy, Energy Information Administration, "U.S. Household Electricity Report," July, 2005, http://www.eia.doe.gov/emeu/reps/enduse/er01_us.html.

10. Energy Star, "History of Energy Star," http://www.energystar.gov/index.cfm?c=about.ab_history.

11. Ibid.

12. Energy Star, "Special Offers and Rebates from Energy Star Partners," http://www.energystar.gov/index.cfm?fuseaction=rebate.rebate_locator.

13. Matthew L. Wald, "A U.S. Alliance to Update the Light Bulb, *New York Times*, 14 March 2007, http://www.nytimes.com/2007/03/14/business/14light.html?pagewanted=print.

14. "Green Light Districts," *Wall Street Journal*, 12 April 2007, p. A14.

15. Energy Star, "Compact Florescent Light Bulbs," http://www.energystar.gov/index.cfm?c=cfls.pr_cfls.

16. "Australia Pulls Plug on Old Bulbs," BBC News, 20 February 2007, http://news.bbc.co.uk/2/hi/asia-pacific/6378161.stm.

17. "Ontario Government to Ban Incandescent Lights by 2012," *Green-Biz News*, 23 April2007, http://www.greenbiz.com/news/news_third.cfm?NewsID=34949.

18. Smithsonian Institution, "Light Emitting Diodes," *The Quartz Watch*, http://www.hrw.com/science/si-science/chemistry/careers/quartz/timeline/diodes.html.

19. Toolbase Services, LED Lighting, *PATH Technology Inventory*, http://www.toolbase.org/Techinventory.

20. Steve Bush, "Organic LEDs Are on the Way," *Electronics Weekly*, 11 November 2004, http://www.electronicsweekly.com/ARTICLES/2004/11/11/33567/Organic+LEDs+are+on+the+way.HTM.

21. See U.S. Department of Energy, Office of Efficiency and Renewable Energy, "Solar Lighting," http://www1.eere.energy.gov/solar/solar_lighting.html.

22. U.S. Green Building Council, "Green Building by the Numbers," June 2007, http://www.usgbc.org/DisplayPage.aspx?CMSPageID=1442.

23. US Environmental Protection Agency,"Green Buildings," http://www.epa.gov/greenbuilding.

24. U.S. Green Building Council, "Green Building by the Numbers."

25. Lime Energy, *Investors Presentation*, September 2007, http://www.lime-energy.com/investors/LimeInvestorsSeptember07.ppt.

26. Pollution figures are derived by Lime Energy from the calculator at http://www.cleanerandgreener.org/resources/emission_reductions.htm.

27. Coal savings are computed by Lime Energy at http://www.usctcgateway.net/tool/.

28. Lime Energy, *Investors Presentation*, September 2007.

CHAPTER 11

The author would like to thank and acknowledge Melvin & Company for permission to use several excerpts and graphics in this chapter that the author originally published in research reports written for Melvin & Company.

1. Global Environment Fund, Center for Smart Energy, *The Emerging Smart Grid: Investment and Entrepreneurial Potential in the Electric Power Grid of the Future*, October 2005, http://www.globalenvironmentfund.com/GEF%20white%20paper_Electric%20Power%20Grid.pdf.

2. Ibid.

3. Federal Energy Regulatory Commission, *Assessment of Demand Response and Advanced Metering*," August 2006, http://www.ferc.gov/legal/staff-reports/demand-response.pdf.

4. Ibid., p. 31.

5. Ibid., vi.

6. Gary Fauth and Michael Wiebe, "Fixed-Network AMR: Lessons for Building the Best Business Case," *AMRA News*, September 2004, p. 5.

7. *Smart Grid Newsletter*, November 2006.

8. Federal Energy Regulatory Commission, *Assessment of Demand Response and Advanced Metering*," August 2006, p. 42.

9. International Energy Agency, *Implementing Agreement on Demand-Side Management Technologies and Programmes*, *2006 Annual Report*, http://dsm.iea.org/Files/Exco%20File%20Library/Annual%20Reports/Annual%20Report%202006%20cvr.pdf.

10. International Energy Agency, *Implementing Agreement on Demand-Side Management Technologies and Programmes*, *2005 Annual Report*, p. 8, http://dsm.iea.org/Files/Exco%20File%20Library/Annual%20Reports/IEADSMAnnualReport2005.pdf

11. Patti Harper-Slaboszewicz, UtiliPoint, "Regulator Interest in AMI and Demand Response," written remarks submitted as panelist, FERC Technical Conference, 5. Cited in Federal Energy Regulatory Commission, "Assessment of Demand Response and Advanced Metering," Staff Report, Docket Number AD-06-2-000, Appendix 1, Figure VII-1. Regulator Treatment of AMI and Demand Response, p. I-10, http://ferc.gov/legal/staff-reports/demand-response.pdf.

12. Patti Harper-Slaboszewicz, "PG&E Throws the First Pitch in the AMI Game," *Issue Alert*, UtiliPoint International, 25 July 2007, http://www.utilipoint.com/issuealert/.

13. Ibid.

14. Itron, Inc., 10k annual report management presentations, 2006.

CHAPTER 12

1. California Integrated Waste Management Board, "Electrical Storage: Present, Past and Future," http://www.ciwmb.ca.gov/WPW/Power/ElectricStor.htm.

2. Stationary Sodium-Sulfur (NAS) Battery, Electric Power Research Institute, http://www.aep.com/newsroom/newsreleases/default.asp?dbcommand=displayrelease&ID=790].

3. "AEP to Deploy Additional Large-scale Batteries on Distribution Grid," American Electric Power press release, Sep. 11, 2007, www.aep.com/newsroom/newsreleases/default.asp?dbcommand=displayrelease&ID=1397.]

4. Institute of Electrical and Electronics Engineers, Inc., *Energy Storage Systems for Advanced Power Applications: Proceedings of the IEEE*, vol. 89, no. 12 (December 2001).

5. Ibid.

6. U.K. Department of Trade and Industry, *Review of Electrical Energy Storage Technologies and Systems and of their Potential for the UK*, 2004, p. 10, http://www.dti.gov.uk/files/file15185.pdf.

7. National Renewable Energy Laboratory, "'Wind to Hydrogen' facility offers new template for future energy production," *Hydrogen and Fuel Cells Research*, 23 April 2007, http://www.nrel.gov/features/04-07_xcel_wind_hydro.html. See also National Renewable Energy Laboratory, "Wind-to-Hydrogen Project, *Hydrogen and Fuel Cells Research*, http://www.nrel.gov/hydrogen/proj_wind_hydrogen.html.

8. Electricity Storage Association, "Applications of Electrical Storage," http://www.electricitystorage.org/technologies_applications.htm.

9. Ibid.

10. Enersys, Inc., corporate presentation, June 2007.

11. Isidor Buchmann, "Battery Statistics," *Battery University*, http://www.batteryuniversity.com/print-parttwo-55.htm. The *Battery University* site is sponsored by Cadex Electonics, Inc.

12. BCC Research, "Global Markets for Capacitors, Flywheels and SMES Systems," http://www.bccresearch.com/egy/EGY041A.asp.

CHAPTER 13

1. U.S. Department of Transportation, Bureau of Transportation Statistics, "United States Fast Facts," 2006, http://www.bts.gov/

publications/state_transportation_statistics/state_transportation_ statistics_2006/html/fast_facts.html.

2. U.S. Environmental Protection Agency, "Greenhouse Gas Emissions from Transportation and Other Mobile Sources," http://www.epa.gov/ otaq/greenhousegases.htm.

3. U.S. Department of Transportation, National Highway Traffic Safety Administration "CAFÉ Overview," http://www.nhtsa.dot.gov/ cars/rules/cafe/overview.htm.

4. "How Clean Diesel Fuel Works," *HowStuffWorks*, http://auto .howstuffworks.com/how-clean-diesel-fuel-works.htm.

5. Bill Harris, "How Natural-Gas Vehicles Work," *HowStuffWorks*, http://auto.howstuffworks.com/ngv.htm.

6. Ed Grabianowski, "How Liquefied Petroleum Gas Works," *HowStuff-Works*, http://auto.howstuffworks.com/lpg.htm.

7. "How a Hydrogen-Boosted Gasoline Engine Works," *How Stuff Works*, http://auto.howstuffworks.com/how-a-hydrogen-boosted-gasoline-engine-works.htm.

8. Moteru Development International, *The Air Car*, http://www.theaircar .com/.

9. Bob Ewing, Air-Car Ready for Mass Production, 30 May 2007, Yahoo! Green, http://green.yahoo.com/index.php?q=node/315.

10. "Car runs on compressed air, but will it sell," Associated Press, 4 October 2004, http://www.msnbc.msn.com/id/6138972.

11. R.L. Polk & Co., "Hybrid Vehicle Registration Growth-Rate Slows in 2006," *Polk News*, 26 February 2006, http://usa.polk.com/news/ latestnews/2007_0226_hybrid_growth_rate.htm.

12. "Worldwide HEV (Hybrid Electric Vehicle) Sales," *MarkLines.com*, http://www.marklines.com/en/numproduct/index.jsp.

13. "U.S. hybrid sales by manufacturer," *HybridCars.com*, June 2007, http://www.hybridcars.com/market-dashboard/jun07-us-sales.html.

14. Ibid.

15. Ibid.

16. Tom Appel, "The Consumer Guide to Hybrid Vehicles," *Consumers Guide Automotive*, http://consumerguideauto.howstuffworks .com/the-consumer-guide-to-hybrid-vehicles-cga.htm/printable.

17. "How Plug-in Hybrid Cars Work," *HowStuffWorks*, http://auto. howstuffworks.com/plug-in-hybrid-car.htm.

18. Kevin Bullis, "Are Lithium-ion Electric Cars Safe?" *Technology Review*, 3 August 2006, http://www.technologyreview.com/Energy/17250/.

19. Johnson Controls, "Hybrid Vehicles: Batteries for vehicles with a hybrid drive," http://www.johnsoncontrols.com/publish/us/en/products/power_solutions/Battery_Technology_Centers/AGM/Hybrid_Vehicle_Systems_Li-Ion_NiMH_.html.

20. "Johnson Controls and Saft launch new joint venture for HEVs," Saft Advanced Power Solutions, January 10, 2006, http://www.saftbatteries.com/000-corporate/pdf/JCI_Saft_JV.pdf.

21. Dale Buss, "Fully Charged," *Edmonds.com*, May 8, 2007, http://www.edmunds.com/advice/alternativefuels/articles/120672/article.html (sign-in required)

22. Ibid.

23. Jim Louderback, "Hands on with the Phoenix Electric Car," *PCMagazine.com*, 25 May 2007, http://www.pcmag.com/article2/0,1895,2136457,00.asp.

24. See Tesla Motors, *Tesla Motors*, http://www.teslamotors.com/index.php.

25. Dan Lienert, "Best Cars 2006," *Forbes*, 11 December 2006, http://www.forbes.com/lifestyle/2006/12/08/best-cars-2006-forbeslife-cx_dl_1211bestcars.html.

26. Bloomberg News, "Toyota Says It Plans Eventually to Offer and All-Hybrid Fleet," *New York Times*, 14 September 2005, http://www.nytimes.com/2005/09/14/automobiles/14toyota.html?ei=5070&en=1fe7c42b0c08d7db&ex=1185768000&pagewanted=print.

27. Pacific Northwest National Laboratory, *Impact Assessment of Plug-In Hybrid Vehicles on Electric Utilities and Regional US Power Grids*, by Michael Kintner-Meyer, Kevin Schneider, and Robert Pratt, http://www.pnl.gov/energy/eed/etd/pdfs/phev_feasibility_analysis_combined.pdf.

CHAPTER 14

1. John M. Urbanchuk, *Contribution of the Ethanol Industry to the Economy of the United States*, 21 February-2006, http://www. ethanol-rfa.org/objects/documents/576/economic_contribution_2006.pdf.

2. Lester Brown, "Distillery demand for grain to fuel cars vastly understated: World may be facing highest grain prices in history," *Earth*

Policy Institute, 4 January 2007, http://www.earth-policy.org/ Updates/2007/Update63.htm.

3. Sarah Tarver-Wahlquist and Tracy Fernandez Rysavy, "Corn Ethanol Isn't the Answer," *Co-op America Quarterly*, no. 72, Summer 2007, http://www.coopamerica.org/pubs/caq/articles/Summer2007cornethanol.cfm.

4. U.S. Department of Energy, Office of Energy Efficiency and Renewable Energy, "Net Energy Balance for Bioethanol Production and Use," http://www1.eere.energy.gov/biomass/net_energy_balance.html.

5. Ibid.

6. Christoph Podewils, "Organized Wastefulness: Biofuel Is the Most Inefficient Renewable Energy. Why Not Fill the Car's Tank Directly with Solar Electricity?" *Photon International*, April 2007, pp. 106–113.

7. A test by Consumer Reports on a Chevrolet Tahoe found that E85 produced 27 percent lower mileage than gasoline, taking the mileage down to 10 mpg from 14 mpg. See Eric Evarts, "Ethanol: Hope or Hype?" *Consumer Reports Cars Blog*, 19 September 2006, http://blogs.consumerreports.org/cars/2006/09/ethanol_hope_or.html.

8. George W. Bush, "Twenty in Ten: Strengthening America's Energy Security," *State of the Union*, 2007, http://www.whitehouse.gov/stateoftheunion/2007/initiatives/energy.html.

9. "American Coalition for Ethanol Clears Confusion Surrounding UL's E85 Safety Decision," *Biofuels Journal*, 31 October 2006, http://www.biofuelsjournal.com/articles/American_Coalition_for_Ethanol_Clears_Confusion_Surrounding_UL_s_E85_Safety_Decision____10_31_2006-38597.html.

10. U.S. Department of Energy, Office of Energy Efficiency and Renewable Energy,"E85 Fueling Stations in California," *Alternative Fuels & Advanced Vehicle Data Center*, http://www.eere.energy.gov/afdc/progs/ind_state.php/CA/E85.

11. The National Ethanol Vehicle Coalition tracks the number of E85 service stations in the United States and showed about 1,250 stations as of July 2007. See www.e85fuel.com.

12. Jeffery Ball, "How California Failed in Efforts to Curb Its Addiction to Oil," *Wall Street Journal*, 2 August 2006.

13. Center for American Progress, *America is to Oil: 10 Tough Questions and Answers for President Bush on Kicking the Oil Habit*, February 2006, p. 2, http://www.americanprogress.org/kf/kicking_the_habit.pdf.

14. Underwriters Laboratories, "Underwriters Laboratories Moves Closer to Completing E85 Fuel Dispenser Requirements," 22 March 2007. http://www.ul.com/newsroom/newsrel/nr032307.html.

15. Renewable Fuels Association, "Annual World Ethanol Production by Country," July 2007, http://www.ethanolrfa.org/industry/statistics/#E.

16. "Brazil in ethanol production vow," BBC News, 18 April 2007, http://news.bbc.co.uk/1/hi/business/6566515.stm.

17. Antonio Regalado and Bernd Radowitz, "Overtures to Brazil Show Differing Ethanol Interests," *Wall Street Journal*, 17 April 2007.

18. Ibid.

19. Ibid.

20. Fiona Harvey, "Wolfowitz calls on U.S. to remove ethanol tariffs," *Financial Times*, 13 March 2007.

21. Renewable Fuels Association, "U.S. Fuel Ethanol Industry Biorefineries and Production Capacity," July 2007, http://www.ethanolrfa.org/industry/locations/.

22. Ibid.

23. The calculation of 3.6 billion bushels of corn is calculated as 15 billion gallons divided by the yield of 2.8 gallons/bushel less 1/3 for distiller dried grain output, which is a corn feed product.

24. Diane Greer, "Creating Cellulosic Ethanol: Spinning Straw into Fuel," April 2005, *BioCycle eNews Bulletin*, May 2005, http://www.harvestcleanenergy.org/enews/enews_0505/enews_0505_Cellulosic_Ethanol.htm.

25. C. Schell and G. Peterson, *Cellulosic Ethanol: The State of the Technology*, U.S. Department of Energy, Project Management Center, Golden Field Office, 13 December 2006, http://cobWeb.ecn.purdue.edu/~lorre/16/Midwest%20Consortium/Schell.2006.pdf.

26. Ibid.

27. "Fuels for the Future: Cellulosic Ethanol," *Co-op America Quarterly*, No. 72, Summer 2007, p. 18.

28. VeraSun Energy Corp., "VersaSun Energy to Acquire 330 Million Gallons of Ethanol Production Capacity," Press Release, 23 July 2007, http://phx.corporate-ir.net/phoenix.zhtml?c=197813&p=irol-newsArticle_Print&ID=1028975&highlight=.

29. VeraSun Energy Corp., "VeraSun Announces Innovative Process for Biodiesel production," Press Release, 3 November 2006, http://

phx.corporate-ir.net/phoenix.zhtml?c=197813&p=iro-newsArticle_
Print&ID=926201&highlight=.

30. The Andersons, Inc., "The Andersons, Inc. and Marathon to Build
    Ethanol Plants," Press Release, 10 July 2006, http://phx.corporate-ir.
    net/phoenix.zhtml?c=96043&p=irol-newsArticle&ID=
    880152&highlight=.

CHAPTER 15

1. Current prices from www.Barchart.com for the energy futures complex, including crude oil and gasoline markets, can be found at
   http://www2.barchart.com/mktcom.asp?section=energies.

2. Worldwatch Institute "Biofuels for Transportation: Selected Trends
   and Facts," Press Release, 7 June 2006, http://www.worldwatch.org/
   node/4081.

3. U.S. Department of Agriculture corn crop information as of July
   30, 2007. See the latest U.S. crop production data at http://usda.
   mannlib.cornell.edu/MannUsda/viewDocumentInfo.do?document
   ID=1046.

4. Ibid.

5. Commodity Research Bureau, "Sugar," *CRB Yearbook 2007* (Chicago:
   Commodity Research Bureau, 2007), p. 266.

6. Susan Reidy, "Europe leads rush to produce biodiesel," *Biofuels-
   business.com*, 1 June 2007, http://www.biofuelsbusiness.com/news/
   biodiesel.asp.

7. Commodity Research Bureau, "Soybean Oil," *CRB Yearbook 2007*
   (Chicago: Commodity Research Bureau, 2007), p. 243.

8. Ibid.

9. Ibid.

10. "Indonesia, Malaysia push a biofuels cartel," *Asian Sentinel*, 14 De-
    cember 2006, http://www.asiasentinel.com/index.php? option=com_
    content&task=view&id=304&Itemid=32.

11. Commodity Research Bureau, "Palm Oil," *CRB Yearbook 2007*
    (Chicago: Commodity Research Bureau, 2007), p. 189.

12. Crude palm oil futures information is available at Bursa Malaysia,
    http://www.klse.com.my/Website/bm/products_and_services/derivativ
    e_resources/derivatives-fcpo.html.

CHAPTER 16

1. International Energy Agency, *Key World Energy Statistics 2006*, p. 44, http://www.iea.org/textbase/nppdf/free/2006/key2006.pdf.

2. "Ontario promises to close coal plants by 2014, reduce greenhouse gas emissions," *The Canadian Press*, 18 June 2007, http://ca.news .yahoo.com/s/capress/070618/national/mcguinty_emissions_targets_2.

3. Clifford Krauss, "With Coal Plans cut Back, Texas Faces Energy Gap," *New York Times*, 8 March 2007.

4. Clifford Krauss and Mathew L Wald, "TXU Announces Plans for 2 Coal Plants Designed to be Cleaner-Burning," *New York Times*, 10 March 2007.

5. Clifford Krauss, "With Coal Plans cut Back, Texas Faces Energy Gap."

6. U.S. Department of Energy, Energy Information Administration, *Annual Energy Review 2006*, June 2007, p. 3 and 221 http://www.eia.doe.gov/emeu/aer/pdf/aer.pdf.

7. U.S. Department of Energy, Energy Information Administration, *International Energy Outlook 2007*, May 2007, http://www.eia.doe.gov/oiaf/ieo/pdf/0484(2007).pdf. p. 49.

8. BP Global, *Statistical Review of World Energy 2007*, http://www.bp.com/productlanding.do?categoryId=6848&contentId=7033471.

9. Source: BP Global, "Global coal consumption increased by 4.5% in 2006," *Statistical Review of World Energy 2007: Coal consumption*, http://www.bp.com/sectiongenericarticle.do?categoryId=9017919&contentId=7033429.

10. Ibid.

11. U.S. Department of Energy, "Advanced Combustion Technologies," *Fossil Energy*, http://www.fossil.energy.gov/programs/powersystems/combustion/index.html.

12. Jeff Goodell, *Big Coal: The Dirty Secret Behind America's Energy Future* (New York: Houghton Mifflin 2006), xviii.

13. Centre for Energy and Greenhouse Technologies, "Turning Low-Grade Coal into High-Grade Fuel," http://www.cegt.com.au/news/news_detail.asp?id=192.

14. African American Environmentalist Association, "Coal Facts," *MSN Groups*, http://groups.msn.com/aaea/coal.msnw.

15. Union of Concerned Scientists, "How Coal Works, Clean Energy," http://www.ucsusa.org/clean_energy/fossil_fuels/offmen-how-coal-works.html.

16. African American Environmentalist Association, "Coal Facts."

17. David Hawkins, Daniel Lashof, and Robert Williams, "What to do about Coal," *Scientific American*, September 2006, www.sciamdigital.com (article available on pay basis).

18. U.S. Department of Energy, "Clean Coal Technology & the Presidents Clean Coal Power Initiative," *Fossil Energy*, http://www.fossil.energy.gov/programs/powersystems/cleancoal/index.html.

19. Edison International, "Edison Mission Group and BP Plan Major Hydrogen Power Project for Southern California," Press Release, http://www.edison.com/pressroom/pr.asp?id=6125.

20. Green Car Congress, "NRG testing Greenfuel Algae Emissions-to-Fuel System at Power Plant," 13 April 2007, http://www. greencarcongress.com/2007/04/nrg_energy_test.html.

21. Optical Society of America, "Cleaning up CO2: Environmental Engineers Use Algae for Carbon Dioxide Cleanup," www.aip.org/dbis/OSA/stories/17038.html.

22. National Renewable Energy Laboratory, "A Look Back at the U.S. Department of Energy's Aquatic Species Program: Biodiesel from Algae," July 1998, p. 3, http://www.nrel.gov/docs/legosti/fy98/24190.pdf.

23. There is an entertaining video at YouTube, MIT Algae Photobioreactor, (http://www.youtube.com/watch?v=EnOSnJJSP5c), in which the actor Alan Alda visits an algae photo-bioreactor that was built on the roof of a building at MIT.

24. For information on hybrid solar lighting, visit the Oak Ridge Solar Technologies Program site at http://www.ornl.gov/sci/solar/. A diagram of the process is at http://www.ornl.gov/sci/solar/poster.htm.

25. A Global Force, Tech Focus by the publishers of Popular Mechanics, in collaboration with Sasol International, "Technologies & Processes," Explore Sasol, http://www.sasol.com/sasol_internet/frontend/navigation.jsp?navid=1600033&rootid=2.

CHAPTER 17

1. James Kanter, "In London's Financial World, Carbon Trading is the New Big Thing," *New York Times*, 6 July 2007, http://www.nytimes.com/2007/07/06/business/worldbusiness/06carbon.html.

2. Chicago Climate Exchange, "About European Climate Exchange (ECX)." http://www.chicagoclimatex.com/content.jsf?id=1042.

3. The Intercontinental Exchange, Inc. Web site can be accessed at http://www.theice.com.

4. Mathew Carr and Saijel Kishan, "Europe Fails Kyoto Standards as Trading Scheme Helps Polluters," *Bloomberg.com*, 16 July 2006, http://www.bloomberg.com/apps/news?pid=20601087&sid=awS1xfKp VRs8&refer=home.

5. Mathew Carr, "China's Pollution Allowances Stoke Fourfold Profit Prospects (Update 1)," *Bloomberg.com*, 27 June 2007, http://www.bloomberg.com/apps/news?pid=20601109&sid=aaqEuN9qUYDs&refer =home.

6. Mathew Carr and Alex Morales, "Emission Permits Advance; Bush Urges Climate Goals (Update 3)," *Bloomberg.com*, 1 June 2007, http://www.bloomberg.com/news/index.html?Intro=intro_news.

7. James Kanter, "In London's Financial World, Carbon Trading is the New Big Thing."

8. Ibid.

9. Ibid.

10. Ibid.

11. Chicago Climate Exchange, "Climate Change and Emissions Trading: Market-based solutions to environmental problems," http://www.chicagoclimatex.com/content.jsf?id=221.

12. U.S. Environmental Protection Agency, "Acid Rain Program," *Clean Air Markets*, http://www.epa.gov/airmarkets/progsregs/arp/basic.html.

13. U.S. Environmental Protection Agency, "Acid Rain Program SO2 Allowances Fact Sheet," *Clean Air Markets*, http://epa.gov/airmarkets/trading/factsheet.html.

14. See Chicago Climate Futures Exchange, "Sulfur Financial Instrument Futures Contract Specifications," http://www.ccfe.com/about_ccfe/products/sfi/contract_specs/SFI_Futures_Contract_Specifications.pdf.

Index

A

ABB Ltd., generator manufacturer, 142
Abengoa, stock holdings, 18
Abengoa Bioenergy Corp., ethanol producer, 270t
AB32 Global Warming Solutions Act, 56
AC. *See* Alternating current
Acciona SA, 80, 146
    stock holdings, 18
    wind capacity ranking, 145f
Active Power, Inc., 234
Advanced electricity storage solutions, usefulness, 226
Advanced Energy Initiative, 160
Advanced metering
    benefits, 212–214
    costs, 212–214
        benchmarks, 213t
    deployments, 212t
    interoperability/industry standards, 214–215
    relationship. *See* Demand response
    Southern California Edison, business case experience, 214
    U.S. regulators response, 216
Advanced metering infrastructure (AMI), 208
    example, 209f
    systems. *See* Two-way advanced metering infrastructure systems
Advanced power storage products, companies (involvement), 234–236
AEP. *See* American Electric Power
Africa
    installed wind capacity, 133f
    renewable energy targets, 51t
Agri-business, 12–13
Algae-based CO_2 absorption, 293–294
All-electric vehicles, 247–249
    companies, involvement, 248–249
Allowance Management System (EPA), 304
Altair Nanotechnologies, Inc., 246, 248
Alternating current (AC), DC conversion, 87
AMCO Water Metering Systems, 221
American Depository Receipt (ADR), listing, 10
American Electric Power (AEP), 292

American National Standards Institute (ANSI), meter communications/data storage standards (issuance), 215
American Solar Energy Society, 7
American Superconductor Corp., 144, 234
    global pure-lay wind power manufacturer, 140t
    stock holdings, 15
American Wind Energy Association (AWEA) solution. *See* Wind power
AMI. *See* Advanced metering infrastructure
Amorphous silicon (aSi), 112
AMR. *See* Automated meter reading; Automatic meter reading
AMRA. *See* Automated Meter Reading Association
Andersons, 269
    ethanol producer, 270t
    partnership. *See* Marathon Oil
Angel investing, 7
Appliance efficiency, 50, 189–190
Applied Materials, production line equipment, 112
APU. *See* Auxiliary power unit
AquaEnergy Ltd., 186
aQuantive, stock holdings, 18
Arab Oil Embargo (1973–1975), 39, 281
Arch Coal, 288
Archer Daniels Midland, 269
    ethanol producer, 270t
Arise, polysilicon producer/startup, 105t
Arizona
    prototype dish/Stirling systems, operation, 80
    solar PV incentives, 93t
    Western Regional Climate Action Initiative, 56–57
ASAlliances Biofuels, 269
aSi. *See* Amorphous silicon
Asia
    installed wind capacity, 133f
    renewable energy targets, 51t
Asian central banks, dollar reserves (reduction), 10
Assets, optimization, 203
Associated Foods, lighting upgrade, 199–200

351